Innovations in Family Therapy for Eating Disorders

Innovations in Family Therapy for Eating Disorders brings together prominent voices of the most esteemed international experts to present conceptual advances, preliminary data, and patient perspectives on family-based treatments for eating disorders. This innovative volume is based partly on a special issue of *Eating Disorders: The Journal of Treatment and Prevention* and includes a section on the needs of carers and couples, "Tales from the Trenches," and qualitative studies of patient, parent, and carer experiences. Cutting edge and practical, this compendium will appeal to clinicians and researchers involved in the treatment of eating disorders.

Stuart B. Murray, DClinPsych, PhD is an assistant professor in the department of psychiatry at the University of California, San Francisco, and also serves as director of the National Association for Males with Eating Disorders, the co-chair for the Academy of Eating Disorders Special Interest Group (SIG) panel on male eating disorders, and an honorary associate at the University of Sydney.

Leslie Karwoski Anderson, PhD is an associate clinical professor and training director at the UC San Diego Eating Disorders Center for Treatment and Research. She is also associate editor for *Eating Disorders: The Journal of Treatment and Prevention*, and co-chair of the Academy of Eating Disorders Special Interest Group (SIG) on Suicide.

Leigh Cohn, MAT, CEDS is the founder and editor in chief of *Eating Disorders: The Journal of Treatment and Prevention* and co-editor of four other Routledge books, including *The Last Word on Eating Disorders Prevention* (2016). He is also publisher of Gürze Books and co-author of several trade books on eating disorders.

"This groundbreaking volume brings together some of the most creative voices to continue the development of family-based treatments, which are founded on the invaluable insight that families are part of the solution, instead of merely part of the problem. In addition, the authors provide an experience-near view of the trials and triumphs the whole family faces in this complex endeavor. Highly recommended, and sure to be referenced for many years to come."

Tom Wooldridge, PsyD, assistant professor
at Golden Gate University

"*Innovations in Family Therapy for Eating Disorders* is a tour de force that advances the field in the treatment of anorexia nervosa and bulimia nervosa. It brings together major theoretical frameworks in one volume and provides novel treatment methods. This book is an invaluable addition for all eating disorder practitioners."

Ray Lemberg, PhD, private practice, Prescott, AZ

"This book is exactly what I have been waiting for. The expert team of editors and authors offers compelling treatment innovations and novel clinical perspectives. This text delivers the wisdom of years of clinical practice in an accessible and academically rigorous format. The editors have artfully crafted an integrated work from both cutting edge, data-based research and the enlightening perspectives of patients, parents, and carers. Those working in the field will find this book to be a valuable resource."

Catherine Cook-Cottone, PhD, associate editor of
Eating Disorders: The Journal of Treatment & Prevention
and associate professor of counseling and school
psychology at the University at Buffalo—SUNY

Innovations in Family Therapy for Eating Disorders

Novel Treatment Developments, Patient Insights, and the Role of Carers

Edited by
Stuart B. Murray, DClinPsych, PhD
Leslie Karwoski Anderson, PhD
Leigh Cohn, MAT, CEDS

Routledge
Taylor & Francis Group

NEW YORK AND LONDON

First published 2016
by Routledge
711 Third Avenue, New York, NY 10017

and by Routledge
2 Park Square, Milton Park, Abingdon, Oxon OX14 4RN

Routledge is an imprint of the Taylor & Francis Group, an informa business

Based partially on a Special Issue of *Eating Disorders: The Journal of Treatment and Prevention*
(Volume 23–24, Summer 2016)

Library of Congress Cataloging in Publication Data
Names: Murray, Stuart, 1982– editor. | Anderson, Leslie, 1976– editor. |
Cohn, Leigh, editor.
Title: Innovations in family therapy for eating disorders: novel treatment
developments, patient insights, and the role of carers /
edited by Stuart Murray, Leslie Anderson, and Leigh Cohn.
Description: New York, NY: Routledge, 2016. |
Includes bibliographical references and index.
Identifiers: LCCN 2016027964| ISBN 9781138648982 (hbk: alk. paper) |
ISBN 9781138648999 (pbk.: alk. paper) | ISBN 9781315626086 (ebk)
Subjects: LCSH: Eating disorders–Treatment. | Family psychotherapy.
Classification: LCC RC552.E18 I52 2016 | DDC 616.85/26–dc23
LC record available at https://lccn.loc.gov/2016027964

ISBN: 978-1-138-64898-2 (hbk)
ISBN: 978-1-138-64899-9 (pbk)
ISBN: 978-1-315-62608-6 (ebk)

Typeset in Baskerville
by Out of House Publishing

Contents

About the Editors

Stuart B. Murray, DClinPsych, PhD is an assistant professor at the University of California, San Francisco, co-director of the National Association for Males with Eating Disorders, and co-chair of the Academy of Eating Disorders Special Interest Group on male eating disorders. He is an active clinician-researcher, and has published over 60 scientific articles and book chapters. Dr. Murray is particularly known for his interest in male eating disorders, and the family therapy-based treatment of eating disorders.

Leslie Karwoski Anderson, PhD is an associate clinical professor and training director at the UC San Diego Eating Disorders Center for Treatment and Research. She is also associate editor for *Eating Disorders: The Journal of Treatment and Prevention*, and co-chair of the Academy of Eating Disorders Special Interest Group on Suicide and Eating Disorders. Her research interests center around the application and dissemination of evidence-based treatment for eating disorders.

Leigh Cohn, MAT, CEDS is publisher of Gürze Books in Carlsbad, CA, editor in chief of *Eating Disorders: The Journal of Treatment and Prevention*, and co-author of several books, including the first publication ever written about bulimia. He has spoken at professional conferences and universities throughout North America, and has received awards from the International Association of Eating Disorders Professionals, the Eating Disorders Coalition, and the National Eating Disorders Association, of which he is a member of the Founders Council.

About the Contributors

Donald H. Baucom, PhD is Distinguished Professor of Psychology and Neuroscience at the University of North Carolina at Chapel Hill. His research focuses on evaluation of couple-based treatments for relationship and individual distress.

Ovidio Bermudez, MD is Chief Clinical Officer and Medical Director of Child and Adolescent Services at the Eating Recovery Center, Denver, CO. He is a board-certified pediatrician and adolescent medicine specialist working with patients and families struggling with eating disorders.

Laura A. Berner, PhD is a postdoctoral research fellow and Davis Scholar at the UC San Diego Eating Disorders Center for Treatment and Research.

Jessica Bezance, DClinPsy is a clinical psychologist working in adult mental health, Berkshire Healthcare NHS Foundation Trust, UK.

Kerri N. Boutelle, PhD is a professor of pediatrics and psychiatry at UCSD and the Director of the Center for Healthy Eating and Activity Research and the Senior Supervising Psychologist at the UC San Diego Eating Disorders Treatment Center.

Abby Braden, PhD is an assistant professor of psychology at Bowling Green State University in Bowling Green, Ohio. Her primary research and clinical interests are in the area of eating disorders and obesity.

Harriet Brown is the author of *Brave Girl Eating: A Family's Struggle with Anorexia* and *Body Of Truth: How Science, History, and Culture Drive Our Obsession with Weight – and What We Can Do About It*, as well as other books. She is an associate professor of magazine journalism at the S. I. Newhouse School of Public Communications at the University of Syracuse, New York.

Cynthia M. Bulik, PhD, FAED is Distinguished Professor of Eating Disorders at the University of North Carolina at Chapel Hill and Professor of Medical Epidemiology and Biostatistics at the Karolinska Institute, Stockholm, Sweden.

Nivia Carballeira Suarez, MD, PhD is a psychiatrist at present working at the Child and Adolescent Psychiatry Clinic in Huddinge, Sweden. At the time of the study she was working in Child and Adolescent Psychiatry at Umeå University Hospital and Umeå University.

Laura L. Connors, PhD is a psychologist employed at the IWK Health Centre in Halifax, Nova Scotia, Canada. She is involved in ongoing research evaluating the use of emotion-focused family therapy for eating disorders and general mental health.

Jennifer Couturier, MD, MSc, FAED is an associate professor, McMaster University, and medical co-director of the Eating Disorders Program at McMaster Children's Hospital. Her research interests include treatments for young people with eating disorders and their uptake into clinical practice.

Anne Cusack, PsyD is a program manager of adult day treatment and intensive outpatient treatment at the UC San Diego Eating Disorders Center.

Joanne Dolhanty, PhD, C.Psych is a psychologist at the Mount Pleasant Therapy Centre in Toronto, Ontario. She co-developed emotion-focused family therapy. She supervises clinicians and teams from organizations across Canada and Europe.

Gina Dimitropoulos, PhD is an assistant professor with the Faculty of Social Work and cross appointed to the Department of Psychiatry at the University of Calgary, Alberta.

Elizabeth Easton, PsyD is Clinical Director of Child and Adolescent Services at the Eating Recovery Center, Denver, CO. She specializes in parent education and empowerment using a family-centered treatment model.

Ivan Eisler, PhD, FAED, FAcSS is Emeritus Professor of Family Psychology and Family Therapy, King's College London and Joint Head of the Child and Adolescent Eating Disorders Service, Maudsley Hospital, London, UK.

Sofie Engman-Bredvik MD was a medical student at Umeå University at the time of the study. Her name is now Koivisto-Engman and she is PRHO/intern at the Hospital of Avesta, county of Dalarna, Sweden.

Natasha Files, MSW, RSW is a family therapist in private practice and at the Looking Glass Residence for Eating Disorders in Vancouver, BC. She is also a sessional instructor in social work at the University of the Fraser Valley.

Melanie S. Fischer, MA is a doctoral student in clinical psychology at the University of North Carolina at Chapel Hill. Her research focuses on psychopathology in the context of intimate relationships and the development and evaluation of couple-based treatments.

Scott Griffiths, PhD is a lecturer in psychology at the University of Canberra, a visiting research fellow at the Australian National University, and an executive board member of the National Association for Males with Eating Disorders.

Joanne Gusella, PhD is a clinical psychologist in private practice in Halifax, NS, and an assistant professor in the Department of Psychiatry at Dalhousie University. She specializes in treating youth and adults with eating disorders and in researching treatment approaches.

Ginger Hartman, RD is a registered dietician at the Eating Recovery Center, Denver, CO. She helped develop the nutrition education modules for the Family in Residence program.

Katherine Henderson, PhD, C.Psych is Co-director and Co-founder of Anchor Psychological Services in Ottawa, Canada, where she specializes in eating disorders and emotion-focused family therapy. She is an adjunct research professor in the Department of Psychology at Carleton University.

Jessica Herschman, BA (Hons), MA is currently completing her Master in Social Work at the Factor-Inwentash Faculty of Social Work at the University of Toronto.

Laura Hill, PhD is the President and CEO of the Center for Balanced Living, a free-standing not-for-profit organization that specializes in the education, treatment, and research of eating disorders.

Joanna Holliday, PhD, DClinPsych is a consultant clinical psychologist working in the Child and Adolescent Eating Disorder Service serving Buckinghamshire and Oxfordshire, UK.

Elizabeth Hughes, PhD is the Lead Research Fellow for Eating Disorders at the Royal Children's Hospital and University of Melbourne, Australia. Her research focuses on the treatment of adolescent eating disorders, particularly family-based treatment for anorexia nervosa.

Katrina Hunt, BSc, DClinPSy is a consultant clinical psychologist for the National and Specialist Child and Adolescent Eating Disorder Service and Service Lead for the National and Specialist CAMHS Dialectical Behaviour Therapy Service, Maudsley Hospital, London, UK.

Craig Johnson, PhD is Chief Science Officer and Director of the Family Institute at the Eating Recovery Center, Denver, CO. He has authored numerous scientific articles and books related to the causes and treatment of eating disorders. He has also been instrumental over the last three decades in developing many of the organizations that have advanced the field.

Walter Kaye, MD is a professor of psychiatry and director of the Eating Disorder Research and Treatment Program, UC San Diego School of

Medicine. He has authored more than 300 publications on anorexia and bulimia nervosa.

Melissa Kimber, PhD, RSW is a post-doctoral fellow within the Offord Centre for Child Studies at McMaster University. Her work focuses on the intersection between eating disorders and family violence, and the implementation of evidence-based practices in adolescent behavioral healthcare.

Jennifer S. Kirby, PhD is Clinical Associate Professor in the Department of Psychiatry at the University of North Carolina at Chapel Hill. She specializes in developing and evaluating couple-based interventions for individual psychopathology, including eating disorders and emotion dysregulation.

Maria C. La Via, MD is Associate Professor of Psychiatry at the University of North Carolina at Chapel Hill, and is the former clinical and medical director of the UNC Center of Excellence for Eating Disorders in Chapel Hill, NC.

Adèle Lafrance Robinson, PhD, C.Psych is an associate professor in the Psychology Department at Laurentian University. She is a psychologist and co-developer of emotion-focused family therapy. She supervises clinicians and teams from organizations across Canada and Europe.

Daniel Le Grange, PhD, FAED is Benioff UCSF Professor in Children's Health, and Eating Disorders Director at the University of California, San Francisco. He is also Emeritus Professor of Psychiatry and Behavioral Neuroscience at the University of Chicago. He is the co-author of several books on adolescent eating disorders.

Richard Levi, MD, PhD, MBA is Senior Consultant in Neurology and Physiatry and Adjunct Professor in Neurological Rehabilitation at Linkoping University and University Hospital, Sweden. At the time of the study, he was Professor of Physical Medicine and Rehabilitation at Umeå University, Sweden.

James Lock, MD, PhD is Professor of Psychiatry and Pediatrics at Stanford University and Director of the Eating Disorders Program in the Department of Psychiatry and Behavioral Sciences. He is the co-author of *Treatment Manual for Anorexia Nervosa: A Family-Based Approach*, *Treating Bulimia in Adolescents*, and *Help Your Teenager Beat an Eating Disorder*.

Katharine L. Loeb, PhD, FAED is Professor of Psychology at Fairleigh Dickinson University. She is on the faculty of the Training Institute for Child and Adolescent Eating Disorders, and is co-editor of the book, *Family Therapy for Adolescent Eating and Weight Disorders: New Applications*.

Pam Macdonald, PhD conducted research into carers at King's College London. She now works as a freelance researcher and coaches carers of people with eating disorders using the New Maudsley method.

Jamie Manwaring, PhD is a therapist at the Eating Recovery Center, Denver, CO, and was a co-creator and facilitator of its Family in Residence program. She has authored several peer-reviewed publications on the subject of eating and weight disorders.

Patricia Marchand, MSW, RSW is the Team Leader and Coordinator of the child and adolescent eating disorders clinic at the Hotel Dieu Hospital in Kingston, ON.

Brittany Matheson, MS is a graduate student researcher in the San Diego State University/UC San Diego Joint Doctoral Program in Clinical Psychology. She is a lead therapist for the UC San Diego Eating Disorders Center's Intensive Family Treatment program.

Shari Mayman, PhD, C.Psych is the Co-founder and Co-director of Anchor Psychological Services, a private practice in Ottawa, ON. She is active in the research and delivery of emotion-focused family therapy, as well as in the training of other professionals.

Patricia Nash, MEd, CCC is the Counselor and Program Facilitator at the Eating Disorder Foundation of Newfoundland and Labrador in St. John's, NL. She is also a mom with lived experience who is passionate about helping families struggling with eating disorders.

Karin Nilsson, PhD is a psychologist, psychotherapist and supervisor in psychotherapy. She is an assistant professor at Umeå University and a psychologist at Umeå University hospital, Sweden. Her main research interests are treatment of eating disorders and families.

Emily Orr, PhD is a clinical psychologist with the Eating Disorders Clinic at Cape Breton Regional Hospital. She also maintains a private practice in the Sydney, NS area.

Erin Parks, PhD is a clinical psychologist with a background in neuroscience research and eating disorder treatment. She currently serves as the Director of Outreach and Admissions at the UC San Diego Eating Disorders Center for Treatment and Research.

Stephanie Knatz Peck, PhD is a clinical psychologist and Program Director for the Intensive Family Treatment (IFT) programs at the UCSD Eating Disorders Treatment and Research Center.

Ana Ramirez, PhD is a licensed clinical psychologist and a manager of the adolescent program at the UCSD Eating Disorders Center for Treatment and Research. She has co-authored several peer-reviewed articles on the treatment and prevention of eating disorders.

Charlotte Rhind, PhD studied those with eating disorders and their carers at King's College London and now works at the South London and Maudsley NHS Foundation Trust as a clinical psychology trainee.

Roxanne E. Rockwell, PhD is a licensed clinical psychologist and Director of the adolescent eating disorder program at the UC San Diego School of Medicine.

Cristin D. Runfola, PhD is Clinical Instructor in the Department of Psychiatry and Behavioral Sciences at Stanford University and Adjunct Assistant Professor at the University of North Carolina at Chapel Hill. She specializes in eating disorder treatment and research.

Grant Salada, LCSW is a therapist at the Eating Recovery Center, Denver, CO. He is a co-creator and facilitator of the Family in Residence program working to educate and empower parents in the treatment process.

Leslie Sanders, MD is a board-certified adolescent medicine physician. She is the Medical Director of the Eating Disorder Program of the Atlantic Health System at the Goryeb Children's Center/Overlook Medical Center in Summit, NJ.

Susan Sawyer, MD, FRACP holds the Geoff and Helen Handbury Chair of Adolescent Health at the University of Melbourne. A pediatrician, she established the specialist eating disorder program at the Royal Children's Hospital where she is Director of the Centre for Adolescent Health.

Jennifer Scarborough, MSW, RSW is a clinician in the eating disorders program at the Canadian Mental Health Association in Waterloo, ON. She is currently completing her PhD at Wilfrid Laurier University with a focus on pediatric eating disorders and parental emotions.

Marjorie Scott, LISW-S is the Assistant Director of the Partial-Hospitalization Program for eating disorders for the Center for Balanced Living, Columbus, OH.

Mima Simic, MD, MSc, MRCPsych is a consultant child and adolescent psychiatrist for the National and Specialist CAMHS DBT Service and Joint Head of the National and Specialist Child and Adolescent Eating Disorders Service, Maudsley Hospital, London, UK.

Cathleen Steinegger, MD, MSc is an adolescent medicine physician and Head of the Eating Disorders Program at the Hospital for Sick Children and Assistant Professor of Pediatrics at the University of Toronto, ON.

Catherine Stewart, BA, PGCE, PhD, DClinPsy is a senior clinical psychologist for the National and Specialist Child and Adolescent Eating Disorders Service, Maudsley Hospital, London, UK.

Amanda Stillar, MA is a doctoral student in counselling psychology at the University of Alberta. She is active in eating disorder research, with a focus on emotion-focused family therapy and the role of parental emotions.

Erin Strahan, PhD is a faculty member in the psychology department of Wilfrid Laurier University. She is active in body image research, with a focus on process models.

Elin Svensson, MD was a medical student at Umeå University at the time of the study. Her name is now Elin Birnefeld and she is a resident in Anesthesiology and Intensive Care at Umeå University Hospital, Sweden.

Gill Todd, RMN, MSc worked for 30 years in the NHS as a psychiatric nurse, spending 27 of those years in the field of eating disorders. Now retired from the NHS, she continues to serve as a motivational enhancement trainer in eating disorders and provides supervision and training for Professor Janet Treasure. She started the annual National Carers Conference for Eating Disorders in 1996.

Alene Toulany, MD, FRCPC is an adolescent medicine specialist at the Hospital for Sick Children and Assistant Professor of Paediatrics in the Faculty of Medicine at the University of Toronto, ON.

Janet Treasure, OBE, PhD, FRCP, FRCPsych has specialized in the treatment of eating disorders at the South London and Maudsley Hospital and has also had an academic career at King's College London for the majority of her career.

Stamatoula Voulgari, BSc, Postgrad Dip, MSc is a senior systemic family psychotherapist, trainer and training co-ordinator for the National and Specialist Child and Adolescent Eating Disorders Service, Maudsley Hospital, London, UK.

Anna Young is an avid cyclist and the proud owner of a Great Dane. She is completing her Bachelor's of Science in Nursing.

Foreword

This volume is part of a gathering body of work in the field of family therapy for eating disorders. It is gratifying to see that the work that started at the Maudsley Hospital in London in the 1980s has brought about a cadre of new clinicians and researchers who all are building on those early foundations. Most notable from this work, perhaps, is that the Maudsley team has elevated the family to being part of the solution as opposed to part of the problem. And now, this volume has put together 25 chapters that discuss different formats of family therapy and in a variety of contexts – each taking a page from that early work that was started in London.

Families with a teen diagnosed with an eating disorder did not always have such great advocates as they might have today. While the role of the family in the context of eating disorders has been acknowledged in the earliest writings (cf. Gull, 1997), the family was seen as a hindrance rather than a resource in treatment. In fact, Gull and his contemporaries, such as Charcot, advocated for patients with anorexia nervosa to be separated from their families, as the influence of the latter was "particularly pernicious." This stance toward families has persisted through much of the twentieth century. In fact, today, well after Gull and others' condemnation of families, many clinicians in our field still resolutely consider the families' involvement in treatment as detrimental to the adolescent and ultimately not helpful in securing a good outcome. It is in this climate that the sea change brought about by the Maudsley pioneers is so significant. Instead of blaming parents for their child's eating disorder, Ivan Eisler and his colleagues (a) saw no evidence for such causality and instead (b) held parents in high esteem *and* elevated them as a resource and as part of the solution. This particular stance built on Salvador Minuchin's and Mara Selvini Palazzoli's earlier work, and solidified a specific family therapy for adolescent anorexia nervosa, i.e. a treatment that purposefully engages parents to support their child through this illness, and in so doing brought about a radical departure from decades of excluding parents from treatment.

Since this work started at the Maudsley Hospital, much has happened regarding family therapy for adolescents with eating disorders. Among the most prominent developments, perhaps, is the publication of two family therapy manuals, one for anorexia nervosa and another for bulimia nervosa (Le Grange & Lock,

2007; Lock & Le Grange, 2013). These manuals have been helpful in promoting training in this approach while at the same time providing opportunities for replicable treatment outcomes research. Several randomized clinical trials have now been published, mostly utilizing these clinician manuals. It must be especially gratifying for our colleagues in London, and equally gratifying for many of the rest of us working in this field, to see this treatment modality with families being implemented in such a systematic way in so many different parts of the world. Numerous families and their adolescent offspring have benefitted from this collective body of work. That said, though, we have much more work to do.

And with that, allow me to turn to the current volume. No treatment is a panacea, and family therapy for adolescent eating disorders is no exception. Therefore, as a field, we need to continue to challenge ourselves, bemoan the modest rates of remission achieved by our best-known treatments, and be prepared to confront the "holy cows" of such treatments. And this volume does that. For instance: should family therapy be restricted to the outpatient setting, should this approach only be conducted in conjoint format, is the family meal necessary, what about convening multiple families instead of single families, and why not test whether incorporating strategies from other evidence-based treatments into family therapy would stand to ultimately improve outcomes for this patient population? These are just some of the many questions that we should ask ourselves and that this volume attempts to address. It does more than just that, though. It also turns to the "trenches," to borrow a phrase from the editors. While we do a lot of talking to the patients and families we work with, this volume reminds us to pay close attention to *what* the families and their offspring have to say, *how* they experience treatment and recovery, and what they can teach us, not just about their therapy needs, but also how we may go about our work in more effective ways. The final "voice" of this volume comes from the therapists themselves. After all, we are in the trenches *with* our patients, and we can all benefit from listening and learning from one another.

We have come a long way since those early pessimistic days that bemoaned the "pernicious" families of patients with anorexia nervosa. Many pioneers of family therapy bravely changed that outlook, and since then, numerous clinicians and researchers have collectively contributed to promoting *and* practicing that positive message. Countless sufferers have benefitted from this family therapy approach, and, although more work needs to be done, this volume contributes in a significant way toward a better understanding of this treatment for youth with eating disorders. The messages to question what we think we know, to think outside the box, and to listen to our families and patients, all come across loud and clear!

Daniel Le Grange, PhD
Benioff UCSF Professor in Children's Health
Eating Disorders Director
Department of Psychiatry, UCSF Weill Institute for Neurosciences
University of California, San Francisco
Emeritus Professor of Psychiatry and Behavioral Neuroscience
University of Chicago

References

Gull, W. W. (1997 [1868]). Anorexia nervosa (apepsia hysterica, anorexia hysterica). *Obesity Research & Clinical Practice*, 5(5), 498–502.

Le Grange, D., & Lock, J. (2007). *Treating bulimia in adolescents: A family-based approach.* New York: Guilford Press.

Lock, J., & Le Grange, D. (2013). *Treatment manual for anorexia nervosa: A family-based approach*, 2nd edition. New York: Guilford Press.

Acknowledgments

We are most grateful to the 70 authors who generously contributed their time and expertise to the chapters in this book. They include many of the most esteemed clinicians and researchers in the eating disorders field. We are also appreciative of the entire staff at Routledge/Taylor & Francis, especially Ngoc Le and Kate Bracaglia, our editors there for *Eating Disorders: The Journal of Treatment and Prevention*, where much of this book's material originated, and Christopher Teja, the Associate Acquisitions Editor, who has been a great supporter of expanding special issues of the journal into comprehensive texts.

Stuart Murray: This book would not have been possible without the friendship, mentorship, and support of Leslie Karwoski Anderson and Leigh Cohn, and I could not imagine a better team to embark on a journey like this with. My deep gratitude also goes to many amazing mentors and teachers, including Elizabeth Rieger and Chris Thornton, who collectively turned a wide-eyed student into a clinical psychologist, and Daniel Le Grange and Walter Kaye, whose passion for furthering our evidence base shaped my approach to scientific inquiry. Thanks to Chris Teja and the team at Routledge for supporting our vision for this book. I'm eternally grateful to my parents, whose guiding hands are evident at every juncture in my life. Lastly, this book is dedicated to Lilliana, Emiliana, and Luciana, who have been my biggest source of support, encouragement, and inspiration.

Leslie Karwoski Anderson: I want to acknowledge my many wonderful professional mentors over the years, especially Walter Kaye, Steve Ilardi, and Terry Schwartz. And, of course, so much gratitude to Stuart Murray for collaborating with me on as many projects as either of us can dream up, and Leigh Cohn, who has become a trusted friend and mentor. Special thanks to my parents, Gail and Chester Karwoski, who showed me how it's done in terms of studying psychology and publishing books. And I am so grateful to my husband, Lucas Anderson, for being my biggest supporter while I balance work and our children and projects like this.

Leigh Cohn: As founding editor of *Eating Disorders: The Journal of Treatment and Prevention*, I've had the opportunity to oversee numerous special issues, several of which have been expanded into books. My collaboration with Stuart and Leslie on this project has been the most enjoyable of those experiences. I have tremendous love and respect for them both.

All editors would like to thank Emily Nauman and acknowledge her wonderful assistance in proofing and indexing this volume.

Introduction

*Stuart B. Murray, Leslie Karwoski Anderson,
and Leigh Cohn*

A cursory glance back over the history of eating disorders illustrates the central role that families have purportedly occupied in illness presentations, since the very first depicted reports of anorexia nervosa (AN). Indeed, the early historical landscape was littered with rich clinical descriptions of how the pernicious influence of one's family both underpinned and maintained AN psychopathology. As such, the prevailing treatment for many years advocated a "parentectomy" to extricate those with AN from their pathogenic parents and family members. However, the late 1970s marked the start of an important shift in our approach to the treatment of eating disorders. During this time, pioneering family therapists Salvador Minuchin and Mara Selvini Palazzoli, despite still retaining the notion that family structure and dynamics were implicated in the pathogenesis of AN, debunked the notion that families were toxic to the recovery process, and instead illustrated how families may drive a series of changes which may ultimately arrive at symptom remission. Subsequent to this, more groundbreaking work by Michael White, and Gerard Russell and colleagues at the Maudsley Hospital in London, actively rejected the notion that families were implicated in the pathogenesis of eating disorders, and, instead, were the greatest allies to the recovery process. This conceptual standpoint forms the basis of contemporary family therapy-based approaches to the treatment of eating disorders.

The last 20 years has witnessed rapid growth in the family therapy-based treatment of eating disorders, and equally rapid progress has been made. To date, the evidence-base for family therapy in the context of eating disorders eclipses that of family therapy for any other psychiatric ailment, and the deeply-seated roots of family therapy for eating disorders continue to spring new crops. Indeed, the precise configuration of family therapy-based approaches for the treatment of eating disorders is becoming increasingly diverse, and the existing evidence-base spans a multitude of data ranging from case studies through to multi-site, randomized controlled trials and manualized treatment manuals.

This book represents a panoramic view from the crest of this growing wave of family therapy treatment for eating disorders, and a look towards the horizon. The conceptual origin of this collected body of works stems, in part, from our liaison with pioneering family therapy groups during a conference on innovative treatment approaches held at the University of California, San Diego in October, 2014. Additionally, the opportunity to edit a Special Edition of *Eating Disorders: The Journal of Treatment & Prevention*, which was entirely devoted to novel family therapy approaches to eating disorders, further galvanized our resolve in bringing this book to fruition. To this end, we've included the original journal articles and have added 15 more chapters to this volume. Its 70 contributors come from several countries and include many of the most prolific voices in this field.

As it stands, *Innovations in Family Therapy for Eating Disorders: Novel Treatment Developments, Patient Insights, and the Role of Carers* aims to address the most recent advances in the field of family therapy for eating disorders, illustrating an array of theoretical models of treatment across a transdiagnostic spectrum of eating disorders in both adolescents and adults alike. Further, we aim to illustrate the patient voice, which conveys a unique "insider knowledge" and expertise, which must be factored in to future clinical treatment developments. Additionally, we address the role of carers, including the parents, spouses, and partners of patients with an array of disordered eating ranging from AN to emotional overeating.

A broad, collected body of works like this naturally lends itself to division into distinct categories. Part I, Innovations in Family Therapy for Anorexia Nervosa and Bulimia Nervosa, relates specifically to novel treatment innovations in the context of AN and bulimia nervosa (BN). The opening chapter, by Stuart Murray and colleagues, outlines the adaptation of family-based treatment (FBT) for adolescent AN across higher levels of patient care. Next, Elizabeth Hughes and colleagues explore the mechanics of delivering parent-only FBT, without the adolescent being present, which was developed in Melbourne, Australia. In the third chapter, Stephanie Knatz Peck and colleagues provide a clinician's overview of a novel multi-family, intensive family therapy program, which was developed for transdiagnostic eating disorder treatment at the University of California, San Diego. The fourth chapter, by Murray and colleagues, revisits the historical roots of family therapy for the eating disorders and proposes an integration of several broader family therapy interventions into the delivery of FBT. Two chapters relating to adolescent BN conclude this section. Leslie Karwoski Anderson and colleagues outline the novel integration of the treatment philosophies underpinning FBT and dialectical behavior therapy (DBT), which is important when considering the emerging evidence for FBT in the context of BN, and the broader evidence supporting the efficacy of DBT in curtailing emotionally dysregulated behaviors. Lastly, Catherine Stewart and colleagues from Maudsley Hospital in London provide a clinical overview of the development of a novel multi-family program for the treatment of adolescent BN.

Part II, Special Topics in Family Therapy for Eating Disorders, includes chapters on diverse topics related to dissemination and implementation of FT. James Lock from Stanford University reviews treatment specificity within the realm of family therapy for eating disorders, noting how specialized family therapy-based treatment offers more potent results than non-specific family therapy treatments. Dovetailing nicely with this chapter, Jennifer Couturier and Melissa Kimber from McMaster University in Ontario, Canada offer a carefully constructed systematic review of the factors implicated in the dissemination and implementation of specialized family therapy treatment. Next, Katherine Loeb and Leslie Sanders explore the roles of multidisciplinary treatment team members, focusing on how the therapist and physician can complement and enhance each other's work. The final two chapters in this part focus on ways to augment treatment response in family therapy for eating disorders. Murray and Scott Griffiths explore the integration of general family therapy techniques into family therapy for eating disorders, with detailed case examples to illustrate how this could be effective. Mima Simic and colleagues, including esteemed professors Ivan Eisler and Walter Kaye, examine ways to augment family therapy with a variety of other evidence-based approaches, including DBT, parent training, and cognitive behavioral therapy.

Part III, Carers, explores the role of family members and loved ones, who are much relied upon in treatment but often overlooked in empirical research. The first two chapters in this section, by Jennifer Kirby and colleagues, present a novel program, "Uniting Couples in the Treatment of Anorexia Nervosa" developed by Cindy Bulik's group at the University of North Carolina, Chapel Hill. They first provide an overview of the approach and then focus more specifically on strategies to engage carers in supporting their loved one in higher levels of care. Next, Janet Treasure and colleagues outline a conceptual overview of their novel treatment, the *New Maudsley Method*, which relates to the carers of adult patients. Elizabeth Easton and colleagues describe how Craig Johnson and Ovidio Bermudez's group at the Eating Recovery Center in Denver has made family involvement an integral part of their residential treatment program, despite the logistical barriers. Peck and colleagues outline a parent-driven treatment of adolescent emotional overeating, focusing specifically on parent coaching. Lastly, doctoral student Amanda Stillar, Professor Adele Lafrance Robinson and 11 Canadian colleagues review several important potential barriers that may stymie the role of carers throughout treatment, namely, fear and self-blame.

Part IV, Tales From the Trenches: Personal Accounts, gives voice to people who have had eating disorders or cared for someone in recovery. First, Harriet Brown, who wrote an inspiring memoir in 2011, and her daughter Anna Young, look back at their experiences doing family therapy for Anna's eating disorder. In the second chapter, Erin Parks and colleagues use a mixed methods design to explore how teenagers feel about having been through family therapy for their eating disorder, once the treatment has concluded. Next are two chapters from Karin Nilsson's Swedish collaborators. Sofie Engman-Bredvik and colleagues share a qualitative study of parental experiences in multi-family therapy in AN; Elin Svensson and colleagues explore the experiences of parents of children with an eating disorder, as well as their experiences caring for the child. Finally, Jessica Bezance and

Joanna Holliday examine the mother's perspective on delivering treatment for their adolescents with AN at home, through interpretive phenomenological analysis.

Finally, Part V, How I Practice, has instructional pieces by clinicians on how they use advanced techniques to enhance their family therapy work with eating disorder patients. Laura Hill and Marjorie Scott describe how they use metaphors and experiential exercises to bring the research on neurobiology of eating disorders to life for patients and their families. Next, Peck outlines how to design and implement behavioral contracts to encourage and support eating disorder recovery within families. Finally, Murray expands upon the classic family technique of circular questioning, including concrete examples of ways to rephrase linear questions into circular questions.

As we pause and take stock to survey the current landscape of family therapy approaches in the treatment of eating disorders, the horizon is broader, brighter, and more diverse than ever before. Our field has come a long way from the days of blaming parents and extricating families from treatment, and the multitude of evidence-based options available to clinicians working with families ought to inspire optimism among both practitioners and families alike. It is our hope that this collection of works may guide clinicians in forging new ways of working with families to overcome eating disorders, and encourage the evolution of emerging clinical practices while retaining the roots of family therapy. As one of the pioneers of family therapy, Salvador Minuchin (1974, p. 47), wrote, "It is only the family, society's smallest unit, that can change and yet maintain enough continuity to rear children who will not be 'strangers in a strange land,' who will be rooted firmly enough to grow and adapt."

Reference

Minuchin, S. (1974). *Families and family therapy*. Cambridge, MA: Harvard University Press.

Part I

Innovations in Family Therapy for Anorexia Nervosa and Bulimia Nervosa

1 Adapting Family-Based Treatment for Adolescent Anorexia Nervosa across Higher Levels of Patient Care

Stuart B. Murray, Leslie Karwoski Anderson, Roxanne Rockwell, Scott Griffiths, Daniel Le Grange, and Walter H. Kaye

Anorexia nervosa (AN) typically demonstrates poor treatment outcomes, high rates of relapse and treatment dropout (Keel & Brown, 2010), elevated rates of premature death related to both medical complications (Steinhausen, 2002) and suicidality (Pompili, Mancinelli, Girardi, Ruberto, & Tatarelli, 2004), and reduced quality of life (Mond, Hay, Rodgers, Owen, & Beumont, 2005). However, when treated during adolescence, favorable treatment outcomes appear somewhat more attainable (Treasure & Russell, 2011). Thus, recent efforts have focused on treatments targeted at adolescent presentations, with family-based treatment (FBT) showing particular promise (Lock & Le Grange, 2013). However, while efforts to disseminate FBT have largely focused on outpatient settings (Couturier, Kimber, & Szatmari, 2013), there is a dearth of evidence detailing the application of FBT to more intensive levels of patient care.

AN is typically treated across a range of treatment contexts based on illness severity, with some arguing that presentations of AN ought to be delineated by stages of severity in order to allow for the most effective and appropriate treatment (Maguire et al., 2009). Indeed, the continuum of care model ensures that treatment dosage can be matched with illness severity, while significantly reducing the overall cost of treatment (Kaye, Enright, & Lesser, 1998; Wiseman, Sunday, Klapper, Harris, & Halmi, 2001).

A patient's transition through levels of care is typically determined by symptom severity, medical status, motivational status, treatment history, and logistical concerns, although with fluctuating levels of motivation for change (Geller, Zaitsoff, & Srikameswaran, 2005) and relapsing symptom severity (Strober, Freeman, & Morell, 1997), movement through the levels of care can be bidirectional. The significance of this multi-tiered level of care system is underscored when considering (a) the medically necessary need for urgent weight restoration in severe AN, (b) the management of clinical complexity and comorbidity, and (c) the need to ensure progress sustainability in the context of the high rates of relapse in AN (Strober et al., 1997). However, few treatment settings currently offer all levels of care within the same setting, and the integration of evidence-based treatment throughout varying levels of care in the treatment of

AN poses many challenges. This may be particularly important as it pertains to the role of families in treatment, given the differing beliefs as to the optimal role of families in the treatment of adolescent AN (Le Grange, Lock, Loeb, & Nicholls, 2010; Murray, Thornton, & Wallis, 2012a).

FBT is characterized by an agnostic stance towards the origin of AN and a conceptualization of parents as the primary resource in restoring their adolescent back to health. The focus of the treatment is orchestrating a parent-driven intervention to restore healthy eating patterns in the adolescent and then gradually transitioning the adolescent back to eating autonomy (Lock & Le Grange, 2013). Empirical evidence suggests that 50–70 percent of adolescents with AN undergoing FBT are weight-restored within a year of commencing treatment, and up to 40 percent being remitted of cognitive symptomatology (Lock et al., 2010). Follow-up studies and meta-analyses further support the efficacy of FBT, suggesting robust symptom remission over time (Couturier et al., 2013; Eisler, Simic, Russell, & Dare, 2007).

The Application of Family-Based Treatment across the Continuum of Care

The lack of clinical research on the efficacy and feasibility of FBT across the continuum of care is particularly important when considering (a) the volume of adolescents with AN who require non-outpatient-based treatment at some stage of their treatment trajectory (Katzman, 2005), and (b) recent findings underscoring the importance of theoretical consistency across treatment providers and levels of care (Murray et al., 2012a; Murray, Griffiths, & Le Grange, 2014). With recent findings documenting that (a) rapid intervention and early treatment mechanisms are indicative of overall treatment outcome (Doyle, Le Grange, Loeb, Doyle, & Crosby, 2010; Le Grange, Accurso, Lock, Agras, & Bryson, 2014), and (b) those with more severe AN psychopathology typically report greater benefit from FBT than those with less marked symptomatology (Le Grange, Lock, Agras, Bryson, & Kraemer, 2012), there appears to be a clear rationale for applying FBT to intensive treatment settings.

However, there are many challenges inherent in practicing FBT across levels of care while maintaining treatment fidelity. Given that higher levels of patient care warrant greater professional involvement, there is a risk of undermining the FBT treatment approach that centralizes parental involvement and decentralizes professional expertise. Indeed, while current clinical practice has advocated the use of FBT in higher levels of care (e.g. Girz, LaFrance Robinson, Foroughe, Jasper, & Boachie, 2013; Henderson et al., 2014; Hoste, 2015), little theoretical guidance exists in its application. We therefore aim to outline a theoretical framework of how FBT may be applied across higher levels of patient care, outlining several key challenges and explicating how the theoretical underpinning of FBT may be applied in a way that ensures treatment fidelity.

Establishing the Role of Parents and the Treatment Team Throughout the Continuum of Care

The central premise of FBT posits that parents ought to be the central architects of their child's recovery, providing a sustainable agent of change that persists beyond any treatment context (Lock & Le Grange, 2013). However, higher levels of care are typically characterized by reduced parental involvement in treatment, despite emerging evidence demonstrating that mechanisms of symptom remission in FBT appear to be driven by empowering parents to take control of their child's eating (Ellison et al., 2012). Thus, any adaptation of FBT to more intensive levels of patient care ought to carefully consider the dialectic of balancing the empowerment of parents while also ensuring thorough clinical management of medical instability.

Clinical Options

Restoring medical stability, offering respite for parents, and delaying the onset of FBT. The clinical reality in inpatient hospital settings is that urgent medical stabilization and caloric restoration take full priority. To this end, strict medical guidelines exist in expediently and safely curtailing the potential scope for medical complications in AN (Katzman, Peebles, Sawyer, Lock, & Le Grange, 2013). In this context, the time required to mobilize disempowered parents into active symptom resolution may likely contravene medical best practice, which urges the most immediate restoration of medical stability. Thus, greater illness severity often necessitates swift medical intervention at the expense of parent-driven symptom reduction.

However, a key distinction was recently drawn between hospital-based medical stabilization and hospital-based weight restoration, with current evidence supporting inpatient medical stabilization and an expedient step-down into less intensive levels of care and parent-assisted weight restoration (Madden et al., 2014). Thus, *inpatient hospital settings* might be most suited to the urgent medical stabilization of acute AN that might preclude full parental involvement, followed by the commencement of FBT once the adolescent is medically stable and parents may play a more central role in treatment. However, with emerging evidence supporting shorter periods of inpatient hospitalization for adolescents with AN and swifter transitions into FBT (ibid), it is important to caution against offering respite for parents beyond a point when they could feasibly be involved in the feeding of their child. Indeed, parental respite beyond this point may alleviate the necessity for swift parental intervention, undermining subsequent treatment (ibid).

Increasing parental involvement as adolescents progress through levels of care. While keeping in mind the medical gravity of severe AN, exploring creative ways to involve the family as much as possible, even at higher levels of care, may be particularly congruent with FBT.

Inpatient hospital settings. While inpatient settings are necessarily oriented towards urgent medical stabilization, these settings are also uniquely placed to orient families towards the early goals of FBT. For instance, FBT clinicians may work alongside medical teams in: (a) raising parental anxiety, which will further mobilize parental resources once FBT commences, and (b) working to create unity between the parents. Concurrently, the medical team may assume the role as expert on the patient's medical status and communicate that information to the parents, further assisting in generating parental anxiety. Similarly, while dietitian involvement is not typically prescribed in outpatient FBT, the imminent weight gain requirements in critically unwell adolescents, coupled with the risk of re-feeding syndrome, may necessitate dietitian involvement. However, integrating parental involvement within the context of dietetic assistance is plausible, for instance by having dietitians convey the calculated caloric requirements and consulting with parents as to how these calories are provided (Katzman et al., 2013).

Residential settings. A feature of residential programs is the temporary removal of adolescents from their home until symptom remission is indicated, which may impinge upon the prescribed and empirically supported role of parents throughout FBT (Ellison et al., 2012). As such, FBT in residential contexts may be inherently challenging, particularly when residential settings are not in the same geographical region as the family home. Endeavors towards this end may include encouraging parents' temporarily residing in the local area, including regular family meetings, the co-construction of treatment goals, and multiple family meals and parent coaching.

Patient hospitalization program/intensive outpatient program settings. Perhaps more amenable to an FBT framework, patient hospitalization program (PHP) and intensive outpatient program (IOP) settings feature day-based clinical treatment, coupled with home-based symptom management outside of program hours. Such settings allow for treatment goals to be oriented towards family psychoeducation and weight restoration in a manner consistent with outpatient FBT, although at a more intensive treatment dose and with more stringent medical monitoring. With respect to the broader treatment team, the physician (typically a pediatrician or psychiatrist), may not necessarily occupy the most central role at this level unless there are imminent medical concerns, instead serving as a consultant to the parents and FBT clinician while monitoring medical status (Katzman et al., 2013). Similarly, dietetic involvement may be downwardly adjusted in conjunction with increasing parental involvement over meal provision. For instance, dietitians at this level of care may serve primarily as a consultant to the family therapist as needed, especially in cases with complicated dietary features (e.g. diabetes, celiac disease, etc.), or in cases in which treatment is not progressing as expected (e.g. weight gain is not occurring, despite the family appearing to appropriately manage their child's behaviors). Furthermore, since patients in PHP/IOP typically attend most meals in program without the support of siblings, an individual therapist might play a role in a PHP/IOP setting by supporting the patient in the same way siblings are encouraged to support the patient in outpatient FBT. Additionally, due to the high level of psychiatric comorbidities in higher levels of care, the individual therapist may concurrently provide other types of evidence-based treatment to address these issues.

Mobilizing and Empowering Parents throughout Treatment in Hospital and Partial-Hospital Settings

Prior to beginning treatment, it is commonplace for many families to feel disempowered and ambivalent about the challenge of weight restoring their child with AN. Indeed, many families report inadvertently accommodating an array of AN-type behaviors in an attempt to allay their child's anxiety (Eisler, 2005). Thus, a crucial tenet of FBT posits that parents ought to be immediately ushered beyond any anxiety or avoidance and charged with the responsibility of urgent intervention in their child's behaviors.

To this end, a therapeutic "double-bind" at the outset of FBT aims to simultaneously elevate parental anxiety and implore parental intervention in reversing their child's symptoms (Dare et al., 1995; Lock & Le Grange, 2013). This is accomplished through a somber discussion of the medical complications of AN, which aims to render the anxiety parents feel about *not* confronting their child's AN greater than any anxiety around confronting their child's symptoms.

However, the timing of this therapeutic double-bind may need adaptation for clinical settings that foster greater staff than parental involvement and thus afford less scope for parental responsibility in symptom reduction. Raising parental anxiety and imploring them to intervene in these settings may contraindicate the empowerment FBT advocates. For instance, it is possible that elevated parental anxiety at the outset of treatment may be more allayed by the child's involvement with the intensive staff-driven program than by their own increasing sense of mastery in managing their child's symptoms. In this respect, therapeutically elevating parental anxiety, when coupled with reduced scope for parental involvement and staff-driven reductions in parental anxiety, may potentially deepen a sense of reliance on staff-driven symptom reduction, which contravenes the mechanism by which the therapeutic double-bind was intended to operate in outpatient settings. Thus it is important that this double-bind at higher levels of care is carefully planned.

Clinical Options

Create greater scope for parental involvement in hospital and partial-hospital settings. Many schools of family therapy posit that the most effective time to mobilize familial anxiety is during the peak of the most intense crisis (Haley, 1980), which for some families facing AN will inevitably fall during admissions to higher levels of care. However, FBT theory would posit that raising parental anxiety and empowerment ought to coincide with the opportunity for parents to act on their raised anxiety and sense of empowerment in curtailing their child's symptoms (Lock & Le Grange, 2013). To this end, one recently developed "family admissions program" involved entire families undergoing a two-week inpatient hospital admission alongside their child with AN, both underscoring the magnitude of the family crisis and simultaneously allowing enhanced scope for parental involvement in symptom reduction (Wallis et al., 2013). Another program, operating at a PHP level, involved 40 hours of intensive FBT-based treatment over one week, allowing parents full scope for involvement at every meal, as well as intensive training on implementing FBT at home (Rockwell, Boutelle, Trunko, Jacobs, & Kaye, 2011). These approaches are predicated on both the theoretical notion and empirical findings stipulating that parental empowerment and influence over symptom reduction is most centrally connected to favorable long-term treatment outcome (Ellison et al., 2012). However, it should be noted that this approach is both time and labor intensive, meaning that very few families may be accommodated at any one time. In treatment settings, this may raise questions as to the practical viability of this approach, given that multiple adolescents typically require medical stabilization in specialized eating disorder units at any given time.

Coordinate several parental anxiety mobilizing meetings, geared towards specific stages of treatment in hospital and partial-hospital settings. An alternative approach may integrate multiple staggered and specifically nuanced crisis meetings with parents at different levels of care, given the importance of not seeking parental involvement beyond what a particular treatment setting can accommodate. For instance, in attending to the most significant crisis around medical instability and urgent hospitalization, FBT clinicians may raise and mobilize anxiety with the goal of having parents commit to urgent hospitalization. In transitioning to a lower level of care, empirical findings suggest that many adolescents with AN do not consistently attend treatment or complete treatment of their own accord (Girz et al., 2013). Thus, the transition to this level of care may be punctuated by a more nuanced therapeutic double-bind in which parental anxiety is raised by being made aware of the rate of relapse to hospital settings following hospital-driven weight restoration and the propensity for treatment dropout in partial-hospital settings (ibid), mobilizing parents into a more active stance in ensuring continued treatment attendance and compliance as the child progresses through the levels of care.

Similarly, the transition to outpatient FBT, which is characterized by the greatest scope for parental involvement, may be marked by a further and qualitatively different therapeutic double-bind, which may place greater emphasis on parents in ensuring long-term symptom remission. Indeed, repeated double-bind sessions are common throughout FBT, either in re-mobilizing parental resources in instances of treatment plateaus or in priming parental resources for the next stage of treatment without endorsing parental complacency (Lock & Le Grange, 2013).

Indices of Parental Efficacy throughout Treatment

The assessment of parental efficacy forms a crucial component of FBT and perhaps the most pivotal barometer of parental efficacy is their child's weight status, which affords direct feedback as to how effective parental efforts at weight restoration have been (Lock & Le Grange, 2013). This feedback is so important that it typically determines the content of every family meeting during the re-feeding phase of outpatient FBT (Lock & Le Grange, 2013), with weight gain resulting in a family discussion amplifying parental strengths, and weight loss resulting in a discussion on the barriers which prevented weight gain (Murray, Wallis, & Rhodes, 2012b). Empirically, the role of adolescent weight status is so centrally implicated in outpatient FBT, that this is thought to be the primary criterion around which overall treatment response versus treatment non-response can be indicated during the early stages of treatment (Doyle et al., 2010; Le Grange et al., 2014).

However, in a higher level of care, it is likely that an adolescent's weight status may be impacted by a multitude of factors external to parental influence, including nasogastric feeding and carefully calculated clinic-based meal programs. Furthermore, failure to gain weight in such settings may be less common, which may further obscure the weight-based indexing of parental efficacy throughout the re-feeding phase of treatment. Thus, alternative methods of indexing parental efficacy may be more appropriate in informing the content of family meetings in hospital and partial-hospital settings.

Clinical Options

Indexing parental efficacy through weight-related data. Unless inpatient hospital settings are able to accommodate full-scale parental involvement, it is unlikely that early weight gain in such settings exclusively indicates parental efficacy. However, as adolescents progress into partial-hospital settings, once medical instability subsides, weight-related data may be utilized creatively to indicate preliminary parental efficacy. In these settings, the adolescent spending weekends in their family home may allow for access to how weight change over weekends compares with weight change during weekdays, offering an insight into how home-based weight restoration compares to in-program weight restoration. Access to these data may be crucial in accessing early indicants of parental efficacy, which may be utilized therapeutically in mobilizing parental anxiety and troubleshooting the parents' efforts to restore healthy eating in their child.

Developing alternate methods of indexing parental efficacy in hospital and partial-hospital settings. When family involvement in hospital and partial-hospital settings is not possible, alternate methods of indexing parental efficacy may be necessary. For instance, in instances when adolescents still require urgent and medically indicated weight restoration, a series of family meals may be employed by FBT therapists within hospital settings, affording an opportunity to assess parental efficacy around re-feeding. Clinical observations of the extent to which parents are able to effectively influence their child's eating behaviors may be utilized to indicate parental efficacy and inform treatment content within hospital and partial-hospital contexts.

Meal Provision and Supervision throughout Treatment

Predicated on the notion that symptomatic adolescents are almost exclusively making decisions that are influenced by the eating disorder, FBT is characterized by the removal of food-based choices from the adolescent, alongside intensive meal supervision. Wherever possible, the overseeing of food-based decisions and supervision of meals ought to be undertaken by parents, who typically have the greatest knowledge, authority over their dependent child, and scope for long-term symptom remission. Empirical evidence illustrates that, in fact, parental control over their child's AN symptom profile is the central predictor of favorable treatment outcome in those undergoing FBT for AN (Ellison et al., 2012). However, the provision and supervision of meals in hospital and partial-hospital settings is most typically undertaken by staff, leading to the potential disparity between the agent of authority in home-based meals and program-based meals. Although a higher level of care could be used to offer respite for parents until the child discharges, with staff devising, serving, and supervising all meals based on dietetic calculation and providing psychological support, that may miss a critically important window in which to build parents' skills and efficacy around re-feeding.

Clinical Options

Create the scope for parents to prepare, serve, and supervise all program-based meals. Perhaps the closest approximation to standard FBT in hospital and partial-hospital settings would involve full-scale parental involvement in meal preparation and supervision within hospital contexts. Practically, this may mean that parents would be present for all meal-based decision making, preparation, and supervision, as well as the supervision of any compensatory behaviors. However, adopting this approach in inpatient settings when urgent medical stabilization is required may impinge upon the rate of weight restoration, potentially contravening medical best practice when urgent nutritional rehabilitation is required. Furthermore, a practical concern in higher levels of care may relate to the necessary structural and time constraints. For instance, idiosyncratic family meal preparation and supervision, several times per day, of differing lengths and emotional intensity, may render a structured treatment program comprising scheduled group and individual meetings with treatment specialists extremely challenging. As such, alternate provisions for integrating parental input around food-based decision making and meal supervision may be required.

Empower parents in the decision-making process. Parents need to be empowered to engage in the decision-making process in terms of what food is served to their child in program-based meals and how staff may assist their child, while taking into account the practical considerations of the treatment setting.

When full-scale family involvement during the meal provision and supervision process is not feasible, creative deviation from the manualized protocol may be required to ensure therapeutic fidelity. For instance, one alternative to parents preparing and supervising all meals in hospital and partial-hospital settings may involve parents preparing and bringing in their child's food for the day at the start of each day, allowing for individually tailored parent-devised dietary regimens without disrupting program feasibility. Whenever possible, allowing parents to individually tailor meals would allow for a greater inclusion of parental expertise, in addition to enhancing the ecological and cultural validity of the food consumed during treatment.

Further integration of parents into meal provision and supervision processes could involve staff calling on parents to assist staff with in-program meal supervision. In the event of challenging meals, FBT clinicians may seek guidance from parents as to which strategies might be most effective in supervising their child's meal. This would underscore the notion that parents themselves are ultimately responsible for refeeding their child, and may also be used to strategically orient parents towards the main tenets of treatment. For instance, consulting with parents directly as to how to be firm without being punitive towards their child during meals may prime parental focus on these areas for home-based meals, provoking reflection on their own use of these strategies. Furthermore, multi-family therapy theory posits that a large component of parental empowerment is garnered from the act of giving other families advice, crystallizing their own sense of agency (Murray & Le Grange, 2014). As such, it is likely that the act of guiding staff on how to coax their child through challenging meals could help parents develop a sense of efficacy, and further underscore the notion that overall responsibility and expertise rests with parents. Staff could also call the parents to have them coach their child if meals are refused while in program. In those instances, parents could take over coaching the child by phone, or even come in and sit with their child to ensure meal compliance.

Conclusion

There can be little doubt surrounding the necessity for intensive levels of patient care in acute and severe presentations of adolescent AN, and the adaptation of FBT from outpatient to these settings may prove to be important in ensuring swift and lasting symptom remission. Indeed, with recent research suggesting that an expedited transition from inpatient care through to outpatient FBT is both cost-effective and clinically recommended (Madden et al., 2014), and that consistency between treatment providers across levels of care significantly relates to FBT outcome (Murray & Le Grange, 2014), the adaptation of FBT across treatment settings is warranted. We have aimed to outline theoretical and practical considerations in assisting clinicians across levels of care in determining the optimal balance between swift and staff-assisted symptom resolution in emergency situations versus parent-driven symptom resolution in less critically unstable situations. However, it should be noted that the recommendations outlined are theoretical in nature, and it is critical that future research evaluates the efficacy of FBT across higher levels of care, as it remains unclear to what extent findings drawn from outpatient settings may translate into more intensive treatment settings.

References

Couturier, J., Kimber, M., & Szatmari, P. (2013). Efficacy of family-based treatment for adolescents with eating disorders: A systematic review and meta-analysis. *International Journal of Eating Disorders*, 46, 3–11,

Dare, C., Eisler, I., Colahan, M., Crowther, C., Senior, R., & Asen, E. (1995). The listening heart and the Chi square: Clinical and empirical perceptions in the family therapy of anorexia nervosa. *Journal of Family Therapy*, 17, 19–45.

Doyle, P. M., Le Grange, D., Loeb, K. L., Doyle, A. M., & Crosby, R. D. (2010). Early response to family-based treatment for adolescent anorexia nervosa. *International Journal of Eating Disorders*, 43, 659–662.

Eisler, I. (2005). The empirical and theoretical base of family therapy and multiple family day therapy for adolescent anorexia nervosa. *Journal of Family Therapy*, 27, 104–131.

Eisler, I., Simic, M., Russell, G. F. M., & Dare, C. (2007). A randomised controlled treatment trial of two forms of family therapy in adolescent anorexia nervosa: A five-year follow-up. *Journal of Child Psychology and Psychiatry*, 48, 552–560.

Ellison, R., Rhodes, P., Madden, S., Miskovic, J., Wallis, A. et al. (2012). Do the components of manualised family-based treatment for anorexia nervosa predict weight gain? *International Journal of Eating Disorders*, 45, 609–614.

Geller, J., Zaitsoff, S. L., & Srikameswaran, S. (2005). Tracking readiness and motivation for change in individuals with eating disorders over the course of treatment. *Cognitive Therapy and Research*, 29, 611–625.

Girz, L., LaFrance Robinson, A., Foroughe, M., Jasper, K., & Boachie, A. (2013). Adapting family-based therapy to a day hospital programme for adolescents with eating disorders: Preliminary outcomes and trajectories of change. *Journal of Family Therapy*, 35, 102–120.

Haley, J. (1980). *Leaving home: The therapy of disturbed young people*. New York: McGraw-Hill.

Henderson, K., Buchholz, A., Obeid, N., Mossiere, A., Maras, D. et al. (2014). A family-based eating disorder day treatment program for youth: Examining the clinical and statistical significance of short-term outcomes. *Eating Disorders*, 22, 1–18.

Hoste, R. R. (2015). Incorporating family-based therapy principles into a partial hospitalization programme for adolescents with anorexia nervosa: Challenges and considerations. *Journal of Family Therapy*, 37, 41–60.

Katzman, D. K. (2005). Medical complications in adolescents with anorexia nervosa: A review of the literature. *International Journal of Eating Disorders*, 37, S52–S59.

Katzman, D. K., Peebles, R., Sawyer, S. M., Lock, J., & Le Grange, D. (2013). The role of the pediatrician in family-based treatment for adolescent eating disorders: Opportunities and challenges. *Journal of Adolescent Health*, 53, 433–440.

Kaye, W. H., Enright, A. B., & Lesser, S. (1998). Characteristics of eating disorders programs and common problems with third-party payers. *International Journal of Eating Disorders*, 7, 573–579.

Keel, P. K., & Brown, T. A. (2010). Update on course and outcome in eating disorders. *International Journal of Eating Disorders*, 43, 195–204.

Le Grange, D., Accurso, E., Lock, J., Agras, W. S., & Bryson, S. W. (2014). Early weight gain predicts outcome in two treatments for adolescent anorexia nervosa. *International Journal of Eating Disorders*, 47, 124–129.

Le Grange, D., Lock, J., Agras, W. S., Bryson, S. W., Jo, B., & Kraemer, H. C. (2012). Mediators and moderators of remission in family-based treatment and adolescent focused therapy for anorexia nervosa. *Behavior Research and Therapy*, 50, 85–92.

Le Grange, D., Lock, J., Loeb, K., & Nicholls, D. (2010). Academy for Eating Disorders position paper: The role of the family in eating disorders. *International Journal of Eating Disorders*, 43, 1–5.

Lock, J., & Le Grange, D. (2013). *Treatment manual for anorexia nervosa: A family-based approach*, 2nd edition. New York: Guilford Press.

Lock, J., Le Grange, D., Agras, W. S., Moye, A., Bryson, S., & Jo B. (2010). Randomized control trial comparing family-based treatment with adolescent-focused individual therapy for adolescents with anorexia nervosa. *Archives of General Psychiatry*, 67, 1025–1032.

Madden, S., Miskovic, J., Wallis, A., Kohn, M., Lock, J. et al. (2014). A randomized controlled trial of in-patient treatment for anorexia nervosa in medically unstable adolescents. *Psychological Medicine*, 14, 1–13.

Maguire, S., Le Grange, D., Surgenor, L., Marks, P., Lacey, H., & Touyz, S. W. (2009). Staging anorexia nervosa: Conceptualizing illness severity. *Early Intervention in Psychiatry*, 2, 3–10.

Mond, J. M., Hay, P. J., Rodgers, B., Owen, C., & Beumont, P. J. V. (2005). Assessing quality of life in eating disorder patients. *Quality of Life Research*, 14, 171–178.

Murray, S. B., & Le Grange, D. (2014). Family therapy for eating disorders: An update. *Current Psychiatry Reports*, 16, 447.

Murray, S. B., Griffiths, S., & Le Grange, D. (2014). The role of collegial alliance in family-based treatment of adolescent anorexia nervosa: A pilot study. *International Journal of Eating Disorders*, 47, 418–421.

Murray, S. B., Thornton, C., & Wallis, A. (2012a). A thorn in the side of evidence-based treatment for adolescent anorexia nervosa. *Australian & New Zealand Journal of Psychiatry*, 46, 1026–1068.

Murray, S. B., Wallis, A., & Rhodes, P. (2012b). The questioning process in Maudsley family-based treatment. Part 1: Deviation amplification. *Contemporary Family Therapy*, 34, 582–592.

Pompili, M., Mancinelli, I., Girardi, P., Ruberto, A., & Tatarelli, R. (2004). Suicidality in anorexia nervosa: A meta-analysis. *International Journal of Eating Disorders*, 36, 99–103.

Rockwell, R., Boutelle, K., Trunko, M. E., Jacobs, M. J., & Kaye, W. H. (2011). An innovative short-term, intensive, family-based treatment for adolescent anorexia nervosa: Case series. *European Eating Disorder Review*, 19, 362–367.

Steinhausen, H. C. (2002). The outcome of anorexia nervosa in the 20th century. *American Journal of Psychiatry*, 159, 1284–1293.

Strober, M., Freeman, R., & Morell, W. (1997). The long-term course of severe anorexia nervosa in adolescents: Survival analysis of recovery, relapse, and outcome predictors over 10–15 years in a prospective study. *International Journal of Eating Disorders*, 22, 339–360.

Treasure, J., & Russell, G. (2011). The case for early intervention in anorexia nervosa: Theoretical exploration of maintaining factors. *British Journal of Psychiatry*, 199, 5–7.

Wallis, A., Alford, C., Hanson, A., Titterton, J., Madden S., & Kohn, M. (2013). Innovations in Maudsley family-based treatment for anorexia nervosa at the Children's Hospital at Westmead: A family admissions programme. *Journal of Family Therapy*, 35(S1), 68–81.

Wiseman, C. V., Sunday, S. R., Klapper, F., Harris, W. A., & Halmi, K. A. (2001). Changing patterns of hospitalization in eating disorder patients. *International Journal of Eating Disorders*, 30, 69–74.

2 Who's in the Room?

Parent-Focused Family Therapy for Adolescent Anorexia Nervosa

Elizabeth K. Hughes, Susan M. Sawyer, Katharine L. Loeb, and Daniel Le Grange

In 1970 family therapy pioneer, Nathan Ackerman, remarked upon the tendency for family therapists to avoid including children in therapy. He called upon therapists to overcome their barriers and bring children into the room as, in his view, without engaging children "there can be no family therapy" (Ackerman, 1970, p. 403). Nearly 30 years later, in a commentary on narrative family therapy, Salvador Minuchin (1998) raised similar concerns regarding "the disappearance of the family from the therapeutic process" (p. 397). Indeed, the practice of excluding children from family therapy has been documented to be commonplace and supported by many in the field. For example, one study found that 39 percent of family therapists routinely excluded children from treatment (Korner & Brown, 1990). In another study, 50 percent of therapists believed that it was fine for family therapists to exclude children when the therapist preferred not to work with children (Johnson & Thomas, 1999).

Several factors have been identified as contributing to the inclusion or exclusion of children from family therapy. These include the therapist's level of training in child development, their perceived skills in engaging children and adolescents, their general sense of comfort in working with children and adolescents or with several family members together, and the availability of appropriate facilities such as an office size sufficient to accommodate a family (Korner & Brown, 1990; Ruble, 1999). Pivotal is the view that children and adolescents are difficult to work with, being either disruptive and restless or silent and reluctant participants. Of interest, family therapists are less likely to include children identified as having externalizing problems rather than internalizing problems (Johnson & Thomas, 1999). These influences aside, some family therapists have argued that it is not necessary to see the child to make changes within the family system or to influence the child themselves (Miller & McLeod, 2001; Tomm, 1998). Furthermore, Minuchin's (1998) suggestion that the family had "disappeared" from family therapy was rejected by some who argued that there was a difference in assumptions about what constitutes working with families (i.e. having members in the room, interviewed one by one, or referred to in conversation; Combs & Freedman, 1998; Tomm, 1998). Indeed, Breunlin and Jacobsen (2014) distinguished "whole family therapy" from "relational family therapy," which they defined as maintaining a systemic lens while involving only a subsystem of the family or even an individual.

Since Ackerman's (1970) call for greater inclusion of children, some advancements have been made to improve therapist training, skills, and comfort in working with parents and children together (e.g. Rober, 2008). However, it is unknown whether these advances have influenced practice, as there are no contemporary quantitative data on inclusion practices in family therapy. In their recent commentary "Putting the 'Family' Back into Family Therapy," Breunlin and Jacobsen (2014) described an ongoing decline in the practice of whole family therapy and foreshadowed its rarity in the future.

Anorexia Nervosa and Family Therapy

In contrast to family therapists' tendency to focus on parents to the exclusion of children, the earliest therapeutic interventions for children and adolescents with eating disorders excluded parents. In the first clinical descriptions of anorexia nervosa (AN), parents were viewed as responsible for the development and maintenance of the illness, and were considered detrimental to recovery. William Gull characterized family members as "generally the worst attendants" (Gull, 1874, p. 26), and Jean-Martin Charcot described them as having a "particularly pernicious" influence (Charcot, 1889, p. 2010). The recommended treatment was isolation, that is, separation of the child from their parents (Silverman, 1997).

In the 1960s and 1970s, as family therapy was hitting its stride, there was a related shift in theoretical formulations of AN whereby families were viewed not only as central to the etiology of the illness, but also its treatment (Minuchin, Rosman, & Baker, 1978; Palazzoli, 1974). Minuchin and colleagues' psychosomatic family model was particularly influential. This model posited that AN developed within a family context characterized by enmeshment, conflict avoidance, and rigidity. Rather than separating the child from their parents, this model insisted that treatment be directed at families in order to address these problematic aspects of the family system. Family functioning in individuals with eating disorders has since been extensively studied, with little empirical evidence emerging to support the psychosomatic family model of AN, or any other "anorexogenic" family type (Dare, Le Grange, Eisler, & Rutherford, 1994; Eisler, 2005; Konstantellou, Campbell, & Eisler, 2012). Nonetheless, the work of Minuchin and others provided the first demonstrations of the potential benefits of including parents in treatment and laid the foundation for current family therapies for AN (Le Grange & Eisler, 2009).

Today, family therapies for AN exist in various forms. Perhaps the most well recognized and researched is the form developed at the Maudsley Hospital in London by Eisler and Dare (cf. Eisler, Dodge, & Wallis, 2015, p. 6), that is, "family therapy for adolescent AN." It was subsequently published in manualized form by Lock and Le Grange (2013) and referred to as family-based treatment (FBT). Influenced by Minuchin, Palazzoli, and others, clinicians at the

Maudsley Hospital in the 1980s developed an intervention for AN that incorporated techniques from existing family therapy paradigms but took a different stance on the role of the family in the pathogenesis of the illness (Dare, 1983; Eisler, 2005; Russell, Szmukler, Dare, & Eisler, 1987).

Their model of treatment took a non-blaming approach to the family, emphasizing the family as a major resource in the recovery process rather than as a target for causative explanations. In fact, the model assumed an explicitly agnostic stance with regard to etiology, reflecting the state of definitive research-driven knowledge in the field. Instead of directly targeting family functioning, this treatment initially focuses on weight restoration through parental meal monitoring and support at home, gradually transferring agency around energy intake and expenditure back to the patient as the illness recedes. In the last stage of treatment, the focus shifts away from eating and weight to other adolescent and family issues that may need to be addressed. A growing number of clinical trials and case series support the effectiveness of FBT for medically stable adolescents with AN (for a review, see Stiles-Shields, Hoste, Doyle, & Le Grange, 2012) and, at this stage, FBT has the strongest evidence base of any adolescent AN treatment (Lock, 2015). Nonetheless, relatively few randomized controlled trials have been conducted, and more research is needed to clarify the benefits of FBT over other treatments. Most recently, a randomized trial of FBT and systemic family therapy found that the treatments achieved equivalent rates of remission at end of treatment and 12-months follow-up, but that weight gain was faster early in treatment for FBT (Agras et al., 2014). In addition, FBT was associated with fewer days in hospital and lower costs per remitted patient. This suggests that, while family therapies that focus primarily on family processes (i.e. systemic family therapy) may result in similar outcomes to those focused on weight and eating (i.e. FBT), the latter may have specific compelling benefits, including more immediate and broad reduction of the burden of illness.

Separating Parents and Adolescents in Treatment for AN

The FBT manual instructs therapists to involve the whole family in treatment, with roles designated for the parent, adolescent, and siblings (Lock & Le Grange, 2013). All family members are expected to attend sessions but in practice there is much variability. In our experience, sibling attendance is the first to become sporadic, if indeed they attend at all. Fathers may also be less frequent attendees when the mother is the primary caregiver, and when leave from work is difficult. Even when families arrive at the clinic together, the therapist may choose to see family members separately for all or part of the session. In fact, two randomized controlled trials of FBT have compared conjoint and separated models; that is, a model in which the whole family is seen together and a model in which the therapist sees the parents alone for part of the session and the adolescent alone for part of the session (Eisler et al., 2000; Le Grange, Eisler, Dare, & Russell, 1992). These studies did not find a significant difference between separated and conjoint models; however, their samples were small ($n = 40$; $n = 18$) and there was some indication that a separated model may be superior for certain families.

Specifically, in the study by Eisler et al. (2000), 80 percent of adolescents from families in which there was high expressed emotion (i.e. criticism from the parent toward the ill offspring) had good or intermediate outcome if they received separated FBT compared to 29 percent if they received conjoint FBT. This pattern of results was also found at five-year follow-up (Eisler, Simic, Russell, & Dare, 2007).

Although conjoint FBT is the usual choice for services implementing FBT (Hughes et al., 2014b; Loeb et al., 2007), some have utilized an approach that combines separated and conjoint sessions (Paulson-Karlsson, Engström, & Nevonen, 2009), and others have developed variations of separated FBT such as acceptance-based separated family treatment (Merwin, Zucker, & Timko, 2013). For some, the use of separated FBT (either in part or fully) may be based on research evidence. However, given what is known about the practice of family therapy more generally, it is also likely that its use is influenced by therapist preferences.

Therapists treating eating disorders may be uncomfortable working with parents, adolescents, and siblings all together. Some of the reasons for this are likely to mirror those conveyed in the family therapy literature such as lack of training, availability of facilities, and concerns about the appropriateness of content (e.g. discussions of the adolescent's menstrual status in front of fathers, or reviewing stark AN mortality rates in the presence of young siblings). Like family therapists, eating disorder clinicians may lack confidence in their ability to manage multiple and sometimes overwhelming or competing emotions and behaviors from several family members. This may be especially so with AN patients who, due to the ego-syntonic nature of the illness, may be opposed to treatment and actively try to derail therapeutic progress. Staying focused in session content and technique, and separating internally developing, broader family-level case conceptualizations from immediate treatment priorities may represent challenges for some therapists. For parents, the illness can provoke a range of distressing emotions, including anger, guilt, and frustration. Therapists who feel unable to manage these emotions, or who feel the manner in which emotions are expressed in sessions is detrimental to progress, may choose to see family members separately. This may be an appropriate decision; as already noted, research suggests that families with high expressed emotion are better suited to separated treatment. More specific to FBT, therapists are often uncomfortable with some components such as the in-session family meal. In a study of 40 therapists treating young people with AN, only 10 reported that they regularly included the family meal (Couturier & Lock, 2006).

Family members may also prefer separated FBT. In a qualitative study of satisfaction with conjoint FBT for adolescent AN (Krautter & Lock, 2004), while most family members expressed that including the whole family in treatment was helpful, several identified the lack of individual support for patients and parents and the involvement of siblings as unhelpful. The desire for more individual support appeared to be related to feeling uncomfortable speaking openly about some issues with the whole family present. Although not explored further in the study, the reluctance to involve siblings may be related to perceived negative impacts on the siblings or to more practical barriers such as school and recreational commitments, an area that warrants more research. Separated FBT has the potential to overcome some of the perceived challenges or deficiencies of conjoint FBT and so may be preferred by some families. In practice, separated FBT has been shown to be acceptable to families and to meet patient and parent expectations (Paulson-Karlsson, Nevonen, & Engström, 2006).

Parent-Focused Treatment for Adolescent Anorexia Nervosa

Given that FBT is primarily focused on parents as the agents of change and that having the therapist see parents and adolescents separately can be as effective as seeing the whole family together, it must be asked whether the same goals can be achieved without the therapist working directly with the adolescent. As shown, many family therapists feel they can exact change within the family and children by working only with parents. Furthermore, various childhood conditions are treated via parents alone. For example, interventions for disruptive behavior disorders often comprise parent training programs that may or may not require direct involvement of the child or adolescent (Eyberg, Nelson, & Boggs, 2008). Intervention and prevention programs for childhood obesity are also often parent focused. Of significance, Golan and colleagues found that a parent-only intervention for obese children was more effective than both a child-only intervention (Golan, Fainaru, & Weizman, 1998) and a combined parent and child intervention (Golan, Kaufman, & Shahar, 2006) at reducing weight and changing eating behaviors in this patient population.

The goals of FBT (described above) have the potential to be achieved by the therapist and parents without the adolescent in the room. Of course, given the medical complications and psychiatric comorbidities associated with AN, the adolescent will require monitoring and management of these issues by an appropriately trained physician, nurse, or mental health professional. In addition, an important feature of FBT is routine monitoring of the adolescent's weight, with changes in weight status setting the tone for the session (Lock & Le Grange, 2013).

Taking these factors into consideration, the Royal Children's Hospital Specialist Eating Disorders Program in Australia developed a separated form of FBT that combines parent-only therapist sessions with brief weight monitoring and supportive counselling by a nurse or medical practitioner (Hughes, Sawyer, Loeb, & Le Grange, 2015). Parent-focused treatment (PFT) for adolescent AN was commenced at the service in 2010 and a randomized controlled trial was due to be completed in early 2016 (Hughes et al., 2014a).

PFT adheres to the FBT manual with regard to the core tenets, goals, and phases of treatment (Lock & Le Grange, 2013). It is delivered at an outpatient clinic in approximately 18 sessions over 6 months. PFT differs from the manual, however, with regard to the structure of each session. In this respect it is similar to earlier models of separated FBT in that the therapist does not see the whole family together. Instead, at each session, the adolescent first meets with a nurse (or medical practitioner) who weighs them, checks their medical and mental status, and provides brief supportive counselling. This usually takes 10 to 15 minutes, after which the nurse communicates the weight to the therapist along with any other pertinent information. The therapist will then see the parents for a 50-minute session. Siblings do not attend treatment sessions and there is no in-session family meal. Medical monitoring is managed by a pediatrician with appointments scheduled approximately every five weeks. The nurse may undertake a physical assessment (e.g. heart rate, blood pressure) during their time with the adolescent if there are concerns regarding medical stability such as dizziness or significant loss of weight, but this is not routine. Concerns regarding the adolescent's mental status, including suicidal ideation, are promptly referred to the team psychiatrist for assessment and management. Further detail about PFT and the randomized controlled trial can be found in Hughes et al. (2014a, 2015), or by contacting the authors for the unpublished manual (Le Grange, Loeb, Hughes, & Sawyer, 2010).

Since introducing PFT, we have observed several recurring themes raised by therapists during clinical supervision that highlight both benefits and challenges of this treatment. Supervision focuses on both research cases that are part of the clinical trial and on cases seen in our clinical service; thus, our impressions reflect a range of presentations and experiences. Of benefit is the simplification of some aspects of FBT; for example, not having the whole family in the room, the absence of the in-session family meal, reduced exposure of the adolescent to parental criticism and distress, and reduced disruption of therapy sessions by adolescents who may be driven by the illness to derail treatment. The model also has the benefits of strongly reinforcing the central role of parents in their child's recovery, and of separate sessions providing an opportunity for parents and adolescents to speak more openly about their struggles than they might otherwise in conjoint sessions. On the other hand, the lack of direct interaction between the therapist and adolescent can pose a challenge for therapists who are accustomed to monitoring progress (or deterioration) in the patient themselves. However, we have found that regular communication within the treating team allows effective identification and management of deterioration in the adolescent's physical or mental state. It also fosters a sense of shared responsibility and ensures a consistent approach to treatment (Katzman, Peebles, Sawyer, Lock, & Le Grange, 2013). In addition, while the absence of the in-session family meal and siblings may simplify treatment, it also requires that therapists find alternative ways to achieve the potential benefits of these aspects of conjoint FBT. This can involve working through detailed retrospective accounts of family meals at home and assisting parents in eliciting support from siblings.

Finally, it is currently unknown whether some families are more suited to PFT than conjoint FBT. Given this, families at our service who were not part of the clinical trial could choose for themselves between PFT and conjoint FBT. Approximately one in five families selected PFT and no clear differences have been observed between the types of family that selected one form over the other. As noted, past research suggests that highly critical families may respond better to a separated model of FBT (Eisler et al., 2000; Le Grange et al., 1992), but whether this extends to PFT will not be known until completion of the current clinical trial (Hughes et al., 2014a). Of further interest will be whether other parent, adolescent, and family factors have utility for individual treatment selection.

Conclusions

The importance of including the whole family in therapy has been fiercely defended by many family therapists. Korner and Brown (1990) went so far as to describe the exclusion of children as a "bastardization of the field" (p. 427). However, the practice continues (Breunlin & Jacobsen, 2014), suggesting there are ongoing factors that sway therapists to work with parents alone. In some cases these may be pragmatic, but increasingly decisions may be guided by evidence for the effectiveness of parent-focused versus whole family approaches (e.g. Eisler et al., 2000; Golan et al., 2006). The development of PFT, and more importantly the forthcoming findings comparing its outcomes to those of conjoint FBT, will make a significant contribution to this evidence for those treating adolescent eating disorders.

Acknowledgments

The authors thank the Royal Children's Hospital Eating Disorders Program staff.

This work was supported by the Baker Foundation. The Murdoch Childrens Research Institute is supported by the Victorian Government's Operational Infrastructure Support Program.

References

Ackerman, N. (1970). Child participation in family therapy. *Family Process*, 9, 403–410.

Agras, W., Lock, J., Brandt, H., Bryson, S. W., Dodge, E. et al. (2014). Comparison of two family therapies for adolescent anorexia nervosa: A randomized parallel trial. *JAMA Psychiatry*, 71, 1279–1286.

Breunlin, D. C., & Jacobsen, E. (2014). Putting the "family" back into family therapy. *Family Process*, 53, 462–475.

Charcot, J.-M. (1889). *Clinical lectures on diseases of the nervosa system*. London: New Sydenham Society.

Combs, G., & Freedman, J. (1998). Tellings and retellings. *Journal of Marital and Family Therapy*, 24, 405–408.

Couturier, J., & Lock, J. (2006). What is recovery in adolescent anorexia nervosa? *International Journal of Eating Disorders*, 39, 550–555.

Dare, C. (1983). *Family therapy for families containing an anorectic youngster*. Columbus, OH: Ross Laboratories.

Dare, C., Le Grange, D., Eisler, I., & Rutherford, J. (1994). Redefining the psychosomatic family: Family process of 26 eating disorder families. *International Journal of Eating Disorders*, 16, 211–226.

Eisler, I. (2005). The empirical and theoretical base of family therapy and multiple family day therapy for adolescent anorexia nervosa. *Journal of Family Therapy*, 27, 104–131.

Eisler, I., Dare, C., Hodes, M., Russell, G. F. M., Dodge, E., & Le Grange, D. (2000). Family therapy for adolescent anorexia nervosa: The results of a controlled comparison of two family interventions. *Journal of Child Psychology and Psychiatry and Allied Disciplines*, 41, 727–736.

Eisler, I., Dodge, L., & Wallis, A. (2015). What's new is old and what's old is new: The origins and evolution of eating disorders family therapy. In K. L. Loeb, D. Le Grange, & J. Lock (Eds.), *Family therapy for adolescent eating and weight disorders: New applications* (pp. 6–42). New York: Routledge/Taylor & Francis.

Eisler, I., Simic, M., Russell, G. F., & Dare, C. (2007). A randomised controlled treatment trial of two forms of family therapy in adolescent anorexia nervosa: A five-year follow-up. *Journal of Child Psychology and Psychiatry and Allied Disciplines*, 48, 552–560.

Eyberg, S. M., Nelson, M. M., & Boggs, S. R. (2008). Evidence-based psychosocial treatments for children and adolescents with disruptive behavior. *Journal of Clinical Child & Adolescent Psychology*, 37, 215–237.

Golan, M., Fainaru, M., & Weizman, A. (1998). Role of behaviour modification in the treatment of childhood obesity with the parents as the exclusive agents of change. *International Journal of Obesity and Related Metabolic Disorders*, 22, 1217–1224.

Golan, M., Kaufman, V., & Shahar, D. R. (2006). Childhood obesity treatment: Targeting parents exclusively v. parents and children. *British Journal of Nutrition*, 95, 1008–1015.

Gull, W. W. (1874). Anorexia nervosa (*apepsia hysterica, anorexia hysterica*). *Transactions of the Clinical Society of London*, 7, 22–28.

Hughes, E. K., Le Grange, D., Court, A., Yeo, M., Campbell, S. et al. (2014a). Parent-focused treatment for adolescent anorexia nervosa: A study protocol of a randomised controlled trial. *BMC Psychiatry*, 14, 105.

Hughes, E. K., Le Grange, D., Court, A., Yeo, M., Campbell, S. et al. (2014b). Implementation of family-based treatment for adolescents with anorexia nervosa. *Journal of Pediatric Health Care*, 28, 322–330.

Hughes, E. K., Sawyer, S. M., Loeb, K. L., & Le Grange, D. (2015). Parent-focused treatment. In K. L. Loeb, D. Le Grange, & J. Lock (Eds.), *Family therapy for adolescent eating and weight disorders: New applications* (pp. 59–71). New York: Routledge/Taylor & Francis.

Johnson, L., & Thomas, V. (1999). Influences on the inclusion of children in family therapy. *Journal of Marital and Family Therapy*, 25, 117–123.

Katzman, D. K., Peebles, R., Sawyer, S. M., Lock, J., & Le Grange, D. (2013). The role of the pediatrician in family-based treatment for adolescent eating disorders: Opportunities and challenges. *Journal of Adolescent Health*, 53, 433–440.

Konstantellou, A., Campbell, M., & Eisler, I. (2012). The family context: Cause, effect or resource. In J. Alexander & J. Treasure (Eds.), *A collaborative approach to eating disorders* (pp. 5–18). New York: Routledge/Taylor & Francis.

Korner, S., & Brown, G. (1990). Exclusion of children from family psychotherapy: Family therapists' beliefs and practices. *Journal of Family Psychology*, 3, 420–430.

Krautter, T., & Lock, J. (2004). Is manualized family-based treatment for adolescent anorexia nervosa acceptable to patients? Patient satisfaction at the end of treatment. *Journal of Family Therapy*, 26, 66–82.

Le Grange, D., & Eisler, I. (2009). Family interventions in adolescent anorexia nervosa. *Child and Adolescent Psychiatric Clinics of North America*, 18, 159–173.

Le Grange, D., Eisler, I., Dare, C., & Russell, G. F. (1992). Evaluation of family treatments in adolescent anorexia nervosa: A pilot study. *International Journal of Eating Disorders*, 12, 347–358.

Le Grange, D., Loeb, K., Hughes, E. K., & Sawyer, S. M. (2010). *Parent-focused treatment for adolescent anorexia nervosa: Treatment manual*. Melbourne, Australia: Royal Children's Hospital.

Lock, J. (2015). An update on evidence-based psychosocial treatments for eating disorders in children and adolescents. *Journal of Clinical Child & Adolescent Psychology*, 44, 707–721.

Lock, J., & Le Grange, D. (2013). *Treatment manual for anorexia nervosa: A family-based approach*, 2nd edition. New York: Guilford Press.

Loeb, K. L., Walsh, B. T., Lock, J., Le Grange, D., Jones, J. et al. (2007). Open trial of family-based treatment for full and partial anorexia nervosa in adolescence: Evidence of successful dissemination. *Journal of the American Academy of Child and Adolescent Psychiatry*, 46, 792–800.

Merwin, R. M., Zucker, N. L., & Timko, C. (2013). A pilot study of an acceptance-based separated family treatment for adolescent anorexia nervosa. *Cognitive and Behavioral Practice*, 20, 485–500.

Miller, L. D., & McLeod, E. (2001). Children as participants in family therapy: Practice, research, and theoretical concerns. *The Family Journal*, 9, 375–383.

Minuchin, S. (1998). Where is the family in narrative family therapy? *Journal of Marital and Family Therapy*, 24, 397–403.

Minuchin, S., Rosman, B. L., & Baker, L. (1978). *Psychosomatic families: Anorexia nervosa in context*. Cambridge, MA: Harvard University Press.

Palazzoli, M. S. (1974). *Self-starvation: From the intrapsychic to the transpersonal approach to anorexia nervosa*. Oxford: Chaucer.

Paulson-Karlsson, G., Engström, I., & Nevonen, L. (2009). A pilot study of a family-based treatment for adolescent anorexia nervosa: 18- and 36-month follow-ups. *Eating Disorders*, 17, 72–88.

Paulson-Karlsson, G., Nevonen, L., & Engström, I. (2006). Anorexia nervosa: Treatment satisfaction. *Journal of Family Therapy*, 28, 293–306.

Rober, P. (2008). Being there, experiencing and creating space for dialogue: About working with children in family therapy. *Journal of Family Therapy*, 30, 465–477.

Ruble, N. (1999). The voices of therapists and children regarding the inclusion of children in family therapy: A systematic research synthesis. *Contemporary Family Therapy: An International Journal*, 21, 485–503.

Russell, G. F., Szmukler, G. I., Dare, C., & Eisler, I. (1987). An evaluation of family therapy in anorexia nervosa and bulimia nervosa. *Archives of General Psychiatry*, 44, 1047–1056.

Silverman, J. A. (1997). Charcot's comments on the therapeutic role of isolation in the treatment of anorexia nervosa. *International Journal of Eating Disorders*, 21, 295–298.

Stiles-Shields, C., Hoste, R. R., Doyle, P. M., & Le Grange, D. (2012). A review of family-based treatment for adolescents with eating disorders. *Reviews on Recent Clinical Trials*, 7, 133–140.

Tomm, K. (1998). A question of perspective. *Journal of Marital and Family Therapy*, 24, 409–413.

3 A Brief, Intensive Application of Multi-Family-Based Treatment for Eating Disorders

Stephanie Knatz Peck, Stuart B. Murray, Brittany Matheson, Kerri N. Boutelle, Roxanne Rockwell, Ivan Eisler, and Walter H. Kaye

Introduction

With current treatments for anorexia nervosa (AN) failing to reach acceptable standards of treatment outcome (Bulik, Berkman, Brownley, Sedway, & Lohr, 2007), the need for innovative treatment approaches is well established (Strober & Johnson, 2012). Amongst contemporary treatment approaches, family therapy approaches have amassed a particularly robust evidence base supporting their application in medically stable adolescent presentations of AN (Downs & Blow, 2013). Family-based therapy for anorexia nervosa (FT-AN) is a manualized family treatment (Lock & Le Grange, 2012) with a specific eating disorder focus, which centrally leverages parental and family resources in directly intervening in an adolescent's behavioral symptom profile. FT-AN demonstrates promising empirical evidence, in that up to 70 percent of patients are weight-restored within a year of commencing treatment (Le Grange & Eisler, 2009), and up to 40 percent of patients are remitted of cognitive symptoms within a year (Lock & Le Grange, 2012).

However, an ongoing challenge of specialized family-based therapy approaches pertains to their widespread dissemination, with a noted scarcity of trained specialists beyond the academic treatment centers in which they were developed (Murray, Labuschagne, & Le Grange, 2014). Currently, the lack of specialized family therapists inhibits the dissemination of these treatments, with both families and clinicians alike noting how the scarcity of specialist providers inhibits treatment access for families and precludes supervised treatment uptake by clinical practitioners (Couturier, Kimber, & Szatmari, 2013).

In response to these barriers, recent endeavors by our group have sought to establish short-term intensive treatment programs, which allow temporary immersion into otherwise inaccessible evidence-based treatment programs, with preliminary reports suggesting promising findings (Marzola et al., 2015; Rockwell, Boutelle, Trunko, Jacobs, & Kaye, 2011). Initially, these short-term intensive treatments were developed for individual families (Rockwell et al., 2011), although recently they have evolved into a more cost-effective multi-family format (Marzola et al., 2015), demonstrating promising outcomes comparable to both outpatient FT-AN (Lock & Le Grange, 2012) and intensive family therapy for individual families (Rockwell et al., 2011). However, alongside the emerging empirical evidence supporting intensive multi-family therapy, it is important that the clinical content of this approach is outlined such that dissemination and widespread implementation are facilitated. Thus, we aim to comprehensively outline the nature of the intensive multi-family therapy program developed at the University of California, San Diego.

Program Description

The program is intended to provide an immersive treatment experience and psycho-education for families. The treatment is delivered to children and adolescents with eating disorders and their families over five days. Treatment is conducted with up to six families and delivered in an intensive format, with families receiving approximately 9 hours of treatment per day, for a total of 40-plus hours of treatment delivered over the course of the week. The program is run in a multi-family group format, such that parents, patients, and other attending family members participate conjointly in the majority of groups. Other components include daily parent-only and patient-only group sessions, and individual family psychiatric and medical evaluations. Multi-family intensive family treatment (IFT) is deemed suitable by families and has demonstrated preliminary efficacy for patients with a broad range of ages (8–27), eating disorder diagnoses (Marzola et al., 2015; Rockwell et al., 2011), and phases of treatment. This heterogeneous group composition serves a number of diverse patient needs including supporting transitions between phases of treatment or levels of care, augmenting traditional individual therapy, and as a booster for patients failing to make gains in outpatient care.

IFT is based primarily on the underlying theoretical principles of FT-AN, which draws on broad systemic family therapy principles with a central focus on conceptualizing parents as a necessary and critical resource in facilitating recovery through managing early eating disorder behavior change (Dare, Eisler, Russell, & Szmukler, 1990; Eisler, Wallis, & Dodge, 2015; Lock & Le Grange, 2012). The overarching goal of IFT is to educate, train, and prepare parents to effectively manage the recovery of their child upon the transition to home-based management whilst motivating the young person to accept their parents' help to return to normal adolescent functioning. Accordingly, the program employs treatment strategies and psycho-education that are focused on mobilizing parents to engage their teen in recovery-oriented behaviors.

Alongside this family systems approach, the guiding principles underlying IFT are also rooted in a contemporary understanding of the neurobiology of eating disorders. Thus, IFT treatment strategies frame eating disorders as neurobiologically-driven illnesses, which assists families in viewing the illness as a medical problem, thereby reducing blame and increasing empathy. In addition, the etiological emphasis allocated to neurobiology allows for treatment strategies to become increasingly congruent with the temperamental and personality-based correlates of those with eating disorders. For instance, IFT treatment strategies have been constructed and/or adopted in response to the recognition that patients, and frequently their family members, exhibit high levels of anxiety and harm avoidance, difficulty with tolerating uncertainty, interoceptive deficits, and altered responsivity to reward and punishment (Kaye, Fudge, & Paulus, 2009; Kaye, Wierenga, Bailer, Simmons, & Bischoff-Grethe, 2013). The perspective that eating disorders emerge as a function of a specific neurobiology is complementary to the FT-AN model because both emphasize the importance of dispelling blame and using existing family and individual characteristics as strengths to overcome the disease. The neurobiological perspective and the FBT approach thus have mutual positive benefits and together make up the general philosophy underlying the IFT model. In keeping, IFT consists of six primary treatment components with very specific aims. These components form the foundation of treatment, with all exercises and activities conducted throughout the program falling under the umbrella of one or more of these components. The six components include family therapy, supervised family meals, parent management training, behavioral contracting, patient skills training, and psycho-education.

Treatment Format

Multi-Family Format

IFT is modeled on multi-family therapy for eating disorders, where multiple families are treated simultaneously in a group format (Dare & Eisler 2000; Simic & Eisler, 2015). Despite the relative novelty of multi-family treatment for eating disorders, the approach has an extensive history (Asen, 2002), and has been successfully applied to a number of child and adolescent issues, where parent involvement is critical (McKay, Harrison, Gonzales, Kim, & Quintana, 2002; Saayman, Saayman, & Wiens, 2006). Delivering family therapy in a group format appears to enhance the uptake of FT-AN principles, as well as accelerate necessary change and movement towards recovery (Salaminiou, 2005; Voriadaki, Simic, Espie, & Eisler, 2015). For instance, families serving as consultants to each other allows for a greater development of agency as opposed to when therapists serve as consultants, and allows for further decentralization of the role of the therapist (Murray et al., 2014). Indeed, the synergistic effect of combining group and family modalities increases the opportunities for learning and change amongst family members by allowing learning to take place from other attending families through direct observation, comparison, and consultation (Asen & Scholz, 2010). A recent multi-center RCT comparing single-family and multi-family treatments for eating disorders showed that multi-family treatment was more effective at post-treatment and early follow-up (Eisler, 2013).

Brevity and Intensity

The intensive nature of IFT is one of the unique features of this program, where families receive approximately 40 hours of treatment over the course of 5 days. Intensive models of treatment have been utilized extensively in the treatment of a range of anxiety disorders (Davis, Ollendick, & Öst, 2009; Mörtberg, Karlsson, Fyring, & Sundin, 2006; Whiteside & Jacobsen, 2010; Whiteside, Brown, & Abramowitz, 2008). Similar to intensive family-based treatment programs for anxiety disorders, IFT participants benefit from the ability to receive massed practice and in-vivo therapist-guided training on key factors involved in recovery. Real-time therapist observation and intervention during target events such as mealtimes, acute emotional outbursts, and family interactions allows parents to receive practical, hands-on training and management skills.

Primary Therapeutic Components

The comprehensive IFT model provides training in parent management of the illness in line with principles of FT-AN in conjunction with other complementary treatment modalities, all of which serve to mobilize parents to take action towards recovery, prepare families to manage recovery in the home, and facilitate rapid and sustained symptom remission within the patient. These objectives are achieved by employing therapeutic strategies that increase parental competency, facilitate a familial framework that supports recovery, and provide a structured plan that promotes consistency in parental approaches that promote recovery-focused behavior on the part of the patient.

Family Therapy

Systemic principles are applied in therapeutic activities through IFT, both in the multi-family group and in single-family sessions. Family therapy approaches are primarily borrowed from principles of FT-AN and multi-family therapy; however, the model also borrows approaches that are rooted in broader systemic theory and application. FT-AN strategies such as the prioritization on weight and physical health, acknowledging and mobilizing parental anxiety, illness externalization, and a pragmatic focus are considered key systemic techniques in IFT, and are employed at the outset of treatment to facilitate parent mobilization.

IFT is modeled on multi-family therapy for eating disorders, where multiple families are treated simultaneously in a group format. The multi-family context is used to introduce and reinforce FT-AN techniques and the underlying philosophy of parents as the champions of recovery. Delivering key FT-AN strategies and approaches in a multi-family format is thought to enhance the uptake of these principles through the construction of group and parent-to-parent solidarity, as well as increased opportunities to learn and receive feedback from others through both observation and direct inter-family feedback (Murray et al., 2014). Broader multi-family therapy activities, such as inter-family role plays and cross-generational interviews amongst group members, are used to assist families in reflecting on structural family changes and systemic family patterns and alliances that will facilitate movement towards recovery.

Family Meals

IFT is unique in that it includes multiple family meals over the course of treatment. On a daily basis, families eat breakfast, lunch, and two snacks under therapist observation/supervision as part of the program, resulting in approximately 15–20 therapist-supported family meals. Mealtimes, particularly in the early stages of treatment, are an opportunity for therapists to assess key mealtime behaviors, both parent and adolescent, in order to formulate target intervention points to reduce eating disorder symptoms. Mealtimes are then used as an opportunity for in-vivo intervention, where parents are led through the use of appropriate strategies to improve adolescent mealtime behavior. Similarly, therapists coach the adolescents on how to effectively use skills to increase compliance while also managing anxiety and other distressing emotions associated with mealtimes. Interventions with parents include direct feedback on the appropriateness of the meal (caloric sufficiency, quantities, and variety of food) and parent coaching on implementing behavioral strategies for maximizing the likelihood of eating and for managing negative affect and/or behavioral issues related to eating. Interventions directed at patients include teaching and modeling positive reinforcement, re-directing, distress tolerance skills, and other appropriate behavioral management strategies. In line with the FT-AN informed stance of therapists as consultants, the majority of therapist feedback is directed towards parents, with the ultimate goal of the therapist being to inform and assist parents in deciding on the appropriate ways to intervene. The parent focus is crucial, as it is ultimately the parents, and not therapists, who deliver the intervention in order to facilitate a successful transition to home-based treatment management.

Parent Skills Training

Throughout the program, parents receive didactic behavioral skills training in an effort to improve their effectiveness in managing eating disorder behaviors. Similar to FT-AN, the IFT model recognizes that parents' existing skill sets can be used to facilitate recovery, while also recognizing that adolescents' strong behavioral reactions to undergoing recovery can be difficult to manage. Although it is true that parents must capitalize on their previous experiences in successfully directing children to healthy behaviors and managing negative emotions, many parents feel unequipped to deal with such powerful reactions like those associated with eating disorders. Additionally, the intensity of reactions in patients with eating disorders may dissuade normally functioning parents from intervening. IFT provides training to parents using skills adapted from the Parent Management Training program (PMT; Kazdin, 1997). PMT is a comprehensive set of parent-directed treatment techniques that were originally developed to enhance motivation and compliance in treatment-resistant youth. The program is based on basic behavioral principles and uses praise, reinforcement, and contingency management to achieve specified target behaviors. Parent training is both didactic and experiential in nature. Parents are taught behavioral management skills in parent-only sessions and coached through effective application of these skills in interactions with their adolescents.

Behavioral Contracting

A substantial portion of treatment provided during the week surrounds the goal of constructing a family behavioral contract. The behavioral contract is intended to be a document that guides families forward in recovery by outlining guidelines for mealtimes and eating behavior, weight recovery, and other cardinal factors on which recovery is based. The contract outlines a stepped behavioral program to reach target benchmarks (such as target weights) to ensure that families possess a roadmap that specifies behaviors that are necessary for achieving recovery. In addition to defining rules and expectations, the contract defines contingencies for each target behavior expected of adolescents. This establishes a parental protocol for responding to adolescent behavior to not only ensure parental consistency in their response sets, but also promote recovery-oriented behavior on the part of the adolescent through the use of positive and negative contingencies. Thus, the contract serves as both a way to enhance adolescent compliance with key behaviors such as eating, and to promote consistent and effective management strategies on parents' behalf. Furthermore, the contract facilitates the construction of a strict and predictable structure surrounding recovery by insisting that families specify a detailed routine for things such as times of meals. This approach may be particularly well suited to individuals with eating disorders who often display difficulty tolerating uncertainty and anticipatory anxiety and avoidance behaviors in response to novel situations (Hildebrandt, Bacow, Markella, & Loeb, 2012). Behavioral contracts are highly individualized and are structured to take into account specific family circumstances, recovery needs, patient motivating factors, caretaker leverage, and patients' sensitivity to reward and punishment. Upon discharge, each family leaves with a signed document constructed in collaboration with treating therapists.

Patient Skills Training

A segment of the IFT program is devoted to teaching patients adaptive coping skills to manage distress and challenging emotions that may arise during recovery. Contemporary neurobiological findings suggest that individuals with eating disorders experience emotion dysregulation that may contribute to eating disorder behaviors such as restricting, binging, and purging (Kaye, Fudge, & Paulus, 2009; Kaye et al., 2013). Both food receipt and the anticipation of food receipt may cause extreme anxiety, which is thought to contribute to avoidance behaviors such as food restriction (Kaye et al., 2013). Patients are taught coping strategies, akin to those taught in dialectical behavior therapy (Linehan, 2015) to tolerate distress, and therapists facilitate opportunities for practice of these skills throughout the program, particularly surrounding mealtimes. The ability for therapists to be present at mealtimes and other times throughout the day where distress levels rise allows for therapist-directed skills practice on an as-needed basis, as patients acquire and master a "toolbox" of skills. While the majority of skills training occurs with patients only, one to two group sessions throughout the week are devoted to "family skills training," in which skills are introduced to the entire group so that family members can utilize skills in managing their own distress while also modeling appropriate skills usage for the patients.

Psycho-Education

Throughout the week, families attend didactic and interactive lectures during which information pertinent to medical and biological aspects of eating disorders is covered. Psycho-education sessions are presented in an informal didactic style by university faculty with expertise in specific eating disorder-related areas and include medical consequences of eating disorders, physiological effects of starvation, temperament and personality contributors to eating disorders, neurobiology of eating disorders, and best medical practices for eating disorders. Additionally, the psychoeducation sessions serve to strengthen the FT-AN guided objectives of mobilizing caretakers by creating urgency, reducing familial blame, and further empowering parents as critical treatment team members in their child's recovery.

Conclusion

The IFT program represents a brief, intensive model of treatment for children and adolescents with eating disorders. The program focuses on delivering a comprehensive treatment that prepares families for engineering a successful recovery from their adolescents' eating disorder by providing skills, education, and immersive practice based on a contemporary and updated understanding of these illnesses. The treatment represents an integrated treatment program that consists of both well-established evidence-based treatment and novel treatment techniques employed with a strong theoretical rationale, resulting in a robust model that promotes familial self-efficacy and improves families' chances of succeeding with recovery in the home.

References

Asen, E. (2002). Multiple family therapy: An overview. *Journal of Family Therapy*, 24, 3–16.

Asen, E., & Scholz, M. (2010). *Multi-family therapy: Concepts and techniques*. London, UK: Routledge.

Bulik, C. M., Berkman, N. D., Brownley, K. A., Sedway, J. A., & Lohr, K. N. (2007). Anorexia nervosa treatment: A systematic review of randomized controlled trials. *International Journal of Eating Disorders*, 40, 310–320.

Couturier, J., Kimber, M., & Szatmari, P. (2013). Efficacy of family-based treatment for adolescents with eating disorders: A systematic review and meta-analysis. *International Journal of Eating Disorders*, 46(1), 3–11.

Dare, C., & Eisler, I. (2000). A multi-family group day treatment programme for adolescent eating disorder. *European Eating Disorders Review*, 8, 4–18.

Dare, C., Eisler, I., Russell, G. F. M., & Szmukler, G. I. (1990). The clinical and theoretical impact of a controlled trial of family therapy in anorexia nervosa. *Journal of Marital and Family Therapy*, 16, 39–57.

Davis, T. E. III, Ollendick, T.H., & Öst, L.-G. (2009). Intensive treatment of specific phobias in children and adolescents. *Cognitive and Behavioral Practice*, 16, 294–303.

Downs, K. J., & Blow, A. J. (2013). A substantive and methodological review of family-based treatment for eating disorders: The last 25 years of research. *Journal of Family Therapy*, 35(S1), 3–28.

Eisler, I. (2013). Family therapy for adolescent eating disorders: A special form of therapy or family therapy with a specific focus? *Journal of Family Therapy*, 35(S1), 1–2.

Eisler, I., Dodge, L., & Wallis, A. (2015). What's new is old and what's old is new: The origins and evolution of eating disorders family therapy. In K. L. Loeb, D. Le Grange, & J. Lock (Eds.), *Family therapy for adolescent eating and weight disorders: New applications* (pp. 6–42). New York: Routledge/Taylor & Francis.

Hildebrandt, T., Bacow, T., Markella, M., & Loeb, K. L. (2012). Anxiety in anorexia nervosa and its management using family-based treatment. *European Eating Disorders Review*, 20, 1–16.

Kaye, W. H., Bulik, C. M., Thornton, L. Barbarich, N., & Masters, K. (2004). Comorbidity of anxiety disorders with anorexia and bulimia nervosa. *American Journal of Psychiatry*, *161*, 2215–2221.

Kaye, W. H., Fudge, J.L., & Paulus, M. (2009). New insights into symptoms and neurocircuit function of anorexia nervosa. *Nature Reviews Neuroscience*, 10, 573–584.

Kaye, W. H., Wierenga, C. E., Bailer, U. F., Simmons, A. N., & Bischoff-Grethe, A. (2013). Nothing tastes as good as skinny feels: The neurobiology of anorexia nervosa. *Trends in Neurosciences*, 36, 110–120.

Kazdin, A. E. (1997). Parent management training: Evidence, outcomes, and issues. *Journal of the American Academy of Child & Adolescent Psychiatry*, 36, 1349–1356.

Le Grange, D., & Eisler, I. (2009). Family interventions in adolescent anorexia nervosa. *Child and Adolescent Psychiatric Clinics of North America*, 18, 159–173.

Linehan, M. M. (2015). *DBT skills training manual*, 2nd edition. New York: Guilford Press.

Lock, J., & Le Grange, D. (2012). *Treatment manual for anorexia nervosa: A family-based approach*. New York: Guilford Press.

Marzola, E., Knatz, S., Murray, S. B., Rockwell, R., Boutelle, K. et al. (2015). Short-term intensive family therapy for adolescent eating disorders: 30-month outcome. *European Eating Disorders Review*, 23(3), 210–218.

McKay, M. M., Harrison, M. E., Gonzales, J., Kim, L., & Quintana, E. (2002). Multiple family groups for urban children with conduct difficulties and their families. *Psychiatric Services*, 53, 1467–1468.

Mörtberg, E., Karlsson, A., Fyring, C., & Sundin, Ö. (2006). Intensive cognitive behavioral group treatment (CBGT) of social phobia: A randomized controlled study. *Journal of Anxiety Disorders*, 20, 646–660.

Murray, S. B., Labuschagne, Z., & Le Grange, D. (2014). Family and couples therapy for eating disorders, substance use disorders, and addictions. In T. D. Brewerton & A. Baker-Dennis (Eds.), *Eating disorders, addictions and substance use disorders* (pp. 563–586). Berlin, Germany: Springer.

Rockwell, R. E., Boutelle, K., Trunko, M. E., Jacobs, M. J., & Kaye, W. H. (2011). An innovative short-term, intensive, family-based treatment for adolescent anorexia nervosa: Case series. *European Eating Disorders Review*, 19, 362–367.

Saayman, R. V., Saayman, G. S., & Wiens, S. M. (2006). Training staff in multiple family therapy in a children's psychiatric hospital: From theory to practice. *Journal of Family Therapy*, 28, 404–419.

Salaminiou, E. E. (2005). Families in multiple family therapy for adolescent anorexia nervosa: Response to treatment, treatment experience and family and individual change. Doctoral dissertation, University of London, UK.

Simic, M., & Eisler, I. (2015). *Multi-family therapy: Family therapy for adolescent eating and weight disorders*. New York: Guilford.

Strober, M., & Johnson, C. (2012). The need for complex ideas in anorexia nervosa: Why biology, environment, and psyche all matter, why therapists make mistakes, and why clinical benchmarks are needed for managing weight correction. *International Journal of Eating Disorders*, 45(2), 155–178.

Voriadaki, T., Simic, M., Espie, J., & Eisler, I. (2015). Intensive multi-family therapy for adolescent anorexia nervosa: Adolescents' and parents' day-to-day experiences. *Journal of Family Therapy*, 37(1), 5–23.

Whiteside, S. P., Brown, A. M., & Abramowitz, J. S. (2008). Five-day intensive treatment for adolescent OCD: A case series. *Journal of Anxiety Disorders*, 22, 495–504.

Whiteside, S. P., & Jacobsen, A. B. (2010). An uncontrolled examination of a 5-day intensive treatment for pediatric OCD. *Behavior Therapy*, 41, 414–422.

4 The Integration of Family-Based Treatment and Dialectical Behavior Therapy for Adolescent Bulimia Nervosa

Philosophical and Practical Considerations

Leslie Karwoski Anderson, Stuart B. Murray, Ana L. Ramirez, Roxanne Rockwell, Daniel Le Grange, and Walter H. Kaye

To date, adolescent bulimia nervosa (BN) has received markedly less empirical attention than adolescent anorexia nervosa, with only two controlled trials demonstrating modest rates of full symptom remission (Le Grange, Crosby, Rathouz, & Leventhal, 2007; Schmidt et al., 2007). Le Grange et al. (2007) found that family-based treatment for adolescent BN (FBT-BN) was more efficacious than supportive psychotherapy, while Schmidt et al. (2007) found that cognitive behavioral therapy (CBT) guided self-care resulted in slightly more rapid reduction of bingeing than family therapy. In essence, BN is a disorder of complex etiology, characterized by frequent episodes of binge eating and purging/compensatory behaviors, which affects approximately 1–3 percent of the American population (Hudson, Hiripi, Pope, & Kessler, 2007; Swanson, Crow, Le Grange, Swendsen, & Merikangas, 2011). Furthermore, alongside core binge/purge-type symptomatology, frequent comorbid complexities include medical and psychological disorders, and impaired psychosocial functioning (Wonderlich & Mitchell, 1997), which may run over a protracted and relapsing illness course (Steinhausen, 2002). In addition to bulimic symptoms, 40 percent of adolescents with eating disorders report self-harming, which co-occurs significantly with binging/purging (Crow, Swanson, Le Grange, Feig, & Merikangas, 2014; Peebles, Wilson, & Lock, 2011). Population-based samples illustrate that among adolescents with BN, 53 percent reported suicidal ideation (SI), 26 percent reported a current plan for suicide, 35 percent reported a previous suicide attempt, and 17 percent reported multiple suicide attempts (Crow et al., 2014). It is important to note that participants for the two controlled studies (Le Grange et al., 2007; Schmidt et al., 2007) were excluded for having acute suicidality, substance dependence, or psychosis, therefore limiting the conclusions that we are able to draw from the existing evidence base about patients with a more complex diagnostic presentation.

More recently, it has been demonstrated that BN symptoms among adults, at least in part, are a means of coping with dysphoric mood states and interpersonal stress (Lavender et al., 2014), which consequently may be recursively reinforced by environmental factors. In addition, a growing consensus suggests that neurobiological vulnerabilities contribute significantly to the pathogenesis of BN (Kaye, 2008; Kaye & Bailer, 2011), suggesting intrapsychic, interpersonal, and neurobiological factors are all salient in presentations of BN. As such, clinical treatments must consider (a) the core behavioral symptom profile of BN, (b) the neurobiological correlates of binge/purge and other impulsive behaviors, and (c) the dysregulated mood states that precipitate and maintain them.

Indeed, treatments mobilizing family members to directly intervene into symptomatic BN behaviors, such as FBT (Le Grange & Lock, 2007), may help override neurobiological vulnerabilities and the ego-syntonic components of BN by installing a framework that protects the symptomatic adolescent from decision-making capacities. Alternatively, dialectical behavior therapy (DBT) centrally focuses on skill development in regulating the intensely experienced affective states characteristic of BN (Linehan, 1993; Safer, Telch, & Chen, 2009), which is thought to mitigate the biologically-driven vulnerability towards emotional dysregulation and vulnerability to negative affect (Smyth et al., 2007) and self-destructive behaviors (Telch, 1997). Preliminary evidence for using DBT with BN in adults (Bankoff, Karpel, Forbes, & Pantalone, 2012) and in adolescents (Fischer & Peterson, 2015; Salbach Andrae, Bohnekamp, Pfeiffer, Lehmkuhl, & Miller, 2008) has been promising. However, keeping in mind that DBT does not fully articulate a role for the family in assisting with recovery, and similarly that FBT-BN's primary focus is on regular eating and not emotional regulation, integration of these two treatments may be warranted to comprehensively encapsulate the full scope of deficits experienced by those adolescents with BN.

Philosophical Similarities

Non-Judgmental Stance

FBT-BN posits that adolescents with a bulimic disorder are not unwell of their own volition, but rather are experiencing a partially ego-syntonic illness whose behavioral symptoms are largely driven towards offsetting the intense anxiety brought about by the illness itself (Le Grange & Lock, 2007). As such, FBT-BN adopts a non-judgmental stance in relation to both parents and adolescents alike throughout treatment. Similarly, DBT assumes that, in the context of emotional dysregulation, the patient and the family members aim to cope as skillfully as possible despite powerfully experienced emotions, and a non-pejorative/non-blaming stance is adopted with family members and adolescents. Furthermore, both FBT-BN and DBT posit that high expressed emotion and parental criticism may help exacerbate symptom severity and undermine treatment (Hoste, Lebow, & Le Grange, 2015), and both FBT-BN and DBT clinicians continually work to shape the language of the teen and parents towards non-judgmental neutrality.

Separating the Adolescent from the Illness

In FBT-BN, the adolescent is not seen as being in control of their own behavior/manipulation; rather, the eating disorder is seen as controlling the adolescent (Le Grange & Lock, 2007). While this distinction is not explicitly made in DBT, this approach does encourage separation between the patient and the illness by helping the adolescent create an identity outside of the illness (Linehan, 1993).

Behavioral Treatment Approach

In FBT-BN, the therapist focuses exclusively on re-establishing healthy eating for the adolescent and disrupting the behavioral features of BN (Le Grange & Lock, 2007). This is central to FBT-BN, and a review of the adolescent's binge/purge log takes place at the outset of every family meeting, allowing the family to target the most symptomatic behaviors. DBT adopts a similar focus on behavioral change, targeting multiple problem behaviors that serve as attempts to regulate emotion. Adolescents complete diary cards to record emotions, urges, and behaviors, as well as the skills that were used throughout each week, and this diary card is used to set the agenda for each session (Miller, Rathus, & Linehan, 2007). Behaviors are targeted in order of priority, such that life-threatening behaviors are addressed first and foremost, followed by therapy-interfering behaviors, and then quality-of-life behaviors.

Focus on Validation

Validation is considered a key strategy in FBT-BN, and parents are taught to support and comfort their child, while the therapist takes a stance of consistently and resolutely holding the parents and their family in positive regard (Le Grange, 2010). In addition, parental expressed emotion, critical comments in particular, toward adolescents correlate negatively with treatment outcome (Hoste et al., 2015), and as such, are immediately modified in FBT (Le Grange & Lock, 2007). DBT places a similar emphasis on validation at the forefront of all DBT interventions by encouraging therapists to maintain a delicate balance between validation of a patient's emotional experience while simultaneously activating change (Linehan, 1993).

Philosophical Differences

FBT-BN and DBT share many commonalities, but there are certain aspects of the treatment approaches that appear somewhat incompatible. In this section these differences are explored and reconciled.

Etiology and Functionality of Behavior

In keeping with the largely unsubstantiated etiological origin of BN, FBT-BN adopts an agnostic stance to etiology, which assists in absolving parents and adolescents of any potential self-blame around "causing" the illness, which in turn assists in mobilizing the family into an active role throughout treatment (Le Grange & Lock, 2007). However, DBT is predicated on the biosocial model, which postulates that a child with a more emotional temperament may display stronger emotions, which, when coupled with an invalidating environment, may result in the more pronounced expression of affective dysregulation (Linehan, 1993). While parents and adolescents are not blamed for this pattern, the dynamic is pointed out to family members so that all involved may work towards shifting this dynamic. Despite differing accounts as to the origin of symptom development, both FBT-BN and DBT remain focused on behavioral symptom expression, which in turn offers concrete goals for treatment to target.

Family Involvement

In FBT-BN, the family is central and pivotal in the process of treatment, especially at the outset. This is due not only to the adolescent being embedded in their family of origin, but also because while ill with BN, the adolescent is seen as being unable to make healthy decisions about eating and related behaviors (Le Grange & Lock, 2007). In contrast, DBT was developed in the context of adult disorders of emotion regulation. As such, the focus of treatment has traditionally been on intervening at the individual level, and on coaching the adult patients themselves on how to intervene in their own environment. However, in the context of adolescence, and particularly when the environment is intransigent and powerful, the family can be included as needed when the patient may not effectively intervene on their own behalf (Linehan, 1993). In a combined approach, the family is involved more centrally, as in FBT-BN, although this can be adjusted according to the capacity and motivation level of the adolescent. For example, parents would be asked to remove objects used in life-threatening target behaviors (e.g. self-harm implements) and would be encouraged to have a contract with the adolescent that would specify behavioral contingencies. Dialectically at the same time, the adolescent would be empowered to act more skillfully, and the parents would be charged with being receptive and validating of the increased skillful behavior.

Mechanisms of Change

In delineating the mechanism of symptom remission, it may appear that FBT-BN and DBT operate via differential pathways of symptom remission. FBT-BN posits that the adolescent's ambivalence about their symptomatic behaviors, coupled with the neurobiological vulnerabilities characteristic of eating disorders, grossly impede the adolescent's ability to make healthy decisions (Murray & Le Grange, 2014). As such, a strong interventive parental framework is required in counteracting all pro-BN behaviors, insulating adolescents from further symptom escalation (Le Grange & Lock, 2007).

In DBT, it is assumed that symptomatic behaviors arise out of dysregulated attempts to cope with intense emotional states, and thus primarily seeks to assist the adolescent in regulating their own affective states. The reported mechanisms of change in FBT-BN and DBT, while different, are not mutually exclusive, and synthesizing the active mechanisms of change in both treatments is possible. This integration may seek a flexible blend of direct parental intervention in pro-BN and life-threatening behavior, while assisting adolescents in their own management of intense affective states that result in symptomatic behaviors. However, in determining the delicate balance of parental versus adolescent-driven symptom remission, it is critically important to frequently assess (a) the severity of symptoms, (b) the adolescent's ability to intervene in their own environment, (c) the transigency of the family, and (d) adolescent willingness/motivation to learn and apply skills.

Confidentiality

In FBT-BN, given the largely conjoint nature of family meetings, little confidentiality is offered to adolescents around what is reported back to parents, and all symptomatic behaviors are necessarily shared with parents to allow for interventive measures. However, DBT typically adopts a firmer stance around adolescent confidentiality, allowing adolescents more scope to decide for themselves whether to report certain behaviors (Miller et al., 2007). For instance, while life-threatening behaviors are reported to parents, symptomatic behaviors are not typically reported by the therapist to the parents, as this may limit adolescent disclosure of behavioral symptoms. In a combined approach, a frank and open discussion upon commencing treatment around which behaviors ought to be reported to parents in order to ensure adolescent safety and target symptom remission may serve well in establishing the bounds of confidentiality. While keeping in mind that parents require feedback to gauge the efficacy of their assistance/interventions, and that adolescents may also benefit from developmentally appropriate autonomy in some areas, it can be beneficial for each family to discuss the risk of specific adolescent behaviors, and collaboratively determine which behaviors warrant a breach of confidentiality and parental assistance.

Prescription

FBT-BN is typically non-prescriptive in that therapists encourage parents to rely on their own judgment in how best to assist their child, asserting only that symptoms need to be swiftly interrupted by any means necessary. On the other hand, DBT is quite prescriptive, often incorporating individual skill use and aspects of behavioral parent training in a didactic manner. In a combined approach, interventions are developed collaboratively, with the therapist taking a more prescriptive role in the context of behaviors that may be inadvertently reinforced. For instance, the DBT therapist would point out that parental efforts to reduce distress may inadvertently reinforce symptoms in some instances, and solicit the family's feedback on how to disrupt that cycle.

Strategies to Include in a Blended Approach

FBT-BN and DBT appear to be philosophically compatible, and offer several complementary strategies that are likely to be useful in treating multidiagnostic BN adolescents. The approaches might be integrated at every level of care for eating disorders, but this section outlines strategies that could be incorporated in most treatment settings.

Family Diary Card Review

Both FBT-BN and DBT sessions typically commence with a review of symptomatic behaviors. In an integrated approach, the diary card includes a record of all target behaviors from the preceding week, and may typically include dietary restriction, binge–purge frequency, self-harm, and impulsive behaviors. Parents are encouraged to discuss whether their observations of behaviors match adolescent reports, and family sessions are structured according to the behaviors disclosed on the diary card.

Family Behavior Chain Analysis

In DBT, behavior chains are typically used to elicit the sequential steps preceding engagement in targeted behaviors, paying particular attention to outlining emotions, thoughts, and actions (Linehan, 1993). In FBT, family-wide sequential analyses are often conducted with a view to identifying helpful and unhelpful family interactions that may impact target outcomes (Murray, Wallis, & Rhodes, 2012). In an integrated approach, family-wide analyses may be used to identify the emotions, thoughts, and actions underpinning engagement in target behaviors, allowing for the development of co-constructed alternate points of intervention.

Family Crisis Plan

Patients in DBT typically develop a crisis plan to use when managing intense urges for impulsive behavior (Linehan, 1993). In integrating the development of this plan into a family-wide context for target behaviors, family members are explicitly involved in each step of the crisis plan. Central parental involvement in this plan allows for a greater degree of accessibility of support for adolescents, and may provide additional emotional support, validation, and distraction when needed for the adolescent. For instance, when managing acute and intense urges to binge or purge, crisis management plans may encourage adolescents to turn towards parents in assisting with emotional validation and distraction until urges subside.

Multi-Family Skills Training

Teaching emotion regulation skills in a group format that included adolescents and caregivers would seem consistent with both FBT-BN and DBT. Given how disruptive an eating disorder is to a family's overall emotional and interpersonal functioning, teaching skills to the family can help regulate the emotions that arise in response to the restoration of normal eating, and those emotions that might be contributing to behaviors. Additionally, these skills can help the parents regulate their own emotions in response to the extremely difficult task of helping their child eat normally and reach Phase III of FBT-BN.

Interpersonal Effectiveness Strategies

In DBT, a number of strategies for interacting with people more effectively are taught to adolescents (Rathus & Miller, 2015). In the context of FBT-BN, using skills can be helpful, particularly around mealtimes when distress may be most elevated, for both adolescents and family members. Thus, co-constructed strategies for effective interpersonal communication may assist parents in effectively intervening in symptomatic behaviors, and may also help adolescents in accurately conveying to parents how help is required.

Telephone Consultation

Phone coaching to assist in the management of acute emotional crises is a central feature of DBT, and has been adapted for use with eating disorder patients (Wisniewski & Ben-Porath, 2005). Additionally, with an integrated approach, the option of phone coaching is extended to parents, who may call the therapist for assistance in the management of acute emotional crises. This approach further centralizes and empowers the parents, which is consistent with FBT-BN, while ensuring that adolescents are able to access swift crisis management support, which is consistent with DBT.

Parent Training and Contracts

A common occurrence among families in adapting to the presence of an eating disorder is a reduced range of family interactions, with family life becoming gradually reorganized around mitigating the eating disorder induced anxiety in the afflicted individual (Eisler, 2005). As a result, parental boundaries may become less firm, as parents often forego calling attention to ordinary boundary violations in favor of maintaining focus on the extraordinary circumstances around the eating disorder. From a behavioral learning perspective, any reduction in natural consequences of problematic behavior may serve to inadvertently reinforce the target problematic behavior. As such, behavioral contracts have been adopted for use in an integrated approach to BN treatment, in balancing the focus on rapid symptom remission with the potential ecological maintaining variables.

Conclusion

FBT-BN and DBT represent two distinct clinical approaches to the treatment of adolescent BN, and may share common theoretical assumptions. While integrating these two approaches presents some philosophical incongruence, their practical integration may offer significant advances in current treatments of adolescent BN, offering a dual therapeutic focus on swift behavioral symptom remission and underlying emotional states of both the adolescent and the family. We have outlined a series of theoretical similarities and discrepancies, and further documented a range of clinical strategies that may be utilized in an integrated approach. Although FBT-BN and DBT have accumulated an impressive amount of evidence for the treatment of adolescent eating disorders and emotion dysregulation, respectively, this conceptual review articulates how these treatment strategies may be integrated in treating adolescent BN. Controlled empirical research is needed in supporting the theoretical framework described in the present article. Pending further empirical support in more controlled trials, more detailed pragmatic guidelines may better assist in the dissemination and clinical application of this integrated treatment model. To date, preliminary evidence demonstrates promising clinical outcomes (Murray et al., 2015), although more controlled long-term assessment is required.

References

Bankoff, S. M., Karpel, M. G., Forbes, H. E., & Pantalone, D. W. (2012). A systematic review of dialectical behavior therapy for the treatment of eating disorders. *Eating Disorders, 20,* 196–215.

Crow, S. J., Swanson, S. A., Le Grange, D., Feig, E. H., & Merikangas, K. R. (2014). Suicidal behavior in adolescents and adults with bulimia nervosa. *Comprehensive Psychiatry, 55,* 1534–1539.

Eisler, I. (2005). The empirical and theoretical base of family therapy and multiple family day therapy for adolescent anorexia nervosa. *Journal of Family Therapy, 27,* 104–131.

Fischer, S., & Peterson, C. (2015). Dialectical behavior therapy for adolescent binge eating, purging, suicidal behavior, and non-suicidal self-injury: A pilot study. *Psychotherapy, 52,* 78–92.

Hoste, R. R., Lebow, J., & Le Grange, D. (2015). A bidirectional examination of expressed emotion among families of adolescents with bulimia nervosa. *International Journal of Eating Disorders*, 48, 249–252.

Hudson, J. I., Hiripi, E., Pope, H. G., Jr., & Kessler, R. C. (2007). The prevalence and correlates of eating disorders in the national comorbidity survey replication. *Biological Psychiatry*, 61, 348–358.

Kaye, W. H. (2008). Neurobiology of anorexia and bulimia nervosa. *Physiology & Behavior*, 94, 121–135.

Kaye, W. H., & Bailer, U. F. (2011). Understanding the neural circuitry of appetitive regulation in eating disorders. *Biological Psychiatry*, 70, 704–705.

Lavender, J. M., Wonderlich, S. A., Peterson, C. B., Crosby, R. D., Engel, S. G., & Mitchell, J. E. (2014). Dimensions of emotion dysregulation in bulimia nervosa. *European Eating Disorders Review*, 22, 212–216.

Le Grange, D. (2010). Family-based treatment for adolescents with bulimia nervosa. *Australian and New Zealand Journal of Family Therapy*, 31, 165–175.

Le Grange, D., & Lock, J. (2007). *Treating bulimia in adolescents: A family-based approach.* New York: Guilford Press.

Le Grange, D., Crosby, R., Rathouz, P., & Leventhal, B. (2007). A controlled comparison of family-based treatment and supportive psychotherapy for adolescent bulimia nervosa. *Archives of General Psychiatry*, 64, 1049–1056.

Linehan, M. M. (1993). *Cognitive-behavioral treatment of borderline personality disorder.* New York: Guilford Press.

Miller, A. L., Rathus, J. H., & Linehan, M. M. (2007). *Dialectical behavior therapy with suicidal adolescents.* New York: Guilford Press.

Murray, S. B., & Le Grange, D. (2014). Family therapy for adolescent eating disorders: An update. *Current Psychiatry Reports*, 16, 2–7.

Murray, S. B., Anderson, L. K., Rockwell, R., Griffiths, S., Le Grange, D., & Kaye, W. H. (2015). Adapting family-based treatment for adolescent anorexia nervosa across higher levels of patient care. *Eating Disorders*. doi: 10.1080/10640266.2015.1042317.

Murray, S. B., Wallis, A., & Rhodes, P. (2012). The questioning process in Maudsley family-based treatment. Part 1: Deviation amplification. *Contemporary Family Therapy*, 34, 582–592.

Peebles, R., Wilson, J. L., & Lock, J. D. (2011). Self-injury in adolescents with eating disorders: Correlates and provider bias. *Journal of Adolescent Health*, 48, 310–313.

Rathus, J. H., & Miller, A. L. (2015). *DBT skills manual for adolescents.* New York: Guilford Press.

Safer, D. L., Telch, C. F., & Chen, E. Y. (2009). *Dialectical behavior therapy for binge eating and bulimia.* New York: Guilford Press.

Salbach-Andrae, H., Bohnekamp, I., Pfeiffer, E., Lehmkuhl, U., & Miller, A. L. (2008). Dialectical behavior therapy of anorexia and bulimia nervosa among adolescents: A case series. *Cognitive and Behavioral Practice*, 15, 415–425.

Schmidt, U., Lee, S., Beecham, J., Perkins, S., Treasure, J. et al. (2007). A randomized controlled trial of family therapy and cognitive behavioral guided self-help for adolescents with bulimia nervosa and related conditions. *American Journal of Psychiatry*, 164, 591–598.

Smyth, J. M., Wonderlich, S. A., Heron, K. E., Sliwinski, M. J., Crosby, R. D., e al. (2007). Daily and momentary mood and stress associated with binge eating and vomiting in bulimia nervosa patients in their natural environment. *Journal of Consulting and Clinical Psychology*, 75, 629–638.

Steinhausen, H. (2002). The outcome of anorexia nervosa in the 20th century. *American Journal of Psychiatry*, 159, 1284–1293.

Swanson, S. A., Crow, S. J., Le Grange, D., Swendsen, J., & Merikangas, K. R. (2011). Prevalence and correlates of eating disorders in adolescents: Results from the national comorbidity survey replication adolescent supplement. *Archives of General Psychiatry*, 68, 714–723.

Telch, C. F. (1997). Skills training treatment for adaptive affect regulation in a woman with binge-eating disorder. *International Journal of Eating Disorders*, 15, 77–81.

Wisniewski, L., & Ben-Porath, D. (2005). Telephone skill-coaching with eating disordered clients: Clinical guidelines using a DBT framework. *European Eating Disorders Review*, 13, 344–350.

Wonderlich, S. A., & Mitchell, J. E. (1997). Eating disorders and comorbidity: Empirical, conceptual, and clinical implications. *Psychopharmacology Bulletin*, 33, 381–390.

5 Multi-Family Therapy for Bulimia Nervosa in Adolescence

Catherine Stewart, Stamatoula Voulgari, Ivan Eisler, Katrina Hunt, and Mima Simic

There is a marked contrast between the strength of the evidence bases guiding treatment of adolescents with anorexia nervosa (AN) and adolescents with bulimia nervosa (BN). It has been recognized that effective treatment for adolescents with AN requires different approaches to that used with adults given the particular developmental stage and life cycle of the family (Dare, Eisler, Russell, & Szmukler, 1990) and it is now well established that psychological treatment for AN should include family interventions that directly target the eating disorder (National Institute for Health and Care Excellence [NICE], 2004). However, while there is a good evidence base for the treatment of adults with BN (Hay, 2013; NICE, 2004), the evidence base for treatment of BN in adolescence is scant.

The Presentation and Treatment of Bulimia Nervosa in Adolescence

BN is an eating disorder which has a typical age of onset spanning adolescence and early adulthood and is characterized by binge eating followed by compensatory behaviors such as purging, excessive exercise, or laxative use. People with BN report feelings of guilt and shame, a sense of being out of control when binge eating, and concerns about body shape. It is common for people with BN to experience comorbid anxiety and depression, as well as impairment in social functioning and drug and alcohol use (Le Grange & Schmidt, 2005). BN in adolescence has not been well described, although there is some evidence that adolescents may present with less binge eating and less laxative use than young adults (Fisher, Schneider, Burns, Symons, & Mandel, 2001). Though the disorder may appear less severe in adolescents, it is not thought to be self-limiting (Striegel-Moore, Seeley, & Lewinsohn, 2003).

To date there have been only two published randomized controlled trials (RCTs; Le Grange, Crosby, Rathouz, & Leventhal, 2007; Schmidt et al., 2007), both evaluating bulimia-focused family therapy (FT-BN) in comparison with guided self-care cognitive behavioral therapy (CBT) or supportive psychotherapy. The studies indicated that both guided self-care CBT and FT-BN result in comparable abstinence rates at post-treatment and follow-up (ibid), although

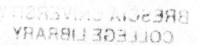

the reported remission rates are lower than those found in AN. Schmidt et al. (2007) highlight a low rate of recruitment because of adolescents' unwillingness to involve their parents in the treatment but those whose treatment included their family continued to make more improvements after the end of treatment than those seen on their own. Le Grange et al. (2007) observed that there is a modest effect of FT on BN, which is comparable to that of CBT in adults and indicative of scope for development of more efficacious treatment.

Developing More Efficacious Treatments for BN in Adolescence

Areas of development in the treatment of BN include (a) the need to involve the family to help overcome low motivation in the young person and to address raised levels of negativity, criticism, or hostility (Duclos, Vibert, Mattar, & Godart, 2012) that may render the young person vulnerable to relapse if stress related to criticism or hostility persists (Medina-Pradas, Navarro, Lopez, Grau, & Obiols, 2011); (b) a low rate of recruitment for family therapy (FT) because the more disturbed adolescents were reluctant to involve their parents (Perkins et al., 2005); and (c) high levels of emotional and behavioral dysregulation (Anestis, Selby, Fink, & Joiner, 2007) that are not addressed in more traditional forms of eating disorders therapy.

Adolescents with BN have particular needs that distinguish them both from adolescents with AN and from adults with BN. First, although the incidence of BN in adolescence is comparable to AN with expected prevalence around 1 percent (Hoek & van Hoeken, 2003), this is not reflected in early help-seeking behavior, which is typically delayed for four–five years after the illness onset (Turnbull, Ward, Treasure, Jick, & Derby, 1996). The reasons for the delay are varied, including a sense of shame and a fear of stigmatization, less evident difficulties than the rapid weight loss and food restriction that alert others to AN, and probably also a lack of effective and credible treatments.

Second, they are clearly at a different developmental stage to adults with BN, and typically living with their family. In common with AN, the presence of an eating disorder places the family under particular stress and can prevent the family from making expected life cycle transitions. Moreover, there is evidence that caregivers of people with BN experience significant practical, emotional, and relational difficulties (Perkins, Winn, Murray, Murphy, & Schmidt, 2004). These include the removal of significant amounts of food from cupboards, blocked drains and other consequences of young people trying to disguise their behaviors, and managing an emotionally dysregulated teen alongside comorbid emotional and behavioral difficulties, often provoking frustration and disgust in caregivers. However, although this is suggestive of the need for family interventions, existing family therapy treatments require modification to increase efficacy and improve acceptability (Le Grange et al., 2007; Schmidt et al., 2007). Indeed, adolescents who report high perceived criticism or hostility from caregivers can find it particularly difficult to engage in FT (Perkins et al., 2005).

Third, the psychological profile of people with BN differs from those with AN, with more marked difficulties with emotion regulation, impulsivity, and distress tolerance (Anestis et al., 2007), leading to risk of dysregulated eating to distract from intolerable affect. As there has been growing recognition of the role that the binge–purge cycle plays in emotion regulation in BN, greater attention has been paid to emotion dysregulation as a therapeutic target. Research examining the efficacy of dialectical behavior therapy (DBT) in adults has indicated that it can significantly reduce bulimic behaviors (Bankoff, Karpel, Forbes, & Pantalone, 2012), though evidence with adolescents is preliminary (Salbach-Andrae et al., 2008).

Fourth, the time course of treatment in BN differs to that of AN where there is an immediacy and urgency to recommence feeding. In contrast, in BN, while there are clear medical risks requiring regular monitoring, the problematic behaviors are more variable in frequency, and food intake has not stopped. Moreover, the difficulties experienced by the young person may have been less visible to those around them, and there is a need for treatment sessions to be spaced to allow families time to practice and build on relational and coping skills over time.

Multi-Family Treatment for BN

The Multi-Family Therapy-BN (MFT-BN) program has been developed by the Child and Adolescent Eating Disorders Service, South London and Maudsley NHS Foundation Trust in London, specifically to build on the evidence provided by the two previous RCTs and address the four particular issues outlined above. MFT-BN has been developed to treat adolescents aged 13–18. MFT-BN incorporates systemic therapy in a multi-family context (Simic & Eisler, 2015), which has been demonstrated to have better outcomes in anorexia than single family therapy (Eisler, 2013), together with elements of CBT and DBT. However, there are significant modifications made to address each of the four outlined issues.

First, it can be difficult to motivate adolescents to engage in therapy that also involves their parents (Perkins et al., 2005). MFT-BN's structure is designed to address this through having the first two sessions as separate young people's and parents' groups. The focus of these sessions for young people is on increased motivation both for recovery and for communication around support and disclosure. This is done alongside psychoeducation around factors involved in the binge–purge cycle. Intervention in the parents' group in these first sessions addresses the second difficulty, of high levels of negativity and criticism. Space is made for expression of difficulties and frustrations before teaching DBT validation skills. Thus, before the young people join together with their parents in the multi-family setting, their parents have started to learn and practice validation so that young people's experience of sharing what they have learned together in their group about the binge–purge cycle receives a response that helps to further motivate them to involve parents in treatment.

These issues are further addressed through the systemic elements of the multi-family approach, the use of the family as a resource, the shared experience of families allowing them opportunities to develop new perspectives, and exploration of new ways of addressing difficulties.

The third issue outlined above was the particular psychological profile of negative affect combined with impulsivity and low distress tolerance hypothesized to be involved in BN. MFT-BN therefore includes specific elements of the DBT skills modules of Distress Tolerance, Emotion Regulation, and Mindfulness, outlined in more detail below.

The fourth issue identified was a more varied time course in BN of exposure to symptoms and opportunities for new behaviors to be tried. This, together with the often greater relational pressures, requires a different therapeutic stance in MFT-BN where the parents are not encouraged to take a very active role in managing their child's eating until the adolescent is more able to regain control themself and the family can negotiate how best to provide support. A key aim in MFT-BN is to help the adolescent become more able to manage emotional difficulties as well as the behaviors associated with dysregulated eating and to increase motivation to allow communication and support from family members. Therefore the structure of MFT-BN has been developed to provide enough regularity for the group to become and remain cohesive, but with time between sessions to allow for the skills learned by family members to be generalized.

Structure of the Program

The program is preceded by an introductory evening, where families meet each other and the treatment team and general expectations are shared around attendants at the group. A formal presentation is given by a medical member of the team outlining the physical risks associated with BN. Information is also shared about the body's digestion of food and absorption of calories, highlighting the ineffectiveness of purging and laxative use as a means to prevent weight gain. The aim of this presentation is to highlight the seriousness of the condition to develop motivation to change in all family members, as well as to convey a sense of expertise held within the team. In this introductory session parents and young people are given the opportunity to meet with members of a graduate family with the aim of engendering hope in the possibility of change.

The program is currently delivered to a closed group of families over a 20-week period with 12 weekly, 1.5 hour-long groups, followed by four fortnightly groups interspersed with individual appointments if required. Medical monitoring is provided alongside these as necessary, particularly for monitoring of weight and blood indicators. We have found that it is helpful for young people to have been known to the service for some weeks prior to the start of the group program so that there is diagnostic certainty (to clearly distinguish symptoms of BN from the symptoms of AN binge–purge subtype) and so that motivation and engagement with the service can be developed individually prior to joining the group program. We have also found that a program with a series of weekly groups initially helps to develop an appropriate level of momentum for the intervention.

Throughout the program a variety of contexts are used for activities. These include multi-family and separate parent/adolescent groups. These allow for management of high negativity and criticism and ambivalence about the involvement of different family members as well as the tailoring of specific input to meet the varying needs of adolescents and parents.

Specific Therapeutic Elements in Treatment

Through a combination of specific therapeutic elements, the program seeks to address:

- Management of the binge–purge cycle, to reduce the behavioral symptoms of bulimia.
- Ability to manage maintaining factors involved in relapse, including psychosocial stressors and emotion dysregulation.
- Burden and stress experienced within families as a result of managing a chronic condition evoking difficult emotions, including guilt, shame, and anger.
- Patterns of family communication and interaction disrupted by an eating disorder.

Systemic Elements

MFT-BN draws on MFT-AN in its use of a range of systemic principles, techniques, and exercises. As with the treatment of AN, there is a focus on working with the family, supporting families to identify their strengths and mobilize their resources. Through the use of information giving, and in the context of a collaborative therapeutic relationship, one of the goals is to support the family to re-discover their strengths and enable the young person to see the family as a resource to their recovery. There is a central focus on helping families to find solutions and reinforcing of the family adaptation processes that enable developmentally appropriate family life-cycle changes (Eisler, Lock, & Le Grange, 2010).

Family life cycle and developmental stages of the adolescent form a conceptual backdrop to the therapy as young people are encouraged to both communicate and to take responsibility, and as parents are supported to maintain boundaries for their child, particularly around food and eating, but also to consider the appropriate level of individuation and experimentation for the developmental stage of their adolescent.

The multi-family environment enables the use of the multiple shared experiences and resources of the families. Bringing together adolescents and their parents with other families helps to combat the stigma associated with BN and supports young people in managing the shame associated with the disorder, through an ongoing practice of the DBT skill of "act opposite" (see below). Moreover, the learning of skills together as a family can serve both to normalize the human experience of negative emotional states and help to develop strategies to manage them. It also provides parents with knowledge of strategies being taught to their adolescents so that they can support them to generalize their use of these outside of the clinic setting. The more open communication about skills that comes from learning them together allows for more effective solution generation to maximize their implementation.

A range of specific activities has been included in the program. For example, cross-generational interviewing, in which parents are interviewed in the role of their adolescent to enhance empathy and show validation of the adolescent's predicament. "Foster families," where a young person is paired with the parent(s) from other families, are used frequently in the program. This allows for families to develop new narratives and draw on more resources in managing their difficulties. In the context of families with high levels of negative emotion, it enables the discussion of emotionally charged topics, such as the possibility of parents helping young people to practice some coping skills to exit binge–purge cycles. The use of this technique is based on the hypothesis that it is easier for young people to discuss difficult issues with an empathic, well-meaning, non-related, neutral adult than within the emotionally charged relationship with their own parent. At the same time, parents witness feedback from their own child and talk issues through with another child. Together, this allows for better sharing of information and the opening of conversations within each family.

Cognitive Behavioral Therapy Elements

A joint CBT formulation of the binge–purge cycle is developed by the adolescent group at the start of the program. This includes external triggers, emotions, and cognitions that are present at each stage of the cycle. Through the drawing out of this cycle, work starts on identifying the range of functions that BN has for each young person and allows for communication of key ideas such as the possibility of exiting the cycle at a range of places and the viciousness of the cycle both with hunger increasing vulnerability to a future binge and the negative emotional impact of harsh judgments of self, provoked by both bingeing and purging.

This group formulation is shared with the parents in a multi-family group session. Prior to this session the parents practice validation skills (cf. Linehan, 1993), a sequencing that is crucial in working with these difficulties given the literature indicating high levels of family stress (Perkins et al., 2004), criticism, guilt, and blame (Anastasiadou, Medina-Pradas, Sepulveda, & Treasure, 2014). Techniques drawn from CBT include challenging thoughts, recognizing negative thinking patterns (such as catastrophizing and black-and-white thinking), and developing plans for exposure to avoided activities.

Dialectical Behavioral Therapy Elements

Specific selected elements of DBT are used and participants are encouraged to use DBT skills taught in the program to exit the cycle of BN and to approach their parents to ask them to support them in using skills and breaking the binge–purge cycle. At the same time, parents are taught skills of validation enabling them to validate difficult feelings and behaviors of their children without responding to those in a hostile manner. Discussing the concept of validation with parents in a group context with other parents makes it easier for parents to consider this without feeling blamed and criticized themselves. Parents are also encouraged to approach young people in-between groups and discuss with them the skills they will attempt to use and the kind of support from parents they will find most useful.

Elements of DBT included in the program are:

- *Motivation techniques:* pros and cons, foot in the door (getting agreement for a small change, e.g. being in the room with parents while the BN cycle is described, and pushing for a larger change, e.g. agreeing to comment on a specific part of the cycle). These techniques are used throughout the program in separate group sessions with young people, as their ambivalence towards recovery can have a significant impact on whether they are willing to allow their parents to know more about the details of their disorder and to support them in implementing skills in breaking the binge–purge cycle.
- *Validation:* learning the skill of being able to acknowledge the validity of another person's experience, even if it is not necessarily agreed with or approved. Validation is presented as a precursor to change.
- *Distress tolerance:* based on the theoretical framework that a low tolerance for negative affect elevates the risk of BN, specific skills for regulating emotion when in a state of negative affect are taught. Young people are supported by their families to develop a distraction plan, and asked to create and use a self-soothe box including means of soothing themselves with each of the five senses. The "Cope Ahead" skill is used to help adolescents develop exposure to thinking about difficulties and ways to cope, and to promote discussion within the family about upcoming challenges and appropriate joint plans to manage these.
- *Emotion regulation:* the intolerable experience of negative affect is further challenged through psychoeducation about the functions of emotions and through development of skills for managing emotions, including opposite action, and working on developing opportunities for experiencing positive emotions.
- *Mindfulness:* to help the young people to develop more awareness of their physical and mental state, and of the urges that lead to impulsive management of difficulties through the binge–purge cycle, mindfulness is taught. It is also used to enhance relationships within families through the introduction of the concepts of Wise Mind, Emotional Mind, and Reasonable Mind and role play of difficult conversations when people are in each of these mind states.

Table 5.1 Cohen's *d* calculated using Morris and DeShon's (2002) Equation 8 to correct for dependence between means

	n	*Pre-group mean (SD)*	*Post-group mean (SD)*	*Effect size, Cohen's d*
Eating Disorder Examination Questionnaire	10	4.31 (0.96)	3.41 (1.88)	0.82
Moods and feelings questionnaire	9	37.67 (17.03)	27.55 (19.29)	0.58
Ways of coping checklist	10	1.39 (0.65)	1.85 (0.64)	1.65

Acceptability of the MFT-BN Program

We have completed five MFT-BN programs over the past five years. Throughout the development of the program we have been guided by formal and informal feedback from participants. This feedback has been broadly consistent with that reported from multi-family groups with other clinical populations, particularly in their sense of the group being a support and noticing improvements in family relationships (Eisler, LeGrange, & Asen, 2003). There are indications from feedback that the groups have served to allow families to incorporate new ways of coping with the disorder and with communicating with each other. A qualitative study using focus groups is underway to further explore the acceptability and perceived benefits of this intervention. Preliminary analysis of clinically collected outcome data indicates reductions in eating disorder symptoms and depression and increase in use of adaptive skills for coping (see Table 5.1).

Future Directions

The evidence to date is that this program is perceived to be beneficial by families who have completed the group sessions. We have found that the utilization of systemic, CBT and DBT elements can be combined in a manner that, according to families' feedback, appears to meet their needs and allows for change to occur. This continues the tradition of MFT drawing on a range of therapeutic modalities. Rates of dropout during the MFT-BN program appear higher than in the MFT-AN groups and there is a need to examine the reasons for this. Future work and evaluation will determine the efficacy and acceptability of the program.

References

Anastasiadou, D., Medina-Pradas, C., Sepulveda, A. R. & Treasure, J. (2014). A systematic review of family caregiving in eating disorders. *Eating Behaviors*, 15, 464–477.

Anestis, M. D., Selby, E. A., Fink, E. L., & Joiner, T. E. (2007). The multifaceted role of distress tolerance in dysregulated eating behaviors. *International Journal of Eating Disorders*, 40, 718–726.

Bankoff, S. M., Karpel, M. G., Forbes, H. E., & Pantalone, D. W. (2012). A systematic review of dialectical behavior therapy for the treatment of eating disorders. *Eating Disorders*, 20, 196–215.

Dare C., Eisler I., Russell G. F. M., & Szmukler G. I. (1990). Family therapy for anorexia nervosa: Implications from the results of a controlled trial of family and individual therapy. *Journal of Marital and Family Therapy*, 16, 39–57.

Duclos, J., Vibert, S., Mattar, L., & Godart, N. (2012). Expressed emotion in families of patients with eating disorders: A review of the literature. *Current Psychiatry Reviews*, 8, 183–202.

Eisler, I. (2013). A multicentre RCT of single and multi-family therapy for adolescent anorexia nervosa. Paper presented at the September meeting of the Eating Disorders Research Society, Bethesda, MA.

Eisler, I., LeGrange, D., & Asen, E. (2003). Family interventions. In J. Treasure, U. Schmidt, & E. van Furth (Eds.), *Handbook of eating disorders* (pp. 150–174). Oxford: Wiley-Blackwell.

Eisler, I., Lock, J., & Le Grange, D. (2010). Family-based treatments for adolescents with anorexia nervosa: Single-family and multi-family approaches. In C. M. Grilo & J. E. Mitchell (Eds.), *The treatment for eating disorders: A clinical handbook* (pp. 291–310). New York: Guilford Press.

Fisher, M., Schneider, M., Burns, J., Symons, H., & Mandel, F. (2001). Differences between adolescents and young adults at presentation to an eating disorders program. *Journal of Adolescent Health*, 28, 222–227.

Hay, P. (2013). A systematic review of evidence for psychological treatments in eating disorders: 2005–2012. *International Journal of Eating Disorders*, 46, 462–469.

Hoek, H. W., & van Hoeken, D. (2003). Review of the prevalence and incidence of eating disorders. *International Journal of Eating Disorders*, 34, 383–396.

Le Grange, D., & Schmidt, U. (2005). The treatment of adolescents with bulimia nervosa. *Journal of Mental Health*, 14, 587–597.

Le Grange, D., Crosby, R. D., Rathouz, P. J., & Leventhal, B. L. (2007). A randomized controlled comparison of family-based treatment and supportive psychotherapy for adolescent bulimia nervosa. *Archives of General Psychiatry*, 64, 1049–1056.

Linehan, M. M. (1993). *Cognitive behavioral treatment of borderline personality disorder*. New York: Guilford Press.

Medina-Pradas, C., Navarro, J. B., Lopez, S. R., Grau, A., & Obiols, J. E. (2011). Dyadic view of expressed emotion, stress, and eating disorder psychopathology. *Appetite*, 57, 743–748.

National Institute for Health and Care Excellence (NICE). (2004). *Eating disorders: Core interventions in the treatment and management of anorexia nervosa, bulimia nervosa and related eating disorders*. Available online at www.nice. org.uk/guidance/cg9 (accessed February 29, 2016).

Perkins, S., Schmidt, U., Eisler, I., Treasure, J., Yi, I. et al. (2005). Why do adolescents with bulimia nervosa choose not to involve their parents in treatment? *European Journal of Child and Adolescent Psychiatry*, 14, 376–385.

Perkins, S., Winn, S., Murray, J., Murphy, R., & Schmidt, U. (2004). A qualitative study of the experience of caring for a person with bulimia nervosa. Part 1: The emotional impact of caring. *International Journal of Eating Disorders*, 36, 256–268.

Salbach-Andrae, H., Bohnekamp, I., Pfeiffer, E., Lehmkuhl, U, & Miller, A. L. (2008). Dialectical behavior therapy of anorexia and bulimia nervosa among adolescents: A case series. *Cognitive and Behavioral Practice*, 15, 415–425.

Schmidt, U., Lee, S., Beecham, J., Perkins, S., Treasure, J. et al. (2007). A randomized controlled trial of family therapy and cognitive behavior therapy guided self-care for adolescents with bulimia nervosa and related conditions. *American Journal of Psychiatry*, 164, 591–598.

Simic, M., & Eisler I. (2015). Multi-family therapy for eating disorders. In K. Loeb, D. Le Grange, & J. Lock (Eds.). *Family therapy for adolescent eating and weight disorders* (pp. 110–138). New York: Guilford Press.

Striegel-Moore, R. H., Seelet, J. R., & Lewinsohn, P. M. (2003). Psychosocial adjustment in young adulthood of women who experienced an eating disorder during adolescence. *American Academy of Child and Adolescent Psychiatry*, 42, 587–593.

Turnbull, S., Ward, A., Treasure, J., Jick, H., & Derby, L. (1996). The demand for eating disorder care: An epidemiological study using the general practice research database. *British Journal of Psychiatry*, 169, 705–712.

Part II

Special Topics in Family Therapy for Eating Disorders

6 Is Family-Based Treatment a Specific Therapy for Adolescents with Anorexia Nervosa?

James Lock

Introduction

There is an ongoing debate about how psychotherapy leads to clinical improvements in patients (Horvath & Symonds, 1991). On the one hand, there is considerable evidence that the effects of psychotherapy are best explained by common factors present in any psychotherapy (e.g. therapeutic alliance, expectancy of improvement, therapeutic context). Data supporting this point of view comes from large meta-analyses of outcome studies (Stevens, Hynan, & Allend, 2000). From this perspective, psychotherapy is generally best viewed as non-specific treatment and those components that are specific to a particular psychotherapy contribute little to the overall outcome. On the other hand, there are data that support that the effects of psychosocial interventions are specific and not solely a result of these common factors (DeRubeis, Brotman, & Gibbons, 2005). Whether a treatment's effects are specific or non-specific is not merely an academic question, because the answer could inform decisions about which treatments to disseminate and implement.

While a number of studies suggest that family therapy is effective for adolescent anorexia nervosa (Lock, 2015), there is debate about whether family therapy is a specific therapy or if common therapeutic factors explain the findings (Lohr, DeMaoi, & McGlynn, 2003; Strober, 2014). If common therapeutic factors such as therapeutic alliance and expectancy effect explain the outcome, then generic therapies might be offered with the expectation of garnering similar patient outcomes (Hovarth, 1988). Generic therapies have the advantage of not requiring extensive training in specific techniques and being potentially applicable to broad populations (i.e. transdiagnostic) so they are likely easier and cheaper to disseminate. On the other hand, if a particular treatment's effects are due to therapeutic ingredients or processes unique to it, then it is probably a specific treatment. If a specific treatment leads to better outcomes, then it is reasonable to consider disseminating the specific treatment rather than a generic one as long as the cost–benefit ratio is also considered. In the case of treatments for adolescent AN, a number have been examined, so dispute in the field about differential effects of specific treatments is understandable. In the case of family therapy for adolescent AN, whether to use a specific manualized version of family therapy or more generic family therapy for AN has been debated (Strober, 2014).

This chapter reviews available data supporting the claim that a specific form of manualized family therapy, family-based treatment for AN (FBT-AN), is a specific therapy that warrants dissemination over generic family therapy or other treatments for adolescent AN (Lock & Le Grange, 2013). What constitutes a specific therapy rather than a therapy whose outcomes are primarily related to the impact of common factors has been variously described (Lohr et al., 2003), but in general, to assess whether a particular therapy is a specific therapy, answers to the following questions are helpful:

(1) Is there data supporting the overall efficacy of the approach? There needs to be compelling data that the approach is effective before answering the question about specificity.
(2) Is there data that suggests that a particular therapy is more effective than comparison therapy? Data suggesting differential efficacy supports the proposition that treatments may differ from one another; however, it is insufficient because two different therapies can lead to the same outcome and still differ from each other by process and mechanism.
(3) Do so-called common factors such as therapeutic alliance, expectancy, and context present in all psychotherapies explain the effect of treatment? If the treatment effects are best explained by the effects of therapeutic alliance, expectation effects, contextual effects, general emotional expression/support, or rationale for treatment, then the treatment is not likely to be specific.
(4) Do different patient groups have differential responses to treatments? If patients respond differently to one treatment rather than another (moderators), this suggests that at least one of the treatments is different and specific.
(5) Does data about response timing and trajectory differ between comparison treatments? If there is a difference in the pattern of response between two treatments, this suggests that there are differences in process that lead to differences in therapeutic action and therefore supports specificity of an approach.
(6) Are there data that support a specific mechanism of action of the therapy that distinguishes it from approaches not utilizing the same therapeutic target? If the mechanisms of action can be identified and the impact of changes related to this mechanism is associated with clinical benefit, these data would support that an approach is specific.
(7) Are there data to support that adherence to specific treatment components affects outcome in treatment? Data that show that therapist fidelity to the treatment ingredients and procedures affects outcome supports the view that a treatment is specific.

This chapter argues that, when taken together, data supports the proposition that manualized FBT-AN is a specific treatment for the following reasons: common factors do not appear to explain the outcome; there are differences in treatment response trajectory in FBT-AN compared to other treatments; moderators of treatment effect have been identified; there are differences in service utilization compared to other treatments when FBT-AN is administered; there are data supporting a specific mechanism that underlies the efficacy of FBT-AN related to parental self-efficacy; and there are data supporting the importance of fidelity to key components of FBT-AN and clinical outcome. The chapter reviews the data supporting these observations and makes the case for dissemination of manualized FBT-AN rather than generic family therapy or other approaches.

Different Family Therapy Manuals and Approaches

The question of whether FBT-AN is a specific treatment arises in part because the database of systematic studies for adolescent AN is complicated by the use of differing versions of family therapy. There are four different manuals of different family therapy approaches (e.g. FBT-AN; Lock & Le Grange, 2013), Family Therapy for AN (FT-AN; Eisler et al., unpublished), Behavioral Family Systems Therapy (BFST; Robin, 2003) and Leeds Systemic Family Therapy (SyFT; Pote, 2001). FBT-AN, FT-AN, and BFST share similar components early in treatment designed to promote parental behavioral management of weight restoration in their child; while the Leeds SyFT manual is focused on family system issues related to more general issues of communication and conflict. The FBT-AN manual has been used in five RCTs to date ($n = 353$). The BFST manual has been used in one study ($N = 37$). The Leeds manual has been used in one study for adolescent AN ($N = 82$). The FT-AN manual, developed at the Maudsley Hospital by Ivan Eisler and colleagues, has not been used in a published RCT. Other published RCTs examining outpatient family therapy for adolescent AN did not use manuals ($N = 76$; Eisler et al., 2000; Le Grange, Eisler, Dare, & Russell, 1992; Russell, Szmukler, Dare, & Eisler, 1987). Thus, although the majority of systematic data is derived from studies utilizing the FBT-AN manual ($353/572 = 62$ percent of patients studied received FBT-AN), this is an insufficient answer to the question of specificity, though it does suggest that conclusions about the effectiveness of family therapy depend largely on those studies that used FBT-AN.

The Evidence Base

There has been a significant increase in systematic treatment studies for adolescents with AN and, overall, data now supports family therapy as the approach with the greatest evidential support (Lock, 2015). Three RCTs in three different research centers, as well as a meta-analysis, have demonstrated that FBT is superior to other therapies examined (Couturier, Kimbler, & Szatmari,

2013b; Lock et al., 2010; Robin et al., 1999; Russell et al., 1987). Three RCTs have also demonstrated that FBT is more efficient in restoring weight and decreasing hospital use than comparison treatments examined (e.g. individual and family therapy; Agras et al., 2014; Lock et al., 2010; Madden et al., 2015). In addition, a dose study has demonstrated that a 10-session/6-month version of FBT is as effective as a 20-session/12-month version of FBT for most patients (see discussion of moderators below) (Lock, Agras, Bryson, & Kraemer, 2005). Taken together, these studies find a recovery rate (weight > 94% EBW and EDE within 1 SD of normal) (Couturier & Lock, 2006) of adolescents with AN treated with FBT ranging between 33 and 42 percent by the end of treatment. A recent comprehensive review argues that FBT-AN has accumulated enough supportive data to conclude it is a well-established treatment for adolescent AN (requires a minimum of two RCTs with rigorous methods at two different sites and a meta-analysis) using American Psychological Association (APA) guidelines (Lock, 2015). However, other studies using family therapy approaches, most of which are broadly systemic, are also probably effective (at least one systematic study demonstrating superior or equivalent efficacy of a known effective treatment) (Agras et al., 2014). It should be pointed out that a limitation of the database supporting FBT-AN is that the majority of RCTs (three studies) were conducted at the sites of the authors of the manual (Luborskey et al., 1999), though in each of these studies an independent data center collected and analyzed the study data. In addition, one of these studies also included six sites that were fully independent (Agras et al., 2014) and a third study took place in a fully independent site (Madden et al., 2015). Nonetheless, allegiance effects are known to influence study outcomes and cannot be fully ruled out as at least one source of treatment effects of manualized FBT-AN (Luborskey et al., 1999).

Common Factors

Common factors in psychotherapy include therapeutic alliance, positive expectancy of benefit of treatment, a therapeutic context, opportunity to express emotions, acquisition and practice of new behaviors, and communication of a therapeutic rationale (Safer & Hugo, 2006). Therapeutic alliance describes the empathetic support and understanding expected in all therapeutic encounters. Positive expectancy is an expression of the patient's evaluation that treatment will be helpful and contributes to the willingness to engage in and continue with treatment. The therapeutic context is the clinical setting wherein treatments are administered and contributes to both expectancy and the processes of treatment. Expressing emotions and feeling, even in behavioral and cognitive approaches, is a necessary aspect of therapy. Learning new skills and practicing them, whether they are expression-based, cognitive, or behavioral, is part of all psychotherapies. To embark on and continue in therapy, an understanding of why the treatment is likely to be helpful is necessary. To distinguish treatment effects of a specific psychotherapy over and above effects expected from common factors, these factors need to be accounted for in the analysis of data to determine their relative role in outcome.

Turning to the problem of specific treatment versus common factors in treatment in the case of studies of adolescent AN requires reviewing recent developments in treatments for this disorder. When researchers at the Maudsley Hospital and Institute of Psychiatry in London developed the family therapy approach they combined treatment interventions from different schools of family therapy, including systemic, structural, strategic, narrative, and feminist schools (Dare & Eisler, 1997). The approach developed was not manualized, though an overall description of contents of the therapy was ultimately published (Dare & Eisler, 1997; Eisler, 2005). This iteration of family therapy for adolescent AN was compared to a form of individual supportive psychotherapy that contained the common factors described above (Russell et al., 1987). At the same time, though, the individual therapy provided was not manualized, was highly unstructured, and did not include dietary advice or have a specific behavioral or cognitive focus, though it did encourage expression of emotions and feelings (ibid). The results of that first study suggested the specific form of family therapy used was superior to supportive therapy for adolescents with short duration AN because those patients who received family therapy did better than those who received supportive therapy. Importantly, this was not true for the other patient groups that were included in the study; thus, adolescents with longer duration (> 3 years) AN, adults with AN, and adults with BN all did the same in both treatments. This early study, then, supports the contention that for adolescents with AN of short duration, the specific family therapy provided at the Maudsley Hospital in this study was superior to that expected as a result of a treatment that included only common factors. However, at the same time, it is important to note that the role of common factors in either treatment was not explicitly examined in this small cohort. Further, because the family therapy used was not manualized, how replicably and consistently the specific interventions in treatment were delivered is uncertain.

As a result of this shortcoming, subsequent to the initial study, family therapy based on the treatment used in Russell and colleagues' study was manualized by two groups. The first manual was developed by Robin and colleagues at Wayne State University (Robin, 2003). The treatment was named Behavioral Family Systems Therapy (BFST) and a summary of it has been published (Robin, 2003). BFST, however, did not completely replicate the approach used in the Russell and colleagues study, but instead added cognitive elements to the approach that were not part of the approach. In designing a comparison study for BFST, Robin and colleagues developed what they considered to be a therapy that not only included common factors but also contained specific therapeutic targets related to adolescent competence, developmental mastery, and self-efficacy. This treatment was manualized and called Ego Oriented Individual Therapy (EOIT; Robin et al., 1999). In a small randomized controlled trial (RCT) ($N = 37$), BFST and EOIT were found to have similar outcomes, but BFST was deemed the superior approach because it resulted in better weight gain and physiologic health (menstruation) than EOIT. These data suggested that BFST performed better than EOIT because of specific rather than common factors, in part because common factors were a part of both treatments and yet the outcomes differed. In addition, though there was an attempt to control for common factors in the treatments by nesting therapists in treatments they supported, these factors were not assessed in either approach.

The first manual to explicitly delineate the type of family therapy that was used in the initial studies at the Maudsley was written in close collaboration with the original developers and published in 2001 (Lock & Le Grange, 2001; Lock, Le Grange, Agras, & Dare, 2001). It was also used in the first study to examine therapeutic alliance explicitly using manualized FBT-AN (Krautter & Lock, 2004). The RCT compared two doses of FBT-AN in 86 adolescents with AN and their parents (Lock et al., 2005). Therapeutic alliance in this study was initially assessed by self-report post-treatment using a Likert-type rating scale. Scores of therapeutic rapport were generally high (adolescent = 4.18; mother = 4.71; father = 4.19), with no significant differences between them (Krautter & Lock, 2004). A more definitive study of this same sample was conducted using the Horvath therapeutic alliance rating scheme that involved independent assessors rating taped sessions at early, middle, and late stages in treatment ($N = 41$; Horvath, Gaston, & Luborsky, 1993; Pereira, Lock, & Oggins, 2006). Results of that study found therapeutic alliance predictive of early weight gain and of staying in treatment. This finding would be consistent with common factor effects; however, end of treatment therapeutic alliance was predicted by mid-treatment weight gain rather than early therapeutic alliance. In other words, although therapeutic alliance was important in setting the stage for treatment using manualized FBT-AN, therapeutic alliance was maintained throughout treatment only if there was evidence of clinical progress (i.e. weight gain). Further, end of treatment changes in eating-related psychopathology as measured by the Eating Disorder Examination (EDE; Cooper & Fairburn, 1987) were predicted by mid-treatment weight progress, not therapeutic alliance. These findings suggest that the treatment effects of FBT-AN in this study were not fully explained by the common factor of therapeutic alliance; rather, they were attributable to other ingredients and processes specific to the approach.

As noted, the Robin and colleagues study was small and therefore questions remained about the conclusion that family therapy (in this case, BFST) was the superior approach. More recently, Lock and colleagues embarked on a significantly larger RCT ($N = 121$) comparing FBT-AN to individual therapy (adolescent-focused therapy   AFT). AFT is modeled directly on EOIT but was further refined and detailed in manual form for this new study (Fitzpatrick, Moye, Hoste, Le Grange, & Lock, 2010). The overall findings of the study suggested that FBT-AN was superior to AFT and therefore reinforced the findings of Robin and colleagues' earlier study. Because establishing an initial therapeutic alliance with the adolescent with AN is a crucial part of AFT, Forsberg and colleagues examined this common factor using independent assessors evaluating taped sessions from early in treatment with the Horvath measure (Forsberg et al., 2013). The study found that therapeutic alliance was generally good for both treatments, but that therapeutic alliance was significantly greater in AFT than FBT-AN (AFT = 5.31; FBT = 4.25; p = 0.001, ES = 1.26). Thus therapists in both treatments were successful in building a therapeutic alliance consistent with common factor theory for effective treatment. However, in contrast to common factor theory, no relationship was found between scores on therapeutic alliance and the clinical outcomes of the study (weight gain and improved psychopathology). These findings suggest that the common factor of therapeutic alliance does not sufficiently explain the treatment effects of either FBT-AN or AFT.

Another common factor said to explain treatment response in psychotherapy is expectancy. Patients and families who embark on treatment have a measurable opinion as to whether the proposed treatment is likely to be helpful. In general, a higher positive expectancy should inflate treatment response, while lower or negative expectancy should diminish treatment response. In three recent RCTs for adolescent AN, baseline expectancy was assessed. Expectancy scores for all treatments delivered (FBT-AN, AFT, and SyFT) were similar to each other, suggesting that outcomes should be similar to one another based on this common factor. As noted, clinical outcomes differed between FBT-AN and AFT; however, clinical outcomes were similar between the two forms of family therapy. These data suggest that the common factor of expectancy likely explains more of the variance in outcomes between the two types of family therapy but not individual therapy (AFT). At the same time, however, expectancy was neither a predictor nor a moderator of outcome in any of these studies, so the effects of expectancy appear to be small overall. This is not surprising given the overall similarity of scores of this measure regardless of treatment type.

The common factor of a therapeutic context for FBT-AN has received comparatively little attention in randomized studies. All of the RCTs thus far have been conducted in academic medical centers with similar specialty clinical programs for youth with eating disorders. However, in this regard, it is useful to consider data related to FBT-AN as practiced in clinical rather than research protocols (Stiles-Shields, Goldschmidt, Lock, & Le Grange, 2013). Five studies examined the treatment effects of FBT-AN in primarily clinical programs (Couturier, Isserlan, & Lock, 2010; Hughes et al., 2013; Loeb et al., 2007; Tukiewicz, Pinzon, Lock, & Fleitlich-Bilyk, 2010; Wallis, Rhodes, Kohn, & Madden, 2007). Data from these studies, conducted in New York, Sydney, Toronto, Melbourne, and São Paolo, found that treatment context did not appear to affect outcomes. Adolescents with AN treated with FBT-AN fared remarkably similarly to those who were treated in controlled studies in terms of improvements in weight and eating-related psychopathology. In addition, data from several of these studies suggested significant effects on hospital utilization after FBT-AN was introduced compared to historic levels, documenting large decreases in admission rates, re-admission rates, and lengths of stay

(Hughes et al., 2013; Wallis et al., 2007). This finding after implementing FBT is not surprising given that data from RCTs documents that FBT uses less hospitalization than individual therapy or other forms of family therapy (Agras et al., 2014; Lock et al., 2010).

Therapeutic Rationale, Response Trajectories and Early Response

In addition to the data discussed so far suggesting that common factors do not fully explain treatment effects of manualized FBT-AN, there are several process variables supporting the view that FBT-AN is a specific treatment. First, data suggests that FBT-AN works more quickly than comparison treatments. In comparisons between FBT-AN and AFT and SyFT, robust weight restoration to normal levels (95 percent expected mean BMI), the target of treatment in FBT-AN, occurs significantly more quickly (Agras et al., 2014; Lock et al., 2010). Further, the impact of rapid weight restoration significantly reduced the need for hospitalization over the course of treatment when FBT-AN is compared to either AFT or SyFT (ibid).

The data related to response trajectory suggest that the process of treatment differs in FBT-AN compared to these other treatments, thereby supporting the view that FBT-AN does not depend only on common factors for its main effects, at least early in treatment. While data suggest that SyFT catches up in terms of weight gain over the course of treatment so that by end of treatment (EOT) (Agras et al., 2014) there are no statistical differences between SyFT and FBT-AN, the difference in weight gain trajectory and pattern between the two treatments suggests that there are likely different mechanisms and processes at work. These results are consistent with the rationale of the two approaches as well. FBT-AN places strong emphasis on rapid weight restoration early in treatment, while SyFT emphasizes the importance of general family processes related to communication and relationships and this emphasis may slow weight gain. Thus, while both treatments may ultimately achieve similar outcomes, the processes associated with this achievement differ, suggesting that something other than common factors is involved in the approaches.

In a related vein, more specific data suggest that longer-term response to FBT-AN can be predicted by weight gain in the first four sessions of treatment. Four studies using four different samples at three different sites have identified weight gain early in treatment in FBT as a surrogate early marker for full weight restoration (> 94 percent EBW) by EOT (Agras et al., 2014; Doyle, Le Grange, Loeb, Celio-Doyle, & Crosby, 2010; Le Grange, Accurso, Lock, Agras, & Bryson, 2014; Lock et al., 2005; Madden et al., 2015). The earliest study compared differing doses of FBT and identified weight gain as early as session 2 as the strongest predictor of weight restoration by EOT (Lock et al., 2005). Doyle and colleagues, using receiver operating curve (ROC) analyses on a clinical sample of adolescents with AN, reported that weight gain of 2.3 kg by session 4 identified those who are unlikely to respond (predictive power) with

71 percent accuracy (Doyle et al., 2010). Le Grange and colleagues (2014), using ROC analyses in a sample of 121 adolescents from an RCT comparing FBT and individual therapy, showed that weight gain of 3.2 kg at session 4 significantly predicted weight restoration by EOT. Most recently, Madden and colleagues, in a sample of 82 adolescents with AN who participated in an RCT that examined two hospitalization protocols (short or long) followed by 20 sessions of FBT, found that weight gain greater than 1.8 kg by session 4 of FBT predicted EOT weight restoration (Madden et al., 2015). In the largest multi-site study of FBT for adolescent AN, Agras and colleagues (2014) found that weight remission at EOT could be predicted with 90 percent accuracy when weight change was greater than 2.4 kg at session 4 of FBT. Although there are some variations in the exact weight gain needed by session 4 to predict EOT remission due to differing samples (e.g. post-hospitalization, treatment settings, etc.), there is a consistent signal that weight gain in the range of 2–3 kg by session 4 is a strong early marker for likely weight remission by EOT and that, specifically, weight gain of 2.4 kg by session 4 is an empirically supported marker for early treatment response to predict weight restoration by EOT. The identification of an early response marker supports the view that FBT-AN is a specific treatment that leads to specific outcomes, particularly early in treatment, that are predictive of longer-term outcomes. No other treatment for adolescent AN has identified a treatment-specific early marker of treatment response for adolescent AN.

Moderators of Treatment Effect

Another argument suggesting that FBT-AN is a specific treatment is found in reviewing the data related to moderators of treatment effect. Moderators are baseline variables that relate to treatment response (Kraemer, Frank, & Kupfer, 2006). When a moderator is found to be correlated with outcome in one treatment but not another, it suggests that the treatments differ from one another and that different patient populations with that characteristic benefit differentially from receiving that specific treatment. In contrast, predictors of treatment response are baseline characteristics that predict treatment response regardless of treatment type. Predictors therefore are not related to treatment type, while moderators support a specific approach for a particular subgroup. Finding moderators of treatment effects therefore supports that a treatment is a specific one and response is not due exclusively to common factors.

Formal moderator identification requires that they be assessed in the context of a randomized treatment study (Kraemer, Wilson, Fairburn, & Agras, 2002). Moderators related to treatment dose of FBT-AN were found in Lock and colleagues' dose study described above (Lock et al., 2005). Obsessive and compulsive features related to eating (Yale-Brown-Cornell Eating Disorder Scale – YBC-ED; Mazure, Halmi, Sunday, Romano, & Einhorn, 1994) and family structure (intact versus non-intact) moderated weight gain, with those with greater obsessive and compulsive features and those from non-intact families requiring longer and more intensive FBT-AN (Lock et al., 2005). In the RCT comparing FBT-AN and AFT also mentioned above (Lock et al., 2010), three moderators were identified: obsessive compulsive features related to eating (YBC-ED), EDE scores, and the presence of binge eating or purging. These features are commonly recognized clinical markers of severity. The study found that those patients with greater severity using any one of these markers did better in FBT-AN. Interestingly, in the Agras and colleagues' (2014) study that compared FBT-AN to SyFT, the only moderator identified was general obsessive compulsive features (Child and Youth Obsessive Compulsive Scale – CYBOCS; Goodman et al., 1989), and participants with this feature who received SyFT did better than those who received FBT-AN. Taken together, these moderator studies support the fact that FBT-AN is differentially effective for different populations, supporting the view that it is a specific treatment. Further, these data also suggest that SyFT may also be a specific treatment based on the finding that this approach is more effective with patients who have general obsessive compulsive features rather than those related to eating and weight.

Treatment Mechanism

No studies have identified a mechanism of action specific to FBT-AN to date. The identification of mediators in randomized clinical trials requires large data sets and these are not available for adolescent AN (Kraemer et al., 2006). Nonetheless, some data are now available that suggest there is likely a specific mechanism to account for the treatment effects of FBT-AN (Lock et al., 2015). Increasing parental self-efficacy specifically as it is related to re-feeding and weight restoration is targeted in the first phase of FBT-AN. Measures of parental self-efficacy and re-feeding using the Parent Versus Anorexia Scale (PVA; Rhodes et al., 2005) show that changes in this measure are correlated with improved weight gain, whereas lower scores predict poorer early weight gain (Lock et al., 2015). Although not a formal moderator analysis, a recent study found that differences in parental self-efficacy related to re-feeding differed at session 2 in FBT-AN between those who ultimately gained weight early and those who did not (ibid).

Treatment Fidelity

Treatment fidelity refers to the ability of therapists to adhere to the specific intervention techniques of a treatment as well as their competence in conducting these techniques in therapy (McHugh, Murray, & Barlow, 2009). Adherence was assessed by a small sample of therapists using FBT-AN (Couturier et al., 2013a). The main finding of that study was that therapists were generally adherent to procedures early in treatment, but were considerably less so in later phases of FBT-AN. Reasons for early adherence likely included greater detail of content in early sessions of FBT-AN in the manual, the highly focused nature of early sessions compared to the widening focus on adolescent development in later sessions, and the emergence of clinical problems other than AN later in treatment that cause therapists to turn to these other dilemmas instead of following the manual. More recently, a standardized measure of fidelity was developed and tested (Forsberg et al., 2015). The new measure was used to assess the quality of FBT delivered and its relationship to outcome in a sample of adolescents treated with manualized FBT-AN. The main finding of that study was that adherence to and competence in interventions promoting *agnosticism* regarding the cause of AN and *externalization* instead of blaming the patient or the family during the first two sessions of FBT-AN are correlated with early weight gain (ibid). Although these data are limited by a small sample size and focused exclusively on early treatment, they support the view that fidelity to the specific interventions manualized in FBT-AN is necessary to obtain good outcomes.

Conclusions

While there are still many open questions about the specificity of FBT-AN, the findings discussed in this chapter generally provide strong empirical support for the specificity of the approach. These data suggest that FBT-AN has better outcomes and/or a different response trajectory than comparison treatments. Furthermore, manualized FBT-AN is differentially effective for adolescents with differing characteristics (e.g. obsessive features) and clinical severity. In addition, early weight gain in FBT-AN leads to different patterns of weight restoration (i.e. faster than other treatments) and decreased hospitalization use during treatment. Other preliminary data suggest that FBT-AN has a specific mechanism of action related to changing parental self-efficacy related to re-feeding. Finally, early studies also suggest that fidelity to the interventions in FBT-AN, especially early in treatment, is necessary for the best clinical outcomes.

The gap between efficacy of a treatment and its dissemination and implementation in routine clinical settings is a large one (McHugh et al., 2009). While it is tempting to consider using more generic treatments that depend on common factors because these treatments might be more easily taught and more acceptable to therapists, the benefits of a specific treatment for some disorders is also evident because of the crucial impact these more specific treatments have on clinical outcome. In a disorder as serious and life-threatening as AN (Stevens et al., 2000), there is less room for the use of a non-specific treatment that delays weight restoration and utilizes high-cost interventions such as hospitalization.

The available data suggest that a short course of FBT-AN will likely lead to recovery in 40–50 percent of adolescents (Lock, 2015). More recent data suggests that the addition of a few additional sessions for those adolescents who do not respond early will convert an additional 20–30 percent of those to responders by the end of treatment (ibid). While there is less compelling data available on the specificity of the later phases of FBT-AN, an 8–10 session dose of this specific form of therapy is likely the best hope for early and effective treatment for adolescents with AN (Lock et al., 2005).

The next challenge is to design a cost-effective strategy for rapid dissemination of FBT-AN. This will likely include web-based training, supervision, and consultation. Early testing of these strategies is underway and preliminary data appear to be promising.

References

Agras, W., Lock, J., Brandt, H., Bryson, S., Dodge, E. et al. (2014). Comparison of 2 family therapies for adolescent anorexia nervosa: A randomized parallel trial. *JAMA Psychiatry*, 72(11), 1279–1286.

Cooper, Z., & Fairburn, C. G. (1987). The Eating Disorder Examination: A semi-structured interview for the assessment of the specific psychopathology of eating disorders. *International Journal of Eating Disorders*, 6(1), 1–8.

Couturier, J., Isserlan, L., & Lock, J. (2010). Family-based treatment for adolescents with anorexia nervosa: A dissemination study. *International Journal of Eating Disorders*, 18, 199–209.

Couturier, J., Kimber, M., Jack, S., Niccols, A., Van Blyderveen, S., & McVey, G. (2013a). Understanding the uptake of family-based treatment in adolescents with anorexia nervosa: Therapist perspectives. *International Journal of Eating Disorders*, 46, 177–188.

Couturier, J., Kimber, M., & Szatmari, P. (2013b). Efficacy of family-based treatment for adolescents with eating disorders: A systematic review. *International Journal of Eating Disorders*, 46, 3–11.

Couturier, J., & Lock, J. (2006). What is recovery in adolescent anorexia nervosa? *International Journal of Eating Disorders*, 39, 550–555.

Dare, C., & Eisler, I. (1997). Family therapy for anorexia nervosa. In D. M. Garner & P. Garfinkel (Eds.), *Handbook of treatment for eating disorders* (pp. 307–324). New York: Guilford Press.

DeRubeis, R., Brotman, M., & Gibbons, C. (2005). A conceptual and methodological analysis of the non-specific argument. *Clinical Psychology: Science and Practice*, 12, 174–183.

Doyle, P., Le Grange, D., Loeb, K., Celio-Doyle, A., & Crosby, R. (2010). Early response to family-based treatment for adolescent anorexia nervosa. *International Journal of Eating Disorders*, 43, 659–662.

Eisler, I. (2005). The empirical and theoretical base of family therapy and multiple family day therapy for adolescent anorexia nervosa. *Journal of Family Therapy*, 27, 104–131.

Eisler, I., Dare, C., Hodes, M., Russell, G., Dodge, E., & Le Grange, D. (2000). Family therapy for adolescent anorexia nervosa: The results of a controlled comparison of two family interventions. *Journal of Child Psychology and Psychiatry*, 41(6), 727–736.

Fitzpatrick, K., Moye, A., Hoste, R., Le Grange, D., & Lock, J. (2010). Adolescent-focused therapy for adolescent anorexia nervosa. *Journal of Contemporary Psychotherapy*, 40, 31–39.

Forsberg, S., Fitzpatrik, K., Darcy, A., Aspen, V., Accurso, E. et al. (2015). Development and evaluation of a treatment fidelity instrument for family-based treatment of adolescent anorexia nervosa. *International Journal of Eating Disorders*, 48, 91–99.

Forsberg, S., Lo Tempio, E., Bryson, S., Fitzpatrick, K., Le Grange, D., & Lock, J. (2013). Therapeutic alliance in two treatments for adolescent anorexia nervosa. *International Journal of Eating Disorders*, 46, 34–38.

Goodman, W. K., Price, L. H., Rasmussen, S. A., Mazure, C., Fleischmann, R. L. et al. (1989). The Yale-Brown Obsessive Compulsive Scale (Y-BOCS) 1: Development, use, and reliability. *Archives of General Psychiatry*, 46(11), 1006–1011.

Horvath, A., Gaston, L., & Luborsky, L. (1993). The therapeutic alliance and its measures. In L. Miller, L. Luborsky, & J. Barber (Eds.), *Psychodynamic treatment and research* (pp. 247–273). New York: Basic Books.

Horvath, A., & Symonds, B. (1991). The relationship between working alliance and outcome in psychotherapy. *Journal of Counseling Psychology*, 38, 139–149.

Hovarth, P. (1988). Placebos and common factors in two decades of psychotherapy research. *Psychological Bulletin*, 104, 214–225.

Hughes, E., Le Grange, D., Yeo, M., Whitelaw, M., Atkins, L., & Sawyer, S. (2013). Implementation of family-based treatment for adolescents with anorexia nervosa. *Journal of Pediatric Health Care*. doi: doi.org/10.1016/j.pedhc.2013.07.012.

Kraemer, H., Frank, E., & Kupfer, D. (2006). Moderators of treatment outcomes: Clinical, research, and policy importance. *Journal of the American Medical Association*, 296, 1286–1289.

Kraemer, H., Wilson, G. T., Fairburn, C. G., & Agras, W. S. (2002). Mediators and moderators of treatment effects in randomized clinical trials. *Archives of General Psychiatry*, 59(10), 877–884.

Krautter, T., & Lock, J. (2004). Is manualized family-based treatment for adolescent anorexia nervosa acceptable to patients? Patient satisfaction at end of treatment. *Journal of Family Therapy*, 26, 65–81.

Le Grange, D., Accurso, E., Lock, J., Agras, W., & Bryson, S. (2014). Early weight gain predicts outcome in two treatments for adolescent anorexia nervosa. *International Journal of Eating Disorders*, 47, 124–129.

Le Grange, D., Eisler, I., Dare, C., & Russell, G. (1992). Evaluation of family treatments in adolescent anorexia nervosa: A pilot study. *International Journal of Eating Disorders*, 12(4), 347–357.

Lock, J. (2015). An update on evidence-based psychosocial interventions for children and adolescents with eating disorders. *Journal of Clinical Child and Adolescent Psychology*, 44, 707–721.

Lock, J., & Le Grange, D. (2001). Can family-based treatment of anorexia nervosa be manualized? *Journal of Psychotherapy Practice and Research*, 10, 253–261.

Lock, J., & Le Grange, D. (2013). *Treatment manual for anorexia nervosa: A family-based approach*, 2nd edition. New York: Guilford Press.

Lock, J., Agras, W. S., Bryson, S., & Kraemer, H. (2005). A comparison of short- and long-term family therapy for adolescent anorexia nervosa. *Journal of the American Academy of Child and Adolescent Psychiatry*, 44(7), 632–639.

Lock, J., Le Grange, D., Agras, W. S., & Dare, C. (2001). *Treatment manual for anorexia nervosa: A family-based approach*. New York: Guilford Press.

Lock, J., Le Grange, D., Agras, W. S., Fitzpatrick, K., Jo, B. et al. (2015). Can adaptive treatment improve outcomes in family-based treatment for adolescents with anorexia nervosa? Feasibility and treatment effects of a multi-site treatment study. *Behaviour Research and Therapy*. doi: 10.1016/j.brat.2015.07.015.

Lock, J., Le Grange, D., Agras, W. S., Moye, A., Bryson, S., & Jo, B. (2010). A randomized clinical trial comparing family-based treatment to adolescent-focused individual therapy for adolescents with anorexia nervosa. *Archives of General Psychiatry*, 67(10), 1025–1032.

Loeb, K., Walsh, B., Lock, J., Le Grange, D., Jones, J. et al. (2007). Open trial of family-based treatment for adolescent anorexia nervosa: Evidence of successful dissemination. *Journal of the American Academy of Child and Adolescent Psychiatry*, 46, 792–800.

Lohr, M., DeMaoi, C., & McGlynn, F. (2003). Specific and nonspecific treatment factors in the experimental analysis of behavioral treatment efficacy. *Behavioral Modification*, 27, 322–368,

Luborskey, L., Diguer, L., Seligman, D., Rosenthal, R., Krause, E. et al. (1999). The researcher's own therapy allegiances: A "wild card" in comparisons of treatment efficacy. *Clinical Psychology: Science and Practice*, 6, 95–106.

Madden, S., Miskovic-Wheatley, J., Wallis, A., Kohn, M., Hay, P., & Touyz, S. (2015). Early weight gain in family-based treatment predicts weight gain and remission at end of treatment and remission at 12-month follow-up for adolescent anorexia nervosa. *International Journal of Eating Disorders*, 48(7), 919–922.

Madden, S., Miskovic-Wheatley, J., Wallis, A., Kohn, M., Lock, J. et al. (2015). A randomized controlled trial of inpatient treatment for anorexia nervosa in medically unstable adolescents. *Psychological Medicine*, 45, 415–427.

Mazure, S., Halmi, C. A., Sunday, S., Romano, S., & Einhorn, A. (1994). The Yale-Brown-Cornell Eating Disorder Scales: Development, use, reliability, and validity. *Journal of Psychiatric Research*, 28, 425–445.

McHugh, R., Murray, H., & Barlow, D. (2009). Balancing fidelity and adaptation in the dissemination of empirically supported treatments: The promise of transdiagnostic interventions. *Behaviour Research and Therapy*, 47, 946–953.

Pereria, T., Lock, J., & Oggins, J. (2006). The role of therapeutic alliance in family therapy for adolescent anorexia nervosa. *International Journal of Eating Disorders*, 39, 677–684.

Pote, H., Stratton, P., Cottrell, D., Boston, P., & Shapiro, D. (2001). Systemic family therapy manual. Available online at www.medhealth.leeds.ac.uk (accessed August 1, 2001).

Rhodes, P., Baillie, A., Brown, J., & Madden, S. (2005). Parental efficacy in the family-based treatment of anorexia: Preliminary development of the Parents Versus Anorexia Scale (PVA). *European Eating Disorders Review*, 13, 399–405.

Robin, A. (2003). Behavioral family systems therapy for adolescents with anorexia nervosa. In A. Kazdin & J. Weisz (Eds.), *Evidence-based psychotherapies for children and adolescents* (pp. 358–373). New York: Guilford Press.

Robin, A., Siegal, P., Moye, A., Gilroy, M., Dennis, A., & Sikand, A. (1999). A controlled comparison of family versus individual therapy for adolescents with anorexia nervosa. *Journal of the American Academy of Child and Adolescent Psychiatry*, 38(12), 1482–1489.

Russell, G. F., Szmukler, G. I., Dare, C., & Eisler, I. (1987). An evaluation of family therapy in anorexia nervosa and bulimia nervosa. *Archives of General Psychiatry*, 44(12), 1047–1056.

Safer, D., & Hugo, E. (2006). Designing a control for behavioral group therapy. *Behavior Therapy*, 37, 120–130.

Stevens, S., Hynan, M., & Allend, M. (2000). A meta-analysis of common factor and specific treatment effects across the outcome domains of the phase model of psychotherapy. *Clinical Psychology: Science and Practice, 7*, 273–290.

Stiles-Shields, C., Goldschmidt, A., Lock, J., & Le Grange, D. (2013). Are adolescent treatment studies of eating disorders utilizing clinically relevant samples? A comparison of RCT and clinic treatment seeking youth with eating disorders. *European Eating Disorders Review, 21*, 420–424.

Strober, M. (2014). Proposition: Family-based treatment is overvalued. *Advances in Eating Disorders: Theory, Research, and Practice, 1*, 1–21.

Tukiewicz, G., Pinzon, V., Lock, J., & Fleitlich-Bilyk, B. (2010). Feasibility, acceptability, and effectiveness of family-based treatment for adolescent anorexia nervosa: An observational study conducted in Brazil. *Revista Brasileira de Psiguiatria, 32*, 169–172.

Wallis, A., Rhodes, P., Kohn, M., & Madden, S. (2007). Five years of family-based treatment for anorexia nervosa: The Maudsley Model at the Children's Hospital at Westmead. *International Journal of Adolescent Medicine and Health, 19*, 277–283.

7 Dissemination and Implementation of Manualized Family-Based Treatment

A Systematic Review

Jennifer L. Couturier and Melissa S. Kimber

Introduction

Despite evidence for the efficacy and cost-effectiveness of family-based treatment (FBT; Agras et al., 2014; Couturier, Kimber, & Szatmari, 2013; Lock, Agras, Bryson, & Kraemer, 2005; Lock, Couturier, & Agras, 2008; Lock, Le Grange, Agras, & Dare, 2001; Lock et al., 2010; Madden et al., 2015) in treating children and adolescents diagnosed with anorexia nervosa (AN), many clinicians continue to use this model without high fidelity to the treatment manual (Couturier et al., 2013; Kosmerly, Waller, & Robinson, 2014). This is one example of the "research–practice" gap; that is, the disjuncture between research evidence and what is actually applied in routine clinical practice. Reductions in the research–practice gap have the potential to reduce patient morbidity and mortality while also decreasing healthcare costs through appropriate assessment and application of evidence-based treatments (Brownson, Colditz, & Proctor, 2012).

Over the past decade, hospitalizations among patients diagnosed with eating disorders have dramatically risen (Canadian Institute for Health Information, 2014). Furthermore, research has emerged documenting the serious and persistent nature of these disorders, suggesting that once they are established, they tend to persist over time and have long-term negative physical and psychological sequelae (Neumark-Sztainer, Wall, Larson, Eisenberg, & Loth, 2011). For these reasons, early and intensive intervention is necessary. One particular intervention that has been shown to interrupt eating disorder symptoms and behaviours among children and adolescents diagnosed with eating disorders is FBT. As an evidence-based treatment (EBT), FBT is an intensive, manualized, outpatient treatment that empowers parents to take control of eating disorder behaviors. A recent meta-analysis by Couturier, Kimber, and Szatmari (2013) indicated that FBT was superior to individualized approaches over the long term for children and adolescents with eating disorders. The treatment has also been found to result in a reduction of hospitalization costs by up to 70 percent (Lock et al., 2008). Therefore, it would be important to understand how this treatment could best be implemented in clinical practice.

A review of definitions as they pertain to the movement of knowledge into the clinical realm is important. Whereas *dissemination* implies the distribution of information by passive means, *knowledge translation* (KT) implies the active process of applying knowledge generated by rigorous scientific inquiry in a systematic way, and *implementation science* is the process of systematically investigating the methods that are used for increasing the uptake and use of EBTs in routine clinical practice (Brownson, Colditz, & Proctor, 2012). Often used interchangeably with KT and dissemination, implementation research differs from the previous two given its focus on evaluating the processes and methods by which evidence-based interventions are integrated within a clinical setting. Furthermore, implementation research encapsulates studies focusing on knowledge dissemination and KT, but extends these investigations one step further by studying the methods by which adequate dissemination and KT occurs within the clinical realm (ibid). In this manner, implementation research represents a purposeful and planful approach for integrating an EBT into routine clinical practice.

Emerging research suggests that applying models of implementation to the adoption of an EBT in practice, as opposed to relying on passive dissemination, results in more ready adoption and a higher degree of fidelity (Brownson et al., 2012; Fixsen, Blase, Metz, & Van Dyke, 2013; Fixsen, Naoom, Blase, Friedman, & Wallace, 2005). However, the extent to which implementation science models have been utilized to increase the uptake of EBTs, particularly FBT, among eating disorder treatment professionals is unclear. Given this information, the objective of this chapter is to systematically review the literature investigating the dissemination and implementation of FBT within the eating disorder treatment field. We will also make recommendations for future research with respect to ensuring adequate implementation and provision of FBT in the clinical practice realm.

Methods

A systematic review was conducted to locate studies focusing on the dissemination or implementation of FBT. Search terms included "effectiveness," "dissemination," or "implementation" and "family-based treatment" and "eating disorders" using the search engine PubMed. Articles were fully reviewed by both authors, and reference lists of these articles were also searched.

Results

There were two main groupings of studies found in the literature on the topic of manualized FBT use in wider treatment settings. These included: (a) studies focusing on clinical outcomes at sites where FBT was adopted into clinical practice (dissemination studies) and (b) studies whose primary outcomes were not clinical, but instead focused on implementation processes and/or outcomes (implementation studies). These two groupings are described below.

Dissemination Studies

Dissemination studies to date have largely focused on clinical variables and report data that compare clinical outcomes pre-uptake to post-uptake of FBT. These studies suggest that FBT can be disseminated to settings beyond those of the primary research (i.e. beyond Stanford and Chicago). Three studies used a similar design of recruiting therapists who were previously unfamiliar with FBT and training them by having them read the manual and attend a two-day workshop by the primary author of the FBT manual. These studies were conducted at three different academic centers, and evaluated the outcomes of the patients that the newly trained therapists had treated. Loeb and colleagues (2007) found that in 20 adolescents, there was a low dropout rate (25 percent), and weight was improved, with two-thirds achieving normal menstruation. In addition, scores on the Eating Disorders Examination (EDE) were significantly improved. A study in Brazil of 11 adolescents found that patients and families accepted FBT (82 percent) and that most patients demonstrated improvements in weight and EDE score (Tukiewicz, Pinzon, Lock, & Fleitlich-Bilyk, 2010). A study by Couturier and colleagues (2010) of 13 adolescents found similar clinical improvements. However, this study also evaluated the fidelity of the clinicians to the treatment manual by rating video-taped sessions. The results indicated high fidelity to the first phase of FBT (72 percent achieved a rating considered acceptable), but that fidelity decreased in subsequent phases (47 percent with acceptable ratings in phase 2, and 54 percent with acceptable ratings in phase 3).

Two additional retrospective studies describing the changes observed with the introduction of manualized FBT have been published. The first of these describes the impact of FBT on decreasing re-admission rates at a children's hospital in Sydney by about 50% over a five-year period (Wallis, Rhodes, Kohn, & Madden, 2007). The second study documents substantial changes in use of hospitalization, including a 56% decrease in admission, a 75% decrease in re-admissions, and a 51% decrease in length of admission (Hughes et al., 2014). In addition, 83% of families treated with FBT completed it (ibid). This study also describes some challenges to the uptake of FBT, obtained by reflective analysis. Some of these included therapist concerns about including patients with comorbidity, and whether families could handle the demands of the treatment. There were also concerns raised about the changes in professional roles for pediatricians, dieticians, and therapists, in that therapists became placed in a lead role, dieticians were not so involved, and the pediatricians were to shift the focus from a more holistic approach to a more narrow approach of ensuring medical stability (ibid).

Implementation Studies

Studies focusing on outcomes relating to FBT implementation processes and outcomes (rather than clinical outcomes) can be categorized into three additional groupings, including: (a) the barriers and facilitators affecting FBT implementation, (b) knowledge transfer or implementation frameworks that can inform the adoption and application of FBT in routine clinician practice, and (c) the decision-making processes involved in the adoption and application of FBT in routine clinical practice. Our search revealed four studies, which are described below.

Barriers and facilitators. In an effort to understand the barriers and facilitators to implementing FBT in clinical practice, Couturier and colleagues (2013a) analyzed qualitative interview data from 40 therapists providing psychotherapeutic intervention to children and adolescents diagnosed with AN. These therapists had varying degrees of knowledge of and training in FBT, but all knew about the model to some degree and had either contemplated using it or were attempting to use it in clinical practice. Content analysis revealed a number of specific factors affecting therapists' ability to implement FBT within their treatment programs; specifically, those factors having to do with the characteristics of the intervention (i.e. FBT), the organization, patients and families, the clinician, the nature of the illness, and systemic issues inherent within the service delivery system. A number of these themes and their related concerns are similar to those that have already been identified in the general mental health literature, including clinician preferences and training (Aarons, 2004) and patient and family preferences (Karver, Handelsman, Fields, & Bickman, 2006).

However, participants did note some unique considerations that seem to be specific to the eating disorder field and FBT, in particular. Therapists perceived the treatment to require a large time commitment. The perceived lack of attention paid to the prevalence of comorbid diagnoses by the FBT model, and the need for intensive family involvement were also mentioned as barriers to routine use of FBT within clinical practice. In addition, therapists were struggling to maintain fidelity to three aspects of the manual; conducting a family meal in the second session, omitting the dietician from the therapeutic process, and weighing the patient at the start of each therapeutic session. Only 10 of the 40 clinicians had ever implemented the family meal during a therapeutic session, with clinicians noting spatial constraints as often being the reason for its omission in practice. In addition, clinicians reported increased levels of interpersonal anxiety when conducting the family meal portion of the FBT model. Finally, the debate about the exclusion of the dietician from the therapeutic process appeared to be a salient concern among clinicians in this sample; with only 6 of the 40 clinicians indicating that they would be comfortable implementing FBT without a dietician. The majority of clinicians indicated that dieticians would be responsible for weighing the patient prior to their sessions and providing guidance on caloric consumption, a component of treatment that a number of clinicians felt was outside their own scope of practice.

In addition to characteristics of the FBT intervention, clinicians also identified a number of organizational and systemic factors influencing their ability to implement FBT in their clinical practice. Perhaps most notably, clinicians acknowledged a seminal role for their administrator (also encompassing managers and directors) in the adoption and implementation of FBT within their organization. Specifically, 30 of the 40 participants indicated that their administrator's approval of the model would be required to implement FBT in practice. In addition, 70 percent of participants indicated that team buy-in to the EBT model would play a key role in whether or not they adopted the therapeutic approach.

Adding to this qualitative data, Kosmerly and colleagues (2014) completed a study using an online survey with 117 clinicians who stated that they used FBT. These authors found that about one-third of the respondents reported delivering FBT that actually deviated significantly from the manual. These respondents incorporated mindfulness techniques, food diaries, motivational interviewing, and individual therapy. Interestingly, correlations were found between clinician-reported levels of anxiety and weighing the patient "occasionally" or "rarely," such that more anxiety was correlated with weighing the patient less frequently (ibid). These authors concluded that the affective states of clinicians can influence their ability to implement a treatment.

A knowledge transfer framework. Couturier and colleagues (2014) completed a secondary data analysis of the qualitative interview data to identify the five elements stipulated by Lavis and colleagues (2003) for successful transmission of research evidence into clinical practice; including: (a) identifying the knowledge needing to be transferred ("the message"), (b) identifying whom the knowledge should be transferred to ("the audience"), (c) assessing by whom should the knowledge be transferred ("the messenger"), (d) how the knowledge will be transferred ("knowledge transfer strategies and infrastructure"), and finally (e) the most appropriate method of demonstrating knowledge transfer ("evaluation"). Analysis revealed that FBT messaging should include both the provision of the research evidence supporting the model's effectiveness and the specific intervention components of the FBT manual. In addition, the "audience" for FBT messaging was identified as therapists, administrators, physicians and community members working within the field of pediatric eating disorders; with the development and dissemination of clinical practice guidelines identified as one seminal strategy to ensure all "audience" members received consistent messaging.

Interestingly, therapists identified local FBT experts as an ideal source for FBT knowledge and training. Specifically, clinicians suggested that local experts in the FBT model could take on the challenge of training less-experienced therapists to alleviate traveling costs associated with undergoing intensive and specialized training. In addition, therapists recognized that protected time to learn, practice, and enhance their FBT skills would be necessary for successful implementation. Relatedly, clinicians acknowledged the importance of clinical supervision in learning a new EBT skill set. Participants reported that, if a roll-out of FBT was encouraged or mandated, ongoing supervision and mentorship would be necessary to prevent fidelity drift, as well as being an essential component of ongoing implementation and evaluation.

Decision-making processes. Kimber and colleagues (2014) completed a secondary data analysis of the Couturier et al. (2013a) qualitative study, as well as purposefully recruited and qualitatively interviewed the administrators of the programs from which the original 40 clinicians worked. The authors identified a multi-stage decision-making process for adopting and implementing any EBT, including FBT, in clinical practice. Respondents identified a seven-stage decision-making model for their uptake and implementation of EBTs in clinical practice, including: (a) individual exposure to the EBT; (b) team exposure to the EBT; (c) evaluating the EBT evidence; (d) determining program fit, (e) training in the EBT model; (f) using the EBT in practice with supervision; and (g) evaluating the EBT in their programs. An inclusive culture of change and involvement of leadership in these decisions were prominent themes.

Discussion

The types of studies to date on the use of manualized FBT in settings outside the primary originating sites fall into two main categories: (a) those studies focusing on clinical outcomes, demonstrating that FBT has effectiveness at other centers (dissemination studies), and (b) those studies focusing primarily on implementation processes and outcomes (implementation studies). To date, several dissemination studies have determined that FBT can achieve good clinical outcomes in various centers that are removed from the primary researchers. However, all of the sites involved in these studies are academic centers. This may pose a risk of bias as academic centers have benefits that community practices do not have, including the encouragement of research endeavors by providing time and salary support. Alternatively, four implementation studies on FBT have focused on the application and uptake of FBT in real-world clinical settings.

Implementation models currently being studied may further our understanding of how to move FBT into clinical practice. For example, the National Implementation Research Network's (NIRN) model of implementation is meant to characterize the overarching process of implementing a single EBT within an organization. The NIRN model posits that successful implementation hinges on the consideration of five successive stages, including: (a) exploration and adoption, (b) program installation, (c) initial implementation, (d) full operation, and (e) innovation. In addition, each implementation stage requires an ongoing consideration of EBT evaluation and sustainability (Fixsen et al., 2013). This model also suggests the use of internal implementation teams, whose role is to oversee and monitor the implementation process and devise procedures and protocols to support the implementation of the EBT within everyday practice in the community.

With this model in mind, a study is currently underway looking at implementation outcomes of FBT. Specifically, our group is in the process of training and supervising four sites in Ontario, Canada on the use of FBT. This study has employed the NIRN model to form implementation teams at each site involving an administrator, physician, and lead therapist. In addition, we are providing monthly supervision calls that focus on therapeutic elements of FBT, as well as monthly implementation calls that focus on process issues associated with implementing FBT. These calls will be transcribed and qualitatively analysed for themes. Other outcomes include quantitative and qualitative data on perceptions of evidence-based treatment and the implementation process in general. We are also examining fidelity to FBT using clinician-, parent-, and researcher-rated scales based on audio-recorded therapy sessions. This study will further develop our knowledge base on implementation of FBT in clinical practice.

In summary, evidence suggests that passively relying on clinicians to adopt evidence-based treatments in the clinical realm has led to their underutilization and, in some cases, inappropriate use within front-line practice. Advances in implementation science suggest that active, purposeful, and supportive implementation can result in greater treatment fidelity and better patient outcomes. Sound qualitative data from FBT implementation studies lend support to tailoring planful and facilitative implementation initiatives. More generally, the lack of FBT use with fidelity within the eating disorder treatment field, as well as knowledge about the specific factors and processes important to treatment professionals in FBT uptake, lend support to the field testing of implementation models in the pediatric eating disorder treatment setting.

References

Aarons, G. A. (2004). Mental health provider attitudes toward adoption of evidence-based practice: The Evidence-Based Practice Attitude Scale (EBPAS). *Mental Health Services Research*, 6, 61–74.

Agras, W. S., Lock, J., Brandt, H., Bryson, S. W., Dodge, E. et al. (2014). Comparison of two family therapies for adolescent anorexia nervosa: A randomized parallel trial. *JAMA Psychiatry*, 71, 1279–1286.

Brownson, R. C., Colditz, G. A., & Proctor, E. K. (Eds.). (2012). *Dissemination and implementation research in health: Translating science to practice*. New York: Oxford University Press.

Canadian Institute for Health Information. (2014). *More young women hospitalized for eating disorders*. Available online at www.cihi.ca/web/resource/en/ eatingdisord_2014_pubsum_en.pdf (accessed January 19, 2015).

Couturier, J., Isserlin, L., & Lock, J. (2010). Family-based treatment for adolescents with anorexia nervosa: A dissemination study. *Eating Disorders*, 18, 199–209,

Couturier, J., Kimber, M., Jack, S., Niccols, A., Van Blyderveen, S., & McVey, G. (2013a). Understanding the uptake of family-based treatment for adolescents with anorexia nervosa: Therapist perspectives. *International Journal of Eating Disorders*, 46, 177–188.

Couturier, J., Kimber, M., Jack, S., Niccols, A., Van Blyderveen, S., & McVey, G. (2014). Using a knowledge transfer framework to identify factors facilitating implementation of family-based treatment. *International Journal of Eating Disorders*, 47, 410–417.

Couturier, J., Kimber, M., & Szatmari, P. (2013b). Efficacy of family-based treatment for adolescents with eating disorders: A systematic review and meta-analysis. *International Journal of Eating Disorders*, 46, 3–11.

Fixsen, D., Blase, K., Metz, A., & Van Dyke, M. (2013). Statewide implementation of evidence-based programs. *Exceptional Children*, 79, 213–230.

Fixsen, D., Naoom, S. F., Blase, K. A., Friedman, R. M., & Wallace, F. (2005). *Implementation research: A synthesis of the literature*. Tampa, FL: University of South Florida and The National Implementation Research Network.

Hughes, E. K., Le Grange, D., Court, A., Yeo, M., Campbell, S. et al. (2014). Implementation of family-based treatment for adolescents with anorexia nervosa. *Journal of Pediatric Health Care*, 28, 322–330.

Karver, M. S., Handelsman, J. B., Fields, S., & Bickman, L. (2006). Meta-analysis of therapeutic relationship variables in youth and family therapy: The evidence for different relationship variables in the child and adolescent treatment outcome literature. *Clinical Psychology Review*, 26, 50–65.

Kimber, M., Couturier, J., Jack, S., Niccols, A., Van Blyderveen, S., & McVey, G. (2014). Decision-making processes for the uptake and implementation of family-based therapy by eating disorder treatment teams: A qualitative study. *International Journal of Eating Disorders*, 47, 32–39.

Kosmerly, S., Waller, G., & Robinson, A. L. (2014). Clinician adherence to guidelines in the delivery of family-based therapy for eating disorders. *International Journal of Eating Disorders*, 48, 223–229.

Lavis, J. N., Robertson, D., Woodside, J. M., McLeod, C. B., & Abelson, J. (2003). How can research organizations more effectively transfer research knowledge to decision makers? *Milbank Quarterly*, 81, 221–248.

Lock, J., Agras, W. S., Bryson, S., & Kraemer, H. C. (2005). A comparison of short- and long-term family therapy for adolescent anorexia nervosa. *Journal of the American Academy of Child and Adolescent Psychiatry*, 44, 632–639.

Lock, J., Couturier, J., & Agras, W. S. (2008). Costs of remission and recovery using family therapy for adolescent anorexia nervosa: A descriptive report. *Eating Disorders*, 16, 322–330.

Lock, J., Le Grange, D., Agras, W. S., & Dare, C. (2001). *Treatment manual for anorexia nervosa: A family-based approach*. New York: Guilford Press.

Lock, J., Le Grange, D., Agras, W. S., Moye, A., Bryson, S. W., & Jo, B. (2010). Randomized clinical trial comparing family-based treatment with adolescent-focused individual therapy for adolescents with anorexia nervosa. *Archives of General Psychiatry*, 67, 1025–1032.

Loeb, K., Walsh, B., Lock, J., Le Grange, D., Jones, J. et al. (2007). Open trial of family-based treatment for adolescent anorexia nervosa: Evidence of successful dissemination. *Journal of the American Academy of Child and Adolescent Psychiatry*, 46, 792–800.

Madden, S., Miskovic-Wheatley, J., Wallis, A., Kohn, M., Lock, J. et al. (2015). A randomized controlled trial of in-patient treatment for anorexia nervosa in medically unstable adolescents. *Psychological Medicine*, 45, 415–427.

Neumark-Sztainer, D., Wall, M., Larson, N. I., Eisenberg, M. E., & Loth, K. (2011). Dieting and disordered eating behaviors from adolescence to young adulthood: Findings from a 10-year longitudinal study. *Journal of the American Dietetic Association*, 111, 1004–1011.

Tukiewicz, G., Pinzon, V., Lock, J., & Fleitlich-Bilyk, B. (2010). Feasibility, acceptability, and effectiveness of family-based treatment for adolescent anorexia nervosa: An observational study conducted in Brazil. *Revista Brasileira de Psiguiatria*, 32, 169–172.

Wallis, A., Rhodes, P., Kohn, M., & Madden, S. (2007). Five years of family-based treatment for anorexia nervosa: The Maudsley Model at the Children's Hospital at Westmead. *International Journal of Adolescent Medical Health*, 19, 277–283.

8 Physician–Therapist Collaboration in Family-Based Treatment for Anorexia Nervosa

What Each Provider Wants the Other to Know

Katharine L. Loeb and Leslie Sanders

Eating disorders (EDs), particularly anorexia nervosa (AN), exert a profound negative impact on a patient's behavioral, cognitive, affective, and physiological states, with psychosocial, psychiatric, and medical sequelae (American Psychiatric Association, 2013). The broad-range insults these disorders introduce in a patient's system require a comprehensive treatment approach that includes perspectives, assessments, and interventions from multiple disciplines. Nowhere is this more critical in the developmental pathway than during childhood and adolescence, where AN can disrupt normal development, at times with irreversible effects (Katzman, 2005). At a minimum, the treatment team for AN will consist of a mental health clinician who can deliver an evidence-based psychological intervention, and a collaborating medical provider. For youth, this team is typically a practitioner of Family-Based Treatment (FBT; Lock & Le Grange, 2013) plus a pediatrician or adolescent medicine specialist.

FBT is a strengths-based intervention that is an alternative to hospitalization for medically stable patients. FBT capitalizes and builds on existing parenting capacities, enlisting mothers and fathers as agents of change in resolving their child's AN. The treatment has three phases; in the first, parents actively modify ED behaviors and renourish their underweight child, functioning as an inpatient treatment team might in providing patient support and symptom management. In the second phase of FBT, parents gradually fade their involvement and the patient transitions to more autonomous functioning with regard to energy intake and expenditure. The third phase of FBT focuses on broader concerns of adolescent development. Sessions begin weekly and decrease in frequency over the course of treatment (Lock & Le Grange, 2013).

FBT, although the primary evidence-based treatment for AN/restrictive ED (Forsberg & Lock, 2015), remains elusive to many practitioners, both mental health and medical. Many professionals still ascribe to the belief that ED treatment is best accomplished by keeping the child in control of their eating while marginalizing the parents' role, by not "forcing" them to eat, and by supporting various diets such as gluten-free and "healthy" eating. When this position is held by one team member and not the other(s), the patient and family will invariably receive mixed messages that undermine the potency of treatment and invite the ED to capitalize on the differing viewpoints. For this reason, the FBT manual recommends that the treatment team be part of the same system (Lock & Le Grange, 2013) (e.g. clinic, hospital, or health system), although this is not always possible. Thus, parallel to the unity and alignment expected of parents in their implementation of FBT, practitioners must also be "on the same page" (ibid). A small but revealing literature on collegial alliance in FBT highlights the importance of clinician unity as a predictor of outcome (Murray, Griffiths, & Le Grange, 2014; Murray, Thornton, Griffiths & Le Grange, 2015; Murray, Thornton, & Wallis, 2012). Ideally, a triadic, complementary expertise model will ultimately be established between the parents, FBT therapist, and physician, in which each party both uses and imparts their knowledge base to create a formidable shield against the ED.

First Steps to a Successful Collaboration

Physicians are an integral member of the consulting team for FBT (Lock & Le Grange, 2013), and their multi-faceted role in facilitating uptake of the treatment is increasingly recognized and delineated in the eating disorders and medical fields (Bass, 2015; Katzman, Peebles, Sawyer, Lock, & Le Grange, 2013; Society for Adolescent Health and Medicine, 2015). A first and important step is to ascertain the medical practitioner's understanding of FBT as well as their commitment to supporting it. Directly inquiring about the medical professional's orientation regarding ED treatment will facilitate a dialogue that fosters a mutual understanding of the treatment approach. Medical professionals, including adolescent medicine physicians, who by virtue of their training have been exposed to ED patients, may report having extensive experience with ED patients. The majority, however, may never have provided medical care for a patient treated with FBT. Although medically competent, they may inadvertently undermine FBT.

Obtaining medical clearance for outpatient treatment is essential. Assessment for medical clearance is a dynamic, not static, process, and the physician will determine whether FBT will need to be delayed in favor of immediate hospitalization, and later, whether FBT may need to be interrupted for a temporary higher level of care to address medical or psychiatric instability or lack of progress (Katzman et al., 2013). Suggested criteria for hospitalization, based on the Society for Adolescent Health and Medicine's eating disorder guidelines (Golden et al., 2013), can be found in the FBT protocol (Lock & Le Grange, 2013). Similarly, the frequency of medical appointments will be determined by the medical professional, and this will likely change over the course of treatment as the patient becomes more (or less) stable (Katzman et al., 2013).

From the initial contact it is imperative to discuss how the team will communicate. The FBT manual suggests that team members convey the following information at the conclusion of each visit: weight, new concerns, and clinical recommendations (Lock & Le Grange, 2013). Secure email or telephone exchanges following each or most visits are efficient means of exchanging information and preventing "splitting" by the family or patient. Many medical providers will not be accustomed to this amount of contact with mental health providers but will quickly see its benefit. For instance, it is not uncommon for parents to "parcel out" what they tell each practitioner. Ongoing communication will "paint the full picture" across treatment modalities.

Chapter Format and Audience

This chapter is co-authored by an adolescent medicine specialist with extensive experience and expertise in EDs (LS) and a clinical psychologist who is an FBT clinician and researcher (KLL). The Introduction and Conclusion are written in the collective voice of the two authors. Each section in-between will focus on a topic relevant to FBT implementation, providing a dual-perspective, dialogue format wherein each author has written what she wants the other's discipline to know, consider, and expect. Specifically, Dr. Loeb will communicate what she would like medical providers involved in the treatment of adolescent AN to know about the tenets and implementation of FBT, and Dr. Sanders will convey what she believes is important for FBT therapists to understand about the medical aspects of AN. Each author's sections can also be a resource for practitioners within their respective disciplines. As the authors have collaborated successfully on FBT cases for many years, the format and content are designed as an analogue for practitioners who are newer to one another's work. It is the authors' hope that this chapter may be shared between providers to facilitate productive and cohesive multidisciplinary efforts in the treatment of youth with AN.

Weight, Part I: Loss, Complications, Targets, and Measurement

The Physician's Perspective

Medical stability and degree of malnutrition, as determined by the medical professional, will include consideration of not only the patient's weight at presentation and amount of weight loss but also the rapidity of weight loss and the presence of consequential medical complications, such as very low heart rate, low blood pressure, orthostatic changes in heart rate and blood pressure, abnormal EKG, or electrolyte abnormalities (Society for Adolescent Health and Medicine, 2015). The medical professional should also judge the patient's risk of re-feeding syndrome, as often heralded by hypophosphatemia (Society for Adolescent Health and Medicine, 2014); severely malnourished patients may need to delay FBT until they are re-fed through the high-risk period of 7–10 days during which they are closely medically monitored in a higher level of care. Updated guidelines for this are now available (Society for Adolescent

Health and Medicine, 2014, 2015). Even such patients can benefit from the application of FBT principles, such as early parental control and monitoring of meals, while in the hospital.

Although monitoring growth parameters is fundamental in pediatric medicine, incomplete growth charts are not an infrequent issue. Having as many data points as possible is essential to determining not only the expected weight but also expected height for the patient at the point of intervention. If the growth chart is not complete it is likely that heights and weights are available and documented in the medical record from historical appointments and can be incorporated to complete a cumulative growth chart. Reviewing the growth chart with both the FBT provider and parents can provide a compelling visual depiction of degree of deviation from what was normal for the patient prior to AN onset, as well as a graphic treatment target, i.e. return to the original growth trajectory. The expectation in children who were not clinically underweight, overweight, or obese prior to the onset of AN is to restore them to their premorbid percentile. In this sense, "normal" or optimal weight is an individualized variable (Society for Adolescent Health and Medicine, 2015). It is important to keep in mind that children may also track downward in height percentiles secondary to malnourishment and appear "proportionate" with weight loss. Restoring them to their premorbid weight percentile will promote height restoration as well.

Not identifying a specific number is essential, especially in younger children who have not completed their growth. They will need to continue to make expected weight gain along their premorbid weight percentile during and following weight restoration (Katzman et al., 2013). Even for adolescents who may have reached their adult height, aging alone will necessitate increases in weight to continue to track on their healthy growth curve percentile. If a specific number is discussed or a range given, especially unilaterally by one of the practitioners on the team, the patient and/or family is likely to fixate on this number or the lowest number in the range and this can undermine progress, erode trust, and potentially trigger ED cognitions and behaviors. The practitioners should not negotiate weight. Even when the child appears to be weight-restored, before the renourishment process is halted the professionals should explicitly discuss from each of their perspectives if weight restoration has been achieved. Are all the medical issues improved? Is the child free of ED behaviors and cognitions? Premature or unilateral declarations of weight normalization can jeopardize full remission.

In female patients, resumption of menses is one important marker of restored health (Society for Adolescent Health and Medicine, 2015). Delayed puberty is an important health consequence of inadequate weight gain, weight loss, or excessive exercise without adequate energy intake. With weight restoration, children should begin to re-enter the normal progression of puberty. The medical professional should be following various laboratory markers such as estradiol and other hormone markers of menstrual status. A baseline estradiol is often obtained at the initial assessment and repeated when the patient has been weight-restored. It may be necessary to repeat it if the weight-restored patient remains amenorrheic after several months. A persistently low value may guide recommendations for additional weight gain. Consideration of other issues interfering with resumption of menses, such as level of exercise, should be kept in mind.

Determining target weights in children with a history of obesity is more difficult. From a medical/health perspective, it is likely that a patient will resume medical and psychological functioning at a lower-than-premorbid point on the growth curve, but well above the 50th percentile. In children who present with insufficient growth or "failure to thrive," determining a point at which they deviated from their previous pattern of growth provides guidance as to where the child should be restored to, even if this occurred at a very young age. Children who have failed to thrive since infancy require special discussion that is beyond the scope of this chapter.

The team should discuss how the child is weighed in each setting. Most mental health practitioners will not weigh ED patients in gowns nor have them void, as the medical professionals do. This leads to increased opportunity for weight manipulation either through water loading, which can inflate weight by several pounds, to hiding objects such as weights under clothing. It is highly likely that there will not be perfect weight agreement between the scales across practitioners' offices. Given this, it may be most helpful and less distressing for the patient and family to learn the weight at only one office, especially at the onset of treatment when both FBT and medical appointments occur as often as weekly. What should be evident is a similar trend in each office; large deviations from the trend, especially gains, are red-flags for weight manipulation.

Many medical professionals will be familiar with the more traditional approach of not discussing the weight with the patient throughout treatment. The mental health practitioner may need to explain the rationale for making the weight "public" at every FBT session. Team members should share the weight obtained in each office so patterns of changes in weight can be tracked. Ultimately, the weight on the medical practitioner's scale will be more "accurate" and should be referred to if there are concerns (Lock & Le Grange, 2013).

The FBT Therapist's Perspective

In FBT for AN, the patient's weight is tracked at every session. Specifically, at the start of each visit the FBT therapist meets one-to-one with the patient to obtain the weight, document it on a chart that will later be reviewed with the family present, and discuss any problems the patient may be experiencing (Lock & Le Grange, 2013). Because change in weight is the variable of interest, absolute and consistent (small) discrepancies between the physician's scale and the FBT therapist's scale will be immaterial.

The measured weight, relative to the prior readings, functions as an important data point that informs evaluation of progress and treatment response, and, by extension, the tone and content of the ensuing family session (ibid).

Weight is communicated with transparency, permitting the parents to adjust or maintain their renourishment efforts in accordance with objective data (barring weight manipulation), and challenging any ED-driven avoidance of weight on the part of the patient. Weighing the patient therefore not only serves a pragmatic function at the family level, but also likely an exposure-based, ultimately anxiolytic one for the patient (Hildebrandt, Bacow, Markella, & Loeb, 2012). Practitioners should keep in mind that patient resistance to how weights are handled in FBT may be exacerbated by a history of either self-directed or treatment-directed "blind weights."

In FBT, the patient's state of functioning (medical, psychological, behavioral) later in the course of treatment informs the determination that the "right" weight has been achieved (Lock & Le Grange, 2013). This is a dramatic departure from interventions that set a defined target weight or weight range and then assess functioning when that point has been met or maintained. That said, a thorough review of a patient's growth curve history, in collaboration with the physician, will help determine which BMI-for-age percentile will likely represent a return to a premorbid, healthy trajectory. Notably, this may be especially difficult to identify for patients with an extended prodrome of AN, in which a longer period of restrictive eating and some weight loss may have predated onset of full AN.

The specific weight that corresponds to return to the pre-ED point on the growth curve will by definition be a moving target as the patient grows in age and height (Katzman et al., 2013; Lock & Le Grange, 2013; Society for Adolescent Health and Medicine, 2015). This is one important reason why a medical provider's declaration of a precise goal weight can undermine full recovery. It is also why the term "weight maintenance" in youth is misleading and should be avoided. Broad projections – for practitioners' use only – can be made by factoring in the current degree of deviation from the individualized growth curve, the expected duration of Phases I and II of FBT when renourishment is accomplished, and the duration of illness (in our experience, among patients with more chronic AN, there may be a longer lag between return to growth curve and psychological symptom relief, in some cases justifying a brief "wait and see" period). However, this number should be treated as a hypothesis only, not a precise prediction, to be modified continuously based on new information. It should not be shared or negotiated with the patient, who will be particularly vulnerable to reference dependence effects within this topic. Exceeding the uttered target weight (or the lower limit of a range), even in the context of significant height growth, may trigger ED cognitions related to fear of fatness, and unintentionally increase patient distress. As one young adult patient with a 10-year history of AN stated, "Anything above my goal weight from my first hospitalization when I was 12 is how I define obesity."

Using prior growth curves to guide individual recovery parameters may be particularly complicated in ED patients with a history of overweightness and obesity. The mental health practitioner should assess for the following in a treatment intake, and discuss the information with the collaborating physician: Was the higher, pre-morbid BMI-for-age percentile a consistent one for the patient, or was there a sudden or gradual shift upward? If the latter, were there any significant stressors that correspond temporally? Any changes in mood, interpersonal functioning, or eating behavior? Was the patient's higher weight status (whether lifetime or temporary) associated with any modifiable variables, such as a sedentary lifestyle or a particular diet? For example, an adolescent female who was always at the 85th percentile, active in sports, and who exhibited no disordered eating prior to AN onset may need to approach that same percentile to experience full recovery. However, an adolescent whose percentile increased from the 50th to the 85th during the transition to middle school, in the context of depressed mood, social withdrawal, and binge eating may do well when they approach the earlier point on the growth curve (provided that the other problem areas are also ultimately addressed).

Weight, Part II: Restoration and Renourishment

The Physician's Perspective

Medical professionals may focus on weight gain as the most important parameter of success. However, an early, positive response to treatment, while conferring prognostic advantage (Doyle, Le Grange, Loeb, Doyle, & Crosby, 2010; Le Grange, Accurso, Lock, Agras, & Bryson, 2014), can also carry risk, which good communication from the FBT therapist to the physician will mitigate. Specifically, the mental health practitioner should keep the physician informed of very rapid weight gain in a patient, especially at the initiation of FBT, so that re-feeding syndrome can be assessed if necessary. If the patient was deemed medically stable enough to initiate treatment, the medical professional may have scheduled a more distal follow-up visit without anticipating rapid weight gain, especially if their FBT experience is limited.

At the onset of treatment, it is essential for the medical professional to understand the experience of the extinction burst (the temporary exacerbation of fear/anxiety-based responses before they become extinguished) and increased resistance, in order to put a seemingly worsening clinical state in context, so the family can be appropriately supported and encouraged. The medical provider, as their trusted advisor, can also reassure parents that it is not essential that their child "like" or "feel connected to" the FBT provider early in treatment (Katzman et al., 2013). This, as well as reinforcing the notion that their child is unlikely to show motivation or buy-in at this stage, will support the work of the FBT therapist. The medical professional, given their knowledge of the family, can also provide the FBT therapist with helpful insights into the family's handling of other crises and how to best support them.

The FBT Therapist's Perspective

It is important for physicians to know that patients undergoing FBT may appear to initially be faring worse, psychologically, even as weight is gained (Katzman et al., 2013). This may be particularly true when there has been a history of well-meaning (and sometimes clinically prescribed) parental symptom accommodation that predates FBT; the introduction of a clear mission and set of strategies to rid the patient of the ED will almost invariably result in (temporary) increased resistance and distress. Physicians can also expect an understandable degree of frustration in the patient about the seeming tautology of the treatment model. For example, patients may find it illogical to expect that they will ultimately feel *better* about their body at a much higher weight when, early in treatment, each increment of weight gain only seems to increase their suffering. Explaining that the relationship between weight gain and psychological symptom relief in AN is less of a "dose-dependent" one and more of a threshold effect may reassure parents but will provide little comfort to the patient. Thus, the notion that a reduction in shape and weight concerns represents one functional marker of recovery will prompt a fear that the treatment team will never deem them "well" and instead continue to increase their weight to catastrophic levels. If the physician inadvertently reinforces this anxiety by expressing doubt about the principles, techniques, or efficacy of FBT to the family, it will be harder for the patient to trust the treatment process. Questions and concerns are best introduced first among the treatment team to resolve any discrepancy in perspectives before they are presented to the family.

Physicians may observe an apparent lack of therapeutic alliance between the FBT patient and the therapist early in treatment (ibid). In fact, research shows that therapist–patient alliance can be achieved in FBT (although therapist–parent alliance is generally stronger) (Forsberg, Lo Tempio, Bryson, Fitzpatrick, Le Grange, & Lock, 2014; Isserlin & Couturier, 2012; Lo Tempio, Forsberg, Bryson, Fitzpatrick, Le Grange, & Lock, 2013), and that by the end of treatment, patients regard FBT as highly acceptable (Krautter & Lock, 2004). These findings highlight the FBT principle of the externalized illness (Lock & Le Grange, 2013): there is a healthy part of the patient that recognizes that the ED is beyond their control and that welcomes adult intervention, even as the AN is loudly asserting the opposite sentiment. To illustrate this, I quote a 14-year-old patient, who stated in session 3 of FBT: "I hate coming here but I also know that my eating disorder will never be happy, no matter how much weight I lose, and that scares me." Similarly, a medical practitioner less familiar with EDs or FBT may be alarmed by an ostensible deterioration in the parent–child relationship early in FBT (Katzman et al., 2013). All members of the treatment team should help parents manage their expectations and remind them that they are fighting against the ED, not their child, even if their child's mindset and identity are currently eclipsed by the AN (Lock & Le Grange, 2013).

A final word about weight restoration in FBT: as noted above, weight gain alone does not define recovery. It is possible to achieve weight physiological recovery while other manifestations of the ED are still active (e.g. food rituals, food avoidance, purging, excessive exercise, etc.); thus, we encourage parents to consider all the ways in which their child's cognitions and behaviors are being "puppeteered" by AN, and to address them in Phases I and II of FBT (ibid). Cross-disciplinary emphasis of this point will help depleted parents mobilize to address the full extent of the AN's influence on their child.

Junctures and Transitions

The Physician's Perspective

A common issue raised in the transition from FBT Phase I to Phase II is return to exercise/sports participation for the patient (Lock & Le Grange, 2013). While the foundation of the timing and nature of this is medical clearance, followed by parental decision making, the issue can be complex and require collaboration between the parents, physician, and FBT therapist, factoring in variables such as risk for compulsivity. Specifically, there needs to be agreement that the child is psychologically ready to return not only to exercise in general but also which form. Return to premorbid exercise routines that were connected to weight loss and the ED may not be possible, particularly if the form sets up expectations for leanness. Key questions, the answers to which can inform the parents' decision to permit or delay their child's resumption of exercise, should be anticipated and reviewed as a team antecedently, and later be reflected back to parents as they consider the best options for their child. For example, can this patient be a healthy participant in ballet or the cross country team? Are the parents up to the challenge of feeding more, in the context of energy expenditure, if necessary? Assessing motivations (including the parents') for return to exercise and discussing alternate forms may be indicated.

Medical professionals are required to complete health clearance forms for participation in school-based activities. Often the forms need to be completed long before a sports season actually begins. FBT therapists should encourage physicians to write a disclaimer regarding re-evaluation at a more proximate time to the season, and to review the rationale for this with the patient and family. Being mindful of the frequency of medical visits, which may be more spread out at this point, is important in terms of obtaining accurate weights and monitoring vital signs during resumption of exercise.

With older adolescents for whom there are plans to transition to independent living (e.g. college), the junctures between Phases II and III, or between Phase III and termination, are critical. It is important for the patient, family, and team to have discussions far in advance about what needs to be in place for this to occur. Establishing a timeline with discrete and evaluable milestones is helpful. What will the parents need to see in their child to feel confident that they will thrive independently? Working backwards to determine the duration of this timeline will help parents assess the likelihood of a successful "on-time" transition that will match the pace of the patient's peers. As much as everyone, the treatment team included, wants the patient to be able to go off to college with their high-school cohort, is this realistic? Like sports participation papers that need to be completed by the medical professional, there will be health clearance forms for college or other post-high school programs as well. Having disclaimers about revoking clearance should be discussed. Advising parents to purchase tuition insurance is important. The team should frame this in a manner that does not discount progress made or discourage optimism about and momentum toward ultimate full recovery. Rather, such contingency plans will increase the ease with which parents can access options to ensure their adolescent's health and safety should the strength of the ED wax and wane.

The FBT Therapist's Perspective

At times, both parents and physicians alike will be concerned that a patient is not ready to transition between phases of FBT, particularly between Phases I and II. This often arises from a misconception of this juncture as reflecting changes that ensue from a complete recovery. In fact, while patients must be well past a dangerous, clearly diagnostic weight threshold, they do not have to be fully weight-restored to begin practicing independence around eating (Lock & Le Grange, 2013). The FBT manual also states that resistance must be significantly decreased and parental confidence in symptom management be high in order to make this transition. These criteria should be honored even when there are worries that the patient will not be able to tolerate even a small return of autonomy. Sometimes, these concerns are generated by behavioral noise, i.e. reflexive verbal objections to eating made by the patient that are more ED habit than a reflection of psychological state, are not correlated with behavioral resistance, and are not necessarily predictive of Phase II success. The FBT therapist, by virtue of their expertise in learning and behavior, is in the best position to explain this in the decision around transition from Phase I to Phase II. The treatment team should focus on the manual's criteria and favor behavioral indicators in determining readiness for Phase II. Notably, the FBT protocol's standard requirement of a gradual transition to independence will permit parents to "test the waters" without risking a major setback (ibid).

Similarly, apprehension about patient readiness may arise in the transition from Phase II to Phase III, or from Phase III to termination. This often centers around residual shape and weight concerns that the parents and physician may worry signal lack of complete recovery and/or propensity for relapse. The FBT therapist should assess the clinical significance of these remaining psychological symptoms to determine if they in fact exceed "normative discontent" (Rodin, Silberstein, & Striegel-Moore, 1984), a phrase used to capture the unfortunate reality that the majority of females in cultures that espouse the thin ideal may be somewhat dissatisfied with their bodies. The FBT therapist, as with earlier decisions, will use the information and criteria in the treatment manual to inform team-based and family determinations about readiness for transition. A persistent focus on shape and weight in adolescent–parent communication can be addressed directly as a family-level concern as part of Phase III (ibid).

When FBT Plus Medical Care Is or Appears to Be Insufficient

The Physician's Perspective

If a child is making insufficient weight gain progress it is helpful to analyze the feeding in detail. Parents may be hesitant to deviate from healthy eating practices; the medical professional can reassure the family that incorporating very high-calorie and high-fat items in a "food as medicine prescription" for AN (Lock & Le Grange, 2013) will not be detrimental to the child's health. They may also help reassure the family that somatic complaints like bloating and abdominal pain, while present, are typically not based on any medical pathology and will improve over time. Additionally, the physician can validate that physical changes can be expected during initial weight restoration, such as disproportionate weight gain in the abdomen (Mayer et al., 2005).

For some families, referral to a registered dietician (RD) may be helpful. Only the parents should consult the RD, who would serve in a consultative role to the parents, not patient. It is also imperative that the RD be familiar with the principles of FBT and not prescribe a rigid meal plan or try to modify the approach. Including the RD as a member of the team to facilitate collaboration is key (Lock & Le Grange, 2013).

It is important to establish and implement assessment and intervention procedures if there is any concern about suicidality, keeping in mind that often emotion dysregulation in the patient in the context of early renourishment efforts may paradoxically signal that treatment is going well, not poorly. Put another way, a "quiet" ED is often an unchallenged ED. Having a unified plan for the parents for responses to violence or threats of violence may also be necessary.

The medical provider will also be able to assess patients for non-suicidal self-injury via clinical observations unavailable to the FBT provider. Examination in a gown is essential to adequately assess for self-harm as it is often inflicted on body parts about which the patient is feeling distressed, such as the thighs and abdomen. The medical provider, given their often lifelong relationship with the patient, may be disturbed by the patient's level of distress and by behaviors that are completely uncharacteristic for the patient and thus not anticipated. Communication with the FBT therapist will help put this in context, and a plan for response to these situations, especially ongoing self-harm, should be discussed.

Although a patient may be deemed medically stable at the outset of FBT there are circumstances when they may become medically unstable as treatment progresses (Katzman et al., 2013), even beyond the initial re-feeding period as discussed above. Ongoing or rapid weight loss, acute food refusal, and frequent purging can all lead to medical instability. If these are occurring, the medical provider should always be informed. The decision about when and how to intervene should be discussed among the team. For example, determining how many missed meals would be tolerated and how this would be handled is important. Options could include brief emergency room management in which the patient would be given an opportunity to eat versus insertion of a nasogastric tube for provision of sufficient calories, following discharge versus admission to the hospital or higher level of care.

An in-person team meeting with the FBT provider, medical professional, and the family can be a very powerful intervention when treatment is not progressing as anticipated. Often these meetings allow the providers to re-empower and invigorate beleaguered parents by together pointing out all that they are doing well and also by acknowledging their challenges. Such a meeting provides a forum for the medical provider to clearly demonstrate support for FBT and alliance with the FBT provider.

The FBT Therapist's Perspective

There are three primary causes for adding adjunctive care to FBT or interrupting it for a higher level of care. The first is medical instability, and determination of this and consequential intervention will be determined primarily by the physician (Katzman et al., 2013), although the FBT therapist should have input regarding inpatient programs that will support the FBT model while providing stabilization. The second is lack of treatment response. As noted above, research shows that early weight gain in FBT carries positive prognostic significance (Doyle et al., 2010; Le Grange et al., 2014). An absence of this early indicator may be best addressed with an augmentation of FBT (Fitzpatrick, Darcy, Le Grange, & Lock, 2015; Lock et al., 2015), rather than by switching interventions, although further research is needed to inform such treatment algorithms. Sustained lack of response to FBT (rather than simply a slower response) will require team-level discussions about alternative treatment options.

The third clinical issue that prompts consideration of adjunctive or alternate care is acute psychological instability, particularly suicidality. The FBT manual (Lock & Le Grange, 2013) is clear that maintaining patient safety is of paramount importance, and can require prioritizing management of risk of self-harm over the AN. However, not all expressions of affect dysregulation (internalized or externalized), especially *passive* suicidal ideation and non-suicidal self-injury, require a change in treatment. Assessing for risk, not just at a single time point but in an ongoing manner, is a non-negotiable cornerstone of good care. What a competent evaluation may reveal is that actual risk for suicide is absent, and that worrisome verbal utterances by the patient, such as "I don't want to be here" or "I'd rather die than eat," are indicators of distress secondary to both the ED and the intervention. It is important for the physician and parents to know that these ED-driven statements may be inadvertently negatively reinforced by a reduction in the feeding task demand whenever they are expressed. The FBT therapist can work with the parents to respond with a judicious blend of empathy and a firm commitment to recovery, e.g. "I know the eating disorder is making you suffer, and that right now getting treatment feels worse than having anorexia. We want to reassure you that we are here to help you get better, no matter what, and that we will not give up on you." There should also be an emergency plan in place in the event that the parent has concerns about their child's safety, at any time. If psychiatric hospitalization is necessary, an immediate return to outpatient renourishment efforts upon discharge will be important to avoid unintentional negative reinforcement of suicidality.

Negative mood and suicidality are exacerbated by AN and low weight. That said, if affect dysregulation and self-harm predate the onset of the eating disorder, it will be harder for the parents and treatment team to reassure themselves that these symptoms will resolve with weight restoration. Additional psychological interventions, such as Dialectical Behavior Therapy for adolescents (Miller, Rathus, & Linehan, 2007), can be applied in conjunction with FBT, provided that certain modifications are made to preserve the FBT model of parents as the primary agents of ED change in Phase I (Anderson, Murray, Ramirez, Rockwell, Le Grange, & Kaye, this volume; Bhatnagar & Wisniewski, 2015). Concurrent treatments have the advantage of ideally reducing patient suffering more broadly and quickly, assuming consistency of messages across providers; family resources (time, money) may be challenged by this approach, however. Alternatively, sequencing interventions may permit more focused attention on each problem area over time, but delay of holistic improvement and possible interim safety risks are potential disadvantages that the team should consider.

Conclusions: A United Front

As FBT therapists tell parents, presenting a united front to their child and to the AN does not require being "clones" of one another. Parents must share their commitment to the mission of FBT, but can bring complementary strengths to the frontline – determining who is best at what becomes one of the early tasks in FBT participation. One parent may be better at planning meals, the other more patient while sitting with the patient as a meal's duration seems endless. This model extends to FBT therapist–physician collaboration in FBT. While clearly having defined and independent roles in the process of helping a young person recover from an ED, unity and collaboration are essential for success. This was echoed in the process of writing this chapter. We framed our mission and topics together, wrote our respective sections apart, and appreciated the degrees of both convergence and divergence as we merged our documents.

Some final words of advice from the authors, to our readers of both disciplines: become comfortable encouraging parents to first try to answer their own questions, and respect parental authority on details of FBT implementation within the framework of the treatment protocol (Katzman et al., 2013). Become comfortable responding to questions that require provider input with, "I'll consult with the team and get back to you." As difficult as it may be to adjust to a model in which you frequently defer to both parental and team-level decisions, it is preferable to be cautious moving forward than to backtrack and undo statements to parents following consultation; not only could this undermine your credibility but it will be confusing to families. We also caution against being territorial or feeling threatened by another's area of expertise (ibid). This will inhibit good communication, ultimately hurting the patient.

FBT, despite the clarity that the manual and research base provide, can be an exhausting experience for all involved. Overwhelmed families can be overwhelming for providers. Frequent, respectful, and open communication between providers will not only optimize the patient's treatment but also provide a rich and rewarding support experience for the team.

References

American Psychiatric Association. (2013). *Diagnostic and statistical manual of mental disorders*, 5th edition. Washington, DC: APA.

Anderson, L. K., Murray, S. B., Ramirez, A. L., Rockwell, R., Le Grange, D. & Kaye, W. H. (2016). The integration of family-based treatment and dialectical behavior therapy for adolescent bulimia nervosa: Philosophical and practical considerations. In S. B. Murray, L. K. Anderson, & L. Cohn (Eds.), *Innovations in family therapy for eating disorders: Novel treatment developments, patient insights, and the role of carers*. New York: Routledge.

Bass, P. S. (2015). Family-based therapy for eating disorders. *Contemporary Pediatrics*, September.

Bhatnagar, K., & Wisniewski, L. (2015). Integrating dialectical behavior therapy with family therapy for adolescents with affect dysregulation. In K. L. Loeb, D. Le Grange, & J. Lock (Eds.), *Family therapy for adolescent eating and weight disorders: New applications* (pp. 305–327). New York: Routledge.

Doyle, P. M., Le Grange, D., Loeb, K., Doyle, A. C., & Crosby, R. D. (2010). Early response to family-based treatment for adolescent anorexia nervosa. *International Journal of Eating Disorders*, 43, 659–662.

Fitzpatrick, K. K., Darcy, A. M., Le Grange, D., & Lock, J. (2015). In vivo family meal training for initial nonresponders. In K. L. Loeb, D. Le Grange, & J. Lock (Eds.), *Family therapy for adolescent eating and weight disorders: New applications* (pp. 45–58). New York: Routledge.

Forsberg, S., & Lock, J. (2015). Family-based treatment of child and adolescent eating disorders. *Child and Adolescent Psychiatric Clinics of North America*, 24(3), 617–629.

Forsberg, S., Lo Tempio, E., Bryson, S., Fitzpatrick, K. K., Le Grange, D. & Lock, J. (2014). Parent–therapist alliance in family-based treatment for adolescents with anorexia nervosa. *European Eating Disorders Review*, 22(1), 53–58.

Golden, N. H., Katzman, D. K., Kreipe, R. E., Stevens, S. L., Sawyer, S. M. et al. (2013). Eating disorders in adolescents: Position paper of the Society for Adolescent Medicine. *Journal of Adolescent Health*, 33, 496–503.

Hildebrandt, T., Bacow, T., Markella, M., & Loeb, K. L. (2012). Anxiety in anorexia nervosa and its management using family-based treatment. *European Eating Disorders Review*, 20, e1–e16.

Isserlin, L., & Couturier, J. (2012). Therapeutic alliance and family-based treatment for adolescents with anorexia nervosa. *Psychotherapy*, 49(1), 46–51.

Katzman, D. K. (2005). Medical complications in adolescents with anorexia nervosa: A review of the literature. *International Journal of Eating Disorders*, 37(Suppl.), S52–S59.

Katzman, D. K., Peebles, R., Sawyer, S. M., Lock, J., & Le Grange, D. (2013). The role of the pediatrician in family-based treatment for adolescent eating disorders: Opportunities and challenges. *Journal of Adolescent Health*, 53, 433–440.

Krautter, T., & Lock, J. (2004). Is manualized family-based treatment for adolescent anorexia nervosa acceptable to patients? Patient satisfaction at the end of treatment. *Journal of Family Therapy*, 26, 65–81.

Le Grange, D., Accurso, E. C., Lock, J., Agras, S., & Bryson, S. W. (2014). Early weight gain predicts outcome in two treatments for adolescent anorexia nervosa. *International Journal of Eating Disorders*, 47(2), 124–129.

Lock, J., & Le Grange, D. (2013). *Treatment manual for anorexia nervosa: A family-based approach*, 2nd edition. New York: Guilford Press.

Lock, J., Le Grange, D., Agras, W. S., Fitzpatrick, K. K., Jo, B. et al. (2015). Can adaptive treatment improve outcomes in family-based therapy for adolescents with anorexia nervosa? Feasibility and treatment effects of a multi-site treatment study. *Behaviour Research and Therapy*, 73, 90–95.

Lo Tempio, E., Forsberg, S., Bryson, S. W., Fitzpatrick, K. K., Le Grange, D. & Lock, J. (2013). Patients' characteristics and the quality of the therapeutic alliance in family-based treatment and individual therapy for adolescents with anorexia nervosa. *Journal of Family Therapy*, 35(Suppl. 1), 29–52.

Mayer, L., Walsh, B. T., Pierson, R. N., Heymsfield, S. B., Gallagher, D. et al. (2005). Body fat redistribution after weight gain in women with anorexia nervosa. *American Journal of Clinical Nutrition*, 82, 1286–1291.

Miller, A. L., Rathus, J. H., & Linehan, M. M. (2007). *Dialectical behavior therapy with suicidal adolescents*. New York: Guilford Press.

Murray, S. B., Griffiths, S., & Le Grange, D. (2014). The role of collegial alliance in family-based treatment of adolescent anorexia nervosa: A pilot study. *International Journal of Eating Disorders*, 47, 418–421.

Murray, S. B., Griffiths, S., Thornton, C., & Le Grange, D. (2015). Collegial alliance and family-based treatment for adolescent anorexia nervosa: A qualitative report of three cases. *Advances in Eating Disorders: Theory, Research and Practice*, 3(3), 251–258.

Murray, S. B., Thornton, C., & Wallis, A. (2012). A thorn in the side of evidence-based treatment for adolescent anorexia nervosa. *Australian and New Zealand Journal of Psychiatry*, 46, 1026–1028.

Rodin, J., Silberstein, L. R., & Striegel-Moore, R. H. (1984). Women and weight: A normative discontent. In T. B. Sonderegger (Ed.), *Nebraska symposium on motivation: Psychology and gender* (pp. 267–307). Lincoln, NE: University of Nebraska Press.

Society for Adolescent Health and Medicine. (2014). Refeeding hypophosphatemia in hospitalized adolescents with anorexia nervosa: A position statement of the Society for Adolescent Health and Medicine. *Journal of Adolescent Health*, 55, 455–457.

Society for Adolescent Health and Medicine. (2015). Position paper of the Society for Adolescent Health and Medicine: Medical management of restrictive eating disorders in adolescents and young adults. *Journal of Adolescent Health*, 56, 121–125.

9 The Integration of Wider Family Therapy Practices into Family-Based Treatment for Adolescent Anorexia Nervosa

Stuart B. Murray and Scott Griffiths

There can be little doubt that family therapy has occupied a particularly central role in the history of eating disorders, with even the very earliest accounts of anorexia nervosa (AN) noting that clinical descriptions of AN would be "incomplete without reference to the patient's home life" (Lasegue, 1873). Indeed, the development of family therapy over the last 40 years has seen many pioneering family therapists demonstrate a sustained interest in the family processes underpinning AN (Dare, 1985; Minuchin, Rosman, & Baker, 1978; Selvini-Palazzoli, 1974; White, 1987), with the easily quantifiable outcome measures (i.e. weight gain) meaning that for the first time family therapists had a straightforward method of indexing the efficacy of their work. As such, AN became something of a paradigm for family therapy, with many theoretical models of family therapy being developed and tested in the context of AN (Dare et al., 1990).

This sustained interest from family therapists cumulatively resulted in the more recent development of a highly sophisticated treatment program, which integrates several key theoretical schools of family therapy into a pragmatic approach to the home-based treatment of AN. This treatment model, family-based treatment (FBT), is a manualized form of eating disorder-focused family therapy that adopts an agnostic approach to the origin of AN and "externalizes" AN as separate to family functioning, whilst conceptualizing the adolescent's parents as the primary resource in restoring their unwell child to full health (Lock & Le Grange, 2013). The notion that parents instinctively know how to feed a healthy child helps empower parents in overcoming the powerful presence of AN, which in many instances can be so overwhelming within families that it coerces parents away from their natural instincts, inadvertently resulting in a level of accommodation to AN symptoms (Eisler, 2005). As such, treatment is initially focused on mobilizing parental strengths in ensuring the nutritional rehabilitation of their child, which takes undivided precedence over other areas of adolescent functioning and typically involves parents temporarily exercising full control over all ecological and individual maintaining features of AN until they are abated. Age-appropriate autonomy and independence are gradually restored to the child upon the reversal of the adolescent's weight loss and a decline in the cognitive and behavioral symptoms of AN. The final stage of treatment focuses less on food specifically and more on general adolescent issues that may have been interrupted by the presence of AN, such as individuation and separation, anxiety, and social integration.

Current empirical evidence continues to support the use of FBT as a first-line treatment for medically stable adolescents with AN, with up to 50–75 percent of adolescents being weight-restored within 12 months of commencing treatment (Le Grange & Eisler, 2009), and a significant number remaining weight-restored at both 12-month (Lock et al., 2010) and 5-year follow-up (Lock et al., 2006). Furthermore, up to 40 percent are likely to be cognitively remitted of all eating disorder symptomatology by the end of treatment, which compares favorably with other forms of adolescent-oriented treatment (Lock et al., 2010), with FBT further demonstrating greater rates of symptom remissions over time (ibid).

However, despite this promising evidence base, not all families respond favorably to FBT (ibid). Indeed, approximately 25–50 percent of adolescents undergoing FBT may not be weight-restored by the end of treatment (Le Grange & Eisler, 2009), and it is likely that a sizeable portion of adolescents will not be remitted of all cognitive symptoms of AN by the end of treatment (Lock et al., 2010), often requiring additional treatment. Furthermore, a minority of patients drop out of treatment prior to completion, further limiting treatment efficacy (ibid). Whilst the extant evidence base has begun to develop an understanding of the complexities that may make full symptom remission less likely in some instances (i.e. in families inclusive of high expressed emotion and single-parent families; Lock & Le Grange, 2013), less research has focused on how to augment treatment in such instances. Thus, further research is perhaps warranted in developing augmentations to enhance the efficacy of FBT in instances in which symptoms do not fully remit during a course of standard FBT.

Indeed, broader comments within the field of eating disorders have called for the development of new and more complex ideas in the treatment of anorexia nervosa, citing in particular the need to identify when augmentative interventions may be indicated (Strober & Johnson, 2012). In the specific context of FBT, empirical research has demonstrated that reliable predictors of treatment non-response may be indicated after only four sessions (Doyle et al., 2010; Le Grange et al., 2014), which affords clinicians and families a particularly valuable opportunity to review treatment response at an early stage with a view to potentially implementing augmentative strategies if treatment non-response is indicated. This chapter is therefore intended to review potential augmentations to standard FBT in instances when symptom remission is not achieved throughout standard treatment.

The Possible Integration of Wider Family Therapy Practices

Recent suggestions have intimated that the manualization of eating disorder-focused family therapy, whilst allowing for standardization, widespread dissemination and rigorously controlled research trials, may have inadvertently resulted in the narrowing of a family therapy lens in the treatment of adolescent AN (Eisler, 2012). Indeed, FBT was originally developed against the backdrop of a rich body of wider family therapy literature, with many earlier family therapists reporting impressive rates of symptom remission in their treatment of adolescents with AN (i.e. Minuchin et al., 1978; Selvini-Palazzoli, 1974). Thus, despite some of the theoretical assumptions and conceptual understanding embedded in previous theoretical models of family therapy for AN subsequently found to be inaccurate (Dare et al., 1994; Eisler, 2005), many therapeutic and interventive practices borne out of these earlier approaches remain central to contemporary FBT practice (Lock & Le Grange, 2013) and have been empirically demonstrated to be crucial in bringing about symptom remission (Ellison et al., 2012).

However, despite aspects of these earlier practices remaining central in contemporary FBT, many other aspects and interventive practices from earlier family-oriented approaches to adolescent AN remain absent from contemporary FBT. One approach that has attempted to integrate wider family therapy practices into the family-based treatment of adolescent AN is multi-family therapy for AN, in which up to six families grappling with AN convene for intensive facilitated group meetings and are encouraged to help each other take charge of their child's AN (Dare & Eisler 2000; Scholz & Asen, 2001). Due to differences in the nature of this treatment (which centralizes group processes), multi-family therapy for AN features interventive techniques from earlier family therapy approaches that were not integrated into standardized FBT, including "goldfish bowl" enactments and discussion forums, role reversals for family meals, and foster parenting at family meals (in which children temporarily rotate into other families for meals), and "greek chorus" style feedback between families (Papp, 1980). Preliminary evidence suggests that multi-family therapy may be a viable alternative to individual FBT (Eisler, 2012), although through a clinical lens multi-family therapy is resource- and time-intensive, typically involving several three–five-day intensive multi-family visits in addition to weekly individual family meetings. However, the preliminary studies demonstrating the efficacy of multi-family therapy (ibid) cumulatively suggest that there may exist a wider array of family therapy practices that may be utilized in assisting families in overcoming their child's AN.

Thus, a potential augmentation to the delivery of standard FBT may involve the reintegration of wider family therapy practices. For instance, preliminary evidence suggests that some practices from multi-family therapy can be applied in individual family-based treatment, which may lead to augmentative outcome effects. For instance, in applying the multi-family therapy practice of connecting "beginning parents" with "graduating parents" (Scholz & Asen, 2001) to individual FBT at the start of treatment, positive effects were found in parents' sense of empowerment and perceived capacity to reflect on changes within their family (Rhodes et al., 2009). Furthermore, the introduction of a facilitated online support forum between parents, which is consistent with the emphasis placed on group processes in multi-family therapy for AN, has also been found to augment individual family-based treatment (Binford-Hopf, Le Grange, Moessner, & Bauer, 2013).

However, a dearth of empirical research exists in examining whether the reintegration of alternate wider family therapy practices may broaden the potential scope for change within individual families undergoing FBT in instances when treatment non-response is indicated. In contrast, wider family therapy practices have been shown to exert further therapeutic effects in an array of psychiatric illnesses in adolescents (Andersen, 1987), and more recent developments in the field of family therapy (subsequent to the manualization of FBT) have also been shown to offer augmentative options upon treatment non-response (Rhodes et al., 2011). This chapter therefore proposes several possible augmentations to standard FBT, including clinical case examples, which are drawn from wider family therapy practices and lie consistent with the core theoretical tenets of FBT, evaluating their possible impact in eating disorder-focused family-based treatment. However in attempting to augmentatively integrate any wider family therapy practices into FBT, careful consideration must be given to the extant evidence base which demonstrates that the core theoretical tenets of FBT are directly related to symptom reduction (Ellison et al., 2012). Thus, any augmentations should support rather than corrupt the core principles of FBT.

Reflecting Teams

The concept of reflecting teams was initially developed as a means of helping families move beyond stuck points in treatment, and typically involves a team behind a one-way screen observing the conversation between the interviewer and the family and subsequently sharing their reflections of what they understood with the interviewer in the presence of the family, who observe this clinical conversation (Andersen, 1987). Borne out of Bateson's (1972) writings on epistemology, the overarching aim of this intervention was to share "different views of the same world," helping to foster an "ecology of ideas" for change in how reality is constructed (Andersen, 1987). This innovation was thought to be particularly helpful in the context of families who had become disempowered by the scope for potential change, as the team's reflections typically possess the tendency to positively connote and magnify overlooked familial interactions and strengths.

Why Apply this to FBT?

Families facing AN typically report a high degree of feeling disempowered and "stuck," in addition to parents being coerced away from acknowledging and utilizing their strengths (Eisler, 2005). Thus, the potential introduction of reflecting teams may augment FBT in helping families develop a broader scope for understanding their capacity for change. In addition, the reflecting team's emphasis on not taking control of the therapy process (whilst, however, accepting that they are a part of it) is theoretically consistent with the core tenets of FBT, which aim to decentralize the authority of clinicians in favor of deferring to the authority of parents (Lock & Le Grange, 2013). However, in describing the content of reflecting team feedback, Andersen warned of the potential for inadvertently strengthening families' attachment to their original ideas should the team's reflections *radically* differ from families' original ideas, or if connotations were negative or perceived to be judgmental (Andersen, 1987). Thus careful thought is warranted in ensuring that the team's reflections are speculative rather than definitive, and that the content of reflections are new to the family but not too unusual.

Case Example

Leena was a 15-year-old girl with a 6-month history of restrictive-type AN, who lived with both parents and her elder brother. During five weeks of FBT the family had not made consistent progress in terms of restoring Leena's weight, and the FBT clinician arranged for a reflecting team (two other FBT clinicians) to observe the next meeting with the family. The reflecting team did not know about this case prior to their reflecting team session, although both were experienced FBT practitioners. During the family meeting, it emerged that Leena had lost a further 1.5 lb despite her parents' ongoing efforts to restore her weight. Upon exploring this weight loss, her parents reported that they had been particularly non-united in their re-feeding efforts, which was reportedly becoming increasingly typical leading up to the development of Leena's AN, and it emerged that Leena's father had been away with work for four days over the course of this particular week. In discussing the impact of her father's absence on the therapeutic goals identified the week before, Leena stated that "Dad's work is more important than me." Follow-up discussion revealed that Leena had felt particularly distant from her father throughout the course of AN, and that in seeing how hurt she had been, Leena's mother found it increasingly difficult to be firm in her interventions around her eating.

   During the reflecting team session, the reflecting team met with the FBT clinician in the presence of the family, and discussed their thoughts regarding the meeting. The team wondered about the history of Leena's relationship with her father, and the FBT clinician reported that Leena had encountered profound difficulties in adapting to her father's transition into managing part-ner of his law firm, previously describing herself as a "daddy's girl." The team shared their own experiences of working with families, noting the difficulties fathers often face in maintaining closeness with their daughters as they pro-gress through various stages of adolescence, particularly in the context of AN, and how *different types* of close relationship may often emerge. The team also wondered about the effect of this distancing in their father–daughter relation-ship on Leena's father, noting that he too may likely be feeling hurt, and fur-ther wondering whether this distancing impacted his perceived authority as a parent. The team finished off by pondering whether the presence of AN may be partially functioning to provide an invitation for Leena's father to step back into a closer role in her life.

In reflecting upon the reflecting team meeting, the family, who were all tear-ful, reported "much deeper insights into what might be going on." In particu-lar, Leena's father reflected upon how lonely it must feel for Leena to have "lost her father at the time when she needed him the most." In the weeks that followed he was able to assert firm boundaries around his work schedule, was present for all of Leena's meals, and also decided to build in some "quality father–daughter time" with her twice a week. Leena's mother decided to take up the same practice with Leena, and both parents individually extended this practice to their son. Leena demonstrated consistent weight gain over the next eight weeks, at which time she reached 98 percent of her expected body weight.

Collegial Systemic Processes

The working alliance between mental health professionals in delivering evidence-based treatments has been of significant concern for many years, with reports of interprofessional conflict being common (Berg, 1986). However, with much research documenting the impact of therapist–patient alliance (Forsberg et al., 2014), and patient–patient alliance in group therapy (Budman et al., 1989), relatively little research has explored the effect of alliance between mental health colleagues upon treatment outcome. Recent and preliminary evidence suggests that, in the context of multi-disciplinary patient care, a focus on helping clinicians develop an understanding of the wider relational processes amongst those involved in the care of their patients may help clinicians move beyond stuck points with their patients (Rhodes et al., 2011). For instance, in the context of caring for those with intellectual difficulties (who typically require clinical involvement from a multitude of services), a "systemic consultation" has been shown to be effective in aiding clinicians move forward with their case, assisting in the development of a richer understanding of the potential collegial restraints to effective intervention (Rhodes et al., 2011). This systemic consultation involves clinicians presenting "stuck" cases to a team of colleagues, who interview the clinician about their case, paying particular attention to the relationships between those being cared for and those caring for them (including the presenting clinician), hypothesizing as to how these collegial relationships may present barriers to effective therapeutic intervention (ibid). Whilst not replicated in controlled trials or in the context of other psychopathologies, this systemic intervention may offer important insights into addressing the impact of collegial alliance on interprofessional patient care.

Why Apply this to FBT?

In illuminating the factors that may impinge upon the efficacy of FBT, recent efforts have begun to investigate the systemic processes amongst the team of clinicians involved in the system of care (Murray, Griffiths & Le Grange, 2014; Murray, Thornton, & Wallis, 2012). Due to their multidimensional nature, the treatment of eating disorders typically involves a wide-ranging team that may span institutional and professional boundaries, and may frequently include psychiatrists, clinical psychologists, social workers, dieticians, pediatricians, and clinical nursing staff alike. This array of practitioners is particularly noteworthy when considering the potential for varying approaches to treatment amongst practitioners and the potential scope for inconsistent messages given to families. For instance, an FBT practitioner working towards the empowerment of parents into an authoritative role may run counter-intuitive to a colleague's goal of working towards the individuation of an unwell adolescent, or another colleague's aim of giving the parents a meal plan to feed their child (Murray, Griffiths, Thornton & Le Grange, 2015a). In this sense, FBT is thought to be particularly vulnerable to "systemic sticking points" amongst the clinicians themselves, as the high degree of parental anxiety, the volume of difficult decisions parents are required to make, and the often disempowered nature of families facing anorexia nervosa may naturally align families with team members who do not require such challenging parental involvement, thus undermining the FBT therapist (Murray et al., 2012, 2015a), and rendering treatment less effective (Murray et al., 2014). Indeed, preliminary evidence suggests that collegial alliance amongst team members involved in coordinating FBT may discriminate between those who drop out and those who complete treatment, and is also positively correlated with the remission of cognitive AN symptomatology (Murray, Griffiths & Le Grange, 2014). Thus, the application of colleague-oriented systemic practices may be particularly indicated in the context of FBT, assisting clinicians in navigating beyond the wider collegial barriers that may deleteriously impact treatment outcome.

Case Example

Trisha was a 16-year-old girl whose family sought FBT following discharge from an inpatient admission in the context of a three-month history of restrictive-type AN. Upon commencing FBT she made rapid progress in the first two weeks, continuing to gain weight beyond discharge weight from hospital, further demonstrating stabilized eating under the guidance of her parents. However, following these first two weeks of FBT, the family therapist noted a sense of disengagement from Trisha's parents, who demonstrated more reluctance in engaging in conversations surrounding their potential interventions to restore Trisha's health. This shift persisted for several weeks, and Trisha's early weight gain first plateaued, and then started to reverse. In attempting to re-mobilize the parents, the family therapist had engineered a second parental anxiety-raising session, hoping to further underscore the centrality of their involvement in their daughter's recovery in this grave situation. However, in response to this session, the parents informed the therapist that they were thinking of dropping out of psychological treatment, in favor of proceeding with the family pediatrician.

At this point, the family therapist requested a team meeting with other family therapy colleagues to discuss the potential complexities of this case. The family therapist was interviewed by two other members of the team, and aimed to outline (i) a visual illustration of everyone involved in Trisha's care, (ii) the history of each person's involvement, (iii) the relationships between each person involved in Trisha's care, including her parents, (iv) the history of Trisha's eating disorder, and (v) any broader family events. Throughout this interview it emerged that two weeks after commencing FBT, Trisha and her parents had attended a pre-arranged post-discharge appointment with their pediatrician. The timing of this visit coincided with the point in treatment at which the family therapist noted a shift away from the family's rapid start towards a more disengaged approach towards FBT. The team hypothesized that, of everyone involved in Trisha's care, the parents might share their closest relationship with Trisha's lifelong pediatrician, who had acted swiftly in recognizing Trisha's emerging eating disorder to avert a potentially life-threatening crisis. As such, the team wondered aloud about the benefits of contacting Trisha's pediatrician and asking for her thoughts regarding the sudden stuck point in treatment.

During this call with Trisha's pediatrician it emerged that she held strong views about the efficacy of FBT, after having had several patients die from complications related to AN throughout her career. In one of these cases, the pediatrician had attempted to assist in the completion of a meal with a patient. During this meal, in the pediatrician's office, the patient "turned on" the pediatrician, and attacked her, reporting that she was unable to complete her meal because of the extra pressure the pediatrician had exerted. Not long after this, the patient died. In discussing Trisha's treatment, the pediatrician stated several times that "Trisha cannot be force-fed into recovery, as she has to *want* to recover for herself." For this reason, the pediatrician recommended "that the parents back off from controlling her food," in favor of supporting Trisha's attempts to pursue her own recovery. Following this disclosure, the family therapist was able to discuss treatment philosophies with the pediatrician, and share empirical articles outlining FBT as the first-line treatment for adolescent AN. Following this, Trisha's pediatrician vowed to support FBT, and the role of the parents in treatment, and Trisha's weight trajectory began to incline once again.

Definitional Ceremonies and Re-Authoring Conversations

One of the central tenets of narrative therapy, which played a significant role in the development of FBT, posits that the narratives and discourses told about our lives contribute to the shaping of our identity (White, 2007). Thus, the objectification of problems as separate to oneself (via externalization of the problem) allows one to develop an identity that is separate from the problem

(White, 1984). However, a crucial step in the active construction of preferred identities and realities, which follows the separation and externalization of "problem-saturated life stories or narratives," is the shared construction of preferred narratives that are more congruent with one's strengths (White, 2007). To this end, White and colleagues developed a specific set of "re-authoring conversations" to locate the historical origins of personal strengths and preferred narratives, which involve the tracing of specific events, both in terms of behaviors undertaken and the intentions when undertaking them. Throughout these re-authoring conversations, the therapist may orient their questions/inquiry along the dimension of "the landscape of action" (i.e. what the person did) and the "landscape of consciousness" (i.e. the intentions behind what the person did). Collectively, these conversations typically aim to "thicken" or develop alternate life narratives that do not centrally implicate an individual's symptoms or difficulties, instead centralizing the person's strengths and qualities that may have been overlooked as a result of the overwhelming presence of their symptom profile.

"Definitional ceremonies" refer to a specific type of re-authoring conversation in which the patient, family member, or therapist invites "outsider witnesses" to take part in a conversation that details a person's (usually the patient's) life story, paying particular attention to exploring and inviting the telling of stories that are reflective of their preferred identity and not necessarily their current problems. Subsequent to this interview the outsider witnesses, who remain in a silent observing role throughout the interview, are invited to re-tell the person's story with the family present, sharing their reflections on aspects of the person's life story that most touched them, whether what they heard evoked any feelings from specific times in their lives, and how they think hearing the person's story will impact their own life (ibid). Following such conversations, those sharing their story may report a sense of validation that helps reinvigorate a preferred sense of identity, and a "lifting of the fog" beyond stuck points in treatment (ibid).

Why Apply this to FBT?

This influence of narrative therapy practices can be clearly observed throughout FBT, through the importance attached to externalizing "the anorexia" as separate from the adolescent. In FBT, the process of externalization is thought to be crucial in alleviating parental guilt, which likely reduces expressed criticism of the child and reduces treatment dropout (Le Grange, Eisler, Dare, & Hodes, 1992), and is empirically reflected in the direct effect of externalization upon treatment outcome (Ellison et al., 2012). However, despite the critical importance of externalizing AN-saturated narratives throughout FBT, therapeutic practices that actively facilitate the re-authoring of preferred identities and realities are absent from FBT. As such, only one half of the re-authoring process (i.e. the externalization of problem-saturated narratives) is included in FBT. This is particularly noteworthy given that difficulty in negotiating a new identity has been cited as a significant barrier to long-term recovery from AN (Lamoureux & Bottorff, 2005). Thus, the rationale for the integration of re-authoring practices such as definitional ceremonies into FBT seems apparent, and is conceptually very similar to externalization of "the anorexia." Further, the inclusion of re-authoring conversations also retains the theoretical agnosticism of FBT, and may help adolescents develop a preferred sense of identity (separate from AN) during the later stages of FBT treatment, which facilitates ongoing adolescent development and reduces the potential scope for relapse.

Case Example

Delilah was a 16-year-old girl who had struggled with AN for approximately three years. She had undergone individual courses of cognitive behavioral therapy and interpersonal therapy, and experienced little symptom remission throughout each course of treatment. Upon becoming aware of the evidence base for FBT, her family sought FBT and commenced treatment with an experienced family therapist. Delilah was entrenched in her illness, and referred to her eating disorder as part of her identity, stating that she "wouldn't know who she was without it." Upon commencing FBT, progress was inconsistent and challenging, although over a period of six months her parents managed to restore her weight to the developmentally adjusted expected weight. However, this restoration of body weight was not met with any accompanying shift in the steadfastness of her eating disorder cognitions, and perhaps expectedly, attempts at fostering Delilah's own ability to manage her food intake was met with marked reductions in her weight. In discussing these downward spirals in her weight, Delilah's parents expressed grave concerns, noting that treatment had done little to impact her "anorexic mindset." Similarly, Delilah herself emphasized the importance of being anorexic because "that's all I am good at now."

In embarking upon a re-authoring conversation, the therapist first sought to trace the origin of AN, paying careful attention to externalizing it and referring to it as separate from Delilah, mapping the impact of AN upon Delilah's life, portraying the AN as a tyrant who crept into Delilah's life without invitation and caused widespread devastation. During this conversation, in which Delilah's parents actively participated, it emerged that the AN had robbed Delilah of her budding sporting prowess, her circle of friends, and her first boyfriend. Additionally, Delilah's almost perfect grades dipped significantly when she became unwell, and her most prized domains of self-efficacy (i.e. athletic performance, school grades, and gregarious nature) were attacked.

Further to these disclosures, the therapist lingered over the question of how both Delilah and those close to her defined her identity before she met the anorexia. This conversation revealed that Delilah held strong feminist beliefs, and was described by her parents as somebody with "lots of integrity, who knew her values, and was prepared to stand up and defend them." Delilah traced these characteristics as far back as seven years of age, when she remonstrated with a school teacher that girls should be allowed to play on the same basketball team as the boys. In recalling this particular incident, Delilah described how she opted to speak up and make a stand for herself and her friends, who enjoyed basketball but couldn't play competitively since the school district did not have a girls' league. Her parents recalled earlier seeds of this character in pre-school, when she would approach children who had snatched toys from other children and make them return them. Many more examples emerged, all of which depicted Delilah as a strong and courageous young woman, who was fearless in the pursuit of following her values.

Following the description of Delilah's true character, the therapist invited Delilah and her family to discuss how the value system of AN relates to the emerging young woman Delilah was becoming. The family noted the irony of how AN had turned a once-aspiring feminist into the personification of the unrealistic objectified female body, which was propagated mainly by males, and was the antithesis of feminism. This resonated with Delilah, who for the first time throughout treatment became angry with the AN. Delilah added that AN had tricked her into thinking that being thinner would make her more attractive, more popular, and more likeable, and for the first time she acknowledged that she would prefer to be the old Delilah. In elaborating upon the person she wished to be, Delilah described a strong, independent woman who was not only able to withstand societal pressure to conform, but was also able to rise up and oppose it. This conversation marked the *re-definition* of Delilah, who vowed to break free of the oppressive shackles of AN and reclaim her value system. Over the following weeks and months, this preferred identity was nurtured and further developed as close family members and friends were invited in to treatment sessions to narrate their own story of Delilah's strengths. Delilah was also encouraged to write letters to herself from the vantage point of being fully recovered, allowing her to immerse herself in her preferred identity whilst encouraging herself beyond challenging moments in the course of recovery. Treatment continued for several more months after this definitional ceremony and Delilah was able to make a full recovery, reconnect with the identity she felt was her true identity, and be empowered by her commitment to her values, in spite of a psychiatric condition that enforced self-objectification.

Videotape Feedback

FBT posits that the overwhelming presence of AN within families is so powerful that it may result in structural changes within family functioning (Eisler, 2005). Whilst parents themselves are thought to possess the necessary skills and instincts to feed their unwell child, the AN-induced coercion away from their instincts may inadvertently help organize family life around AN (promoting the power of the unwell child within the family system), thus accommodating any structural changes brought about by the illness. As such, the realigning of these structural changes is a crucial endeavor throughout treatment, such that parents are freed to once again rely on their natural instincts and authority as parents. Indeed, several key tenets of FBT are oriented, to an extent, towards encouraging families to revisit any structural changes brought about by AN, including parental control, parental unity, and sibling support.

In the history of family therapy, videotape feedback of home-based family interactions around problem behaviors has been used effectively to identify structural changes occurring within family systems as a result of problem behavior (Haley, 1971). The identification of alliances, coalitions, and complex behavioral sequences around challenging behavior through videotape feedback has been demonstrated to result in enhanced parental capacity and efficacy in coping with children who demonstrate challenging behaviors (Meharg & Lipsker, 1991), leading to self-reported improvements in conduct and a direct reduction in problematic behaviors (Webster-Stratton, 1992).

Why Apply this to FBT?

Given the high propensity for structural adaptations and modified family functioning in families facing AN (Eisler, 2005), the use of videotape feedback may be particularly indicated throughout FBT, where particular family sequences (around food consumption) are magnified and focused on during treatment sessions. The placing of family members in an observing stance (rather than the experiential and participating stance of being questioned directly) may better position family members to develop their own objective understanding of family interactions occurring around AN, which is consistent with the theoretical underpinnings of FBT, emphasizing the role of empowering families in their own process of change. Similar techniques have been implemented in multi-family therapy for AN, in which familial interactions often take place under the "fishbowl"-like observation of other group members, with feedback being offered. Indeed, observations of and feedback on family interactions constitute one of the central features of multi-family therapy for AN (Scholz & Asen, 2001), and its integration into FBT may be expected to bring about augmentative effects.

Case Example

Donny was a 14-year-old boy with a three-month history of restrictive-type AN. Donny and his family underwent a course of FBT, although after six weeks of treatment his weight gain had been very modest, and he did not show early signs of a favorable treatment response (Le Grange et al., 2014). For several weeks, Donny's parents left each treatment session with sensible interventions planned around both the caloric volume of food and the level of supervision required in ensuring proper food consumption. However, each week they reported that they were unable to carry out their plans effectively. In discussing the barriers to executing their well-made plans, each parent held the other one accountable for Donny's lack of progress. Donny's father reported that his mother "abandoned the plans when the going got tough, and was more concerned with Donny feeling okay," whereas Donny's mother reported that his father "became almost militant and hostile in feeding Donny, and didn't care about how hard it was for him." This pattern prevailed for several weeks, and the therapist was unable to engineer reflective conversations around each parent's role without a highly primed defensiveness emerging. Further, attempts to encourage each parent to reflect on the other's observations resulted in each parent suggesting that the therapist was aligning with the other and insinuating that the therapist was doing a bad job in caring for their son.

As such, the therapist recommended that the family use their cell phones to record each meal at home throughout the week, and suggested a parent-only meeting where they brought in footage of the most challenging meal. Additionally, the therapist invited the parents to sit and review the most challenging meal from each day. At the planned parent-only meeting, Donny's parents then presented as being much more united and reported gaining great benefit from watching daily footage of their family's interaction around food. In reviewing footage with the therapist, Donny's parents pointed out that he would respond to instructions issued by his father during meals by turning to his mother and complaining that his father was too hard on him. This commonly resulted in his mother initiating a conversation with Donny's father about whether they needed to follow through his suggestion entirely. The therapist further discussed this sequence with the parents, who reasoned that this interaction was effectively aligning Donny and his mother, leaving his father feeling undermined and "standing alone on what they agreed on in therapy." As a result, Donny's father became quickly frustrated with his mother, and compensated for her "leaving the ranks" by becoming more firm and angry with Donny, which, in turn, caused his mother to become more protective to compensate for his father's firmness. They realized that Donny was successfully coming between them and turning them against each other, and that they had allowed themselves to be divided and rendered less effective. As a result of these observations and insights, Donny's parents developed scripts before each meal, and planned how to respond to Donny's behavior without dividing themselves. As such, they were able to be much more effective in carrying out their plans, and Donny's weight went up accordingly.

Concluding Comments

FBT is currently established as the first-line evidence-based treatment for adolescent anorexia nervosa, with an accumulating body of evidence demonstrating impressive rates of symptom remission in medically stable adolescents with short illness duration (Le Grange et al., 2012; Lock et al.,

2010). However, equally consistent findings have demonstrated that a consistent minority of patients do not experience full symptom remission during a standard course of FBT (Fisher et al., 2010; Lock et al., 2010), which has necessitated a shift in empirical focus towards the identification of augmentative treatment interventions that may enhance outcome in instances in which FBT is less likely to bring about symptom remission. Indeed, current research has advocated for a thorough understanding of the mediators and moderators of treatment outcome in FBT, identifying sub-groups of patients for whom FBT may be less effective, and further identifying therapeutic processes that may enhance or inhibit treatment (Le Grange et al., 2010; Murray, Loeb & Le Grange, 2015b).

What is currently clear is that under conditions in which FBT is less likely to result in symptom remission, or when early treatment progress indicates likely treatment non-response, an intensified form of treatment is warranted. We argue that, in intensifying FBT, augmentative practices may seek to examine the potential efficacy of wider and pre-existing family therapy practices, which had previously been utilized in the treatment of adolescent AN prior to the manualization of FBT. However, in light of the impressive body of evidence supporting the use of FBT, demonstrating that the core tenets of FBT are directly related to favorable treatment outcome (Ellison et al., 2012), it should also be underscored that FBT ought to remain as the starting point for treatment, and that augmentative measures complement rather than contaminate the core theoretical principles of FBT. Furthermore, we also recommend that all augmentative adaptations to treatment be subject to rigorous empirical testing before being streamlined into treatment protocol. This may be a particularly crucial endeavor for our field as the developing evidence-base continues to illuminate factors that may mediate and moderate the efficacy of FBT, leading naturally to a greater emphasis on the development of treatment augmentations.

References

Agler, I., & Hogan, P. (1967). The use of videotape recording on involvement in conjoint marital therapy. *American Journal of Psychiatry*, 123, 1425–1429.

Andersen, T. (1987). The reflecting team: Dialogue and meta-dialogue in clinical work. *Family Process*, 26, 415–428.

Bateson, G. (1972). *Steps to an ecology of mind*. New York: Ballatine Books.

Berg, M. (1986). Towards a diagnostic alliance between psychiatrist and psychologist. *American Psychologist*, 41, 52–59.

Binford-Hopf, R. B., Le Grange, D., Moessner, M., & Bauer, S. (2013). Internet-based chat support groups for parents in family-based treatment for adolescent eating disorders: A pilot study. *European Eating Disorder Review*, 21, 215–223.

Budman, S. H., Soldz, S., Demby, A., Feldstein, M., Springer, T., & Davis, M. S. (1989). Cohesion, alliance and outcome in group psychotherapy. *Psychiatry*, 52, 339–350.

Couturier, J., Isserlin, L., & Lock, J. (2010). Family-based treatment for adolescents with anorexia nervosa: A dissemination study. *Eating Disorders*, 18, 199–209.

Dare, C. (1985). The family therapy of anorexia nervosa. *Journal of Psychiatric Research*, 19, 435–453.

Dare, C., & Eisler, I. (2000). A multi-family group day program treatment programme for adolescent eating disorder. *European Eating Disorder Review*, 8, 4–18.

Dare, C., Eisler, I., Russell, G. F. M., & Smuckler, G. L. (1990). The clinical and theoretical impact of a controlled trial of family therapy in anorexia nervosa. *Journal of Marital and Family Therapy*, 16, 39–57.

Dare, C., Le Grange, D., Eisler, I., & Rutherford, J. (1994). Redefining the psychosomatic family: Family processes of 26 eating disorder families. *International Journal of Eating Disorders*, 16, 211–226.

Doyle, P. M., Le Grange, D., Loeb, K., Doyle, A. C., & Crosby, R. D. (2010). Early response to family-based treatment for adolescent anorexia nervosa. *International Journal of Eating Disorders*, 43, 659–662.

Eisler, I. (2005). The empirical and theoretical base of family therapy and multiple family day therapy for adolescent anorexia nervosa. *Journal of Family Therapy*, 27, 104–131.

Eisler, I. (2012). Multiple family therapy for anorexia nervosa. Workshop presented at Eating Disorders: Building Partnerships, May 16, Sydney, Australia.

Ellison, R., Rhodes, P., Madden, S., Miskovic, K., Wallis, A. et al. (2012). Do the components of manualised family-based treatment for anorexia nervosa predict weight gain? *International Journal of Eating Disorders*, 45, 609–614.

Fisher, C. A., Hetrick, S. E., & Rushford. N. (2010). Family therapy for anorexia nervosa (review). *Cochrane Database of Systematic Reviews*, Issue 6.

Forsberg, S., Lo Tempio, E., Bryson, S., Fitzpatrick, K., Le Grange, D., & Lock, J. (2014). Parent–therapist alliance in family-based treatment for adolescents with anorexia nervosa. *European Eating Disorders Review*, 22, 53–58.

Haley, J. (1971). *Changing families: A family therapy reader*. New York: Grune & Stratton.

Lamoureux, M. H., & Bottorff, J. L. (2005). Becoming the real me: Recovering from anorexia nervosa. *Health Care for Women International*, 26, 170–188.

Lasegue, E. (1883). De l'anorexie hysterique. *Archives Generales de Medecine*, 21, 384–403.

Le Grange, D., & Eisler, I. (2009). Family interventions in adolescent anorexia nervosa. *Child and Adolescent Psychiatric Clinics of North America*, 18, 159–173.

Le Grange, D., Accurso, E., Lock, J., Agras, W. S., & Bryson, S. W. (2014). Early weight gain predicts outcome in two treatments for adolescent anorexia nervosa. *International Journal of Eating Disorders*, 129.

Le Grange, D., Eisler, I., Dare, C., & Hodes, M. (1992). Family criticism and self-starvation: A study of expressed emotion. *Journal of Family Therapy*, 14, 177–192.

Le Grange, D., Lock, J., Agras, W. S., Moye, A., Bryson, S. W. et al. (2012). Moderators and mediators of remission in family-based treatment and adolescent focussed therapy for anorexia nervosa. *Behavior Research and Therapy*, 50, 85–92.

Le Grange, D., Lock, J., Loeb, K., & Nicholls, D. (2010). Academy for eating disorders position paper: The role of the family in eating disorders. *International Journal of Eating Disorders*, 43, 1–5.

Lock, J., & Le Grange, D. (2013). *Treatment manual for anorexia nervosa: A family-based approach*, Second edition. New York: Guilford Press.

Lock, J., Couturier, J., & Agras, W. S. (2006). Comparison of long term outcomes in adolescents with anorexia nervosa treated with family therapy. *Journal of the American Academy of Child and Adolescent Psychiatry*, 45, 666–672.

Lock, J., Le Grange, D., Agras, W. S., & Dare, C. (2001). *Treatment manual for anorexia nervosa: A family-based approach*. New York: Guilford Press.

Lock, J., Le Grange, D., Agras, W. S., Moye, A., Bryson, S. W., & Jo, B. (2010). Randomized clinical trial comparing family-based treatment with adolescent-focussed individual therapy for adolescents with anorexia nervosa. *Archives of General Psychiatry*, 67, 1025–1032.

Meharg, S. S., & Lipsker, L. E. (1991). Parent training using videotape self-modelling. *Child & Family Behavior Therapy*, 13, 1–26.

Minuchin, S., Rosman, B., & Baker, L. (1978). *Psychosomatic families: Anorexia nervosa in context.* Cambridge, MA: Harvard University Press.

Murray, S. B., Griffiths, S., & Le Grange, D. (2014). The role of collegial alliance in family-based treatment of adolescent anorexia nervosa: A pilot study. *International Journal of Eating Disorders*, 47, 418–421.

Murray, S. B., Griffiths, S., Thornton, C., & Le Grange, D. (2015a). Collegial alliance and family-based treatment for adolescent anorexia nervosa: A qualitative report of three cases. *Advances in Eating Disorders: Theory, Research & Practice*, 3, 251–258.

Murray, S. B., Loeb, K., & Le Grange, D. (2015b). Mediators and moderators of treatment outcome in adolescent eating disorders. In M. Maric, P. J. M., Prins, & T. H. Ollendick (Eds.), *Mediators and moderators of youth treatment outcomes*. New York: Oxford University Press.

Murray, S. B., Thornton, C., & Wallis, A. (2012). A thorn in the side of evidence-based treatment of adolescent anorexia nervosa. *Australian & New Zealand Journal of Psychiatry*, 46, 1026–1028.

Papp, P. (1980). The Greek chorus and other techniques of paradoxical therapy. *Family Process*, 19, 45–57.

Rhodes, P., Brown, J., & Madden, S. (2009). The Maudsley model of family-based treatment for anorexia nervosa: Qualitative evaluation of parent-to-parent consultations. *Journal of Marital and Family Therapy*, 35, 181–192.

Rhodes, P., Whatson, L., Mora, L., Hansson, A., Brearley, K., & Dikian, J. (2011). Systemic hypothesising for challenging behaviour in intellectual disabilities: A reflecting team approach. *Australian & New Zealand Journal of Family Therapy*, 32, 70–82.

Scholz, M., & Asen, E. (2001). Multiple family therapy with eating disordered adolescents: Concepts and preliminary results. *European Eating Disorders Review*, 9, 33–42.

Selvini Palazzoli, M. (1974). *Self-starvation: From the intrapsychic to transpersonal approach.* London: Chaucer.

Strober, M., & Johnson, G. J. (2012). The need for complex ideas in anorexia nervosa: Why biology, environment, and psyche all matter, why therapists make mistakes, and why clinical benchmarks are needed for managing weight correction. *International Journal of Eating Disorders*, 45, 155–178.

Webster-Stratton, C. (1992). Individually administered videotape parent training: Who benefits? *Cognitive Therapy and Research*, 16, 31–35.

White, M. (1984). Pseudo-encopresis: From avalanche to victory. From vicious to virtuous cycles. *Journal of Family Systems Medicine*, 2, 150–160.

White, M. (1987). Anorexia nervosa: A cybernetic perspective. *Family Therapy Collections*, 20, 117–129.

White, M. (2007). *Maps of narrative practice*. New York: Norton.

10 When Family Therapy Isn't Enough

New Treatment Directions for Highly Anxious and Dysregulated Adolescents with Anorexia Nervosa

Mima Simic, Leslie Karwoski Anderson, Laura A. Berner, Stephanie Knatz Peck, Katrina Hunt, Walter H. Kaye, and Ivan Eisler

Introduction

Eating disorders-focused family therapy (FT-AN)[1] has been shown through about a dozen randomized controlled trials (RCTs) to be the first-line treatment for adolescents with anorexia nervosa (AN) (Couturier et al., 2013). Studies show that FT-AN leads to full remission by the end of treatment in between 35 and 50 percent of patients (Lock, 2015), while between 10 and 40 percent have a poor outcome (Le Grange et al., 2014; Lock, 2015). Thus, there is a need to modify the standard family treatment or add additional elements to address the needs of adolescents who do not respond to existing family therapy treatment approaches.

A few studies have attempted to delineate the factors that moderate response to treatment for adolescents with AN. Two sets of factors have been linked to poorer outcomes in the literature: (1) overall severity of coexisting psychopathology, such as obsessionality, anxiety, or depression; and (2) family functioning impairment and emotional dysregulation.

It is not exactly clear why adolescents with higher levels of anxiety and obsessionality, or those with pronounced emotional and behavioral dysregulation tend to be more treatment refractory. Examining the literature on neurobiology of AN and its comorbid disorders as well as the literature on attachment relationships in families with AN offers some possible directions for treatment modification, development, and augmentation. Neuroimaging research in individuals without AN suggests that efficacious individual psychotherapy for anxiety and dysregulation potentiates brain-based changes in patients (Brooks & Stein, 2015; Goodman et al., 2014). No studies to date have examined the brain-based effects of psychotherapy for AN; however, existing neuroimaging findings support two forms of modification to standard FT-AN for treatment-refractory adolescents: (1) adding individual therapy to target the same neural circuitries that are altered in the treatments for anxiety disorders and behavioral and affective dysregulation; and (2) modifying family-based interventions to promote behavior change in highly anxious or dysregulated adolescents to either alter their neurobiology or, if this cannot be achieved, helping parents and adolescents to manage it. Temperament, by definition, is very difficult to change; however, individual therapeutic interventions targeted to specific personality traits appear important in helping people to cope better with their temperamental characteristics and tendencies (Kaye et al., 2015), and may impact neural impairments. At the same time, it is just as important to target interventions towards parents, so that they can support their child's recovery in a way that takes into account the powerful neurobiology involved. In families where there are unresolved attachment or other difficult relationship issues, these may need to be addressed early on in treatment in order to facilitate behavioral change in the young person.

To explore the issue of non-response in family therapy for eating disorders, we will review factors that have been shown to moderate treatment response in FT-AN, how the biological bases of some of these factors may not be addressed by current family therapy for eating disorders, and modifications to treatment that have been trialed with the aim of improving response in these groups. We will then propose a framework for enhanced treatment modifications and explore directions for the future.

Anxiety and Obsessionality

Roughly two-thirds of individuals with eating disorders have also had an anxiety disorder or obsessive-compulsive disorder (Kaye et al., 2004). Many obsessive, depressive, and anxiety symptoms encountered at treatment initiation are associated with starvation and preoccupation with anorexic cognitions and usually greatly improve after weight gain and disruption of maintaining behaviors over time (Pollice, Kaye, Greeno, & Weltzin, 1997). However, anxiety, harm avoidance, depression, and obsessive-compulsive symptoms are often also present before the onset of the eating disorder and commonly persist after remission and, for those whose anxiety does not remit as the eating disorder behaviors resolve, recovery may be much more difficult to maintain (Holtkamp, Mueller, Heussen, Remschmidt, & Herpertz-Dahlmann, 2005; Wagner et al., 2006).

A growing body of evidence suggests that the severity of eating-related psychopathology, but even more so, the degree of anxiety and obsessionality, moderates treatment outcome in family therapy for eating disorders. Lock and colleagues' 2006 study on predictors of dropout and remission in family therapy found that comorbid psychiatric symptoms of depression, anxiety, and obsessionality (as measured by the Yale-Brown-Cornell Eating Disorder Scale – YBC-ED) led to higher dropout and lower rates of remission

In Agras and colleagues' (2014) study comparing FT-AN with a more generic systemic family therapy (SyFT), adolescents with higher levels of obsessionality demonstrated at baseline higher levels of eating pathology, depression, anxiety, and compensatory behaviors, and had poorer outcomes in FT-AN than adolescents with lower levels of obsessionality. Adolescents with higher obsessionality gained significantly more weight in SyFT, implying that the broader focus of treatment may better address obsessional or anxiety symptoms leading to better outcome of the eating disorder. Thus, research indicates that high anxiety, depressive symptoms, and obsessionality moderate treatment outcomes in family-based interventions for adolescents with AN and that a broader focus on more than just eating and weight normalization may be necessary in these cases.

Family Functioning Impairment and Emotional Dysregulation

While early models of family therapy for eating disorders assumed that there was an underlying family dysfunction (Minuchin, Rosman, & Baker, 1978) that the therapy had to address, this assumption has not been supported by empirical findings (Konstantellou & Campbell, 2011). More recent models (for example, Eisler, Wallis, & Dodge, 2015) focus on the process of family reorganization in response to the ED, which may undermine parental sense of competence and/or serve to maintain the disorder. Self-ratings from patients and their family members report some impairment in one or more areas of family functioning, but on average these tend to be only slightly elevated compared to community norms and generally normalize with improvements in the eating disorder (Ciao, Accurso, Fitzsimmons-Craft, Lock, & Le Grange, 2015). There are, however, consistent findings that family functioning impairment, particularly family conflict, parental criticism, and hostility, are associated with treatment dropout and poor treatment outcome (Szmurker, Eisler, Russell, & Dare, 1985; van Furth et al., 1996) or may moderate response to different forms of family intervention (Eisler et al., 2000; Eisler, Simic, Russell, & Dare, 2007). For instance, a study comparing separated and conjoint family therapy for AN noted a particularly important role for maternal criticism (ibid). At end of treatment and at five-year follow-up, families with raised levels of maternal criticism had shown the least improvement in core eating disorder symptoms, including lack of weight gain and persistent amenorrhea, particularly if they were seen in conjoint family sessions.

Research suggests that greater family functioning impairment is found with more severe ED pathology, and that in addition young people with the binge eating/purging subtype of AN (AN-BP) have overall worse outcome in FT-AN compared to the restrictive subtype (Agras et al., 2014; Le Grange et al., 2012). There are a number of possible explanations for these findings but recent research suggests that key areas might be difficulties in emotional regulation (Anestis, Selby, Fink, & Joiner, 2007; Selby, Anestis, & Joiner, 2008; Selby et al., 2015) and/or the quality of the adolescents' attachment to their parents (Jewell et al., 2015). For instance, Pace, Cacioppo, and Schimmenti (2012) found that a group of late-adolescents who reported binge eating symptoms scored significantly lower on secure attachment, while on the insecure attachment subscales, they had significantly higher scores on the preoccupied and fearful subscales of the attachment measure, but not on the avoidant subscale. The link between attachment and emotional dysregulation is also highlighted by Van Durme, Braet, and Goossens (2014), who found that maladaptive emotional regulation mediated the effect of attachment avoidance and anxiety on eating restraint and eating pathology.

These findings suggest that family functioning, especially high parental criticism and/or hostility, insecure attachment, and emotional dysregulation, are potentially important moderators and possibly also mediators of treatment that may need to be directly targeted in treatment with some families.

Conceptualizing Comorbid Anxiety and Obsessionality

Neurobiology

Premorbid anxiety is associated with more severe AN illness trajectories and lower lifetime BMIs (Dellava et al., 2010; Raney et al., 2008), and a genetic predisposition to more extreme anxiety may serve as a risk factor for treatment-resistant AN (Bloss et al., 2011; Dellava et al., 2010; Raney et al., 2008). After illness onset, individuals with AN have increased frequency of comorbid anxiety disorders and anxious mood (Kaye et al., 2004; Raney et al., 2008), exaggerated anxiety related to food and eating (Steinglass, Walsh, & Stern, 2006), elevated intolerance of uncertainty (Frank et al., 2012), and exaggerated harm avoidance (HA), which is a multifaceted temperament trait that contains elements of anxiety, inhibition, and inflexibility (Cassin & von Ranson, 2005; Klump et al., 2004; Lilenfeld, 2011; Wagner et al., 2006).

The brain-based mechanisms that are likely to contribute to pervasive anxiety and obsessionality in AN may shed light on why these characteristics are associated with poor response in FT-AN and inform the development and additions of adapted and novel treatments. Anxiety and HA in adult AN are associated with altered function, particularly of dopamine (DA) and serotonin (5-HT), in brain regions classically implicated in anxious, avoidant behaviors – dorsal caudate (DC) and limbic regions (Bailer et al., 2012a, 2005; Frank et al., 2005; Kaye, Wierenga, Bailer, Simmons, & Bischoff-Grethe, 2013). For example, DC DA release is normally associated with an experience of euphoria (Brauer & de Wit, 1996; Gabbay, 2003), but in women remitted from AN, DA release in the DC was associated with increased anxiety (Bailer et al., 2012b). If individuals with AN, even after remission, experience DA release as anxiogenic, rather than enjoyable, it may explain avoidance of food and eating as an effective way of diminishing such aversive feelings, especially among individuals high in obsessionality and anxiety.

Limbic DA signals are also involved in the anticipation of upcoming stimuli and it has been shown that individuals with AN experience elevated levels of anxiety in anticipation of eating, and increased anticipatory anxiety predicts reduced food intake (Steinglass et al., 2010). Neuroimaging data have shown that individuals ill with, and remitted from, AN have similar exaggerated anticipatory brain responses to both food cues and pain (for a review, see Kaye et al., 2013). The brains of individuals with AN, even after remission, may anticipate and encode food as both aversive and dangerous. Thus, restriction may be an inhibitory response pursued in an effort to avoid the expected negative consequences of eating (Steinglass et al., 2010) that can interfere with AN recovery.

Treatment Modifications for Comorbid Anxiety and Obsessionality

Given the poorer prognosis observed for adolescents with anxiety and AN, and the associated high rates of comorbidity (Kaye et al., 2004), finding improved ways to address this treatment-interfering moderator may improve overall rates of remission from AN and, further, may broaden the range of individuals for whom currently available treatments such as FT-AN are effective. This section will outline treatment directions for adolescents who present with strong comorbid anxiety and obsessionality, and their parents.

CBT for anxiety following weight restoration

Research has shown that being over-anxious is a risk factor for the development of an eating disorder (Bulik, Sullivan, Fear, & Joyce, 1997), that anxiety leads to higher dropouts from treatment and lower rates of remission (Lock et al., 2006), and if anxiety does not remit during treatment, recovery may be much more difficult to maintain (Holtkamp, Mueller, Heussen, Remschmidt, & Herpertz-Dahlmann, 2005; Wagner et al., 2006). Studies have confirmed that anxiety in young people with AN most commonly takes the form of social phobia and generalized anxiety disorder (GAD) (Godart, Flament, Lecrubier, & Jeammet, 2000; Kaye et al., 2004). CBT is an effective treatment for anxiety disorders in children and adolescents (Compton et al., 2004) and, more specifically, the treatment target in CBT for GAD (Dugas, Gagnon, Ladouceur, & Freeston, 1998) is the intolerance of uncertainty, which has been found to be elevated in AN (Frank et al., 2012). In order to test if it is possible to reduce the level of anxiety and improve overall treatment outcome in the subgroup of patients who fulfilled criteria for comorbid non-remittent GAD, we conducted a pilot case series study (Simic, Eisler, Bevan, & Perrin, unpublished data) by adding CBT for GAD after initial weight gain in FT-AN. CBT was a manualized 10-session treatment, based on the cognitive model of worry developed by Dugas et al. (1998). In addition to intolerance of uncertainty, treatment also targeted cognitive avoidance, positive beliefs about worry, and negative problem orientation. Behavior experiments and imaginal exposure were set up by therapists for patients to trial in and outside of sessions. When parents were involved in sessions, their role was to support adolescents in conducting behavioral experiments at home. All adolescents who participated in the study, aged 13–17, fulfilled the diagnosis of GAD and experienced significant levels of anxiety and worries not related to their eating disorder prior to starting CBT. However, once CBT treatment started, the main issues identified as causing anxiety tended to be around food or weight, thus making it difficult for the young people to identify and engage in experiments around generalized fears and worries, both in and out of sessions. Though all participants showed consistent reduction of severity of anxiety and improvement in psychological well-being over the course of CBT on a number of self-report measures, nonetheless the overall response to treatment was qualitatively different compared to young people treated under the same conditions with GAD who did not have comorbid AN. Clinical impressions suggested that it took young people with AN longer to engage in behavioral experiments and generalize to other situations as compared to non-AN GAD cases. Nevertheless, unlike non-AN GAD cases, the behavioral experiments were the most important factor in creating change as they found it even more difficult to engage in imaginal exposure to the feared event or situation. In some cases, while they were able to visualize the feared event, they were not able to connect with any emotion and therefore were unable to fully engage in the exercise, which might reflect a difference in their neurobiology compared to other young people with GAD. This may indicate that incorporating behavioral experiments progressing from anxieties linked with eating to more generalized fears and worries might be a more beneficial treatment approach in cases with comorbid AN and GAD.

Radically Open DBT (RO-DBT)

Another promising avenue for augmenting FT-AN for patients with high levels of anxiety and obsessionality is radically open dialectical behavior therapy (RO-DBT). There are a number of reasons why RO-DBT is of particular conceptual relevance. First, RO-DBT (Lynch, Hempel, & Dunkley, 2015) is a transdiagnostic treatment model designed for a hard-to-treat spectrum of disorders that might overlap neurobiologically, e.g. anorexia nervosa, treatment-resistant anxiety disorders, chronic depression, and obsessive-compulsive personality disorder. The conceptual model informing RO-DBT hypothesizes that the persistence of the above symptoms is connected to maladaptive over-control (OC). Support from this comes from research showing that OC is linked to many personality traits found to be heightened in individuals with AN, namely, threat sensitivity, harm avoidance, and behavioral and cognitive rigidity (Cassin & von Ranson, 2005; Klump et al., 2004; Lilenfeld, 2011; Wagner et al., 2006), maladaptive perfectionism (Halmi et al., 2000), heightened detailed-focused processing (Lopez et al., 2008), and inhibited emotional expression and resulting social isolation.

In addition to social phobia being present in 22 percent of individuals with AN (Kaye et al., 2004), it has also been shown that individuals with AN are less facially expressive and report feeling less positive emotion than healthy controls (Davies, Schmidt, Stahl, & Tchanturia, 2011; Lang et al., 2016). They report subjectively experiencing significantly higher levels of negative emotions, even though they do not express more negative emotions than healthy controls (Lang et al., 2016), and consequently are more avoidant of negative stimuli (Davies et al., 2011). It has been shown (Hambrook et al., 2011) that AN patients compared to healthy controls were more likely to judge themselves by external standards, endorse statements reflecting a tendency to put the needs of others before themselves, and present an outwardly socially compliant image of themselves whilst feeling hostile within. They also reported more maladaptive beliefs regarding the experience of having negative thoughts and feelings and revealing these emotions to others.

In the RO-DBT model, it is hypothesized that the bio-temperamental predispositions for high threat sensitivity, diminished reward sensitivity, high inhibitory control, and heightened detail-focused cognitive processing, in interaction with environmental responses that value correctness, achievement and self-control, may reinforce or moderate maladaptive OC behaviors (Lynch et al., 2015). This can result in a risk-avoidant, emotionally constrained, and aloof-vigilant style of coping in social relationships, often leading to social isolation (ibid). Defensive arousal and anxiety that are secondary to heightened threat sensitivity also impair social signaling/emotional expression and openness to critical feedback, and impede the formation of social bonds. Lack of social bonds can then circularly result in the reinforcement of social anxiety, social isolation, and behavioral and cognitive rigidity.

RO-DBT interventions aim to give patients the skills to be more receptive and open to new experiences and to disconfirm feedback from others in order to develop more flexible control that allows them to adapt to changing environmental conditions; they also help establish and sustain connectedness and intimacy with others. The treatment targets OC social-signaling deficits in three main ways, by providing the patient with skills to: (1) activate a state of social safety and reduce threat sensitivity; (2) signal cooperation and friendliness to others by changing body posture and facial expressions, and develop social bonds; and (3) self-disclose personal information, share when they feel vulnerable, and signal understanding to others to enable more flexible emotional expression and overall reduction of anxiety and rigidity. In weekly individual sessions combined with skills classes, either with patients only or in a multi-family setting, the core deficits of over-control are addressed alongside teaching skills that encourage engagement in new behaviors, learning to be playful and spontaneous, and more forgiving and kind to the self and others.

RO-DBT has been adapted for patients with anorexia nervosa (Chen et al., 2015) and its effectiveness in reducing eating-disorder symptoms and psychological distress while increasing quality of life has been positively evaluated in an adult inpatient population (Lynch et al., 2013). At the Maudsley Hospital we are currently evaluating modified RO-DBT in adolescents with anorexia nervosa delivered as individual therapy alongside skills classes in later stages of FT-AN in outpatient treatment and skills classes in the intensive day treatment program. Initial experience of RO-DBT as an adjunctive treatment to FT-AN has been positive, although further work is needed to demonstrate improved outcomes and confirm the hypothesized change mechanisms.

Parent Training

Family therapy's effectiveness is diminished by adolescent anxiety (Lock et al., 2006), which raises questions about why the mechanisms that facilitate change are weakened by the presence of anxious psychopathology in adolescents. Augmenting FT-AN with parent skills training focused on teaching parents specific strategies and methods for responding to and managing anxiety may improve outcomes by equipping parents with more effective methods for managing symptoms that may interfere with recovery. We now understand that due to the complex neurobiology underlying AN, individuals undergoing recovery will likely experience both physical and psychological pain and discomfort in response to recovery-related behaviors (Kaye et al., 2013). Accordingly, a strong reaction or resistance to being directed to engage in recovery-related behaviors is understandable and, in fact, should be expected based on these contemporary findings. It is not unusual for clinicians to see cases of severe AN in which parents are having a difficult time putting forth the changes prescribed in FT-AN, such as increasing caloric intake, due to an adolescent's negative reaction.

Parent training, focused on teaching parents specific skills and methods for responding to anxiety and other negative reactions, can be delivered in conjunction with family or multi-family therapy to enhance parental ability to work towards overcoming AN. Although the unique effect of the parent-only sessions is not known, outcomes from at least one program are promising, with 87.8 percent of participants' children achieving either a full or a partial remission maintained at a 30-month follow-up (Marzola et al., 2015). This is also consistent with research in child anxiety disorders showing that parent training improves outcome of individual CBT particularly if parents themselves are anxious (Kendall, Hudson, Gosch, Flannery-Schroeder, & Suveg, 2008).

In this model, parents are taught that anxiety and anxiety disorders tend to be highly comorbid with AN and educated about the overlapping traits that present themselves in both illnesses, including rigidity, intolerance of uncertainty, obsessiveness, harm avoidance, and excessive anticipation of future events (Kaye et al., 2004, 2013). This helps parents to understand why negative reactions may be occurring, and they are taught to see reactions that may be difficult to manage as rooted in anxiety rather than willfulness. Applying a biological framework and explanation to anxiety is used as a therapeutic technique to reduce blame and increase empathy among parents consistent with the way in which the family is engaged in the treatment process in FT-AN (Eisler, Le Grange, & Lock, 2016).

Psychoeducation is also provided on operant conditioning of anxiety, and, specifically, the way in which anxiety can be reinforced and/or extinguished through parent responses. This information is conveyed to help parents to view their response sets as a powerful factor in influencing their children's behaviors over time that will help them recover. This framework sets the tone for skills training in which parents are directed to evaluate their response sets and their influence on their children's behavior, and ultimately learn response sets that both increase the likelihood of and reinforce recovery-oriented behaviors. Key concepts covered include extinction bursts, habituation, reinforcement, and punishment. Anxiety, and its unique presentation in AN, is presented as a feature that requires a corresponding unique set of parent responses that may not be intuitive or natural within the repertoire of parenting an average adolescent.

Conceptualizing Family Functioning Impairment and Emotional Dysregulation in AN to Guide Treatment Development

Adolescents from families with high levels of expressed emotion and hostility tend to have a poorer response to treatment. These are often adolescents who themselves have higher levels of emotional dysregulation, which might be a catalyst for, and/or a reaction to, the family dysfunction. As with anxiety and obsessionality, there is evidence for powerful neurobiology involved with emotional and behavioral dysregulation. Complicating matters further is a possibility that attachment difficulties may interfere with the traditional FT-AN's focus on empowering the parents to take control of the eating disorder. Because of the potential relationship between adolescent emotional dysregulation and family functioning, treatment directions should focus on interventions to increase self-regulatory skills in both the adolescent and the family.

Neurobiology

As previously noted, there is evidence that young people with AN-BP may not respond as well to the usual FT-AN treatment (Agras et al., 2014; Le Grange et al., 2012). Improved understanding of the potential biological drivers of behavioral and emotional dysregulation may also point to treatment modifications for adolescents with AN-BP. Individuals with AN-BP have difficulty resisting urges to purge and interrupting eating during binge episodes, defined by a sense of "loss of control." In addition, AN-BP, compared with the restrictive subtype (AN-R), is associated with higher rates of Cluster B personality disorders (Jordan et al., 2008), emotional instability (Selby et al., 2015), and a high frequency of other co-occurring impulsive behaviors, including non-suicidal self-injurious behavior, shoplifting, risky sexual behaviors, and substance use disorders (Favaro & Santonastaso, 1997; Garfinkel, Moldofsky, & Garner, 1980). Patients with AN-BP are also more likely than those with AN-R to report a history of childhood sexual trauma, which some neurocognitive evidence suggests is associated with impaired inhibitory control (Demir et al., 2016; Marshall et al., 2016). Despite this dysregulation in multiple domains, individuals with AN-BP engage in extreme dietary restriction leading to objectively low weight, suggesting that over-control may also play a role in the disorder.

The alternating binge eating and fasting characteristic of AN-BP may result from a disrupted balance of self-regulatory control and reward sensitivity. Individuals with AN-BP show impaired performance on inhibitory control tasks (Wu, Hartmann, Skunde, Herzog, & Friederich, 2013), but an increased willingness compared with controls to forgo immediate rewards in order to gain larger later rewards (Decker, Figner, & Steinglass, 2015; Steinglass et al., 2012). This preference for delayed over earlier rewards is less pronounced among individuals with AN-BP compared to those with AN-R. Taken together, these findings may explain why individuals with AN-BP acutely and rigidly control their intake, but for a limited period of time before their eating is dysregulated.

Very few imaging studies have focused on AN-BP, specifically, but results from studies of individuals with bulimia nervosa and borderline personality disorder (BPD; e.g. Schmahl & Bremner, 2006) suggest that the behavioral and emotional dysregulation characteristic of AN-BP may result from impairments in the frontostriatal and frontolimbic circuits that control behavior and emotions. Altered development of these circuits has been documented in children with early life trauma (Demir et al., in press; Thomason & Marusak, 2016), suggesting that early trauma could contribute to or exacerbate dysregulation in AN-BP. Neuroimaging data show abnormal activation in control-related regions during inhibitory control tasks in adolescents with binge–purge syndromes (Lock et al., 2011), adults and adolescents with BN (Marsh et al., 2009, 2011), and adults with BPD (Silbersweig et al., 2007). Thus, in AN-BP an inability to appropriately recruit frontolimbic and frontostriatal resources may underlie unstable affect, difficulty stopping eating during binge episodes, and difficulty resisting urges to purge or engagement in other impulsive behaviors.

Emotional Dysregulation and Attachment

Adolescents with AN-BP may struggle to regulate their emotions and control their behavior because of neurobiological vulnerabilities, but these difficulties may be exacerbated by a possible interactional insecure attachment with their parents. Indeed, evidence suggests that adolescents with AN-BP may not respond as well to typical FT-AN because of a difference in the quality of the adolescents' attachment to their parents (Jewell et al., 2015).

Adolescents lacking security in attachment that leads to attachment preoccupation often display on-going anger towards attachment figures and tend to find it difficult to let go of past grievances in their attachment relationships. This experience of anger toward attachment figures may result in young people finding it difficult to experience the therapeutic context as containing and safe and they may experience parental management of eating as primarily controlling rather than caring. This can result in them rebelling against, or dismissing, the initial parental management of their food intake as encouraged in the FT-AN model. Furthermore, the young people's binge–purge behaviors are more likely to be experienced by parents as purposeful and attacking, particularly if these happen in the context of insecure attachment relationships. This may lead to escalation in the parent–child interactions that both young people and parent/s experience as highly negative and invalidating. Parents with a low sense of self-worth and self-efficacy are likely to either withdraw or fluctuate between trying harder to be a "perfect parent" (often experienced by the young people as controlling) and giving up because of their sense that their efforts are not appreciated by their child (and perhaps also the other parent). Low parental self-worth (particularly in mothers) may also be associated with self-blaming for the young person's illness, which may lead to criticism or hostility (Besharat, Eisler, & Dare, 2001).

Treatment Directions for Family Functioning Impairment and Emotional Dysregulation in AN

This section will review individual interventions for targeting emotion dysregulation in adolescents and interventions to increase parental effectiveness in helping their child fight the eating disorder, in spite of existing difficulties in the family system.

Dialectical Behavior Therapy

One reason that young people who present with AN-BP are more difficult to treat is that they often have comorbid difficulties with emotion dysregulation and self-harm. Thus dialectical behavior therapy (DBT; Linehan, 1993) appears promising as a way to augment treatment. DBT has been adapted for use with patients with eating disorders (for a review, see Bankoff, Karpel, Forbes, & Pantalone, 2012). DBT is predicated on the notion that self-destructive behaviors, including eating disorder behaviors, represent an attempt by the young person to regulate their emotions. Difficulties with emotion regulation are hypothesized to be a result of the biosocial model. The biosocial model suggests that the interaction between a child with difficulties in regulating emotion, and a parent becoming increasingly intolerant and invalidating towards that child through an interplay of lack of understanding and exhaustion, results in an increasingly destructive cycle of intolerance of those difficulties in emotion regulation. For young people whose presenting difficulties are based on difficulties in emotion regulation, a DBT approach with them, alongside parent skills training, can be very effective. DBT helps young people to identify their current attempts to regulate emotion, which tend to be self-destructive in nature, and lay them out in a treatment hierarchy with the goal of replacing the self-destructive means of regulating emotion with more adaptive skills. Within DBT the young person's motivation to change is repeatedly addressed, whilst balancing this with validation and acceptance strategies. The young person is supported in realizing the benefits of taking increased responsibility for engaging in regular eating, interrupting binge–purge cycles, and using alternative skills to replace the functions of self-harm.

Parent Training and other Interventions to Enhance Family Functioning

The recruitment of specialized parental support is pivotal in the treatment of eating disorders for which dysregulated mood plays a central role in the development and maintenance of eating disorder behaviors. This is particularly important for those young people for whom problems around managing emotions and feelings are part of a broader picture of relationship difficulties in the family that may pre-date the development of the illness but will have inevitably been exacerbated by the illness. Despite studies demonstrating preliminary efficacy (Anderson et al., 2015; Robinson, Dolhanty, & Greenberg, 2015; Stewart, Voulgari, Eisler, Hunt, & Simic, 2015; Zucker & Marcus, 2006), more parent-supported approaches are needed that are specifically focused on helping parents to effectively address both dysregulated mood and resulting dysfunctional eating behaviors.

To address this need, the UCSD eating disorders program has adapted these existing parent training models for dysregulation aimed at providing parents with psychoeducation and two complementary skill sets (Anderson et al., 2015). Using the biosocial theory as the guiding framework (Linehan, 1993), psychoeducation is designed to empower parents by educating them on mood dysregulation, validation, and positive reinforcement.

Psychoeducation is presented to parents in order to convey that a unique set of parenting skills is necessary to respond effectively due to the unique (and biosocially justified) emotional temperament style of adolescents with problems of dysregulation. Studies have shown that individuals who experience difficulties in emotion regulation may experience emotional arousal more intensely and for a longer duration compared to those with better abilities to self-regulate (Harrison, Sullivan, Tchanturia, & Treasure, 2010). Thus it may be more difficult to withstand without engaging in a behavioral outlet. The model of problematic eating behavior proposed by Safer, Telch, and Chen (2009) is used to assist parents in understanding the link between mood dysregulation and eating disorder behaviors to further bolster the perspective that eating behaviors have a cause, and dispel the myth that the adolescent can easily control them. The biological causes for this abnormality are somewhat out of their adolescents' control, and these biological determinants may be responsible for social experiences that have not allowed their adolescent to progress in developing appropriate mood regulation skills.

Parents are taught emotion-focused skills based on the emotion-focused therapy model (Greenberg, 2002; Robinson et al., 2015), aimed at preventing and reducing the propensity for emotion dysregulation and appropriate methods of

responding to eating disorder behaviors based on underlying behavioral principles (Kazdin, 1997). Parents are taught to accurately gauge their own and their
child's emotional experiences and effective use of contingencies to prevent eating disorder behaviors.

Where there is significant negativity or hostility in the family it is often helpful
to see the young person and the parents in separate sessions (Eisler et al., 2000,
2007). These will in part have the same focus as conjoint family sessions (i.e.
in the early stage of treatment discussing how parents can best help their child
to eat) but will also provide a context for the emotion-focused interventions
described above or attachment-based family therapy interventions (Diamond,
2014). These have not yet been evaluated in eating disorders but have shown
to be effective with depressed and suicidal adolescents (Diamond, Diamond,
Siqueland, & Isaacs, 2002; Diamond et al., 2010).

Conclusions

In this chapter we have described two subgroups of young people with AN
who generally respond less favorably to family therapy than outcome research
would predict. The first group comprises patients with high levels of comorbid
anxiety and obsessionality who tend to be highly emotionally inhibited and
inflexible. The second group is characterized by emotional dysregulation and
impulsivity, and their clinical presentation frequently includes binge–purge
behaviors and self-harm. In addition, patients in this second group often have
more difficult family relationships that may include high expressed emotions
and insecure and ambivalent attachment relationships.

It is our view that it is imperative that current knowledge of neurobiology
of AN is used when developing treatment modifications for young people who
do not respond to eating disorder-focused family therapy. In this chapter we
described treatments that we have modified and piloted, or treatment models that we have integrated as adjuncts for these subgroups of patients. For
example, at UCSD, parent training, psychoeducation about the neurobiology
of eating disorders, and key elements of DBT are integrated with a range of
Maudsley-informed family and multi-family interventions that are the core of
its partial-hospitalization program. At the Maudsley Hospital, a number of
individual treatments are being tested with added multi-family/family components as adjunct treatment options in later stages of FT-AN. Individual
treatments target possible predisposing or maintaining factors for AN, namely,
generalized anxiety disorder (CBT), bio-temperamental predispositions that
result in over-control (RO-DBT), or emotional and behavioral dysregulation
(DBT). Emotion-focused and attachment-based family interventions may be
a useful adjunct to current treatments where problematic relationships make
engagement in effective treatment difficult, but have not yet been evaluated in
eating disorders.

Initial evaluations of the treatments described have indicated the potential value of these approaches for augmenting FT-AN, and they appear

well received by young people and their families. Further research will, however, be needed to establish the extent of their efficacy in progressing the recovery of young people with these particular presentations.

Notes

1 A range of terms, including Maudsley family therapy, family-based treatment (FBT), Family therapy-behavioral (FT-B), behavioral family systems therapy for anorexia nervosa (BFST), has been used to describe a number of conceptually very similar treatments. While there are differences between the manualized accounts of these treatments (for an account of the historical development of these approaches and their overlap and differences, see Eisler, Wallis, & Dodge, 2015), the terminology is often confusing and used ambiguously to refer either to ED-focused treatments in general or to the use of a specific manual. We have used the term FT-AN throughout regardless of any specific treatment manual being used in particular studies to emphasize the commonality of a treatment approach that draws on family systems theory and uses a broad range of family therapy intervention techniques while its specificity derives from its focus on treating anorexia nervosa.

References

Agras, W., Lock, J., Brandt, H., Bryson, S., Dodge, E. et al. (2014). Comparison of 2 family therapies for adolescent anorexia nervosa: A randomized parallel trial. *JAMA Psychiatry*, 71(11), 1279–1286. doi: doi:http://dx.doi.org/10.1001/jamapsychiatry.2014.1025.

Anderson, L., Murray, S., Ramirez, A., Rockwell, R., Le Grange, D., & Kaye, W. (2015). The integration of family-based treatment and dialectical behavior therapy for adolescent bulimia nervosa: Philosophical and practical considerations. *Eating Disorders*, 23(4), 325–335. doi: 10.1080/10640266.2015.1042319.

Anestis, M., Selby, E., Fink, E., & Joiner, T. (2007). The multifaceted role of distress tolerance in dysregulated eating behaviors. *International Journal of Eating Disorders*, 40(8), 718–726.

Bailer, U. F., Frank, G. K., Henry, S. E., Price, J. C., Meltzer, C. C. et al. (2005). Altered brain serotonin 5-HT_{1A} receptor binding after recovery from anorexia nervosa measured by positron emission tomography and [^{11}C]WAY100635. *Archives of General Psychiatry*, 62(2), 1032–1041.

Bailer, U., Frank, G., Price, J., Meltzer, C., Becker, C. et al. (2012a). Interaction between serotonin transporter and dopamine D2/D3 receptor radioligand measures is associated with harm avoidant symptoms in anorexia and bulimia nervosa. *Psychiatry Research: Neuroimaging*, 211(2), 160–168. doi: 10.1016/j.pscychresns.2012.06.010.

Bailer, U., Narendran, R., Frankle, W., Himes, M., Duvvuri, V. et al. (2012b). Amphetamine induced dopamine release increases anxiety in individuals recovered from anorexia nervosa. *International Journl of Eating Disorders*, 45(2), 263–271. doi: 10.1002/eat.20937.

Bankoff, S., Karpel, M., Forbes, H., & Pantalone, D. (2012). A systematic review of dialectical behavior therapy for the treatment of eating disorders. *Eating Disorders*, 20(3), 196–215. doi: 10.1080/10640266.2012.668478.

Besharat, M., Eisler, I., & Dare, C. (2001). The Self- and Other-Blame Scale (SOBS): The background and presentation of a new instrument for measuring blame in families. *Journal of Family Therapy*, 23(2), 208–223.

Bloss, C., Berrettini, W., Bergen, A., Magistretti, P., Duvvuri, V. et al. (2011). Genetic association of recovery from eating disorders: The role of GABA receptor SNPs. *Neuropsychopharmacology*, 36(11), 2222–2232. doi: 10.1038/npp.2011.108.

Brauer, L., & de Wit, H. (1996). Subjective responses to D-amphetamine alone and after pimozide pretreatment in normal, healthy volunteers. *Biological Psychiatry*, 39, 26–31.

Brooks, S., & Stein, D. (2015). A systematic review of the neural bases of psychotherapy for anxiety and related disorders. *Dialogues in Clinical Neuroscience*, 17(3), 261–279.

Bulik, C. M., Sullivan, P. F., Fear, J. L., & Joyce, P. R. (1997). Eating disorders and antecedent anxiety disorders: A controlled study. *Acta Psychiatrica Scandinavica*, 96(2), 101–107.

Cassin, S., & von Ranson, K. (2005). Personality and eating disorders: A decade in review. *Clinical Psychology Review*, 25(7), 895–916.

Chen, E., Segal, K. W., Zeffiro, T. A., Gallop, R., Linehan, M. et al. (2015). Adapting dialectical behavior therapy for outpatient adult anorexia nervosa: A pilot study. *International Journal of Eating Disorders*, 48(1), 23–132. doi: 10.1002/eat.22360.

Ciao, A., Accurso, E., Fitzsimmons-Craft, E., Lock, J., & Le Grange, D. (2015). Family functioning in two treatments for adolescent anorexia nervosa. *International Journal of Eating Disorders*, 48(1), 81–90. doi: 10.1002/eat.22314.

Compton, S., March, J., Brent, D., Albano, A. t., Weersing, R., & Curry, J. (2004). Cognitive-behavioral psychotherapy for anxiety and depressive disorders in children and adolescents: An evidence-based medicine review. *Journal of the American Academy of Child and Adolescent Psychiatry*, 43(8), 930–959.

Couturier, J., Kimber, M., & Szatmari, P. (2013). Efficacy of family-based treatment for adolescents with eating disorders: A systematic review and meta-analysis. *International Journal of Eating Disorders*, 46(1), 3–11. doi: 10.1002/eat.22042.

Davies, H., Schmidt, U., Stahl, D., & Tchanturia, K. (2011). Evoked facial emotional expression and emotional experience in people with anorexia nervosa. *International Journal of Eating Disorders*, 44(6), 531–539. doi: 10.1002/eat.20852.

Decker, J., Figner, B., & Steinglass, J. (2015). On weight and waiting: Delay discounting in anorexia nervosa pretreatment and post-treatment. *Biological Psychiatry*, 78(9), 606–614. doi: 10.1016/j.biopsych.2014.12.016.

Dellava, J., Thornton, L. H., Strober, M., Plotnicov, K., Klump, K. et al. (2010). Childhood anxiety associated with low BMI in women with anorexia nervosa. *Behaviour Research and Therapy*, 48(1), 60–67. doi: 10.1016/j.brat.2009.09.009.

Demir, Ö., Voss, J., O'Neill, J., Briggs-Gowan, M., Wakschlag, L., & Booth, J. (2016). Early-life stress exposure associated with altered prefrontal resting-state fMRI connectivity in young children. *Developmental Cognitive Neuroscience*, 19, 107–114. doi: 10.1016/j.dcn.2016.02.003.

Diamond, G. (2014). Attachment-based family therapy interventions. *Psychotherapy (Chic)*, 51(1), 15–19. doi: 10.1037/a0032689.

Diamond, G. S., Diamond, G. M., Siqueland, L., & Isaacs, L. (2002). Attachment-based family therapy for depressed adolescents: A treatment development study. *Journal of the American Academy of Child and Adolescent Psychiatry*, 41(10), 1190–1196.

Diamond, G. S., Wintersteen, M., Brown, G., Diamond, G. M., Gallop, R. et al. (2010). Attachment-based family therapy for adolescents with suicidal ideation: A randomized controlled trial. *Journal of the American Academy of Child and Adolescent Psychiatry*, 49(2), 122–131.

Dugas, M., Gagnon, F., Ladouceur, R., & Freeston, M. (1998). Generalized anxiety disorder: A preliminary test of a conceptual model. *Behaviour Research & Therapy*, 36(2), 215–226.

Eisler, I., Dare, C., Hodes, M., Russell, G., Dodge, E., & Le Grange, D. (2000). Family therapy for adolescent anorexia nervosa: The results of a controlled comparison of two family interventions. *Journal of Child Psychology and Psychiatry*, 41(6), 727–736.

Eisler, I., Le Grange, D., & Lock, J. (2016). Family therapy for adolescent eating disorders. In T. Sexton & J. Lebow (Eds.), *Handbook of family therapy*, 4th edition (pp. 387–406). New York: Routledge.

Eisler, I., Simic, M., Russell, G., & Dare, C. (2007). A randomised controlled treatment trial of two forms of family therapy in adolescent anorexia nervosa: A five-year follow-up. *Journal of Child Psychology and Psychiatry*, 48(6), 552–560.

Eisler, I., Wallis, A., & Dodge, E. (2015). What's new is old and what's old is new: The origins and evolution of family therapy for eating disorders! In K. Loeb, D. Le Grange, & J. Lock (Eds.), *Family therapy for adolescent eating and weight disorders: New applications*. New York: Routledge.

Favaro, A., & Santonastaso, P. (1997). Suicidality in eating disorders: Clinical and psychological correlates. *Acta Psychiatrica Scandinavica*, 95(6), 508–514.

Frank, G., Bailer, U. F., Henry, S., Drevets, W., Meltzer, C. C. et al. (2005). Increased dopamine D2/D3 receptor binding after recovery from anorexia nervosa measured by positron emission tomography and [^{11}C]raclopride. *Biological Psychiatry*, 58(11), 908–912.

Frank, G., Roblek, T., Shott, M., Jappe, L., Rollin, M. et al. (2012). Heightened fear of uncertainty in anorexia and bulimia nervosa. *International Journal of Eating Disorders*, 45(2), 227–232. doi: 10.1002/eat.20929.

van Furth, E., van Strien, D., Martina, L., van Son Maarten, J., Hendrickx, J., & van Engeland, H. (1996). Expressed emotion and the prediction of outcome in adolescent eating disorders. *International Journal of Eating Disorders*, 20(1), 19–31.

Gabbay, F. (2003). Variations in affect following amphetamine and placebo: Markers of stimulant drug preference. *Experimental and Clinical Psychopharmacology*, 11, 91–101.

Garfinkel, P., Moldofsky, H., & Garner, D. (1980). The heterogeneity of anorexia nervosa: Bulimia as a distinct subgroup. *Archives of General Psychiatry*, 37(9), 1036–1040.

Godart, N. T., Flament, M. F., Lecrubier, Y., & Jeammet, P. (2000). Anxiety disorders in anorexia nervosa and bulimia nervosa: Co-morbidity and chronology of appearance. *European Psychiatry*, 15(1), 38–45.

Goodman, M., Carpenter, D., Tang, C., Goldstein, K., Avedon, J. et al. (2014). Dialectical behavior therapy alters emotion regulation and amygdala activity in patients with borderline personality disorder. *Journal of Psychiatric Research*, 57, 108–116. doi: 10.1016/j.jpsychires.2014.06.02.

Greenberg, L. (2002). *Emotion focused therapy: Coaching clients to work through their feelings*. Washington DC: American Psychological Association.

Halmi, K. A., Sunday, S. R., Strober, M., Kaplan, A., Woodside, D. B. et al. (2000). Perfectionism in anorexia nervosa: Variation by clinical subtype, obsessionality, and pathological eating behavior. *American Journal of Psychiatry*, 157(11), 1799–1805.

Hambrook, D., Oldershaw, A., Rimes, K., Schmidt, U., Tchanturia, K. et al. (2011). Emotional expression, self-silencing, and distress tolerance in anorexia nervosa and chronic fatigue syndrome. *British Journal of Psychiatry*, 50(3), 310–325. doi: 10.1348/014466510X519215.

Harrison, A., Sullivan, S., Tchanturia, K., & Treasure, J. (2010). Emotional functioning in eating disorders: Attentional bias, emotion recognition and emotion regulation. *Psychological Medicine*, 40(11), 1887–1897. doi: 10.1017/S0033291710000036.

Holtkamp, K., Mueller, B., Heussen, N., Remschmidt, H., & Herpertz-Dahlmann, B. (2005). Depression, anxiety, and obsessionality in long-term recovered patients with adolescent-onset anorexia nervosa. *European Journal of Adolescent Psychiatry*, 14(2), 106–110.

Jewell, T., Collyer, H., Gardner, T., Tchanturia, K., & Simic, M. F., & Eisler, I. (2015). Attachment and mentalization and their association with child and adolescent eating pathology: A systematic review. *International Journal of Eating Disorders*. doi: 10.1002/eat.22473.

Jordan, J., Joyce, P. R., Carter, F., Horn, J., McIntosh, V., Luty, S. et al. (2008). Specific and nonspecific comorbidity in anorexia nervosa. *International Journal of Eating Disorders*, 41(1), 47–56.

Kaye, W., Bulik, C., Thornton, L., Barbarich, N., Masters, K. et al. (2004). Comorbidity of anxiety disorders with anorexia and bulimia nervosa. *American Journal of Psychiatry*, 161(12), 2215–2221.

Kaye, W., Wierenga, C., Bailer, U., Simmons, A., & Bischoff-Grethe, A. (2013). Nothing tastes as good as skinny feels: The neurobiology of anorexia nervosa. *Trends in Neuroscience: Special Issue on Neural Control of Appetite*, 36(2), 110–120. doi: 10.1016/j.tins.2013.01.003.

Kaye, W., Wierenga, C., Knatz, S., Liang, J., Boutelle, K. et al. (2015). Temperament-based treatment for anorexia nervosa. *European Eating Disorders Review*, 23(1), 12–18. doi: 10.1002/erv.2330.

Kazdin, A. (1997). Parent management training: Evidence, outcomes, and issues. *Journal of the American Academy of Child and Adolescent Psychiatry*, 36(10), 1349–1356.

Kendall, P., Hudson, J., Gosch, E., Flannery-Schroeder, E., & Suveg, C. (2008). Cognitive-behavioral therapy for anxiety disordered youth: A randomized clinical trial evaluating child and family modalities. *Journal of Consulting and Clinical Psychology*, 76(2), 282–297. doi: 10.1037/0022-006X.76.2.282.

Klump, K., Strober, M., Johnson, C., Thornton, L., Bulik, C. et al. (2004). Personality characteristics of women before and after recovery from an eating disorder. *Psychological Medicine*, 34(8), 1407–1418.

Konstantellou, A., & Campbell, M. E. (2011). The family context: Cause, effect or resource? In J. Alexander & J. Treasure (Eds.), *A collaborative approach to eating disorders*. London: Routledge.

Lang, K., Larsson, E., Mavromara, L., Simic, M., Treasure, J., & Tchanturia, K. (2016). Diminished facial emotion expression and associated clinical characteristics in anorexia nervosa. *Journal of Psychiatric Research*, 236, 165–172. doi: 10.1016/j.psychres.2015.12.004.

Le Grange, D., Lock, J., Accurso, E., Agras, W., Darcy, A. et al. (2014). Relapse from remission at two- to four-year follow-up in two treatments for adolescent anorexia nervosa. *Journal of the American Academy of Child and Adolescent Psychiatry*, 53(11), 1162–1167. doi: 10.1016/j.jaac.2014.07.014.

Le Grange, D., Lock, J., Agras, W., Moye, A., Bryson, S. et al. (2012). Moderators and mediators of remission in family-based treatment and adolescent focused therapy for anorexia nervosa. *Behaviour Research and Therapy*, 50(2), 85–92. doi: 10.1016/j.brat.2011.11.003.

Lilenfeld, L. (2011). Personality and temperament in eating disorders. *Current Topics in Behavioral Neuroscience*, 6, 3–9.

Linehan, M. (1993). *Skills training manual for treating borderline personality disorder.* New York: Guilford Press.

Lock, J. (2015). An update on evidence-based psychosocial treatments for eating disorders in children and adolescents. *Journal of Clinical Child and Adolescent Psychology*, 12, 1–15.

Lock, J., Couturier, J., Bryson, S., & Agras, W. (2006). Predictors of dropout and remission in family therapy for adolescent anorexia nervosa in a randomized clinical trial. *International Journal of Eating Disorders*, 39(8), 639–647. doi: 10.1002/eat.20328.

Lock, J., Garrett, A., Beenhalder, J., & Reiss, A. (2011). Aberrant brain activation during a response inhibition task in adolescent eating disorder subtypes. *American Journal of Psychiatry*, 168(1), 55–64. doi: 10.1176/appi.ajp.2010.10010056.

Lopez, C., Tchanturia, K., Stahl, D., Booth, R., Holliday, J., & Treasure, J. (2008). An examination of the concept of central coherence in women with anorexia nervosa. *International Journal of Eating Disorders*, 41(2), 143–152.

Lynch, T., Gray, K. L. H., Hempel, R. J., Titley, M., Chen, E. Y., & O'Mahen, H. (2013). Radically open-dialectical behavior therapy for adult anorexia nervosa: Feasibility and outcomes from an inpatient program. *BMC Psychiatry*, 13, 293. doi: 10.1186/1471-244X-13-293.

Lynch, T., Hempel, R., & Dunkley, C. (2015). Radically open-dialectical behavior therapy for disorders of over-control: Signaling matters. *American Journal of Psychotherapy*, 69(2), 141–162.

Marsh, R., Horga, G., Wang, Z., Wang, P., Klahr, K. et al. (2011). An fMRI study of self-regulatory control and conflict resolution in adolescents with bulimia nervosa. *American Journal of Psychiatry*, 168(11), 1210–1220. doi: 10.1176/appi.ajp.2011.11010094.

Marsh, R., Steinglass, J., Gerber, A., Graziano O'Leary, K., Wang, Z. et al. (2009). Deficient activity in the neural systems that mediate self-regulatory control in bulimia nervosa. *Archives of General Psychiatry*, 66(1), 51–63. doi: 10.1001/archgenpsychiatry.2008.504.

Marshall, D. P., Ryan, K., Kamali, M., Saunders, E., Pester, B. et al. (2016). Deficient inhibitory control as an outcome of childhood trauma. *Psychiatry Research*, 235, 7–12. doi: 10.1016/j.psychres.2015.12.013.

Marzola, E., Knatz, S., Murray, S., Rockwell, R., Boutelle, K. et al. (2015). Short-term intensive family therapy for adolescent eating disorders: 30-month outcome. *European Eating Disorders Review*, 23(3), 210–218. doi: 10.1002/erv.2353.

Minuchin, S., Rosman, B., & Baker, L. (1978). *Psychosomatic families: Anorexia nervosa in context.* Cambridge, MA: Harvard University Press.

Pace, U., Cacioppo, M., & Schimmenti, A. (2012). The moderating role of fathers' care on the onset of binge eating symptoms among female late adolescents with insecure attachment. *Child Psychiatry & Human Development*, 43(2), 282–292. doi: 10.1007/s10578-011-0269-7.

Pollice, C., Kaye, W. H., Greeno, C. G., & Weltzin, T. E. (1997). Relationship of depression, anxiety, and obsessionality to state of illness in anorexia nervosa. *International Journal of Eating Disorders*, 21(4), 367–376.

Raney, T., Thornton, L., Brandt, H., Crawford, S., Fichter, M. et al. (2008). Influence of overanxious disorder of childhood on the expression of anorexia nervosa. *International Journal of Eating Disorders*, 41(4), 326–332. doi: 10.1002/eat.20508.

Robinson, A., Dolhanty, J., & Greenberg, L. (2015). Emotion-focused family therapy for eating disorders in children and adolescents. *Clinical Psychology & Psychotherapy*, 22(1), 75–82. doi: 10.1002/cpp.1861.

Safer, D., Telch, C., & Chen, E. (2009). *Dialectical behavior therapy for binge eating and bulimia.* New York: Guilford Press.

Schmahl, C., & Bremner, J. (2006). Neuroimaging in borderline personality disorder. *Journal of Psychiatric Research*, 40(5), 419–427.

Selby, E., Anestis, M., & Joiner, T. (2008). Understanding the relationship between emotional and behavioral dysregulation: Emotional cascades. *Behavioral Research & Therapy*, 46(5), 593–611. doi: 10.1016/j.brat.2008.02.002.

Selby, E., Cornelius, T., Fehling, K., Kranzler, A., Panza, E. et al. (2015). A perfect storm: Examining the synergistic effects of negative and positive emotional instability on promoting weight loss activities in anorexia nervosa. *Frontiers in Psychology*, 31(6), 1260. doi: 10.3389/fpsyg.2015.01260.

Silbersweig, D., Clarkin, J., Goldstein, M., Kernberg, O., Tuescher, O. et al. (2007). Failure of frontolimbic inhibitory function in the context of negative emotion in borderline personality disorder. *American Journal of Psychiatry*, 164(12), 1832–1841. doi: 10.1176/appi.ajp.2007.06010126.

Steinglass, J., Figner, B., Berkowitz, S., Simpson, H., Weber, E., & Walsh, B. (2012). Increased capacity to delay reward in anorexia nervosa. *Journal of the International Neuropsychological Society*, 18(4), 773–780. doi: 10.1017/S1355617712000446.

Steinglass, J., Sysko, R., Mayer, L., Berner, L., Schebendach, J. et al. (2010). Pre-meal anxiety and food intake in anorexia nervosa. *Appetite*, 55(2), 214–218. doi: 10.1016/j.appet.2010.05.090..

Steinglass, J., Walsh, B., & Stern, Y. (2006). Set shifting deficit in anorexia nervosa. *Journal of the International Neuropsychological Society*, 12(3), 431–435.

Stewart, C., Voulgari, S., Eisler, I., Hunt, K., & Simic, M. I. (2015). Multi-family therapy for bulimia nervosa in adolescence. *Eating Disorders*, 23(4), 345–355. doi: 10.1080/10640266.2015.1044348.

Szmurker, G., Eisler, I., Russell, G., & Dare, C. (1985). Anorexia nervosa, parental "expressed emotion" and dropping out of treatment. *British Journal of Psychiatry*, 147, 265–271.

Thomason, M., & Marusak, H. (2016). Toward understanding the impact of trauma on the early developing human brain. *Neuroscience*, *16*, 145–147.. doi: 10.1016/j.neuroscience.2016.02.022.

Van Durme, K., Braet, C., & Goossens, L. (2014). Insecure attachment and eating pathology in early adolescence: Role of emotion regulation. *Journal of Early Adolescence*, 35(1), 54–78. doi: 10.1177/0272431614523130.

Wagner, A., Barbarich, N., Frank, G., Bailer, U., Weissfeld, L. et al. (2006). Personality traits after recovery from eating disorders: Do subtypes differ? *International Journal of Eating Disorders*, 39(4), 276–284.

Wu, M., Hartmann, M., Skunde, M., Herzog, W., & Friederich, H.-C. (2013). Inhibitory control in bulimic-type eating disorders: A systematic review and meta-analysis. *PLOS One*, 8(12), e83412. doi: 10.1371/journal.pone.0083412.

Zucker, N., & Marcus, M. B. (2006). A group parent-training program: A novel approach for eating disorder management. *Eating and Weight Disorders*, 11(2), 78–82.

Part III

Carers

11 Couple-Based Interventions for Adults With Eating Disorders

Jennifer S. Kirby,[1] *Cristin D. Runfola,*[1] *Melanie S. Fischer, Donald H. Baucom,*[2] *and Cynthia M. Bulik*[2]

Since the early 2000s, the landscape for eating disorder treatment of children and adolescents has gradually shifted from a focus on individual to family-based intervention. This shift has been based on two key findings. First, interpersonal factors have been found to play an important role in illness persistence (Arcelus, Haslam, Farrow, & Meyer, 2013; Goddard et al., 2011). Second, including family members in the treatment of adolescents with eating disorders has improved outcome (Lock, 2015). Whereas marked shifts in the care of adolescent patients have yielded positive benefits, typical treatment for adults with eating disorders has remained individual therapy and outcomes, which are modest at best, have stagnated (Berkman et al., 2006; Brown & Keel, 2012). To help improve outcome and recovery rates for adults with eating disorders, we created couple-based interventions that incorporate the partner into treatment in a developmentally appropriate and evidence-informed manner. In this chapter, we survey the empirical literature supporting the treatment of adults in a couple context and describe our existing and emerging couple-based interventions for eating disorders.

Why Couple-Based Treatments for Eating Disorders?

Individuals who have recovered from eating disorders describe supportive relationships as vital to their recovery (Linville, Brown, Sturm, & McDougal, 2012; Tozzi, Sullivan, Fear, McKenzie, & Bulik, 2003). Contrary to popular opinion, adults with eating disorders appear to enter into committed relationships at a rate comparable to healthy peers (Maxwell et al., 2010). However, some may struggle with maintaining healthy relationships in the midst of an eating disorder as the disorder is taxing not only on the individual but also the partner and the relationship. Couples with eating disorders report significant relationship distress, reduced levels of positive interaction, and more negative communication than couples without eating disorders (Van den Broucke, Vandereycken, & Vertommen, 1995a; Whisman, Dementyeva, Baucom, & Bulik, 2012; Woodside, Lackstrom, & Shekter-Wolfson, 2000). Difficulties around sexual functioning and intimacy in the relationship are also common (Pinheiro et al., 2010; Van den Broucke, Vandereycken, & Vertommen, 1995b).

Challenges within the romantic relationship are likely due to many patient and partner factors (including biological, temperamental, behavioral, and environmental) related and unrelated to the disorder. For example, many individuals with anorexia nervosa (AN) are emotionally avoidant and struggle to express their feelings, which may negatively affect their ability to articulate their needs, tolerate distress in the relationship, or remain close with others (Schmidt & Treasure, 2006; Van den Broucke et al., 1995a). Adults with bulimia nervosa (BN) generally lack constructive communication skills and tend to be impulsive (van Buren & Williamson, 1988; Van den Broucke et al., 1995a), which may contribute to negative interactions within the relationship. Individuals with binge-eating disorder (BED) experience emotions intensely and have been described as having difficulties with boundary setting and over-involvement in relationships, which may contribute to their experience of interpersonal relationships as stressful (Riener, Schindler, & Ludvik, 2006). Characteristic of eating disorders are body distress and shame, which likely contribute to a patient's anxiety around exposing their body to partners and engaging in intimate acts. Moreover, hormonal changes in the context of eating disorders result in reduced libido and, thus, interest in sex, which can be confusing to the couple.

Partners also struggle relative to the eating disorder and within the relationship. Partners commonly report difficulty understanding the eating disorder and finding the secrecy surrounding eating disorder behaviors challenging to live with (Huke & Slade, 2006). Many describe feelings of powerlessness and their well-intentioned attempts at supporting their loved one as appearing to backfire. Some partners become fearful of saying or doing something hurtful or counterproductive and, thus, become avoidant whereas others become critical or blaming. This behavior can inadvertently support or exacerbate the patient's shame, secrecy, and self-critical nature. Partners often want to help but do not know what to do. These challenges can cause caregiver distress and burden (Fischer, Baucom, Kirby, & Bulik, 2015; Zabala, Macdonald, & Treasure, 2009), and may contribute to escalating conflict or issues in the relationship.

Such distress and conflict within the relationship is noteworthy as a distressed, critical, or hostile relationship has been shown to elevate the risk for illness persistence and relapse in various psychiatric disorders (Baucom, Belus, Adelman, Fischer, & Paprocki, 2014). Fortunately, cognitive-behavioral couple therapy (CBCT; Epstein & Baucom, 2002) that targets interpersonal dynamics to enhance relationship satisfaction, has demonstrated effectiveness in treating a variety of psychiatric disorders, including two highly comorbid with eating disorders – depression and anxiety (Baucom et al., 2014). These data, which suggest that couple-based interventions for eating disorders may help more effectively treat the disorder, lead us to develop the first manualized couple-based intervention for AN.

Uniting Couples in the Treatment of Anorexia Nervosa (UCAN)

Uniting Couples in the treatment of Anorexia Nervosa (UCAN; Bulik, Baucom, Kirby, & Pisetsky, 2011) integrates CBCT and cognitive-behavioral therapy (CBT) for AN to treat the disorder. Given the complexity of AN, UCAN was designed as an augmentation to individual therapy, nutritional counseling, and medication management to ensure treatment appropriately addresses all aspects of the disorder. Unlike family-based treatment with children and adolescents (Lock, Le Grange, Agras, & Dare, 2001), which initially provides significant others (i.e. parents) with control over the renourishment and recovery process, UCAN works with loved ones (i.e. couples) to reach joint decisions regarding treatment and recovery from AN. In this way, the partner is incorporated into treatment as a partner of equal status in a developmentally appropriate manner.

UCAN is believed to benefit couples by facilitating three broad mechanisms of change: two focal to AN and one addressing broader relationship functioning. First, the UCAN therapist works to create conditions that allow the *secrecy and avoidance commonly associated with AN to be addressed* and to decrease (mechanism 1). Bringing AN into the open enables the patient to receive support from the partner, enhances understanding of illness, and helps to increase patient accountability. Throughout treatment partners are kept informed about the patient's progress and are actively involved in team discussions regarding the need for higher levels of care. Critically, at times when patients are struggling and motivation to stay in treatment decreases, the partner and the relationship can be "leveraged" to keep the patient engaged in treatment. UCAN also brings partners into treatment more specifically by *helping the couple work as a team to address AN* (mechanism 2). Throughout treatment, the couple is taught how to work effectively against the AN, including addressing mealtimes, responding when a patient feels the urge to restrict or purge, or developing strategies for social outings or holidays. Third, as described above, AN and relationship difficulties can negatively influence one another; a distressed relationship can be a source of chronic stress for the individual with AN, and AN places considerable strain on the relationship. Therefore, to reduce stress on the patient and facilitate recovery from AN, we *address overall relationship functioning within UCAN when needed* (mechanism 3).

UCAN Treatment

Phase One: Creating a Foundation for Later Work

The UCAN treatment begins by helping the couple build a supportive foundation for addressing AN effectively as a team by targeting three goals: (1) understanding the couple's experience of AN, (2) providing psychoeducation about AN and the recovery process, and (3) teaching the couple communication skills. These treatment procedures aim to reduce the secrecy and avoidance surrounding AN and build the couple's ability to communicate effectively; thus, all three mechanisms described above are in play from the outset of UCAN.

Assessment and psychoeducation. UCAN begins with a thorough assessment of the couple's relationship, AN symptoms, and AN-associated features. Each AN symptom (e.g. low weight, fear of weight gain, restricting) is presented to the couple, and both partners share their experiences and observations of each characteristic. This same process is conducted for comorbid conditions, such as depression, anxiety, substance abuse, etc. The therapist then discusses biologi cal and environmental risk and maintenance factors for AN, as well as details about the recovery process, addressing any questions or misconceptions either partner may have. By discussing this psychoeducation material with both members of the couple, UCAN decreases the secrecy around AN and works to create a comprehensive and shared understanding of AN to help foster the couple's teamwork.

Communication training. Phase one of UCAN concludes with teaching the couple communication skills to help them share their thoughts and feelings with each other, along with strategies for making sound decisions. Through didactic instruction and extensive in-session and out-of-session practice, the couple learns how to express thoughts and feelings, listen responsively, and solve problems/make decisions as a team. More specifically, the emotional expressiveness skills focus on couples sharing their personal experiences in a subjective and specific manner, including their emotions related to the AN, one another, and the relationship. These conversations facilitate the couple taking risks in terms of being more open and vulnerable. The couple is taught how to respond to such disclosures using active listening skills. These listening skills help partners demonstrate that they have heard one another accurately, and that they accept each other's experiences even if they do not agree. This distinction between "acceptance and agreement" – that it is possible to accept one another's experience as being valid and authentic, and yet not have to agree – is paramount for couples experiencing AN. Frequently, the patient and partner have different perspectives relative to the disorder, with some of these having significant implications, such as whether the patient is indeed ill, underweight, or needs a higher level of care. The emotional expressiveness skills create a way for couples to have such conversations, so that both partners feel understood even when their perspectives differ. Couples are also taught how to make decisions together by first articulating what is important to each partner and then working to honor these needs and compromise on a mutually agreed decision. The above skills are applied in couple therapy across a broad set of issues, but in UCAN, the application of these skills involves couples' conversations about the AN. Couples also are encouraged to apply these skills outside of session to issues within their general relationship, so they may also contribute to improvements in the couple's overall relationship quality.

Phase Two: Addressing Anorexia Nervosa within a Couples Context

Resuming a healthy body weight and developing healthy eating behaviors (e.g. avoidance of restricting and purging) are major treatment goals for individuals with AN. Phase two, the majority of the UCAN treatment, parallels the patient's efforts in individual therapy by concurrently helping the couple develop a good support system for this individual work.

Addressing eating disordered behavior. In phase two, the couple works together to address a series of AN challenges to foster healthful eating, exercise, and other relevant behavioral patterns, including arranging to eat together, addressing concerns around eating in public, and changing unhelpful couple interaction patterns by using more appropriate strategies. With the help of their UCAN therapist, the couple is guided in a thoughtful consideration of AN features they find most challenging, and then how to employ their communication skills in responding to these challenges more successfully together. Consistent with the exposure principle of working toward more challenging behaviors over time, the couple selects a lower level AN behavior to address first, such as creating a more positive family mealtime environment. Regarding mealtimes, both patients and partners commonly describe feeling anxious and worrying about what the other is thinking or may do. The patient may worry that the partner is acting like the "food police," and the partner may be frightened that the patient is not eating enough or unsure what to say about or do with this concern. The therapist guides the couple in developing specific strategies to help mealtimes be more calm and conducive to healthy eating (e.g. creating a regular schedule for meals, or a plan for what to discuss and not discuss during meals).

Body image concerns. Phase two of UCAN continues by broadening the AN focus to encompass body image and physical intimacy issues. Applying their communication skills, the couple discusses body image issues and how they can better interact around this challenging domain. Body image distortions and body dissatisfaction can be two of the most confusing and challenging features of AN for the partner; therefore, it is important that the couple has an opportunity to increase understanding of and empathy for each other's body image experiences. Once they have a greater appreciation of how each partner experiences this domain, the couple can use their decision-making skills to create supportive ways of interacting around body image that are conducive to recovery. For example, the couple may decide that the (female) patient will describe to the partner how she feels about her body without focusing on "being fat," and the partner will practice using active listening to express his understanding of her feelings and offer a hug provided the patient finds physical closeness to be supportive. By using the emotional expressiveness skills of the patient being subjective and specific and the partner communicating that he accepts (without having to agree with) the patient's distress, the couple is better able to discuss this topic, helping both parties to feel more supported and understood.

Physical intimacy and affection. Building from the body image domain, phase two concludes with a consideration of the couple's physical intimacy relative to AN. The therapist discusses how sex and physical affection can affect and be affected by the experience of negative body image and an eating disorder, incorporating the couple's specific experiences throughout this discussion. Included in this exploration is how the couple experiences challenges within their physical relationship more broadly as well. Because couples vary widely in their physical and sexual relationships, UCAN is tailored to the patient's and couple's current level of functioning and assists them in developing healthier patterns within their physical relationship. For example, couples who have not been physically close may first work on discussing the possibility of physical touch or beginning to hold hands. Other couples who continue to have physical closeness may focus on building greater quality or quantity of physical intimacy in their lives.

Phase Three: Relapse Prevention and Termination

Phase three of UCAN brings the treatment to a close, focusing on relapse prevention and the couple's next steps in the AN recovery process. The therapist provides psychoeducation on recovery and relapse prevention to help ensure that the couple has realistic, shared expectations for the nonlinear recovery typical of AN. With the therapist's guidance, the couple develops appropriate agreed-upon responses should a slip or full relapse occur for both (a) the patient's eating-disordered behaviors and related symptoms, and (b) the couple's approach to addressing the disorder. Thus, the couple might address how they will discuss their concerns if the patient returns to restricted eating, rather than avoiding the issues as a couple. The treatment concludes with a review of the UCAN experience and a consideration of how the couple needs to continue working together toward recovery from AN.

UCAN Initial Observations

The UCAN program is currently undergoing extensive evaluation with couples in committed relationships. However, results from the pilot trial (Bulik & Baucom, 2012) are highly encouraging, and clinical observations suggest that including partners in the treatment process is of considerable value. First, partners helped keep patients in treatment – only 5 percent of patients dropped out from our initial UCAN trial in comparison to the ~25–40 percent dropout rate observed in previous clinical trials of medication and behavioral interventions for AN (Berkman et al., 2006). Second, UCAN resulted in much greater weight gain over the course of treatment than other clinical interventions (M_{BMI} increase of 2.9 versus 1 kg/m^2; Berkman et al., 2006), suggesting that it was more effective at restoring the patient to physical health. Third, psychological functioning also improved for UCAN patients, with eating disorder symptoms reducing in severity. Fourth, the couples reported experiencing improvements in their relationship functioning. Thus, preliminary data suggest that the UCAN program improves outcome for adults with AN. Since the development of UCAN, case reports of adult patients with eating disorders receiving couple therapy to augment their individual therapy have been published and show promise as well (Murray, 2014; Reyes-Rodriguez, Baucom, & Bulik, 2015).

Extension of UCAN to Other Eating Disorders (UNITE)

The benefit of UCAN in AN recovery naturally raised the question of whether couple-based interventions could also be of benefit for patients and partners affected by other eating disorders – namely, BN and BED. Thus far, we have designed a couple-based intervention for BED that builds on the UCAN foundation and is tailored to the specific features of BED. Uniting Couples in the Treatment of Eating Disorders–Binge-Eating Disorder (UNITE–BED) tackles delicate issues such as how weight is discussed by the couple, including the role of weight stigma; encourages couples to focus on health rather than weight; and addresses fundamental misunderstandings regarding the nature of BED as an illness, not a choice. This program is undergoing pilot testing, with recruitment data thus far suggesting couples are very interested in the program.

If proven effective, these couple-based programs (UCAN and UNITE) have the potential to transform clinical practice for adults with eating disorders who are in relationships. We aim to develop readily accessible dissemination platforms that will enable training of therapists around the world in these promising interventions.

Acknowledgments

We would like to thank Emily Pisetsky, Kathryn Nowlan, Camden Matherne, Robert Hamer, Brian Baucom, Jennifer Belus, and McKenzie Roddy for their contributions to this research. Jennifer S. Kirby and Cristin D. Runfola contributed equally to this chapter and share the role of first author. Donald H. Baucom and Cynthia M. Bulik are co-directors of the UCAN/UNITE treatment program and contributed equally to this chapter. Dr. Bulik is a consultant and grant recipient from Shire Pharmaceuticals.

This research was supported in part by grants MH082732-01 and MH093615 from the National Institute of Mental Health to Cynthia M. Bulik and Donald H. Baucom, MPIs. Cristin D. Runfola was supported by the Global Foundation for Eating Disorders (www.GFED.org; PIs: Bulik and Baucom). UNITE is also supported by a grant from the Hilda and Preston Davis Foundation. The project described was supported by the National Center for Research Resources and the National Center for Advancing Translational Sciences, National Institutes of Health, through Grant Award Number UL1TR000083. The content is solely the responsibility of the authors and does not necessarily represent the official views of the NIH.

142   *Jennifer S. Kirby et al.*

Notes

1 Co-first authors.
2 Co-senior authors.

References

Arcelus, J., Haslam, M., Farrow, C., & Meyer, C. (2013). The role of interpersonal functioning in the maintenance of eating psychopathology: A systematic review and testable model. *Clinical Psychology Review*, 33, 156–167.

Baucom, D. H., Belus, J. M., Adelman, C. B., Fischer, M. S., & Paprocki, C. (2014). Couple-based interventions for psychopathology: A renewed direction for the field. *Journal of Family Therapy*, 53, 445–461.

Berkman, N. D., Bulik, C. M., Brownley, K. A., Lohr, K. N., Sedway, J. A. et al. (2006). *Management of eating disorders: Evidence report/technology assessment no. 135* (Prepared by the RTI InternationalUniversity of North Carolina Evidence-Based Practice Center under contract no. 290-02-0016.) AHRQ Publication NO. 06-E010. Rockville, MD: Agency for Research and Quality.

Brown, T. A., & Keel, P. K. (2012). Current and emerging directions in the treatment of eating disorders. *Substance Abuse*, 6, 33–61.

Bulik, C. M., & Baucom, D. H. (2012). *Uniting couples (in the treatment of) anorexia nervosa (UCAN)*. Workshop presented at the International Conference on Eating Disorders, Austin, TX.

Bulik, C. M., Baucom, D. H., Kirby, J. S., & Pisetsky, E. (2011). Uniting couples (in the treatment of) anorexia nervosa (UCAN). *International Journal of Eating Disorders*, 44, 19–28.

Buren, D. J. van, & Williamson, D. A. (1988). Marital relationships and conflict resolution skills of bulimics. *International Journal of Eating Disorders*, 7, 735–741.

Epstein, N. B., & Baucom, D. H. (2002). *Enhanced cognitive-behavioral therapy for couples: A contextual approach*. Washington, DC: American Psychological Association.

Fischer, M. S., Baucom, D. H., Kirby, J. S., & Bulik, C. M. (2015). Partner distress in the context of adult anorexia nervosa: The role of patients' perceived negative consequences of AN and partner behaviors. *International Journal of Eating Disorders*, 48, 67–71.

Goddard, E., Macdonald, P., Sepulveda, A. R., Naumann, U., Landau, S. et al. (2011). Cognitive interpersonal maintenance model of eating disorders: Intervention for carers. *British Journal of Psychiatry*, 199, 225–231.

Huke, K., & Slade, P. (2006). An exploratory investigation of the experiences of partners living with people who have bulimia nervosa. *European Eating Disorders Review*, 14, 436–447.

Linville, D., Brown, T., Sturm, K., & McDougal, T. (2012). Eating disorders and social support: Perspectives of recovered individuals. *Eating Disorders*, 20, 216–231.

Lock, J. (2015). An update on evidence-based psychosocial treatments for eating disorders in children and adolescents. *Journal of Clinical Child and Adolescent Psychology*, 44(5),707–721. doi:10.1080/15374416.2014.971458.

Lock, J., Le Grange, D., Agras, W. S., & Dare, C. (2001). *Treatment manual for anorexia nervosa: A family-based approach*. New York: Guilford Press.

Maxwell, M., Thornton, L. M., Root, T. L., Pinheiro, A. P., Strober, M. et al. (2010). Life beyond the eating disorder: Education, relationships, and reproduction. *International Journal of Eating Disorders*, 44, 225–232.

Murray, S. B. (2014). A case of strategic couples therapy in adult anorexia nervosa: The importance of systems in context. *Contemporary Family Therapy*, 36, 392–397.

Pinheiro, A. P., Raney, T. J., Thornton, L. M., Fichter, M. M., Berrettini, W. H. et al. (2010). Sexual functioning in women with eating disorders. *International Journal of Eating Disorders*, 43, 123–129.

Reyes-Rodriguez, M. L., Baucom, D. H., & Bulik, C. M. (2015). Culturally sensitive intervention for Latina women with eating disorders: A case study. *Mexican Journal of Eating Disorders*, 5, 135–145.

Riener, R., Schindler, K., & Ludvik, B. (2006). Psychosocial variables, eating behavior, depression, and binge eating in morbidly obese subjects. *Eating Behavior*, 7, 309–314.

Schmidt, U., & Treasure, J. (2006). Anorexia nervosa: Valued and visible. A cognitive interpersonal maintenance model and its implications for research and practice. *British Journal of Clinical Psychology*, 45, 343–366.

Tozzi, F., Sullivan, P. F., Fear, J. L., McKenzie, J., & Bulik, C. M. (2003). Causes and recovery in anorexia nervosa: The patient's perspective. *International Journal of Eating Disorders*, 33, 143–154.

Van den Broucke, S., Vandereycken, W., & Vertommen, H. (1995a). Marital communication in eating disorder patients: A controlled observational study. *International Journal of Eating Disorders*, 17, 1–21.

Van den Broucke, S., Vandereycken, W., & Vertommen, H. (1995b). Marital intimacy in patients with an eating disorder: A controlled self-report study. *British Journal of Clinical Psychology*, 34, 67–78.

Whisman, M. A., Dementyeva, A., Baucom, D. H., & Bulik, C. M. (2012). Marital functioning and binge eating disorder in married women. *International Journal of Eating Disorders*, 45, 385–389.

Woodside, D. B., Lackstrom, J. B., & Shekter-Wolfson, L. (2000). Marriage in eating disorders comparisons between patients and spouses and changes over the course of treatment. *Journal of Psychosomatic Research*, 49, 165–168.

Zabala, M. J., Macdonald, P., & Treasure, J. (2009). Appraisal of caregiving burden, expressed emotion and psychological distress in families of people with eating disorders: A systematic review. *European Eating Disorders Review*, 17, 338–449.

12 Helping Couples Address Higher Level of Care Treatment for Anorexia Nervosa

Jennifer S. Kirby, Donald H. Baucom, Maria C. La Via, and Cynthia M. Bulik

Clinical guidelines for the treatment of anorexia nervosa (AN) converge in recommending treatment in the least restrictive environment (i.e. outpatient or day patient care), reserving hospital admission for those at risk of medical and/or psychological compromise (American Psychiatric Association, 2006; Beumont, Hay, & Beumont, 2003; Hay et al., 2014; National Institute for Clinical Excellence, 2004). According to these guidelines, a higher level of care (HLC) such as inpatient treatment is warranted when specific medical, psychiatric, and social situations arise, such as acute medical instability relating to the complications of malnutrition, suicidality, severe family environment or social problems, and a decline in weight despite maximally intensive outpatient care. As described elsewhere in this volume (Kirby, Runfola, Fischer, Baucom, & Bulik, 2016), UCAN (Uniting Couples in the treatment of Anorexia Nervosa; Bulik, Baucom, Kirby, & Pisetsky, 2011) is a 22-session treatment for patients with AN and their partners that integrates cognitive-behavioral couple therapy and cognitive-behavioral therapy for AN. UCAN is provided in conjunction with individual therapy, nutritional counseling, and medication management to ensure treatment appropriately addresses all elements of the disorder. UCAN reflects the clinical guidelines mentioned above by delivering multidisciplinary care and is an example of maximally intensive outpatient treatment. Even during the course of such intensive intervention, the need for HLC can emerge. In the following sections, we discuss the strategies used in UCAN focal to HLC decisions. Specifically, we present techniques used to orient couples to the concept of HLC, prevent HLC, address when HLC is imminent, and facilitate the transition to and from HLC. (For additional detail on the UCAN program, see Bulik et al., 2011; Fisher, Kirby, Raney, Baucom, & Bulik, 2015).

UCAN is believed to benefit couples by decreasing the secrecy and avoidance commonly associated with AN, helping the couple work as a team to address AN, and improving overall relationship functioning as needed. Primary interventions include: (a) psychoeducation about AN and how it manifests within the couple's relationship; (b) communication skills training (i.e. emotional expressiveness training, which consists of both partners sharing thoughts and feelings, and the couple making decisions as a team); and (c) applying these communication skills around domains focal to AN (e.g. the couple develops a mealtime schedule that supports the patient in increasing caloric intake, and spends time together after meals to assist the patient with physical and emotional discomfort, refrain from purging, etc.).

Orienting Couples to HLC

The role of HLC in the treatment of AN is introduced early in UCAN treatment. Initial sessions are dedicated to psychoeducation, assessment of the patient's AN symptoms, and formulation of treatment goals (i.e. weight gain, dietary plan, coping skills, etc.) to help the couple reach a shared understanding of the team's impressions of the patient's status and what to expect during recovery. The role of the treatment team is discussed at length and includes close monitoring of the patient/couple's progress in treatment, regular feedback to the couple (i.e. every four weeks or more often as needed), and recommendations for HLC when medically necessary. Conditions when an HLC may be considered are presented to the couple in a frank, matter-of-fact and caring manner, with the clarification that UCAN treatment may no longer be provided if the team's recommendations are not adhered to. These conversations demonstrate that we will work with the couple around HLC in as collaborative and flexible a manner as possible, while also being clear that we will not avoid nor shy away from clear recommendations for more intensive treatment. It also is effective to discuss HLC early in treatment when it is not needed since it is easier for couples to absorb when they are not confronting the distress that often accompanies an HLC recommendation.

Preventing HLC

To help prevent HLC, the UCAN program keeps couples informed of the patient's illness status, treatment progress, and any potential need for HLC. By remaining in close communication with the team throughout treatment, patients and partners can monitor the patient's trajectory and work together to make needed behavioral changes to promote recovery and avoid HLC (i.e. increase caloric intake, decrease exercise, etc.). Clinical deterioration is discussed in couple therapy so both partners hear the same message. If, for example, weight is dropping over consecutive weeks, the couple can consider how to reverse the downward trend by focusing on a specific agreed-upon behavior, and using their communication skills to develop a plan to make needed changes (e.g. increasing portion size at dinner, eating meals together to increase patient accountability). In this manner, the couple can actively work with the therapist to prevent HLC. Specific UCAN interventions to help patients and partners work together to target specific eating disordered behaviors are described in greater detail elsewhere (Bulik et al., 2011; Fisher et al., 2015).

Addressing when HLC is Imminent

The nature of AN is such that, at times, HLC is unavoidable and medically necessary. Examples of such situations include consistent weight loss, medical instability, re-emergence of uninterruptable unhealthy behaviors (e.g. purging, laxative abuse, cutting), and suicidality. After team discussion, the UCAN therapist shares the team's concerns and recommendation for HLC with the couple. Depending on community resources, options and appropriate levels of HLC are discussed based on patient status (e.g. intensive outpatient, partial-hospitalization, residential, specialist inpatient, or medical admission). These discussions help partners support patients in making wise decisions about HLC. Couples are then guided through a discussion of their reactions to the prospect of HLC and associated practical considerations (i.e. disruption to work, childcare, etc.). Common challenges in helping couples anticipate HLC are provided below.

Denial or minimization of need for HLC. Helping couples prepare for HLC effectively requires recognition of the severity of the patient's illness and inability to continue safely or effectively in outpatient treatment. Patients commonly underestimate the severity of their illness, ranging from failure to acknowledge that they even have an eating disorder to acknowledging the disorder but being adamant that they can improve without HLC. In the UCAN program, partners more often recognize the need for HLC and are responsive to the team's recommendations. However, partners who are less assertive may defer to the patient's judgment and, believing that they are being supportive, act in a manner that they believe shows respect for the patient's right to decide. When patients and partners agree that HLC is in order, the process can be seamless. When disagreement occurs, these conversations can be protracted, emotional, and challenging and can lead to the UCAN team having to determine that outpatient treatment is no longer a safe or appropriate option for the patient. Whereas the patient makes the ultimate decision regarding HLC, the treatment team is clear in its recommendations, and the UCAN therapist helps to guide the couple's conversation such that all relevant information and emotional responses are addressed. In the unlikely event that the patient is seen to be medically or psychiatrically unstable (e.g. hypokalemia with EKG changes, loss of consciousness, or suicidality) and the patient continues to refuse HLC, then the UCAN team will consider and, if appropriate, pursue involuntary treatment at HLC, discussing this decision with both the patient and partner.

AN-associated features. Common psychological attributes of individuals with AN can interfere with sound judgments and decisions about HLC. Perfectionism can reduce receptiveness to HLC as patients may view needing HLC as a sign of failure or personal weakness. In addition, a high need to maintain control is often present in AN, and HLC by its very nature consists of healthcare providers taking greater control over the patient's treatment. AN also is a very private disorder, and HLC is a much more public acknowledgment of problems, not only to staff, but also to people in the patient's environment. Persistent weight loss or low weight that is non-responsive to outpatient care can also exacerbate rigid thinking, which interferes with processing new information, and challenges flexible consideration of HLC treatment options. Finally, anxiety is a hallmark feature of AN (Kaye et al., 2004), including worry, fear of the unknown, and difficulty tolerating uncertainty, thus rendering the prospect of HLC very frightening. Furthermore, these features can compound and exacerbate one another (e.g. anxiety leading to greater rigidity and fear of loss of control), making discussions and decisions about HLC even more challenging.

Partner features. Partners also present with psychological attributes that can interfere with making sound judgments about HLC or participating effectively in HLC decision making. A commonly observed pattern is generally passive partners who refrain from sharing their perspectives, defer to the patient's wishes, and fail to challenge the patient's reluctance to consider HLC. In this way, partners risk "sitting on the sidelines," and patients do not benefit from their encouragement or greater clarity of perspective. Anxious partners may also be reluctant to consider HLC because of their own perceptions of risk and uncertainty. Lastly, partners who deny or fail to recognize the severity of the illness can be less receptive to considering HLC as a necessary component of the patient's treatment.

Raising numerous concerns with HLC. HLC in adults can create logistical challenges for patients and partners. However, these challenges are viewed by the treatment team as secondary to the patient's well-being and should be considered in much the same way as hospitalization for any other major medical condition would be handled by a family. Such challenges can include securing time off from work or school, arranging childcare, and financial considerations. Patients (and partners) can present these challenges as being insurmountable, and therefore conclude that HLC is impossible. In such situations, the partner's response is pivotal. If they side with the patient in saying that the logistical issues cannot be addressed, patients can firmly resist HLC. If partners express confidence and willingness to help address the logistics at hand (i.e. taking time off from work to help with childcare), navigating alternatives and marshaling resources can help patients consider HLC independent of logistical barriers. Once patients and partners are on board with the possibility of HLC, they are guided through how best to prepare for HLC, as described below.

Guiding Couples through HLC Discussions

As discussed above, UCAN teaches couples to communicate effectively (i.e. sharing thoughts and feelings, and making decisions), and these skills are used throughout the patient's treatment and when HLC is being considered (for greater detail on communication skills training, see Epstein & Baucom, 2002). When discussing potential HLC, the UCAN therapist first talks with the couple in a three-way conversation, in which the therapist's role is to present the recommendation of HLC, elicit each partner's initial reactions to the recommendation, and validate concerns and distress regarding the patient's illness severity or HLC, being careful not to side with either partner or to pit the treatment team against the couple. This conversation is mostly funneled through the therapist, providing a helpful structure for these initial exchanges, which can be tense or emotional based on the couple's reactions to HLC. Then, if the couple has proficient communication skills, the UCAN therapist asks the patient and partner to speak directly with each other about HLC. (If the couple is early in treatment and/or highly argumentative, the therapist may continue the conversation in a three-way format.) In all discussions, the therapist ensures that both the patient and partner have time to share their perspective, demonstrating that the partner is viewed as a full member of the team, and the consideration of HLC is not done solely by the patient.

Expressing thoughts and feelings about HLC. UCAN teaches couples emotional expressiveness skills (i.e. sharing personal experiences, and actively listening without having to agree), and these skills play an important role in helping patients and partners consider HLC decisions together. Patients and partners are encouraged to share their thoughts and emotions, which may include their reactions to the team's assessment of the patient's illness severity, anticipated experiences of being in HLC, and the implications of seeking or not seeking HLC. Couples are encouraged to speak subjectively and specifically, describing their own personal experience rather than stating what they view as fact or objective truth. This allows patients and partners to understand each other and accept any differences of opinion more readily. For example, if a partner describes feeling afraid that the patient's health will continue to deteriorate if HLC is not pursued (e.g. "I'm very scared something will happen to you if you don't go in the hospital, and I don't want to lose you"), versus judging the patient's reluctance to accept HLC (e.g. "This is crazy. How can you not see how sick you are?"), the patient is more likely to listen to the partner's concerns and be open to the team's recommendation for HLC.

In addition, couples are asked to identify and express their specific emotions, especially feelings of vulnerability (e.g. fear of loss, feeling sad, love toward each other, etc.), versus focusing solely on feelings of frustration or anger. The expression of these softer emotions, particularly when related to the relationship, has the potential to heighten the couple's connection, and build motivation toward recovery and HLC. Active listening skills help partners demonstrate that they have heard one another accurately, and that they accept each other's experiences even if they do not agree with them. Respecting each other's perspectives in this way allows both partners to experience their feelings, while also acknowledging those of their partner – an important communication process for couples navigating challenging conversation topics, such as HLC.

Making decisions about HLC. UCAN also teaches couples how to make effective decisions as a team – deciding whether the patient will seek HLC may be one of the most significant decisions the couple makes in the patient's recovery. Decision-making skills consist of identifying what is important to each partner, and working to honor these needs to arrive at a mutually agreed upon decision. Within the context of HLC, patients and partners are encouraged to identify needs relative to level of care (e.g. inpatient, residential, partial-hospitalization), location of care (e.g. local resources versus traveling for care), arranging child-care coverage, navigating work responsibilities, paying for the costs of HLC, telling others about HLC admission, etc. Once these needs are articulated, the couple works together to create the best solution, compromising when necessary and possible. Notably, the most challenging decision for couples tends to be whether the patient will seek HLC – sharing thoughts and feelings regarding HLC as described above plays a crucial role in making these decisions effectively. Once the couple has agreed on HLC, decisions focusing on how best to implement HLC can be more straightforward.

Transitioning to and from HLC

Once a couple has decided to pursue HLC, the UCAN treatment team makes the referral, orients the HLC team to the patient's status and treatment needs, and maintains contact with the couple throughout the transition to HLC. When possible, the UCAN therapist conducts a brief check-in with the patient and partner during HLC to help maintain treatment continuity and provides encouragement to both members of the couple. Following HLC discharge, the UCAN team providers meet with the patient as soon as possible, in an effort to support any treatment gains the patient may have made in HLC. The UCAN therapist discusses with the couple how they can work together to provide a smooth transition back to outpatient care, leveraging the greater accountability, structure, and support that is inherent to HLC. For example, upon discharge from HLC, the partner may spend more time with the patient, the couple may eat more meals together, and sessions with the outpatient team may occur more frequently. As the patient gains a firmer footing in outpatient care, the couple can transition the partner's role as appropriate.

When HLC is Refused

The strategies described above facilitate a couple's consideration of HLC to help ensure a smooth transition to and from the UCAN program. However, despite these efforts, couples may continue to have significant concerns regarding the pursuit of HLC. When the team has recommended HLC to boost the patient's progress in treatment (e.g. a partial-hospitalization), and there are no significant medical concerns with the patient remaining in outpatient care, the team may offer the patient a time-limited opportunity to continue outpatient care in the UCAN program under an explicit agreement. For example, if the patient is able to gain a prescribed amount of weight in the subsequent two weeks and eat dinner on a predetermined number of days, the couple can continue to be treated in UCAN. If these benchmarks are not met, then HLC would be required in order to remain in the UCAN program.

In cases when HLC is deemed necessary, and the patient refuses despite multiple efforts by the treatment team, the patient is operating against medical advice, and therefore can no longer safely participate in UCAN. The couple is then withdrawn from UCAN, a transition is made back to the care of their primary care physician and any other community providers, and a notification letter is sent to the patient's primary care physician indicating that we are no longer overseeing the patient's care. If the patient refuses HLC and is considered to be medically or psychiatrically unstable (e.g. hypokalemia with EKG changes, loss of consciousness, or suicidality), then the UCAN team may pursue involuntary treatment at HLC, discussing this decision with both the patient and partner. Although the team makes every effort for these circumstances not to eventuate, safety and appropriateness of care is of paramount importance.

Conclusion

The UCAN program helps patients and partners work together towards recovery from AN. When patients are struggling and HLC is clinically indicated, patients are at a critical juncture in treatment, and partners can serve an invaluable role providing emotional and practical support. In UCAN, couples are encouraged to express their thoughts and feelings about HLC, make sound decisions, and prepare for HLC together as a team. We believe these same strategies can be utilized with any loved ones involved in a patient's treatment for AN. Parents, other family members, close friends, and partners all can be allies in recovery. We recommend identifying these supportive individuals, and welcoming them into the patient's care, especially during pivotal times such as potential HLC. Loved ones' support can play a key role in helping patients to remain engaged in treatment for AN and receive the appropriate level of care they need.

References

American Psychiatric Association. (2006). *Practice guideline for the treatment of patients with eating disorders*, 3rd edition. Available online at www.psychiatryonline.com/pracGuide/loadGuidelinePdf.aspx?file=EatingDisorders3ePG_04-28-06 (accessed 4 June, 2015).

Beumont, P., Hay, P. J., & Beumont, R. (2003). Summary Australian and New Zealand clinical practice guideline for the management of anorexia nervosa. *Australasian Psychiatry*, 11, 129–133.

Bulik, C. M., Baucom, D. H., Kirby, J. S., & Pisetsky, E. (2011). Uniting Couples (in the treatment of) Anorexia Nervosa (UCAN). *International Journal of Eating Disorders*, 44(1), 19–28. doi:10.1002/eat.20790.

Epstein, N., & Baucom, D. H. (2002). *Enhanced cognitive-behavioral therapy for couples: A contextual approach*. Washington, DC: American Psychological Association.

Fischer, M. S., Kirby, J. S., Raney, T. J., Baucom, D. H., & Bulik, C. M. (2015). Integrating couple-based interventions into the treatment of adult anorexia nervosa: A case example of UCAN. In H. Thompson-Brenner (Ed.), *Casebook of evidence-based therapy for eating disorders* (pp. 220–245). New York: Guilford Press.

Hay, P., Chinn, D., Forbes, D., Madden, S., Newton, R. et al. (2014). Royal Australian and New Zealand College of Psychiatrists' clinical practice guidelines for the treatment of eating disorders. *Australian and New Zealand Journal of Psychiatry*, 48(11), 977–1008. doi:10.1177/0004867414555814.

Kaye, W., Bulik, C., Thornton, L., Barbarich, B. S., Masters, K., & Group, P. F. C. (2004). Comorbidity of anxiety disorders with anorexia and bulimia nervosa. *American Journal of Psychiatry*, 161, 2215–2221.

Kirby, J. S., Runfola, C. D., Fischer, M. S., Baucom, D. H., & Bulik, C. M. (2016). Couple-based interventions for adults with eating disorders. In S. Murray, L. Anderson, & L. Cohn (Eds.), *Innovations in family therapy for eating disorders: Novel treatment developments, patient insights, and the role of carers* (pp. 331–351). Abingdon: Routledge.

National Institute for Clinical Excellence. (2004). Eating disorders: Core interventions in the treatment and management of anorexia nervosa, bulimia nervosa and related eating disorders. Available online at www.nice.org.uk/page.aspx?o=101239 (accessed May 15, 2015).

13 Collaborative Care

The New Maudsley Model

Janet Treasure, Charlotte Rhind, Pam Macdonald, and Gill Todd

Introduction

Anorexia nervosa (AN) has a profound interpersonal impact and often develops at a time of transition within the family. The family and the wider social network have the potential resources to remediate many of the problems faced by individuals with eating disorders. One individual, for example, used the word "isolation" to describe her personal journey through her illness (McKnight & Boughton, 2009). The continued connection to the family can ameliorate loneliness and isolation. Nevertheless, families often report that they are not given the information and skills that they need to manage all phases of the illness (Haigh & Treasure, 2003).

Family-based therapy (FBT) is the gold standard treatment for adolescent patients in the early stage of illness and families are encouraged to be involved in providing direct care to support eating (Lock, 2015). Devised by Gerald Russell and colleagues at the Maudsley Hospital in the 1970s, FBT was shown to have benefits over individual therapy. Interestingly, however, this intervention was not of superior benefit for those in a later stage of the illness and for those who had an adult onset (Eisler et al., 1997; Russell, Szmukler, Dare, & Eisler, 1987).

Various adaptations to FBT have been made. One variation was to make it more suitable for adult patients. This adaptation of FBT was of equivalent benefit to specialist individual therapy (cognitive analytical and focal dynamic; Dare, Eisler, Russell, Treasure, & Dodge, 2001). It has now been further adapted as the New Maudsley Collaborative Care approach to address the complex needs of families of people in the severe enduring stage of AN. In essence, the family, individual, and treatment team work in partnership towards a shared understanding of and approach to management. The guidance and support for families is similar to the training and supervision offered to staff on specialized inpatient units since the same problems, dilemmas, and interpersonal difficulties occur in both the home and hospital (Treasure, Crane, McKnight, Buchanan, & Wolfe, 2011).

Families and individuals in the later stage of AN have different needs from families seen within the first few months of onset, as the time-related changes have a profound effect on both biological and psychosocial functioning; see

Table 13.1 A summary of needs for both the individual patient and the family at the severe enduring stage of illness

Patient problems	Carer problems
Secondary consequences of prolonged starvation and entrenched habits of abnormal eating behavior. Increased anhedonia and anxiety.	Problems with social cognition, depression, and emotional regulation (the consequences of starvation) adding to the complex mix of psychopathology.
Increased obsessive compulsive and autistic spectrum traits.	May be caught in web of maintaining factors such as inadvertently accommodating or enabling the illness.
Capacity for eating-related decisions is impaired. Automatic habits.	Managing the balance of dependency and autonomy.
Interpersonal problems – impaired social cognition and isolation.	Managing the distancing and isolating.
Interrupted vocational functioning.	Financial and other support.

Table 13.1 (Treasure, Stein, & Maguire, 2014). Carers may find themselves on the periphery of illness management, due to confidentiality issues and/or because of an increased desire for independence and responsibility on the part of the patient themselves. The goal of our collaborative skills training is to equip carers with skills that allow them to best support their loved one in a spirit of collaboration and compassion towards a healthier future.

Some of the differences between FBT (Lock, Le Grange, Agras, & Dare, 2001) and the New Maudsley Collaborative Care (NMCC) model (Treasure, Smith, & Crane, 2007) are shown in Table 13.2. Most variations are due to the fact that the interventions target the different needs at the two stages of illness. Both have the ultimate aim of empowering parents to support recovery. The goals for each phase of treatment have to be realistic. Studies in both the early (Agras et al., 2014) and late (Le Grange et al., 2014) stages of the illness find that duration of illness is a key prognostic feature and the Australian and New Zealand guidelines suggest that harm reduction rather than full medical recovery is an appropriate goal for the severe enduring phase of illness. In such cases a better quality of life for both patient and carer is an important goal. The NMCC approach offers a flexible format. Carers are taught how to care for themselves and to manage their own stress reaction to their loved one's disorder. Skills-based training provides an evidence-based template giving information and targeted caregiving skills.

Overview of the Intervention

For the NMCC approach, "carers" are defined as individuals who provide unpaid help and support, such as a parent, child, partner, relative, friend, or

Table 13.2 A comparison between FBT (earlier Maudsley model) and (New Maudsley Collaborative Care)

Family-based care	New Maudsley Collaborative Care
Evidence base: Strong. For people < 18 years, < 3 years illness. Atheoretical.	Evidence base: Emerging. Neuroprogressive changes due to prolonged malnutrition compounds the psychopathology. This complexity increases carer stress.
Moderator. Less successful when high expressed emotion in carer or high obsessive traits in patients.	Theoretical targets. Aim 1. To reduce objective and subjective caregiving burden. Aim 2. To reduce expressed emotion, and accommodating and enabling behaviors.
Goal to increase parental anxiety. Increase parental control over eating.	Goal to decrease parental anxiety. Nutritional goal negotiated as behavioral experiment (extinction hierarchy).

neighbor. Initially this intervention was delivered as a training workshop for several families. The workshops (course of six for two hours) are led by team members with expertise in family work, conjointly with a paid recovery guide (i.e. an individual who has recovered from anorexia nervosa). These individuals are "expert patients," and have flexible contracts with the National Health Service. This joint work is particularly beneficial, as it inspires hope that recovery can occur and leads to a shared understanding of recovery.

More recently, we have delivered the intervention in the form of self-management materials (with guidance). Materials include a manual, set of five instructional DVDs, and series of telephone coaching sessions.

Underpinning Theory and Rationale for Treatment

The theoretical maintenance model that forms the basis of collaborative care is shown in Figure 13.1. This model involves (a) coping with the caregiving role and (b) managing caregiving behaviors towards the ill individual.

The carer coping model is based on the standard stress coping model. Stress inevitably results from the caregiving role, including both objective and subjective burden. There are also protective factors that buffer this effect, but anxiety and depression can result if there is a lack of balance between the stress and protective factors. We teach carers an approach called "C" style, which includes compassion and cooperation with a collaborative and consistent approach with close others. Thus, carers are taught to reflect on their own approach to the illness, utilize emotional intelligence, and reduce enmeshment by encouraging their loved one to take responsibility for their own well-being in the context of agreed boundaries, i.e. eating is non-negotiable. We set the scene

Figure 13.1   Model of carer coping and the interpersonal maintenance component from the cognitive interpersonal model of anorexia nervosa

by emphasizing how the curriculum matches that used for training professionals in specialized eating disorder units. This clears any implicit assumption that carers are to blame or are deficient in some way. We explain that these core skills take health professionals years of training, practice, and supervision to master and we do not expect them to be proficient with 12 hours of training.

First Steps: Building Resilience

We use the airplane analogy – attending to their own oxygen supply before helping anyone else to put on an oxygen mask – to explain how caring for themselves is important. We explain that this model is good coping behavior for the person with an eating disorder. We explore the need for tolerating compromise, not perfection, and also instill a sense of hope, by "seeing the bigger picture."

We then provide psychoeducation on the three levels of maintenance in anorexia: (a) underlying risk factors and vulnerabilities (Schmidt & Treasure, 2006); (b) neuroprogression – the consequences of starvation and abnormal eating behaviors on brain structure and function (Treasure et al., 2014); and (c) social functioning and judging the reactions of others (Treasure & Schmidt, 2013).

Communication Skills

The foundation is built upon motivational interviewing skills. These are used by the facilitators of the workshop to encourage carers to change their own behaviors. This is a surprise for some carers who came for help to change their child's behaviors. The stages of change within the trans-theoretical model (Prochaska, DiClemente, & Norcross, 1992) are brought to life as carers recognize that they are ambivalent or in precontemplation about changing their own behaviors. Role plays and observations of live or recorded interactions form the core aspect of this training. Carers are asked to critique and analyze the processes during the observed interactions, before practicing themselves with role play.

Emotional Regulation Skills

Eating disorders elicit a mixture of intense emotional reactions. We have used animal metaphors to describe the most common reactions, including over-emotional (jellyfish), avoidant (ostrich), critical (terrier), hostile (rhinoceros), and over-protective, avoidant (kangaroo). Participants are encouraged to use these metaphors in order to step back from these hot emotional reactions and behaviors. The goal is for carers to agree to a middle ground in terms of a collaborative and consistent approach in addressing the symptoms. The metaphor of a "dolphin" or a "St. Bernard" is used to describe the ideal "C" style of "collaborative caring." Carers may need to have conversations around joint behavior change styles and goals, such as planning meal support, reducing accommodating and enabling behaviors, and managing over- or under-controlled behaviors.

Accommodation and Enabling

Carers frequently find themselves being pulled into accommodating and enabling problematic behaviors and we use the metaphor of an anorexic bully to describe this. Mothers may clean up the bathrooms after an episode of purging, for example, in order to "keep the peace" or to hide behaviors from the rest of the family. Alternatively, they may drive to six different supermarkets for one special salad dressing. Accommodating and enabling behaviors become automatic and may not register as problematic, and prompting with examples or a self-report instrument may be needed to encourage self-reflection (Sepulveda, Kyriacou, & Treasure, 2009). Consequently, accommodation and enabling behaviors often require a functional analysis of the individual's and carer's behavior in order to examine how the antecedents or consequences of the behavior are modified by the carer's behavior. These behaviors are under the direct control of the carer and can be an important lever for change. Carers are, therefore, taught the principles of extinction learning, whereby gradual goal-setting is applied to tackle fearful scenarios. Accommodating behaviors are more likely to arise if the amount of contact time is high and if the carer or the individual with AN has high levels of anxiety. Change therefore involves overcoming fears about what would happen if the family stopped accommodating.

The following scenario offers an illustration of New Maudsley collaborative care techniques. The therapist role models the same behavior she would like to encourage Paula and David to use with their daughter: calmness, reflective listening, open questioning, rolling with resistance, use of affirmations, and providing psychoeducational information:

> *Paula and David are the parents of Jess, their 19-year-old daughter with anorexia nervosa. Jess is currently seeing her therapist and her GP on a weekly basis. In the following excerpt the therapist engages both parents into adopting a more collaborative stance.*

THERAPIST: Last week you said you would monitor your caregiver behaviors. David, I think you said you were often in rhino mode and Paula, you were often a jelly fish or kangaroo. How have things been going?

DAVID: I know I don't always deal with it the way I should. Work is tough-going at the moment and I'm tired when I get home. Paula really needs to let go a bit more. She's got to begin to trust Jess at some point. She's 19, for God's sake.

PAULA: I'd love to be able to let go a bit more… It's so difficult to carry it out, though.

THERAPIST: Last session we all spoke about how changing habits is really tough-going. How do you feel if we work with this scale to reflect on your responses … to look at where you are in relation to each other? I'm hearing agreements on the need for change from both of you and also quite a bit of uncertainty as to how to put these changes into place. *[summary of last session + open question + complex reflection + giving information]* So let's take a scale [writing '5–4–3–2–1 … 0… 1–2–3–4–5' on a piece of paper] that's full-on rhino on the left-hand side and full-on kangaroo on the right-hand side, and each of you give yourselves a score independently. We can then compare.

DAVID: I would say it's a 4 at the rhino end for me.

PAULA: And yeah… a 5 at the kangaroo end for me. Wouldn't it be great to have a bit more balance?

THERAPIST: So that's interesting – you feel you're at opposite ends of the scale, but you would *like* to develop a more middle ground. How about you, David – what are your thoughts? *[complex reflection + open question]*

DAVID: Yeah, well, same goes for me. We could definitely use coming together a bit more on a few things. Be good for Jess, too, I guess.

THERAPIST: So my next question is, how *confident* are you that you can move closer? *[open question]*

PAULA: Not very … I'd say a 3 for me.

DAVID: I'd go with a 5 … If I saw some give from Paula here, then I can surely work on my attitude.

THERAPIST: Change is tough for everybody…. David, you say that you would address your rhino tendencies if you saw some changes in Paula. Tell me a bit more about that? *[MI adherent (empathy) + simple reflection + open question]*

DAVID: [turning to Paula] Well, everything freaks you out. You want to know what Jess is eating, when she's eating, how much she exercises, who she's going out with, what time she'll be back. The atmosphere can be toxic at times. I worry about your own mental health, too, having this cloud of doom hang over you every minute of the day.

PAULA: Well, actually … I have been thinking of looking for some therapy for myself.

THERAPIST: You know, we do advise putting your own oxygen mask on first, so well done for considering your own needs, Paula. How might you like to see David establish a more middle ground? *[giving information + affirmation + open question]*

PAULA: I'd like you to become a bit more patient … patient with me *and* Jess. Sometimes – and I know you're busy at work – but you can be so short-tempered.

DAVID: I'm aware of that, and that's something I need to work on.

THERAPIST: You both seem to be very clear on what changes are needed. What help and support would you need from each other? *[simple reflection + open question]*

The session continues with the therapist discussing what help they might need from each other (and others), what obstacles might lie in the way and how they would address these obstacles. The session ends with them each setting a small goal for themselves in preparation for their next meeting.

Evidence Base

The workshops were found to be feasible, acceptable, and effective for reducing distress in carers and burden following completion of the program and at three-month follow-up (Pepin & King, 2013; Whitney, Currin, Murray, & Treasure, 2012a; Whitney et al., 2012b). The intervention successfully targeted the processes that maintain the illness; for example, levels of expressed emotion were reduced (Sepulveda et al., 2010). Moreover, the patients themselves reported positive benefits (Goddard et al., 2011).

More recently we have tested a guided self-help skills form of intervention. There were high levels of acceptability of this format (Goddard et al., 2013). The intervention was effective for reducing carer distress. Carers perceived improvements not only in their own outcomes, but also in those of the patient. In a recent trial using guided self-help for people with severe enduring illness following inpatient care, small sustained improvements in symptoms and reduced bed use are seen in the intervention group. Moreover, caregivers were less burdened and spent less time providing care (Hibbs et al., 2015).

Conclusion

Family involvement and individual work needs to be judiciously matched to severity and stage of the illness. We have given a summary of the New Maudsley Collaborative Care approach that can be used across stages of illness. In essence, this involves improving carers' resilience and behavior change skills through sharing information, teaching communication techniques, and working with a team approach.

References

Agras, W. S., Lock, J., Brandt, H., Bryson, S. W., Dodge, E. et al. (2014). Comparison of 2 family therapies for adolescent anorexia nervosa: A randomized parallel trial. *JAMA Psychiatry*, 71, 1279–1286.

Dare, C., Eisler, I., Russell G., Treasure, J., & Dodge, L. (2001). Psychological therapies for adults with anorexia nervosa: Randomised controlled trial of out-patient treatments. *British Journal of Psychiatry*, 178, 216–221.

Eisler, I., Dare, C., Russell, G. F., Szmukler, G., Le Grange, D., & Dodge, E. (1997). Family and individual therapy in anorexia nervosa: A 5-year follow-up. *Archives of General Psychiatry*, 54, 1025–1030.

Goddard, E., Macdonald, P., & Treasure, J. (2011). An examination of the impact of "the Maudsley eating disorder collaborative care skills workshops" on patients with anorexia nervosa: A qualitative study. *European Eating Disorders Review*, 19, 150–161.

Goddard, E., Raenker, S., Macdonald, P., Todd, G., Beecham, J. et al. (2013). Carers' assessment, skills and information sharing: Theoretical framework and trial protocol for a randomised controlled trial evaluating the efficacy of a complex intervention for carers of inpatients with anorexia nervosa. *European Eating Disorders Review*, 21, 60–71.

Haigh, R., & Treasure, J. (2003). Investigating the needs of carers in the area of eating disorders: Development of the Carers' Needs Assessment Measure (CaNAM). *European Eating Disorders Review*, 11, 125–141.

Hibbs, R., Magill, N., Goddard, E., Rhind, C., Raenker, S. et al. (2015). Clinical effectiveness of a skills training intervention for caregivers (ECHO, Experienced Caregivers Helping Others) in improving patient and caregiver health following inpatient treatment for severe anorexia nervosa: Pragmatic randomised controlled trial. *British Journal of Psychiatry Open*, 1, 56–66.

Le Grange D., Fitzsimmons-Craft, E. E., Crosby, R. D., Hay, P., Lacey, H. et al. (2014). Predictors and moderatores of outcome for severe and enduring anorexia nervosa. *Behaviour Research and Therapy*, 56, 91–98.

Lock, J. (2015). An update on evidence-based psychosocial treatments for eating disorders in children and adolescents. *Journal of Clinical and Child Adolescent Psychology*, 12, 1–15.

Lock, J., Le Grange, D., Agras, W. S., & Dare, C. (2001). *Treatment manual for anorexia nervosa: A family-based approach*. New York: Guilford Press.

McKnight, R., & Boughton, N. (2009). A patient's journey. Anorexia nervosa. *British Medical Journal*, 339. doi:10.1136/bmj.b3800.

Pepin, G., & King, R. (2013). Collaborative Care Skills Training workshops: Helping carers cope with eating disorders from the UK to Australia. *Social Psychiatry & Psychiatric Epidemiology*, 48, 805–812.

Prochaska, J. O., DiClemente, C. C., & Norcross, J. C. (1992). In search of how people change: Applications to addictive behaviors. *American Journal of Psychology*, 47, 1102–1114.

Russell, G., Szmukler, G., Dare, C., & Eisler, I. (1987). An evaluation of family therapy in anorexia nervosa and bulimia nervosa. *Archives of General Psychiatry*, 44, 1047–1056.

Schmidt, U., & Treasure, J. (2006). Anorexia nervosa: Valued and visible. A cognitive interpersonal maintenance model and its implications for research and practice. *British Journal of Clinical Psychology*, 45, 343–366.

Sepulveda, A. R., Kyriacou, O., & Treasure, J. (2009). Development and validation of the accommodation and enabling scale for eating disorders (AESED) for caregivers in eating disorders. *BMC Health Services Research*, 9, 171. doi:10.1186/1472-6963-9-171.

Sepulveda, A. R., Todd, G., Whitaker, W., Grover, M., Stahl, D., & Treasure, J. (2010). Expressed emotion in relatives of patients with eating disorders following skills training program. *International Journal of Eating Disorders*, 43, 603–610.

Treasure, J., & Schmidt, U. (2013). The cognitive-interpersonal maintenance model of anorexia nervosa revisited: A summary of the evidence for cognitive, socioemotional and interpersonal predisposing and perpetuating factors. *Journal of Eating Disorders*, 1, 13. doi:10.1186/2050-2974-1-13.

Treasure, J., Crane, A., McKnight, R., Buchanan, E., & Wolfe, M. (2011). First do no harm: Iatrogenic maintaining factors in anorexia nervosa. *European Eating Disorders Review*, 19, 296–302.

Treasure, J., Smith, G., & Crane, A. (2007). *Skills-based learning for caring for a loved one with an eating disorder: The New Maudsley method.* London: Routledge.

Treasure, J., Stein, D., & Maguire, S. (2014). Has the time come for a staging model to map the course of eating disorders from high risk to severe enduring illness? An examination of the evidence. *Early Intervention in Psychiatry*, 9(3), 173–184. doi:10.1111/eip.12170.

Whitney, J., Currin, L., Murray, J., & Treasure, J. (2012a). Family work in anorexia nervosa: A qualitative study of carers' experiences of two methods of family intervention. *European Eating Disorders Review*, 20, 132–141.

Whitney, J., Murphy, T., Landau, S., Gavan, K., Todd, G. et al. (2012b). A practical comparison of two types of family intervention: An exploratory RCT of family day workshops and individual family work as a supplement to inpatient care for adults with anorexia nervosa. *European Eating Disorders Review*, 20, 142–150.

14 Family in Residence Program

A Family Empowerment Model for Higher Levels of Care

Elizabeth Easton, Jamie Manwaring, Grant Salada, Ginger Hartman, Ovidio Bermudez, and Craig Johnson

Introduction

Family-based treatment (FBT; Lock & Le Grange, 2013) and the Maudsley Method (Russell, Szmukler, Dare, & Eisler, 1987) have clearly demonstrated that children and adolescents with anorexia nervosa (AN) benefit from active parent involvement in the behavioral management of weight restoration and other symptoms of the illness (Lock, 2015). Randomized controlled trials comparing FBT to individual therapy (Lock, Le Grange, Agras, Moye, Bryson, & Jo, 2010) and systemic family therapy (Agras et al., 2014) have demonstrated FBT to be more effective at follow-up. Further, FBT is a recommended treatment for both AN (American Psychiatric Association, 2006a; Lock, 2015; Lock et al., 2010), and bulimia nervosa (Le Grange, Lock, Agras, Bryson, & Booil, 2015).

FBT and the Maudsley Method have taught us that, with children and adolescents, parents are the best resource for managing a complex discharge plan requiring multiple interventions daily. The literature is clear that even without the challenge of a serious mental illness, children and adolescents are not reliable managers of their own health (e.g. Loeb & Le Grange, 2009). FBT was designed for outpatient treatment, and has been found to be particularly helpful for patients with less severe forms of the illness (i.e. shorter duration of illness, moderate weight loss, and low psychiatric comorbidity; Accurso, Fitzsimmons-Craft, Ciao, & Le Grange, 2015; Le Grange et al., 2012; Lock, Couterier, Bryson, & Agras, 2006). However, the use of the principles and techniques of FBT at higher levels of care, such as partial-hospital, residential, and inpatient settings, has not been fully explicated or systematically investigated.

This chapter describes an FBT-informed treatment program for children and adolescents who have complex clinical presentations, meet APA criteria for inpatient/residential/partial-hospitalization program care (APA, 2006b; see Table 14.1), and usually have histories of failed outpatient treatment. It is also designed for families who have to travel great distances to access care, thus creating barriers to implementing important face-to-face family therapy and education.

Table 14.1 American Psychiatric Association level of care guidelines for patients with eating disorders

	Level 1: Outpatient	Level 2: Intensive outpatient	Level 3: Partial-hospitalization (full-day outpatient care)[a]	Level 4: Residential treatment center	Level 5: Inpatient hospitalization
Medical status	Medically stable to the extent that more extensive medical monitoring, as defined in Levels 4 and 5, is not required			Medically stable to the extent that intravenous fluids, nasogastric tube feedings, or multiple daily laboratory tests are not needed	For adults: Heart rate < 40 bpm; blood pressure < 90/60 mmHg; glucose < 60 mg/dl; potassium < 3mEq/L; electrolyte imbalance; temperature <97.0°F; dehydration; hepatic, renal, or cardiovascular organ compromise requiring acute treatment; poorly controlled diabetes For children and adolescents: Heart rate near 40 bpm, orthostatic blood pressure changes (> 20 bpm increase in heart rate or > 10 mmHg to 20 mmHg drop), blood pressure < 80/50 mmHg, hypokalemia,[b] hypophosphatemia, or hypomagnesemia
Suicidality[c]	If suicidality is present, inpatient monitoring and treatment may be needed depending on the estimated level of risk				Specific plan with high lethality or intent; admission may also be indicated in patient with suicidal ideas or after a suicide attempt or aborted attempt, depending on the presence or absence of other factors modulating suicide risk

Weight as percentage of healthy body weight[d]	Generally > 85%	Generally > 80%	Generally > 80%	Generally < 85%	Generally < 85%; acute weight decline with food refusal even if not < 85% of healthy body weight
Motivation to recover, including cooperativeness, insight, and ability to control obsessive thoughts	Fair-to-good motivation	Fair motivation	Partial motivation; cooperative; patient preoccupied with intrusive, repetitive thoughts[e] for more than 3 hours/day	Poor-to-fair motivation; patient preoccupied with intrusive repetitive thoughts[e] 4–6 hours a day; patient cooperative with highly structured treatment	Very poor to poor motivation; patient preoccupied with intrusive repetitive thoughts[e]; patient uncooperative with treatment or cooperative only in highly structured environment
Co-occurring disorders (substance use, depression, anxiety)	Presence of comorbid condition may influence choice of level of care				Any existing psychiatric disorder that would require hospitalization
Structure needed for eating/gaining weight	Self-sufficient	Self-sufficient	Needs some structure to gain weight	Needs supervision at all meals or will restrict eating	Needs supervision during and after all meals or nasogastric/special feeding modality
Ability to control compulsive exercising	Can manage compulsive exercising through self-control	Some degree of external structure beyond self-control required to prevent patient from compulsive exercising; rarely a sole indication for increasing the level of care			
Purging behavior (laxatives and diuretics)	Can greatly reduce incidents of purging in an unstructured setting; no significant medical complications, such as electrocardiographic or other abnormalities, suggesting the need for hospitalization		Can ask for and use support from others or use cognitive and behavioral skills to inhibit purging		Needs supervision during and after all meals and in bathrooms; unable to control multiple daily episodes of purging that are severe, persistent, and disabling, despite appropriate trials of outpatient care, even if routine laboratory test results reveal no obvious metabolic abnormalities

Table 14.1 (cont.)

	Level 1: Outpatient	Level 2: Intensive outpatient	Level 3: Partial-hospitalization (full-day outpatient care)[a]	Level 4: Residential treatment center	Level 5: Inpatient hospitalization
Environmental stress		Others able to provide adequate emotional and practical support and structure	Others able to provide at least limited support and structure	Severe family conflict or problem; or absence of family so patient is unable to receive structured treatment in home; patient lives alone without adequate support system	
Geographic availability of treatment program		Patient lives near treatment setting		Treatment program is too distant for patient to participate from home	

Source: American Psychiatric Association, 2006, Table 8.

Note: In general, a given level of care should be considered for patients who meet one or more criteria under a particular level. These guidelines are not absolutes, however, and their application requires physician judgment.

[a] This level of care is most effective if administered for at least 8 hours/day; 5 days/week; less intensive care is demonstrably less effective.

[b] If the patient is dehydrated, whole-body potassium values may be low even if the serum potassium value is in the normal range; determine concurrent urine-specific gravity to assess for dehydration.

[c] Determining suicide risk is a complex clinical judgment, as is determining the most appropriate treatment setting for patients at risk for suicide. Relevant factors to consider are the patient's concurrent medical conditions, psychosis, substance use, other psychiatric symptoms or syndromes, psychosocial supports, past suicidal behaviors, and treatment adherence and the quality of existing physician–patient relationships. These factors are described in greater detail in the APA's *Practice Guideline for the Assessment and Treatment of Patients with Suicidal Behaviors.*

[d] Although this table lists percentages of expected healthy body weight in relation to suggested levels of care, these are only approximations and do not correspond to percentages based on what constitutes a healthy body weight in relation to "norms." For example, for some patients, a healthy body weight may be 110% of the standardized value for the population, whereas for other individuals it may be 98%. Each individual's physiological differences must be assessed and appreciated. For children, also consider the rate of weight loss. Finally, weight level per se should never be used as the sole criteria for discharge from inpatient care. Many patients require inpatient admission at higher weights and should not be automatically discharged just because they have achieved a certain weight level unless all other factors are appropriately considered. See text for further discussion regarding weight.

[e] Individuals may experience these thoughts as consistent with their own deeply-held beliefs (in which case they seem to be ego-syntonic and "overvalued") or as unwanted ego-alien repetitive thoughts, consistent with classic obsessive-compulsive disorder phenomenology.

Family in Residence Program

From admission to discharge, the Family in Residence program is guided by a parent empowerment model with three main elements, as described below: education, motivation, and liberation. The foundational FBT principles incorporated include: neither the parents nor the adolescent are to blame for the illness; providers must unite with the family against the eating disorder; the essential focus on weight restoration (minimum two pounds per week) and symptom reduction; the benefits of externalizing the illness; and the need for parental empowerment in order for them to become effective agents of change (Lock & Le Grange, 2013).

The typical course of treatment for child and adolescent patients at Eating Recovery Center starts with 24-hour care (inpatient and residential levels of care) followed by the partial-hospitalization program (PHP; 7 days per week, 11 hours per day), which includes the Family in Residence programming. The patient's level of care and length of stay are individually determined in collaboration with referral sources, families, and largely in-network insurance providers. Once the patient has been admitted, length of stay and level of care are concurrently reviewed every 3–7 days based on APA (2006b) guidelines.

During the initial weeks of treatment, caregivers participate in weekly family therapy (in person or by phone/video conferencing), and a weekly update call. As the patient nears the transition from residential treatment to the PHP, parents are asked to reside in Denver (average stay of 23 days) to begin intensive training of five days per week/five hours per day of programming. Parents typically reside in a local Ronald McDonald House or nearby hotels. In conjunction with the scheduled programming, a crucial element of the Family in Residence program is the patient progressively spending more time with their parents outside the treatment center. The modules described below are carried out in a variety of settings, including family therapy (twice-weekly sessions), family days (three-days per month educational program), group lectures (five days per week, two hours per day), parent support groups (two days per week for one hour), and multi-family groups (one–two days per week for one and a half hours).

Education

The Family in Residence Program places a strong emphasis on education, as this component is essential to the parent empowerment process (Lock & Le Grange, 2013; Strober & Johnson, 2012).

Admission Assessment

The education begins with the admission assessment. Parents are educated about the eating disorder, as well as possible comorbid disorders, by the masters-level clinical assessment therapists as they complete the admission interview with caregivers and, at times, the patients. The clinicians guiding this process help parents explore the onset of illness, severity of behaviors and health consequences, and best trajectory to enter into the treatment process. They also normalize and validate the caregiver experience, as well as the patient experience, of being overcome by the illness. Parents are then asked to commit to their involvement in the Family in Residence program, with the goal of parent empowerment, prior to returning home.

Patients and caregivers are then further educated in the Initial Team Assessment process, which entails a 90-minute in-person interview on the day of admission with their primary therapist, registered dietitian, and physician (in addition to a health and physical assessment by an internal medicine physician and complete nursing assessment by a registered nurse). Parents are given the opportunity to provide further perspectives on their child and their journey as they begin to partner with the treatment providers to individualize the course of care. Patients are involved in this initial assessment for different lengths of time based on their developmental and functional age, as well as the level of conflict and stability.

Nutrition Modules

Registered dietitians in this family-centered treatment model work closely with medical providers to support nutritional rehabilitation, and with therapists to support behavioral exposure work. The dietitian primarily meets with the child in the early stages of treatment to assess, build alliance, and work on gradual food exposures. They then shift to working primarily with caregivers in individual, group, and family therapy sessions, in order to provide education and empower parents to take over the management of the meal plan.

Nutritional education goals during treatment include: providing accurate nutritional information and helping to debunk common myths and misconceptions; helping individuals establish a healthier relationship with food (i.e. no "good and bad food" distinctions); encouraging balance, moderation, variety, and flexibility; and helping to normalize eating and eating behaviors. In-depth discussions occur during group sessions about the basics of nutrition, meal planning and support, and myths and misconceptions that stem from the media and opinions of others. These and family therapy sessions are an avenue for caregivers to face their anxieties, frustrations, and even shame around not being successful in meal support prior to admission. Parents explore the techniques (e.g. direct eating prompts) and research (e.g. White et al., 2015) supporting the most effective approach with their child, centered on being empathic while firm with directives. In the Family in Residence program, this is commonly referred to as "empathy with expectations."

Another topic covered in group and family therapy sessions is re-incorporating exercise. Prior to returning to exercise and athletics, it is important to explore with parents what it means and would look like for their child to have a "normal" relationship with activity. This includes defining over-exercise, and examining appropriate modes of exercise within the context of eating disorder recovery. Dietitians also provide education on what to expect regarding changes to the meal plan as activity is incorporated back into their lives.

Meal Support Modules

Family meal exposures begin toward the end of 24-hour care or at the beginning of PHP. Parents are asked to eat with their child, with a treatment team member (primary therapist or registered dietitian) present, when indicated. Generally the family starts with snacks and progresses to meals, from the patient's easiest to most challenging foods for gradual exposure. The team member will eat with the family while assessing and modeling the meal support process. Parents have often attended one or more sessions with the primary therapist and/or registered dietitian before this meal in order to be given education on the meal plan, meal selection, and basic training of meal support redirections. Following these meals, parents debrief with the clinician(s). These conversations tend to focus on eating disorder behaviors present at the meal, questions and concerns about meal plan/support needs, and next steps for meal exposures with parents.

Experiential training in portioning and plating a meal is also provided for caregivers. After learning the meal plan and beginning to choose the child's meals and snacks, parents are asked to walk through a buffet line with the support of a registered dietitian. Following this meal planning exposure, the parents will either join the child in a family meal exposure or place the meal on the table for the child to eat with staff. Either way, this begins the child's exposure to their parents choosing their meals and portions.

The last part of the exposure process is off-unit passes. The child joins their family for snacks and meals progressively until discharge, typically ending in full and/or multiple day passes. Typically, families start off-unit passes with preparing meals in a kitchen at their temporary residences. However, they tend to progress quickly to restaurant exposures, as this environment was often the most challenging in the past. The pace of the off-unit passes is determined by parental empowerment: passes are planned with their team as parents report increased understanding of and confidence in their role. Off-unit passes may also include body image challenges, such as shopping; activity redirections, such as spending time at a park without excessive movement; and mindful activity, with extra food provided to the child for the activity.

Family-Centered Treatment Modules

In order for caregivers to sustain their child's recovery, they need education to feel empowered in their parenting approach, both individually and through dyadic approaches (Byrne, Accurso, Arnow, Lock, & Le Grange, 2015). Any caregiver who will be involved in supporting the child's treatment and recovery, including extended family members and family friends, are key collaborators in recovery. The goal is to present a unified front in meal support and setting limits.

Parents may need to re-learn what it means to set limits with their child and examine potential barriers to this approach, including appropriate reinforcements/consequences, while balancing the child's growing need for autonomy and identity. Ultimately, parents learn from lectures, their experiences with their child in the evenings and on passes, and from other parents' experiences of how limits and boundaries provide a sense of safety and security for children in general, but especially for a child affected by a mental illness. These lectures are not just focused on behavior modification for eating disordered behaviors, but also general limits around child and adolescent independence (i.e. sleepovers, technology and the internet, driving, peer relationships, dating, etc.). For instance, the Acceptance and Commitment Therapy (ACT)-influenced course on limit-setting is for parents to find ways to be direct with and supportive of their child, while setting appropriate boundaries and recognizing their own individual strengths and barriers. Concepts such as knowing when to disengage from an argument, remain nonreactive, and accept the child and their recovery process require extensive discussion and even role-playing before being mastered.

It is important to teach parents the same therapeutic skills their child learns from the treatment team; if parents can both model and reinforce the use of therapeutic skills, the chances of success, even in the toughest of moments, increase. In these lectures, parents are taught that emotional regulation difficulties may continue even after prominent eating disorder symptoms have abated (Haynos, Roberto, Martinez, Attia, & Fruzzetti, 2014). In addition to providing education on eating disorders, the Family in Residence program provides extensive education on ACT (Juarascio et al., 2013), cognitive-behavioral therapy (CBT; Grave, Calugi, Doll, & Fairburn, 2013), and dialectical behavior therapy (DBT; Safer, Couturier, & Lock, 2007; Safer, Telch, & Chen, 2009), all of which have varying levels of evidence supporting their effectiveness in adolescent eating disorders.

It is also essential for parents to understand their child in the context of both their stage of development and their mental illness. The foundational underpinnings of growth, resiliency and vulnerability are provided through examining various factors of development during childhood and adolescence. Exploring the temperament styles of the child and caregivers fosters greater understanding of what influences connection and interactions. Parents can then learn how to more effectively de-code their child's behavior and respond based on their temperaments (Treasure, Smith, & Crane, 2007). The bio-psycho-social complexities of adolescence and how different temperaments can be impacted by these developmental challenges is also covered (Johnson, Sansone, & Chewning, 1992).

Parents report finding it informative when current knowledge of brain growth and development in childhood is reviewed (Bava, Thayer, Jacobus, Ward, Jernigan, & Tapert, 2010; Casey, Galvin, & Hare, 2005), how sequential maturation of different brain areas influences behavior and emotion regulation (e.g. Casey & Caudle, 2014; Somerville, Jones, Ruberry, Dyke, Glover, & Casey, 2013), how amygdala predominance renders less mature brains more reactive and emotionally driven (e.g. Arain et al., 2013), and how full development of the pre-frontal cortex does not occur until the mid-twenties (Sowell, Thompson, Holmes, Jernigan, & Toga, 1999). The subsequent discussion focuses on how parents and treating professionals can use this information to address specific needs of children, as well as why full nutritional rehabilitation and full weight restoration is imperative to support normalization of brain function and potentiating ongoing brain development.

The material covered in these modules is extensive and encompasses far more areas than can be described in this chapter. However, three essential topics that should be highlighted are medical complications of eating disorders, technology, and body image. It has been both educational and empowering to teach families about the medical complications of eating disorders and how they can be managed. Three core issues are covered: (1) an understanding of adaptive physiology to malnutrition or nutritional chaos; (2) a blueprint on how organ systems may respond to these insults; and (3) an explanation as to "why we do some of the things we do and why we do not do others" in the clinical care of patients. Finally, there are lectures that focus on how to understand, identify, and protect against relapse.

Technology and its influence on the child and family is examined, specifically how children afflicted by an eating disorder may fall prey to using technology to perpetuate their illness, connect to other ill individuals, and seek out additional maladaptive coping techniques or behaviors. Parents are asked to consider the many types of social media to better understand how to set limits/boundaries and ensure a recovery-focused environment at home. Lastly, the impact of societal, media, and peer influences on body acceptance is explored. This abstract concept is examined from a research and clinical perspective, including body dissatisfaction predictors, maintaining factors, and diagnostic features of eating disorders (e.g. Roy & Meilleur, 2010; Striegel-Moore, Franko, Thompson, Barton, Schreiber, & Daniels, 2004).

The parent community that develops through attending these educational modules has been identified by parents as one of the most crucial components of their child's treatment. Parents validate each other's frustration, anxieties, and disappointments; normalize the stages of treatment and the recovery process; and normalize their reactions to their children's behaviors through these modules as well as through twice-weekly parent support groups. Also, weekly multi-family experiential sessions are provided to caregivers, patients, and even siblings, when possible. This group also allows parents to be validated by directly observing other families struggling with similar issues.

Motivation

As patients move from 24-hour care to the PHP, caregivers are asked to engage in additional family therapy sessions. The focus moves from psychoeducation on eating disorders and co-occurring disorders to the specific symptoms and support needs presented by their child. The treatment team now fully integrates parents into the team. Thus begins the transition from the treatment team managing the child's needs with significant parental input, to the caregivers managing their child's needs with the team's input.

During the family work in PHP, patients and caregivers are encouraged to move from acquisition to application of the skills they are learning. For instance, when reviewing a challenging interaction, the family is asked to review the skills they used, attempted to use, and could use the next time this situation occurs. Given that caregivers are taught the same or similar therapeutic skills as their children, they are asked to discuss their own process of emotion regulation and problem solving, while being careful to not undercut their empowerment as the agent of change for their child. Lastly, each family member's attempts to engage differently and more effectively in meal times and communication are noted and reinforced. Various concepts are threaded throughout the family work in order to support intentional, empowered parenting.

Check Guilt at the Door

Parents are not globally "good" or "bad," despite their fleeting thoughts. Yet "guilt and shame" tend to impact parents during the recovery process. If parents do not face the possibility that they are experiencing a sense of shame in response to having an ill child, they will never be able to be fully open and present in their work with providers or be engaged with their child during treatment. Eating Recovery Center clinicians work to provide a compassionate space to identify, explore, and re-explore how this shame of being a "bad parent" sneaks up on them, even without their awareness, as they work through the treatment process. It is important to note that these opportunities to acknowledge the shame and have it empathized with do not always occur in family sessions.

Expressed Emotion

Expressed emotion has been identified as one of the best predictors for family therapy outcomes (e.g. Lock, Couturier, Bryson, & Agras, 2006). The role of parents in family-centered work is often discussed, but lacks guidance on how to navigate the emotional toll it can take. A parent's ability to identify and effectively express their emotions can be pivotal to their family's success with treatment. The phrase "respond, don't react" is frequently used within the program. Parents' initial reactions can provide good data on how to judge the situation but are not necessarily the best responses to effect change. Parents are encouraged to slow their responses to their child's behavior and engage more intentionally. Educating parents on mindfulness and breath work is often essential in helping them notice and cope with their reactions.

Lastly, parents are asked to carefully consider their support system. Caregivers need to educate those who support them about the treatment approach, even providing specific comments for others to repeat back to them in moments of distress. On a broader scale, parents need to identify individuals who can be non-judgmental and empathetic.

Accommodation Pitfalls

Parents accommodate because it is excruciating to see their child in distress and they feel guilty because they think they may be making the situation worse. They may even feel a sense of shame, believing they could have caused their child's illness in the first place. Normalizing the accommodation response is essential, following the same principle of "check your guilt at the door." If parents learn that allowing their child to avoid distressing stimuli could make them sicker and more overwhelmed in the long term, they are likely to become more mindful of this response and make changes.

Parents receive a lecture entitled "Accommodation Pitfalls." The concepts they are introduced to are returned to through much of the family therapy and meal support training. The theoretical approach, research, and techniques behind exposure therapy are discussed and emphasized, even if the child does not have an anxiety disorder (e.g. Chansky, 2004). The various forms that accommodation may take are discussed, such as giving into a child's demands for a change in meal, allowing them to stay at a weight lower than professionals have advised, and permitting movement and exercise without supplementation. The messages inadvertently given to the child are then reviewed, including "you were in real danger and must be rescued from your anxiety" and "I, as your parent, am responsible for handling your emotions for you." In addition, reassurance is explored as a form of accommodation, specifically helping parents see how ineffective providing repeated reassurance can be in the long term. Lastly, support techniques are reviewed to help the caregivers replace accommodation and reassurance reactions to their child's distress with more effective limit-setting and empowering responses.

Align or Perish

Parents are constantly impressed by how their child's illness has divided them. This division speaks less about their relationship and more about the illness itself. Communication becomes more challenging and collaboration feels less attainable. Empowering parents to remain aligned starts with helping each of them identify their strengths or ways in which they have been effective in supporting their child, even if it is just aligning in the decision to seek help. Many parents have lost sight of their strengths as parents, especially regarding their child's recovery process. Providers should not shy away from asking parents directly about the potential barriers they face in supporting their child. They should even ask that they critique each other without their child present. Although this sounds risky when attempting to build alignment, it allows space for open discussion without guilt or shame. All parents have strengths and barriers in this process, and they will need to be able to discuss them directly with each other and their treatment team. The sooner and more often they can identify what they bring to this process, the more effective they will be.

Liberation

The Family in Residence program stresses that parents are the experts on their child. Through the process of educating them about their child's eating disorder and motivating them to respond with intention, they become the most effective agents of change (Byrne et al., 2015). In the early stages of the treatment, disempowered caregivers often want to rely on providers to educate and help them re-establish their roles in the process. While parents help educate providers as the experts on their child, they in turn are asked to explore their perspectives, opinions, and myths regarding the illness and health in general. Their questions are answered by focusing them on what they know about their child, and what other caregivers in similar situations have done. In the next stage, parents are motivated to join the process in more fundamental ways. They are handed the reins and constantly empowered to explore their ideas on how to respond. Parents become more aware, intentional, and directive in their parent–child relationship. Parents attend classes, engage in on-site training, and then gradually practice further and further away from providers and the security of the program grounds. The final stage hinges on returning to that curiosity of their parental perspective, now that they have integrated their expert knowledge of their child with the expertise of eating disorder recovery. As the caregivers, and many times the child, prove that they have acquired the necessary knowledge, clinicians need to reflect that growth and capability back to them. Thus begins the process of trial and error involved in transitioning back into "real life" away from the treatment program. The complexities of home, academic, and social distractions begin to test the intentionality related to discharge planning.

The focus of aftercare planning is to foster the family's connection to outpatient providers in their home communities. If providers need to be established, caregivers are supported in interviewing therapists, registered dietitians, and physicians in order to find the most effective fit. Throughout the treatment, identified outpatient providers receive treatment plans and update calls to foster collaboration. When possible, outpatient clinicians may be part of discharge sessions to demonstrate alignment between caregivers and the home team, as well as to create plans for session frequency and focus.

A detailed "Wellness Plan" is completed by the patient prior to discharge with the purpose of outlining for caregivers and their outpatient team the child's current struggles, how they can manage these struggles, and the types of support that are most helpful to them. Included in this plan are topics such as body image, technology/social media, coping skills, and signs of relapse.

A "Recommendation Form" is created by the various disciplines of Eating Recovery Center's treatment team, providing suggestions on everything from meal selection to returning to school. Providers have discussions with home clinicians concerning their recommendation for frequency of sessions, and encourage parents to set their appointments based on that plan. Allowing for exercise, grocery shopping, and the return to technology are all addressed. As the child's world becomes bigger again, it is essential to lay out expectations and determine the best course to return to more developmentally appropriate independence. These recommendations are child- and family-specific, and typically developed with considerable input from all providers and caregivers, including teachers and coaches as applicable.

Conclusion

A goal of our field should be to have all levels of informed care available to patients and families within driving distance of their homes. Unfortunately, too many patients and families have to travel great distances to receive higher levels of care. Historically, this has interfered with being able to engage in intensive, face-to-face family therapy, which is particularly important in the treatment of eating disorders. The Family in Residence program was designed to overcome this obstacle, equipping parents with the knowledge and confidence needed to fully prepare for their family member's return home through a combination of educational and experiential modules, support groups, family therapy, and meal support interventions. Data from 2014–2015 demonstrate that 85.6 percent of weight-restoring child and adolescent patients at Eating Recovery Center achieved at least 95 percent of their ideal body weight at discharge. On average, weight-restoring patients gained an average of 2.27 pounds per week, with an admission-to-discharge weight-restoration effect size of 2.3.

Despite the significant burden of time and expense, the families at Eating Recovery Center report high levels of satisfaction with the Family in Residence program. All parents who attended the Family in Residence program between 2012 and 2015 were asked to answer questions about their experience of it within two days of discharge, and no data were systematically excluded. Of the 418 parents who answered whether their experience at ERC was helpful, 98 percent agreed or strongly agreed. Of the 465 parents who answered whether they would recommend ERC to others, 97 percent agreed or strongly agreed. Their satisfaction is a promising start; however, we recognize the need for systematic research to further assess the impact of the program. Validated assessments addressing parental alignment, anxiety, and empowerment are currently being collected in order to further refine and strengthen the Family in Residence program.

References

Accurso, E. C., Fitzsimmons-Craft, E. E., Ciao, A. C., & Le Grange, D. (2015). From efficacy to effectiveness: Comparing outcomes for youth with anorexia nervosa treated in research trials versus clinical care. *Behaviour Research and Therapy*, 65, 36–41.

Agras, W., Lock, J., Brandt, H., Bryson, S. W., Dodge, E. et al. (2014). Comparison of 2 family therapies for adolescent anorexia nervosa: A randomized parallel trial. *JAMA Psychiatry*, 71, 1279–1286.

American Psychiatric Association. (2006a). *Treatment of patients with eating disorders*, 3rd edition. Washington, DC: American Psychiatric Association.

American Psychiatric Association. (2006b). *Practice guideline for the treatment of patients with eating disorders*, 3rd edition. Washington, DC: American Psychiatric Association.

Arain, M., Hague, M., Johal, L., Mathur, P., Nel, W. et al. (2013). Maturation of the adolescent brain. *Journal of Neuropsychiatric Disease and Treatment*, 9, 449–461.

Bava, S., Thayer, R., Jacobus, J., Ward, M., Jernigan, T. L., & Tapert, S. F. (2010). Longitudinal characterization of white matter maturation during adolescence. *Brain Research*, 1327, 38–46.

Byrne, C. E., Accurso, E. C., Arnow, K. D., Lock, J., & Le Grange, D. (2015). An exploratory examination of patient and parental self-efficacy as predictors of weight gain in adolescents with anorexia nervosa. *International Journal of Eating Disorders*, 48, 883–888.

Casey, B. J., & Caudle, K. (2013). The teenage brain: Self control. *Current Directions in Psychological Science*, 22, 82–87.

Casey B. J., Galvin, A., & Hare, T. A. (2005). Changes in cerebral functional development during cognitive development. *Current Opinion in Neurobiology*, 15, 239–244.

Chansky, T. (2004). *Freeing your child from anxiety: Powerful, practical solutions to overcome your child's fears, worries, and phobias*. New York: Broadway Books.

Grave, R. D., Calugi, S., Doll, H. A., & Fairburn, C. G. (2013). Enhanced cognitive behaviour therapy for adolescents with anorexia nervosa: An alternative to family therapy? *Behaviour Research and Therapy*, 51, R9–R12.

Haynos, A. F., Roberto, C. A., Martinez, M. A., Attia, E. & Fruzzetti, A. E. (2014). Emotion regulation difficulties in anorexia nervosa before and after inpatient weight restoration. *International Journal of Eating Disorders*, 47, 888–891.

Johnson, C. L., Sansone, R. A., & Chewning, M. (1992). Good reasons why young women would develop anorexia nervosa: The adaptive context. *Pediatric Annals*, 21, 731–737.

Juarascio, A., Shaw, J., Forman, E., Timko, C. A., Herbert, J. et al. (2013). Acceptance and commitment therapy as a novel treatment for eating disorders: An initial test of efficacy and mediation. *Behavior Modification*, 37, 459–489.

Le Grange, D., Lock, J., Agras, S., Bryson, S., & Booil, J. (2015). Randomized clinical trial of family-based treatment and cognitive-behavioral therapy for adolescent bulimia nervosa. *Journal of the American Academy of Child and Adolescent Psychiatry*, 54, 886–894.

Le Grange, D., Lock, D., Agras, S., Moye, A., Bryson, S. et al. (2012). Moderators and mediators of remission in family-based treatment and adolescent focused therapy for anorexia nervosa. *Behaviour Research and Therapy*, 50, 85–92.

Lock, J. (2015). An update on evidence-based psychosocial treatments for eating disorders in children and adolescents. *Journal of Clinical Child and Adolescent Psychology*, 44, 707–721.

Lock, J., & Le Grange, D. (2013). *Treatment manual for anorexia nervosa: A family-based approach*, 2nd edition. New York: Guilford Press.

Lock, J., Couturier, J., Bryson, S., & Agras, S. (2006). Predictors of dropout and remission in family therapy for adolescent anorexia nervosa in a randomized clinical trial. *International Journal of Eating Disorders*, 39, 639–647.

Lock, J., Le Grange, D., Agras, W. S., Moye, A., Bryson, S. W., & Jo, B. (2010). Randomized clinical trial comparing family-based treatment with adolescent-focused individual therapy for adolescents with anorexia nervosa. *Archives of General Psychiatry*, 67, 1025–1032.

Loeb, K. L., & Le Grange, D. (2009). Family-based treatment for adolescent eating disorders: Current status, new applications and future directions. *International Journal of Child and Adolescent Health*, 2, 243–254.

Roy, M., & Meilleur, D. (2010). Body image distortion change during inpatient treatment of adolescent girls with restrictive anorexia nervosa. *Eating and Weight Disorders*, 15, e108.

Russell, G. F., Szmukler, G. I., Dare, C., & Eisler, I. (1987). An evaluation of family therapy in anorexia nervosa and bulimia nervosa. *Archives of General Psychiatry*, 44, 1047–1056.

Safer, D. L., Couturier, J. L., & Lock, J. (2007). Dialectical behavior therapy modified for adolescent binge eating disorder: A case report. *Cognitive and Behavioral Practice*, 14, 157–167.

Safer, D. L., Telch, C., & Chen, E. Y. (2009). *Dialectical behavior therapy for binge eating and bulimia*. New York: Guilford Press.

Somerville, L. H., Jones, R. M., Ruberry, E. J., Dyke, J. P., Glover, G., & Casey, B. J. (2013). The medial prefrontal cortex and the emergence of self-conscious emotion in adolescence. *Psychological Science*, 24, 1554–1562.

Sowell, E. R., Thompson, P. M., Holmes, C. J., Jernigan, T. L., & Toga, A. W. (1999). In vivo evidence for post-adolescent brain maturation in frontal and striatal regions. *Nature Neuroscience*, 2, 859–861.

Striegel-Moore, R. H., Franko, D. L., Thompson, D., Barton, B., Schreiber, G. B., & Daniels, S. R. (2004). Changes in weight and body image over time in women with eating disorders. *International Journal of Eating Disorders*, 36, 315–327.

Strober, M., & Johnson, C. (2012). The need for complex ideas in anorexia nervosa: Why biology, environment, and psyche all matter, why therapists make mistakes, and why clinical benchmarks are needed for managing weight correction. *International Journal of Eating Disorders*, 45, 155–178.

Treasure, J., Smith, G., & Crane, A. (2007). *Skills-based learning for caring for a loved one with an eating disorder: The new Maudsley method*, 1st edition. New York: Routledge.

White, H. J., Haycraft, E., Madden, S., Rhodes, P., Miskovic-Wheatley, J. et al. (2015). How do parents of adolescent patients with anorexia nervosa interact with their child at mealtimes? A study of parental strategies used in the family meal session of family-based treatment. *International Journal of Eating Disorders*, 48, 72–80.

15 Parent Coaching Model for Adolescents with Emotional Eating

Stephanie Knatz Peck, Abby Braden, and Kerri N. Boutelle

Introduction

A common dysfunctional eating behavior is emotional eating (EE), or eating in response to negative emotional states, as 15–43 percent (Jääskeläinen et al., 2014; Nguyen-Rodriguez, Unger, & Spruijt-Metz, 2009) of healthy adolescents and 63 percent (Shapiro et al., 2007) of treatment-seeking youth report EE. Youth who eat for emotional reasons may eat in response to feelings of anger, anxiety, frustration, or depression (Tanofsky-Kraff et al., 2007) and EE may function as an escape from negative affect (Heatherton & Baumeister, 1991). EE is associated with overeating (van Strien, Engels, Leeuwe, & Snoek, 2005), eating disorder symptoms (Goossens, Braet, Van Vlierberghs, & Mels, 2009), and depression, anxiety, and appearance overvaluation (Stice, Presnell, & Spangler, 2002).

Based on the biosocial model (Linehan, 1993), youth with EE are thought to have a predisposition toward a high level of emotional sensitivity, with a tendency to experience emotions intensely, and for a long duration. Coupled with an environment that mismatches responses to emotional experiences, an adolescent with a high level of emotional sensitivity may not effectively learn how to regulate emotions, increasing the likelihood of EE. Consequently, when experiencing negative emotions, adolescents who do not have adaptive emotion regulation skills may resort to EE as a way of reducing negative affect.

Parents are considered central to the treatment of adolescent eating disorders (Le Grange, Lock, Loeb, & Nicholls, 2010). In terms of the treatment of youth with EE, parental involvement has the capacity to increase the efficacy of interventions for EE. To date, no parent-focused treatments have been studied specifically for youth who emotionally eat. The role of parents in the treatment of youth with EE should be considered within the biosocial framework of emotion dysregulation, which describes emotion regulation difficulties as occurring because of both biological and social influences (Linehan, 1993). Parents may simply lack an understanding of their child's emotional vulnerability and, as a result, fail to adopt a response set that is appropriate for someone with high emotional sensitivity. Thus, this unique biosocial vulnerability predisposes an adolescent to experience emotional arousal that can lead to maladaptive coping behaviors such as EE. Considering these findings, it is possible that a unique interpersonal skill set may be necessary to successfully interact with adolescents who are vulnerable to emotion dysregulation and EE.

Parents of youth with EE may require education on underlying causes of EE and, more importantly, training on appropriate emotional responding. A parent intervention focused on teaching parents to successfully respond to and interact with their child's emotional experiences could potentially mitigate emotion dysregulation and thereby decrease episodes of EE. Promoting parenting practices that facilitate appropriate emotional processing may enhance an adolescent's ability to cope with future emotional challenges in constructive ways rather than through dysfunctional behaviors such as EE (Greenberg, 2002). Furthermore, an intervention focused on tailoring emotional responding to prevent EE episodes, rather than intervening directly in EE episodes, may be more appropriate for adolescents, where direct intervention may pose negative consequences or be rejected (Liddle, Rowe, Dakof, & Lyke,1998).

Thus, we have developed an intervention based on underlying theoretical principles of emotion-focused therapy (EFT) and adapted from emotion-focused family therapy (EFFT) (Greenberg, 2004; Lafrance Robinson, Dolhanty, & Greenberg, 2013). EFT was originally designed for depression (Greenberg & Watson, 2006), and focuses on facilitating appropriate emotional processing by guiding individuals through emotional experiences in a way that facilitates learning to interact with their emotional landscape in healthy ways (Elliott, Watson, Goldman, & Greenberg, 2004; Greenberg & Pascual-Leone, 2006; Greenberg, Warwar, & Malcom, 2008). Greenberg (2002) posits that, in childhood development, caregivers can influence healthy emotional development by the way in which they respond to their child's emotions. Caregivers who are attuned to their child's emotions and who respond to the array of emotions in validating and corrective ways promote healthy emotional functioning through the lifespan. On the contrary, maladaptive or mismatched responses can lead to unhealthy emotional coping styles and dysregulation. EFFT, developed from this model, represents a family-focused intervention to improve emotional transactions between children and their caregivers. EFFT positions parents as their child's "emotion coach" and seeks to teach caregivers effective methods for recognizing and responding to emotional experiences (Lafrance Robinson et al., 2013). Models of EFFT show preliminary promise for use with eating disorders (Lafrance Robinson et al., 2013; Lafrance Robinson, Dolhanty, Stillar, Henderson, & Mayman, 2014). This model may be particularly suitable for parents of youth with EE, where appropriate parental responses could prevent or reduce emotion dysregulation and thereby decrease vulnerability to EE.

Treatment

Overview

Emotion-focused parent training for youth with EE (EFPT-EE) facilitates the positioning of parents as their child's "emotion coach." Parents are guided to understand overeating episodes as a function of emotion dysregulation. The aim of the parent intervention is to learn to successfully intervene in overwhelming emotional experiences (considering the unique biological and social vulnerabilities of children with emotion regulation difficulties) to mitigate EE episodes. Parents are empowered to view their role as pivotal in preventing and intervening in emotion dysregulation by reciprocating with corrective responses that serve to "down-regulate" or "re-regulate" emotion dysregulation. This process is explained as a primary and critical method for preventing the use of maladaptive behaviors, in this case EE, to control or thwart emotional experiences.

This rationale positions parents to adopt the stance that children with emotion regulation difficulties require "emotion coaching" and that they must become an emotion coach by learning a unique emotional skill set to assist their child. In EFPT-EE, parents are led through progressive steps to becoming an emotion coach based on Greenberg's model (2002, 2004) of emotion coaching, which includes (a) attending to emotional experiences by acknowledging their presence, (b) labeling the emotion, (c) validating the emotional experience, and (d) meeting the emotional need. Parents are taught the multiple roles that they must play in coaching adolescents, which include using corrective emotional responding, modeling, problem solving, and facilitating skills usage. Most importantly, the role of emotion coach is framed as a method for responding to a dysregulated emotional style explained using the biosocial model.

Structure

EFPT-EE consists of eight sessions and is conducted in a parent-only format. EFPT-EE can be delivered to parents in either a group or individual format. Group interventions have the benefit of making use of potent group effects including parent-to-parent consultation, comradery, and the ability to observe and learn from others. An individually delivered treatment allows for more opportunity for tailoring the interventions to each particular participant. Our clinical laboratory has delivered the interventions in both formats, and to date, adherence and retention rates suggest that both treatments are feasible and acceptable. The program can be run as a stand-alone treatment, or alongside adolescent-focused interventions of interest to this population, such as dialectical behavior therapy (DBT) or behavioral weight loss. Indeed, due to focus on emotion dysregulation, EFPT-EE is highly suitable to be run in conjunction with adolescent-only or multi-family DBT skills training. When run in tandem (EFPT-EE and DBT), the treatments represent a comprehensive model whereby adolescents learn positive coping skills to self-intervene and, simultaneously, parents learn skilled ways of intervening with their adolescent to further reduce the risk of EE.

Target Population

EFPT-EE is appropriate for parents of adolescents between the ages of 13 and 17 years who engage in maladaptive coping behaviors in an effort to control or manage emotions. Although the protocol was developed to address EE specifically, because of the emphasis on emotion dysregulation as the underlying theoretical cause and primary point of intervention, the protocol can be easily adapted to address other issues of emotion dysregulation that present in adolescence such as self-harm, substance use, and suicidality. Since EE occurs as a result of emotion dysregulation, it is likely that adolescents of participating parents will also present with other comorbid issues stemming from emotion dysregulation difficulties. Due to the focus on intervening on emotional arousal in general, comorbidities do not preclude the participation of a parent–adolescent dyad with multiple presenting issues. Participating caregivers can be any adult in a caregiver role who is present to assist with emotional episodes, and preferably one that is living in the same household.

Treatment Description

The focus on EFPT-EE is on positioning parents as their child's emotion coach. In the first two sessions, the focus is on providing a theoretical rationale for learning a unique skill set for emotional responding using the biosocial framework. Parents are oriented to potential biological and social vulnerabilities that predispose their child to become emotionally aroused, and EE is explained as a maladaptive response to being emotionally overwhelmed. This is done to mobilize parents to take action in a nonjudgmental and empathic manner.

With this rationale, parents are presented with a step-by-step model to becoming an effective emotion coach. Each session is focused around one sequential step to becoming an emotion coach. Steps include: (a) understanding the multiple roles involved in caregiving an adolescent and their function in intervening in EEs; (b) self-assessing emotional response tendencies; (c) identifying and attuning to adolescents' emotions; (d) using empathy and validation; and (e) using specific corrective responses for each emotion.

Parents are taught a method for emotional responding by "attuning, intervening, assessing, and re-intervening." In this model, parents learn the importance of recognizing slight behavioral and cognitive indicators of emotion so that they are attuned to the initiation of even a low-level emotional experience within their child. They use learned response sets (specific to particular emotions) to attend and respond to emotional reactions, and are taught to self-assess their efficacy in down-regulating emotional experiences, and, lastly, to continue to intervene if necessary. Parents are taught effective ways to respond to specific emotional experiences, with an emphasis on the primary emotional triggers of overeating, which can be a wide array of emotions but most often include anxiety, sadness, loneliness, tiredness, and anger (Masheb & Grilo, 2006). Additionally, they are taught empathy and validation and encouraged to use these skill sets as a ubiquitous foundation for emotional responding. Lastly, lessons focus on teaching parents how to anticipate the emotional needs of their child through the use of sincere empathy and then to choose a response that appropriately matches their child's emotion. Specific skill sets that serve as antidotes to negative emotions are then taught and practiced

Table 15.1 List of sessions in the emotion-focused parent training for emotional eating (EFPT-EE) program

Number	Topic	Primary objectives
1	Parenting a teen with emotion dysregulation	• Introduce the biosocial model of emotion dysregulation • Review implications for parenting • Introduce model of emotion coaching to prevent EE (via emotion regulation)
2	Parenting an adolescent with EE: The multiple roles of caregivers	• Review primary parenting roles (teammate, facilitator, psychologist, enforcer, role model) • Discuss specific interventions for EE related to multiple roles • Facilitate parent reflection on ways in which to use each role effectively
3	Know your own response tendency	• Review common models of parent response tendencies to adolescent emotional arousal using metaphorical animal models • Facilitate reflection on typical response tendencies and desired change • Present an ideal model of emotion intervention (using metaphorical animal model)
4	Staying attuned: Becoming an emotional detective	• Identify emotions that trigger EE • Learn cognitive, verbal, facial, and behavioral characteristics associated with specific emotional experiences • Practice recognizing low-level emotional experiences and common triggers
5	Empathy: Seeing your child's emotions from their shoes	• Frame negative emotions as an opportunity for intimacy and teaching • Review function of responding empathically • Facilitate an imaginal exercise to build empathy • Direct parents to use empathy to guide their response sets to emotional experiences
6	Using validation to down-regulate experiences of emotion	• Explain validation as the behavioral expression of empathy • Frame validation as the core universal response to emotional experiences • Review levels of validation • Practice validation
7	What does my teen need? Corrective responses to specific emotions	• Introduce a parent response class for each emotional trigger of EE (cognitive, behavioral, nonverbal, verbal) • Review validation as a common element • Teach specific response class for each emotion (anxiety, sadness, boredom, guilt, shame)
8	Being an effective emotion coach	• Provide an integrative model of emotion coaching by combining all steps • Review comprehensive emotion coaching model • Facilitate continued practice of integrative model

as a way to facilitate a corrective emotional experience, such as responding to sadness through soothing or anxiety through the demonstration of safety. Skill sets include training on appropriate verbal, nonverbal, and behavioral response sets for each particular emotion. In parallel, parents are led through activities that build awareness of their particular emotional response tendencies that are rooted in their own biosocial history and past emotional experiences (Lafrance Robinson et al., 2013). Additionally, this traditional model of emotion coaching is bolstered by teaching parents to (a) problem-solve with their child (Lafrance Robinson et al., 2014), (b) model usage of appropriate methods of managing emotional experiences in their own lives in the presence of their child, and (c) use regular family meetings and reflective questioning after unsuccessful episodes to guide improvements in emotion coaching (see Table 15.1 for list of sessions).

Case Example

Mia was a 16-year-old female of Samoan origin. Mia and her biological aunt Grace, who was her primary guardian, signed up for EFPT-EE after her aunt noticed extreme episodes of binge eating that seemed to be triggered by familial and social stress. Mia was obese, with a BMI in the 99th percentile for girls her height and age. Grace reported that Mia had gained over 30 pounds in the past 2 years. She reported that the weight gain occurred as a result of "stress eating," which began when Mia's mother was placed in jail for theft. Grace assumed legal custody of Mia due to parental neglect resulting from her mother's issues with substance use. Mia met criteria for major depressive disorder and binge eating disorder, and reported that she ate in response to feeling sad and anxious. Prior to EFPT-EE, Grace had made attempts at helping Mia control her eating by ensuring a healthy home environment and minimal access to unhealthy foods. Despite this, she reported that Mia continued to gain weight and engaged in binge eating at school. Grace was unsure how to help Mia and, furthermore, was becoming accustomed to her new role as a parent figure for Mia. She stated that Mia was erratic in her emotions, often irritable or alternatively "shut-down," where she isolated herself and refused to speak about what she was feeling.

During initial sessions of EFPT, Grace learned that Mia was likely engaging in binge eating as a way to manage her emotions. She learned that social experiences, such as Mia's history of familial stress including extreme neglect by her mother, likely contributed to her lack of ability to manage or tolerate emotions. Grace reported that often Mia self-proclaimed that she "doesn't do emotions" and appeared to be very uncomfortable expressing any emotional experiences. Likewise, throughout EFPT sessions, Grace also learned and reflected on her difficulty in tolerating Mia's emotions due to her propensity to be someone more comfortable with reason and logic, rather than the emotional realm. Throughout the time in the program, Grace reflected on how she was often not able to identify what Mia was feeling, and further how uncomfortable she felt when Mia expressed emotion due to her lack of experience with parenting a teen and the experience of her own upbringing. By reflecting on this, Grace realized that her discomfort often led her to avoid the situation or escape when she felt Mia was experiencing a negative emotion. Initially, Grace was led through skills to learn to more accurately use the signs that Mia was showing to identify specific emotional experiences that she was having. Through this practice, she learned that Mia was often sad, and that her primary ways of showing sadness were by becoming quiet and isolating herself. Grace was surprised to learn that this was in fact sadness, having previously assumed that Mia was angry when she displayed this type of behavior. Next, Grace practiced using more validating responses to Mia's sadness after recognizing that her escape tendencies were likely very invalidating to Mia. Grace was taught appropriate ways to respond to sadness through soothing. She learned that in fact Mia craved physical affection and that her presence during Mia's episodes of sadness significantly reduced her negative emotionality. In addition to Grace attending EFPT-EE sessions, Mia participated in a coping skills training group and one-on-one behavioral monitoring sessions with a therapist. Throughout the time she was in treatment and through Grace's continuous practice and application of these skills, Mia lost 15 pounds without any specific dietary intervention. Mia reported using skills independently, but maintained that the most effective tool was being able to rely on her aunt for emotional support.

Conclusion

EFPT-EE is a parent-focused model that targets parents effectively responding to their child's emotions to avoid emotional over-arousal that leads to maladaptive eating behaviors. EFPT-EE considers the biological and social vulnerabilities that predispose particular youth to eat in response to emotion and positions parents as critical agents of change in reducing not only EE, but also emotion dysregulation in general. EFPT-EE is adapted from EFFT, which has demonstrated preliminary promise in youth with eating disorders. However, despite a robust clinical and theoretical rationale for emotion-focused training as a point of intervention for youth with EE, more research is needed to determine the effectiveness of this approach. A clinical trial led by our group is currently underway to assess the feasibility and efficacy of a family treatment intervention for overweight adolescents with EE (13–17 years old) and their parents. Primary outcomes include EE episodes and weight loss. Data will be collected on 30 parent–adolescent dyads receiving EFPT-EE in conjunction with parent–child skills training and behavioral monitoring. We hypothesize that EFPT-EE will assist parents in supporting their adolescents in managing their emotional dysregulation, and thus will reduce their EE over time. Reducing EE may result in greater overall functioning and well-being, as well as weight loss. Future directions for research include trials comparing EFPT to other parent-focused interventions, and trials examining whether EFPT enhances outcomes compared to adolescent-only interventions. Furthermore, this model should be explored in relation to other adolescent issues of emotion dysregulation.

References

Elliott, R., Watson, J. C., Goldman, R. N., & Greenberg, L. S. (2004). *Learning emotion-focused therapy: The process-experiential approach to change.* Washington, DC: American Psychological Association.

Goossens, L., Braet, C., Van Vlierberghs, L., & Mels, S. (2009). Loss of control over eating in overweight youngsters: The role of anxiety, depression, and emotional eating. *European Eating Disorders Review*, 17, 68–78.

Greenberg, L. J., Warwar, S. H., & Malcom, W. M. (2008). Differential effects of emotion-focused therapy and psychoeducation in facilitating forgiveness and letting go of emotional injuries. *Journal of Counseling Psychology*, 55, 185–196.

Greenberg, L. S. (2002). *Emotion-focused therapy: Coaching clients to work through their feelings.* Washington, DC: American Psychological Association.

Greenberg, L. S. (2004). Emotion-focused therapy. *Clinical Psychology & Psychotherapy*, 11, 3–16.

Greenberg, L. S., & Pascual-Leone, A. (2006). Emotion in psychotherapy: A practice-friendly research review. *Journal of Clinical Psychology*, 62, 611–630.

Greenberg, L. S., & Watson, J. C. (2006). *Emotion-focused therapy for depression.* Washington, DC: American Psychological Association.

Heatherton, T. F., & Baumeister, R. F. (1991). Binge eating as escape from self awareness. *Psychological Bulletin*, 110, 86–108.

Jääskeläinen, A., Nevanperä, N., Remes, J., Rahkonen, F., Järvelin, M. R., & Laitinen, J. (2014). Stress-related eating, obesity and associated behavioural traits in adolescents: A prospective population-based cohort study. *BMC Public Health*, 14, 321. doi:10.1186/1471-2458-14-321.

Lafrance Robinson, A., Dolhanty, J., & Greenberg, L. (2013). Emotion-focused family therapy for eating disorders in children and adolescents. *Clinical Psychology & Psychotherapy*, 22(1), 75–82. doi:10.1002/cpp.1861.

Lafrance Robinson, A., Dolhanty, J., Stillar, A., Henderson, K., & Mayman, S. (2014). Emotion-focused family therapy for eating disorders across the lifespan: A pilot study of a 2-day transdiagnostic intervention for parents. *Clinical Psychology & Psychotherapy*, 23(1), 14–23. doi:10.1002/cpp.1933.

Le Grange, D., Lock, J., Loeb, K., & Nicholls, D. (2010). Academy for Eating Disorders position paper: The role of the family in eating disorders. *International Journal of Eating Disorders*, 43, 1–5.

Liddle, H. A., Rowe, C., Dakof, G., & Lyke, J. (1998). Translating parenting research into clinical interventions for families of adolescents. *Clinical Child Psychology and Psychiatry*, 3, 419–443.

Linehan, M. M. (1993). *Skills training manual for treating borderline personality disorder.* New York: Guilford Press.

Masheb, R. M., & Grilo, C. M. (2006). Emotional overeating and its associations with eating disorder psychopathology among overweight patients with binge eating disorder. *International Journal of Eating Disorders*, 39, 141–146.

Nguyen-Rodriguez, S. T., Unger, J. B., & Spruijt-Metz, D. (2009). Psychological determinants of emotional eating in adolescence. *Eating Disorders*, 17, 211–224.

Shapiro, J. R., Woolson, S. L., Hamer, R. M., Kalarchian, M. A., Marcus, M. D., & Bulik, C. M. (2007). Evaluating binge eating disorder in children: Development of the children's binge eating disorder scale (C-BEDS). *International Journal of Eating Disorders*, 40, 82–89.

Stice, E., Presnell, K., & Spangler, D. (2002). Risk factors for binge eating onset in adolescent girls: A 2-year prospective investigation. *Health Psychology*, 21, 131–138.

Tanofsky-Kraff, M., Theim, K. R., Yanovski, S. Z., Bassett, A. M., Burns, N. P. et al. (2007). Validation of the emotional eating scale adapted for use in children and adolescents (EES-C). *International Journal of Eating Disorders*, 40, 232–240.

Van Strien, T., Engels, R., van Leeuwe, J., & Snoek, H. (2005). The Stice model of overeating: Tests in clinical and non-clinical samples. *Appetite*, 45, 205–214.

16 The Influence of Carer Fear and Self-Blame when Supporting a Loved One with an Eating Disorder

Amanda Stillar, Erin Strahan, Patricia Nash, Natasha Files, Jennifer Scarborough, Shari Mayman, Katherine Henderson, Joanne Gusella, Laura Connors, Emily S. Orr, Patricia Marchand, Joanne Dolhanty, and Adèle Lafrance Robinson

Introduction

There is mounting evidence in support of carer involvement in the treatment of eating disorders (EDs) across the lifespan. In children and adolescents, randomized clinical trials provide robust findings supporting the active involvement of parents in the context of family-based therapy (FBT; for reviews, see Downs & Blow, 2013; Lock, 2011). FBT engages parents as key resources in the therapy and the FBT clinician is tasked with empowering parents to adopt a primary role in their child's treatment process. Parental self-efficacy is emerging as a variable of particular interest in FBT. In a qualitative study exploring the core principles of FBT for adolescents with anorexia nervosa, clinicians identified parental self-efficacy as crucial for a positive outcome (Dimitropoulos, Freeman, Lock, & Le Grange, 2015). In the context of research, Lafrance Robinson, Strahan, Girz, Wilson, and Boachie (2013b) reported that, through the course of adapted FBT for adolescents with ED, positive changes in parental self-efficacy predicted reductions in their child's ED, depression, and anxiety symptoms, which were maintained at three and six months post-treatment. Byrne, Accurso, Arnow, Lock, and Le Grange (2015) mirrored and extended these findings. The results of their study revealed that increases in parental self-efficacy predicted adolescent weight gain, whereas increases in self-efficacy in the adolescents themselves did not.

Among adult populations, the New Maudsley Model (NMM) also enlists the family in actively supporting their loved one throughout the recovery process, while targeting carer anxiety and burden in order to decrease the negative impact of these states on helping behaviors (Treasure, Smith, & Crane, 2007; Whitney et al., 2012). Specifically, and among other interventions, carers are trained in the use of communication tools influenced by principles of motivational interviewing to help support their loved one to engage in the tasks of recovery. Macdonald, Murray, Goddard, and Treasure (2011) investigated the impact of an NMM skills-based training program for carers of adults with an ED. Carer skills training was associated with an increase in carer self-efficacy as well as with reductions in carer distress, anxiety and burden, the latter of which are hypothesized to have the potential to maintain ED symptoms (ibid). A second study examining the outcomes of an NMM self-help intervention for carers of adults with an ED revealed that carer self-efficacy was related to improvements in both carer distress in terms of anxiety and depressive symptomology and client outcomes, including ED functioning and symptoms (Goddard, Macdonald, & Treasure, 2011).

Emotion-focused family therapy (EFFT; Lafrance Robinson, Dolhanty & Greenberg, 2013a) is another model of family therapy whereby parents and carers are regarded as essential partners in the treatment process and are recruited as recovery and emotion coaches to support their loved one, regardless of age. An integral part of the treatment model also includes attending to and supporting the processing of strong carer emotion – that is, any emotional reaction, such as fear or self-blame, that could potentially interfere with parental self-efficacy and caregiving efforts. The results of a pilot study examining the outcomes of a two-day EFFT group for parents of children (of any age) with an ED revealed a decrease in parental fears and self-blame over time, as well as an increase in parental self-efficacy (Lafrance Robinson, Dolhanty, Stillar, Henderson, & Mayman, 2014). Parents also reported feeling more determined to engage in behaviors supportive of their child's behavioral and emotional recovery.

Emotion and Self-Efficacy

The impact of emotions and their relationship to self-efficacy are clearly important to consider in the context of family-oriented therapies for EDs. A wealth of research has shown that affect is associated with self-efficacy (Bandura, 1977; Forgas, Bower, & Moylan, 1990; Heimpel, Wood, Marshall, & Brown, 2002), including in the caregiving domain. When carers experience intense emotion (e.g. fear), they lose access to their caregiving instincts, acquired knowledge, and learned skills (Siegel, 2010). For instance, in the context of ED treatment, carers may resist implementing treatment tasks such as reintroducing challenging foods, if they fear that doing so may lead their child to stop eating altogether or, worse, that the distress associated with the intervention could lead them to becoming suicidal. This failure to comply in the parent is thought to be related to both the feared outcome (suicidality) and a crippling fear that they will not be able to handle the crisis that may ensue (low self-efficacy) should they implement the agreed-upon interventions in the face of their loved one's resistance.

Parental self-blame appears similarly to rob the parent of their capacity to engage in recovery tasks effectively. The ED field has emerged from a long history of parental blame (Mondini, Favaro, & Santonastaso, 1996) and, despite a general consensus among clinicians that parents do not cause EDs, many parents blame themselves for having caused the illness (Lafrance Robinson et al., 2014) and for not seeking help soon enough (Perednia & Vandereycken, 1989). In fact, many parents *fear* they are to blame and that others will blame them and so it is possible that fear and self-blame are in fact separate but related processes that negatively influence carers' capacity to help.

The present study examined the manner in which carer fear and self-blame influence carer self-efficacy and accommodating and enabling behaviors. We conjectured that carer fear and self-blame would predict carer empowerment and accommodating and enabling behaviors. That is, we expected that the more caregivers felt fear in relation to their loved one's illness and the more they blamed themselves, the less empowered they would feel in terms of helping their loved one with recovery and the more likely they would be to engage in behaviors that contribute to the maintenance of the illness.

Method

Participants

A parent intervention was delivered to parents of adolescent and adult children with EDs at eight sites in various treatment settings (hospital, community mental health, and private practice) across Canada. The sample included 137 participants, including 126 biological parents (87 mothers), 8 step-parents (3 stepmothers), 2 romantic partners, and 1 relative. Carers were recruited in several ways to participate in an intervention for EDs. Posters were displayed at reception desks of eating disorder clinics and therapists approached (a) carers involved in their loved one's ED treatment, (b) parents of adult clients who were not currently involved in treatment, and (c) parents of adolescents or adults who were on a waiting list for treatment. The measures were administered to the participants in a group setting and were completed by paper and pencil. Measures were administered in the same order and in the same manner across study sites, prior to the commencement of the intervention. Participants were given as much time as they needed to complete the measures. Data collection typically took between 30 and 45 minutes to complete. No exclusion criteria were used.

The mean age of the affected individual was 18 years (SD = 5.06) and ranged from 12 to 41 years. Carers were recruited from a variety of different settings (private practice, hospital, and community mental health agencies). Nineteen percent of carers had a loved one on the waiting list for ED treatment, 56.2% of carers had a loved one involved in active treatment for an ED for an average of one year (range = 2 weeks to 8 years), while 18.2% of families were engaged in services not specific to an ED.[1] Primary symptoms of concern were reported to include restricting in 84.7% of cases, bingeing in 39.4%, over-exercising in 48.2%, purging in 34.3%, and use of laxatives in

7.3%; 12.4% reported other symptoms (examples include self-harm, misuse of insulin and involuntary spitting). In terms of symptom onset, according to caregiver report, 56.2% of loved ones first displayed ED symptoms less than one year ago, 14.6% between one and two years ago, and 12.4% more than two years ago (range = 2 to 20 years).

Measures

Carer Fear Scale

Fear was measured with the Carer Fear Scale. The Carer Fear Scale is a newly developed measure designed to assess the degree to which carers feel vulnerable to fears that can interfere with their ability to re-feed their child and interrupt ED symptoms (Lafrance Robinson, 2014). Items were developed on the basis of clinical experience and carer feedback. Carers were asked to rate on a seven-point Likert scale (ranging from "not at all likely" to "extremely likely") the extent to which they feel vulnerable to four different fear items when supporting their child's behavioral recovery. Sample items include "Fear of breaking down or burning out throughout the process" and "Fear of pushing my child too far with treatment and leading them to depression, running away or suicide." Scale total scores can range from 7 to 28 ($\sim = 0.71$). A higher total scale score on this measure indicates a higher level of carer fear related to their engagement in recovery tasks.

Carer Self-Blame Scale

Self-blame was measured with the Carer Self-blame Scale. This scale was designed to assess the degree to which carers feel they are to blame for their child's ED (Lafrance Robinson, 2014). Items for this scale were also developed on the basis of clinical experience and carer feedback. Carers were asked to rate on a seven-point Likert scale (ranging from "not at all likely" to "extremely likely") the extent to which they felt responsible for their child's ED. Sample items include "Fear of being blamed or to blame", "My worst fears will have come true – I will be to blame" and "Others will blame me." Total scale scores can range from 7 to 14 ($\sim = 0.80$). A higher total scale score on this measure indicates a higher level of self-blame with respect to their child's ED.

Carer Self-Efficacy

Carer self-efficacy or empowerment was assessed using a revised version of the Parent versus Anorexia Scale (PvA; Rhodes, Baillee, Brown, & Madden, 2005).[2] The PvA was designed to study parental self-efficacy, that is, the "ability of a [carer] to adopt a primary role in taking charge of the [eating disorder] in the home setting for the purpose of bringing about the recovery of their loved one" (p. 401). Seven items make up the scale and these are rated on a five-point Likert scale (ranging from "strongly disagree" to "strongly agree"). Total scale scores range from 7 to 35. A lower scale score indicates a lower level of self-efficacy whereas a higher scale score indicates a higher level of self-efficacy. Sample items include "I feel equipped with specific strategies for the task of bringing about the complete recovery of my loved one in the home setting" and "It is more my responsibility than my loved one's to bring them to a healthy weight." The scale yields adequate psychometric properties (Rhodes et al., 2005).

Accommodation and Enabling Scale for Eating Disorders

The Accommodation and Enabling Scale for Eating Disorders (AESED; Sepulveda, Kyriacou, & Treasure, 2009) is a 33-item self-report scale developed to measure the degree to which carers engage in behaviors that may accommodate and enable the symptomology of a relative with an ED. The total scale score can range from 0 to 138. A higher score indicates a higher level of accommodating and enabling of ED symptoms. This measure also consists of five subscales: control of family (sample items: "Does your child's eating disorder control cooking practice and ingredients you use?" and "Does your child's eating disorder control the choices of food that you buy?"); reassurance seeking (sample items: "Does your child engage any family member in repeated conversations asking for reassurance about whether they will get fat?" and "Does your child engage any family member in repeated conversations asking for reassurance about whether it is safe or acceptable to eat a certain food?"); meal ritual (sample items: "Do any family members have to accommodate to what tableware is used?" and "Do any family members have to accommodate to what time food is eaten?"); turning a blind eye (sample item: "Do you choose to ignore aspects of your child's eating disorder … such as if food disappears or money is taken?"); and avoidance and modifying family routine (sample items: "Have you modified your leisure activities because of your child's needs?" and "Have you modified your family routine because of your child's symptoms?"). All items are rated on a five-point Likert scale (ranging from "never" to "daily") except item 24, which is rated on an 11-point Likert scale (ranging from "none at all" to "completely"). This scale yields adequate psychometric properties (ibid).

Results

Predictor Variables and Dependent Measures

The mean for carer fear was 4.55 (SE = 0.12) and for carer self-blame was 2.94 (SE = 0.15), suggesting that carers experienced a moderate degree of fear and self-blame (see Table 16.1). The total mean on the PvA was 18.09 (SE = 0.33) and was comparable to the self-efficacy scores of other carers studied (Byrne et al., 2015; Girz, Lafrance Robinson, Foroughe, Jasper, & Boachie, 2013;

Table 16.1 Means and standard errors
for dependent variables: Carer fear,
carer self-blame, carer self-efficacy, and
accommodating and enabling behaviors

Subscale	Mean	SE
Carer fear	4.55	0.120
Carer self-blame	2.94	0.154
Self-efficacy	18.09	0.33
Accommodating and enabling behaviors	54.32	2.57
Control of family	8.98	0.38
Reassurance seeking	12.60	0.74
Meal ritual	5.65	0.55
Turning a blind eye	2.93	0.32
Avoidance/modifying	24.36	1.14

Lafrance Robinson et al., 2014), suggesting similarly low self-efficacy across this diverse group of participants. The total mean on the AESED was 54.43 (SE = 2.57), which is similar to other carer samples (Goddard et al., 2011; Grover et al., 2011) and suggests considerable accommodating/enabling of ED symptoms.

Link between Carer Fear and Self-Efficacy and Accommodating and Enabling Behaviors

We predicted that carer fear would predict both carer self-efficacy and accommodating and enabling behaviors. To assess this, we conducted two separate regression analyses. In the first analysis, carer fear was the predictor variable and self-efficacy was the dependent variable. In the second regression analysis, carer fear was the predictor variable and accommodating/enabling behaviors was the dependent variable. We found that fear negatively predicted carer self-efficacy: the more fear carers experienced, the less empowered they felt (results for these analyses are reported in Table 16.2). We also found that fear positively predicted accommodating/enabling behaviors: the more fear carers felt, the more likely they were to engage in accommodating/enabling behaviors with their child.

Given that each AESED subscale assesses a unique aspect of accommodating and enabling behaviors within the household, such as reassurance seeking or modifying family routines, we sought to explore the unique relationships between carer fear and each of the AESED subscales. Regression analyses were conducted using fear as the predictor variable and each of the subscales as the dependent variables. Given that strong emotions are suspected to have a negative impact on caregiving efforts by leading carers to engage in behaviors that maintain their child's symptoms (Goddard et al., 2011a; Schmidt & Treasure,

Table 16.2 Regression results for carer fear on carer self-efficacy and accommodating and enabling behaviors and each of the AESED subscales

Subscale	B	T	p	R^2
Self-efficacy	−0.24	−2.77	0.006	0.06
Accommodating and enabling behaviors	0.36	3.68	< 0.001	0.13
Control of family	0.22	2.47	0.015	0.05
Reassurance seeking	0.24	2.67	0.009	0.06
Meal ritual	0.17	1.86	0.07	0.03
Turning a blind eye	0.13	1.39	0.17	0.02
Avoidance/modifying	0.40	4.39	< 0.001	0.16

Note: Predictor in both cases is carer fear.

2006), we expected that carer fear would positively predict each of the AESED subscales. We found that fear positively predicted the following subscales: control of family, reassurance seeking and avoidance/modifying behaviors (results are provided in Table 16.2). The more fear carers experienced, the more likely they were to allow their loved one's ED to control the family, the more likely they were to allow their loved one to engage in reassurance-seeking behaviors, and the more likely they were to modify the family routine. There was a marginal effect for the link between fear and meal rituals: the stronger their fear, the more carers allowed their loved one's ED to alter the family's meal rituals. Carer fear did not predict turning a blind eye to symptoms.

Link between Carer Self-Blame and Self-Efficacy and Accommodating and Enabling Behaviors

We also expected that carer self-blame would predict both carer self-efficacy and accommodating/enabling behaviors. We conducted a second set of regression analyses with carer self-blame as the predictor variable and carer self-efficacy and accommodating/enabling behaviors as the two dependent variables. The same phenomenon was found as with carer fear. Carer self-blame negatively predicted carer self-efficacy and positively predicted accommodating/enabling behaviors (results for these analyses are reported in Table 16.3). Thus, the more carers blamed themselves, the less empowered they felt and the more they engaged in accommodating/enabling behaviors with their loved one.

Next, we looked at the link between carer self-blame and each of the subscales of the AESED. We found that carer self-blame positively predicted control of family, accommodation of meal rituals, and avoidance/modifying family routine (results are shown in Table 16.3). The more carers blamed themselves, the more likely they were to allow their loved one's ED to control the family, the more likely they were to accommodate meal rituals, and the more likely they were to modify the family routine. Carer self-blame did not significantly predict

Table 16.3 Regression results for carer self-blame on carer self-efficacy and accommodating and enabling behaviors and each of the subscales of the AESED

Subscale	B	t	p	R^2
Self-efficacy	−0.27	−3.10	0.002	0.07
Accommodating and enabling behaviors	0.25	2.50	0.01	0.06
Control of family	0.19	2.17	0.03	0.04
Reassurance seeking	0.15	1.64	0.11	0.02
Meal ritual	0.21	2.29	0.02	0.04
Turning a blind eye	0.07	0.75	0.46	0.005
Avoidance/modifying	0.21	2.12	0.04	0.04

Note: Predictor in both cases is carer self-blame.

reassurance seeking, although the link was in the expected direction (the more carers blamed themselves, the more they allowed their loved one to engage in reassurance-seeking behaviors). As with fear, carer self-blame did not predict turning a blind eye to symptoms.

Discussion

The results of the current study indicated that the more fear carers reported, the less empowered they felt about actively supporting their loved one's ED recovery *and* the more likely they were to engage in recovery-interfering behaviors. The same phenomenon was observed with carer self-blame. The more carers blamed themselves, the less empowered they felt *and* the more they reported engaging in accommodating and enabling behaviors. Those accommodating and enabling behaviors that were most vulnerable to the influence of fear and self-blame included the degree to which the ED was allowed to control the family (e.g. how food is prepared), the modification of meal rituals (e.g. what tableware is used), the avoidance and modification of routines (e.g. work schedule or leisure activities), and reassurance seeking (e.g. asking whether they look fat in certain clothes).

Our findings contribute to the literature by demonstrating a clear link between fear and self-blame in carers and low self-efficacy, lending support to the hypothesis that these emotional experiences can lead the carer to become inflexible and reactive, losing access to their instincts and acquired skills (Siegel, 2010). These findings also lend support to the cognitive-interpersonal mainte-nance model of eating disorders (Goddard et al., 2011a; Schmidt & Treasure, 2006), which suggests that carers can experience high emotional arousal that can then lead them to engage in behaviors that can inadvertently maintain their loved one's illness. Our study empirically demonstrates that, in the face of strong emotions such as fear and self-blame, carers are in fact more likely to accommodate and enable ED symptoms. Given that considerable attention is being paid to the active role of carers in the treatment of EDs across the lifespan, it is important for researchers and clinicians alike to become cognizant of the link between carer emotion and therapy-interfering behaviors. This is especially true since emotions are amenable to and accessible for change, and can be evoked and transformed in the context of brief psychotherapy (Greenberg & Paivio, 2003). When clinicians attend to and process carer fear and self-blame, the carer can become better equipped and their loved one better supported. Until now, there have been no studies that point to the ways in which this process can be facilitated and we believe this is reason for hope.

The results relating to self-blame are consistent with FBT, NMM, EFFT, and other family therapy models for EDs, in that they highlight the importance of clinicians reducing carer self-blame in the context of treatment (Lafrance Robinson et al., 2013a; Lock & Le Grange, 2012; Treasure, Schmidt & Macdonald, 2009). Family-oriented ED therapies make recommendations regarding how to accomplish this therapeutic task, such as reassuring caregivers that they are not to blame for their loved one's ED, in both FBT and NMM (Lock & Le Grange, 2012; Treasure et al., 2009). In EFFT, and in line with emotion theory, there is active processing of the presenting emotions in carers (Lafrance Robinson et al., 2013a). When carers present with self-blame, for example, the self-blame is actively attended to and expressed, and the person's emotions are validated. In fact, working through the self-blame becomes the main focus of the session, given the belief that, if not fully processed, it will continue to lead to unspoken dynamics that will negatively influence the carer's ability to support their loved one effectively, and can in fact lead to therapy-interfering behaviors.

In this study, the additional finding that increased parental fear actually reduces carer empowerment begs the question as to whether the increasing of parental anxiety in the context of FBT may have the potential to work in the opposite manner and paradoxically decrease the parent's ability to feel empowered. In FBT, the therapist works to prompt parental action, and thereby increase empowerment, by increasing "anxiety" around the impact of the ED and the potential serious consequences of failing to act quickly to restore normal eating and physical health (Lock & Le Grange, 2012). The discussion of the balance or tension between raising parental anxiety in the service of mobilizing to action, on the one hand, and reducing parental fears in terms of increasing empowerment or self-efficacy, on the other, can be considered in light of the principles of motivational interviewing (MI), fundamental in the NMM (Treasure et al., 2009), and in particular how these principles relate to self-efficacy. A core principle of MI is to "develop discrepancy." The caveat, however, is that in the context of low self-efficacy such as that found in individuals with EDs and their families, the appropriateness of this principle is re-evaluated (Treasure & Ward, 1997). This is because increased discrepancy, or heightened awareness of and concern about one's circumstances, in the face of low self-efficacy in regard to one's ability to change them, is seen to increase a hopeless despair due to the perceived incapacity and lack of confidence in the ability to change. In other words, when carer self-efficacy is low, raising anxiety for the purpose of mobilization could have the opposite effect than what was intended.

Because anxiety and other strong emotional states also lead to a heightened state of physiological arousal, and high physiological arousal leads to decreased access to instincts and learned skills, we would argue that raising anxiety in carers who are already anxious or even emotionally activated – whether overtly or covertly – would be counter-productive. For example, if a parent is afraid their involvement will anger their child and this fear is already immobilizing, heightening that anxiety may further rob the carer of their innate capacity to respond in a calm way that conveys both support and confidence.

The question would then be: are these two constructs – parental anxiety in FBT and parental fear in EFFT – the same or different animals? In FBT, the goal is to incite urgency to act in parents by increasing anxiety around health concerns (Lock & Le Grange, 2012). In EFFT, the identified fears are a mix of those concerning the serious consequences of their loved one's health status, those on an emotional level, such as feeling they will push their child too hard and lose them in some way, and a sense that they have done something to damage their child and thus caused the illness (Lafrance Robinson et al., 2013a). What again can offer hope to the field is that engaging in emotional tasks that reveal and then process previously "dormant" parental fears can free parents from both types of fear.

In light of these findings, it will be very important for clinicians across the disciplines to resist the urge to discount the appropriateness of carer involvement when the carers present as emotional and disempowered, or even when they engage in behaviors that bluntly interfere with treatment. This may be especially pertinent in the context of adult treatment since there is a belief in the field that some adult clients should move towards a more independent recovery, especially when their carers present as unsupportive. These clinical presentations do not in fact suggest that the carers in question are unable or unmotivated. Rather, the results of this study suggest that these carers are quite likely paralyzed by or acting in response to fear or self-blame. Most importantly, we believe that the results of this study can serve to renew our faith and belief in the ability of all carers to transform feelings of defeat, fear and debilitating self-blame in order to contribute actively and positively to their loved one's recovery, and thus improve long-term outcome.

Notes

1 Services included independent counselling, unspecified outpatient services, and psychological treatment for another mental illness.
2 The revision of the scale was minor. Statements referring to "anorexia" were revised to reflect the different eating disorder symptoms.

References

Bandura, A. (1977). Self-efficacy: Toward a unifying theory of behavioral change. *Psychological Review*, 84, 191–215. doi: 10.1037/0033-295X.84.2.191.

Byrne, C. E., Accurso, E. C., Arnow, K. D., Lock, J., & Le Grange, D. (2015). An exploratory examination of patient and parental self-efficacy as predictors of weight gain in adolescents with anorexia nervosa. *International Journal of Eating Disorders*, 48, 883–888. doi: 10.1002/eat.22376.

Dimitropoulos, G., Freeman, V. E., Lock, J., & Le Grange, D. (2015). Clinician perspective on parental empowerment in family-based treatment for adolescent anorexia nervosa. *Journal of Family Therapy*. doi: 10.1111/1467-6427.12086.

Downs, K. J., & Blow, A. J. (2013). A substantive and methodological review of family-based treatment for eating disorders: The last 25 years of research. *Journal of Family Therapy*, 35, 3–28. doi: 10.1111/joft.2013.35.issue-s1.

Forgas, J. R., Bower, G. H., & Moylan, S. (1990). Praise or blame? Affective influences on attributions for achievement. *Journal of Personality and Social Psychology*, 59, 809–819. doi: 10.1037/0022-3514.59.4.809.

Girz, L., Lafrance Robinson, A., Foroughe, M., Jasper, K., & Boachie, A. (2013). Adapting family-based therapy to a day hospital programme for adolescents with eating disorders: Preliminary outcomes and trajectories of change. *Journal of Family Therapy*, 35, 102–120. doi: 10.1111/joft.2013.35.issue-s1.

Goddard, E., Macdonald, P., Sepulveda, A. R., Naumann, U., Landau, S. et al. (2011a). Cognitive interpersonal maintenance model of eating disorders: Intervention for carers. *British Journal of Psychiatry*, 199, 225–231. doi: 10.1192/bjp. bp.110.088401.

Goddard, E., Macdonald, P., & Treasure, J. (2011b). An examination of the impact of "the Maudsley collaborative care skills training workshops" on patients with anorexia nervosa: A qualitative study. *European Eating Disorders Review*, 19, 150–161. doi: 10.1002/erv.v19.2.

Greenberg, L. S., & Paivio, S. C. (2003). *Working with emotions in psychotherapy*, Volume 13. New York: Guilford Press.

Grover, M., Naumann, U., Mohammad-Dar, L., Glennon, D., Ringwood, S. et al. (2011). A randomized controlled trial of an internet-based cognitive-behavioural skills package for carers of people with anorexia nervosa. *Psychological Medicine*, 41, 2581–2591. doi: 10.1017/S0033291711000766.

Heimpel, S. A., Wood, J. V., Marshall, M. A., & Brown, J. D. (2002). Do people with low self-esteem really want to feel better? Self-esteem differences in motivation to repair negative moods. *Journal of Personality and Social Psychology*, 82, 128–147. doi: 10.1037/0022-3514.82.1.128.

Lafrance Robinson, A. (2014). Examining the relationship between parental fears and accommodating and enabling behaviors in parents caring for a child with an eating disorder. Unpublished manuscript.

Lafrance Robinson, A., Dolhanty, J., & Greenberg, L. (2013a). Emotion-focused family therapy for eating disorders in children and adolescents. *Clinical Psychology & Psychotherapy*, 23(1), 14–23. doi: 10.1002/cpp.1861.

Lafrance Robinson, A., Dolhanty, J., Stillar, A., Henderson, K., & Mayman, S. (2014). Emotion-focused family therapy for eating disorders across the lifespan: A pilot study of a two-day transdiagnostic intervention for parents. *Clinical Psychology & Psychotherapy*, 23(1),14–23 . doi: 10.1002/cpp.1933.

Lafrance Robinson, A., Strahan, E., Girz, L., Wilson, A., & Boachie, A. (2013b). "I know I can help you": Parental self-efficacy predicts adolescent outcomes in family-based therapy for eating disorders. *European Eating Disorder Review*, 21, 108–114.

Lock, J. (2011). Evaluation of family treatment models for eating disorders. *Current Opinion in Psychiatry*, 24, 274–279. doi: 10.1097/YCO.0b013e328346f71e.

Lock, J., & Le Grange, D. (2012). *Treatment manual for anorexia nervosa: A family-based approach*. New York: Guilford Press.

Macdonald, P., Murray, J., Goddard, E., & Treasure, J. (2011). Carer's experience and perceived effects of a skills based training programme for families of people with eating disorders: A qualitative study. *European Eating Disorders Review*, 19, 475–486. doi: 10.1002/erv.v19.6.

Mondini, A., Favaro, A., & Santonastaso, P. (1996). Eating disorder and the ideal of feminine beauty in Italian newspapers and magazines. *European Eating Disorders Review*, 4(2), 112–120.

Perednia, C., & Vandereycken, W. (1989). An explorative study on parenting in eating disorder families. In W. Vandereycken, E. Kog, & J. Vanderlinden (Eds.), *The family approach to eating disorders* (pp. 119–146). New York: PMA Publishing.

Rhodes, P., Baillie, A., Brown, J., & Madden, S. (2005). Parental efficacy in the family-based treatment of anorexia: Preliminary development of the Parents versus Anorexia Scale (PvA). *European Eating Disorders Review*, 13, 399–405. doi: 10.1002/(ISSN)1099-0968.

Schmidt, U., & Treasure, J. (2006). Anorexia nervosa: Valued and visible. A cognitive interpersonal maintenance model and its implications for research and practice. *British Journal of Clinical Psychology*, 45, 343–366. doi: 10.1348/014466505X53902.

Sepulveda, A. R., Kyriacou, O., & Treasure, J. (2009). Development and validation of the Accommodation and Enabling scale for Eating Disorders (AESED) for caregivers in eating disorders. *BMC Health Sciences Research*, 9, 171–184. doi: 10.1186/1472-6963-9-171.

Siegel, D. J. (2010). *Mindsight*. New York: Bantam Books.

Treasure, J., & Ward, A. (1997). A practical guide to the use of motivational interviewing in anorexia nervosa. *European Eating Disorders Review*, 5, 102–114. doi: 10.1002/(ISSN)1099-0968.

Treasure, J., Schmidt, U., & Macdonald, P. (Eds.). (2009). *The clinician's guide to collaborative caring in eating disorders: The New Maudsley Method*. London: Routledge.

Treasure, J., Smith, G., & Crane, A. (2007). *Skills-based learning for caring for a loved one with an eating disorder*. London: Routledge.

Whitney, J., Murphy, T., Landau, S., Gavan, K., Todd, G. et al. (2012). A practical comparison of two types of family intervention: An exploratory RCT of family day workshops and individual family work as a supplement to inpatient care for adults with anorexia nervosa. *European Eating Disorders Review*, 20, 142–150. doi: 10.1002/erv.v20.2.

Part IV

Tales from the Trenches

Personal Accounts

17 Looking Back on *Brave Girl Eating*

Harriet Brown and Anna Young

In 2005, soon after our daughter's fourteenth birthday, my husband and I began to notice things that weren't quite right. Little things, for the most part, like the way her friends didn't come around as much and the way she seemed so much more emotional. She cried more easily; seemed more anxious sometimes. Other times, she was her usual cheerful self.

We chalked it up to puberty, which she was just about hitting. We joked about 14 being the "lost year," the worst time in a teen's life and maybe in a family's life too. We worried, of course, and wondered if a therapist would help. Our daughter insisted she didn't need one, that she just wanted to spend more time with us. That rang a few alarm bells – don't most 14-year-olds want to *escape* their parents? Her younger sister cornered me one day to ask whether Anna had an eating disorder. "I don't know," I said. But I think I did know. At her eighth-grade graduation we sat high in the bleachers of the auditorium, looking for Anna in a room full of hundreds of other kids. We found her by the bright orange dress she wore, and by the fact that she was thinner by far than any of the other girls. My husband and I looked at each other, our eyes full of dread. I called the pediatrician the next day.

That began the worst year of our lives, as we struggled to wrap our minds around the words *anorexia nervosa* and then struggled even harder to understand that the treatments on offer were not going to help. It's bad enough realizing your child has a potentially fatal disease. To realize on top of that that the best the medical field has to offer is useless (or worse), that the professionals you turned to were either inaccessible, ineffective, judgmental, or all three – *that* was terrifying.

By great good luck, I stumbled on a description of family-based treatment. I knew immediately we needed to try it. The closest treatment team was four hours away and didn't have an opening, so we decided, with the support of our pediatrician and a therapist who wasn't trained in FBT, to do it ourselves.

Below is an account of that time and treatment as Anna and I recall it. My husband, Jamie, and our younger daughter played crucial roles as well, and my words here represent their perspectives too.

ANNA: I remember being in sixth grade (age 11) and writing a research paper on eating disorders. And I remember thinking to myself, *that will never be me.* Honestly, the eating disorder was almost an accident. It wasn't about wanting to lose weight at first. It was about health. You get so many reinforcing messages from everybody about eating healthy, especially in the public school system. *Make sure your portions aren't too big! Everyone eats too much!* Those scare tactics worked on me. I wasn't confident in my body; I didn't like it. But I don't think I ever made the active connection at first between my actions and the eating disorder.

HARRIET: I remember that research paper too, and thinking the exact same thing: *That's one worry I can cross off the list.* I thought *knowing* about eating disorders would protect her from *developing* one. Of course that reflected my complete ignorance about them, as well as the fact that I must have believed eating disorders were on some level a choice. I thought our daughter was too smart and too knowledgeable to choose that.

Around eighth grade Anna started training on a competitive gymnastics team. She'd always been athletic, and we encouraged that because sports are good for you, right? The team practiced most nights from 6 to 9 p.m. We'd always eaten dinner together as a family, but on those nights Anna got into the habit of eating dinner on her own before practice. We weren't checking what she ate or watching her. She had always been a very logical child, a reliable reporter. So we didn't pay attention or watch closely, and as a result, as we realized later, we had no idea what was actually going on.

ANNA: I remember portioning out food and it almost became a competition, a game: how much did I *really* need to eat? Because at that point it wasn't about losing weight. I had not made the connection then that I was falling down a hole I couldn't get out of. The body image stuff came later for me.

HARRIET: And then there was a day in May when Anna broke down crying on a family bike ride and couldn't be consoled. She told me she was worried but wouldn't tell me what she was worried about.

ANNA: That was the day when I was like, this isn't right, something's wrong. It had gone too far, and I didn't know how to turn it around. That's when I talked to my mom.

HARRIET: We offered to call a therapist but she insisted she could handle it. Whatever *it* was. We talked it over and decided to watch her more closely. For all we knew this was a typical adolescent moment, nothing more. We were so conditioned to believe that our job as parents was to start stepping back during this part of her life. Anorexia didn't really cross my mind then, partly because of that research paper and partly because Anna hadn't lost any weight. At some point in there I did think back to her 14-year checkup, six months earlier; she'd grown an inch and not gained any weight. I'd asked the pediatrician if we should worry, and she said no, everything looked fine. That reassured me. Sort of. Our culture prizes autonomy and the development of the individual; the worst thing you can do, as a middle-class parent, is hover and micro-manage. We didn't want to be helicopter parents. But we were worried, no question.

In retrospect the signs were there and I feel terrible about not spotting them sooner. Earlier that spring Anna had asked for a subscription to *Gourmet* magazine so she could plan an elaborate dinner for my birthday – in October. That seemed odd at the time, especially for a kid who'd never shown the slightest interest in cooking. She'd also started a behavior that was new for her, of asking me on a Monday what we would be having for dinner that Friday, and insisting that she had to know. That was extremely unusual; Anna had always been a flexible, go-with-the-flow kind of child. I remember feeling annoyed and pressured to make plans, which doesn't come naturally to me. Looking back, I don't know what I was thinking, except that it couldn't be anorexia because she hadn't suddenly dropped a lot of weight.

ANNA: There's such a misunderstanding as to what an eating disorder is and how it comes to be and what the intentions are of the person. I hear it all the time on college campuses. You hear groups of girls, or girls and guys, talk about people with eating disorders with so much disdain and judgment. I've even heard girls with eating disorders, who won't admit they have them, openly bash other girls with eating disorders. I want to say to them, "You know how much she's suffering because you're suffering." It upsets me. I feel like no matter how much research and knowledge there is out there, this society will always stigmatize eating disorders and see them as a choice and a cry for attention. When you have a group of people saying "That anorexic bitch" or "That girl has such an eating disorder" – we should know better at this point.

So it's hard to acknowledge you have an eating disorder, because that is the attitude people have toward it. How do you expect someone who's suffering to ask for help or admit they have a problem if society looks at it like you're just some attention whore? This disease affects people with type-A personalities, who are more inclined to feel very judged, to feel shame, to be incredibly caught up with what people think of them, to be constantly worried about other people's opinions. I think that's one reason girls won't ask for help and a lot of people are scared to admit they have a problem.

HARRIET: It's also hard to understand or acknowledge what's going on when you're 14 years old and very sick, or when you have no idea what anorexia is. Once we did understand, we felt a lot of that same shame. Early on, Anna got dangerously dehydrated and wound up in the hospital for five days, and I still remember the looks some of the nurses and residents on the ward gave us. No one came out and said, "This is your fault," but I know they were thinking it. They looked at us with such judgment.

And the first few professionals we came across didn't help with that, or with much else. Our pediatrician was extremely supportive, but the first therapist we found who was on our insurance plan and had an opening was awful. She talked to Anna in a little baby voice and told us Anna would be sick for the rest of her life. I left her office determined to find another way. Our pediatrician suggested residential treatment, which our insurance wouldn't cover. We looked at a day treatment program at a local adolescent psychiatric hospital, but it wasn't specifically for teens with eating disorders and it didn't seem like the right place for her.

And then I stumbled across a description of family-based treatment, and knew immediately that's what we should pursue. By that point we'd spent several months trying to persuade Anna to eat, with no success. She was getting sicker, and no one seemed to have any idea what to do. I could see how terrified she was of eating; I was quite sure she *couldn't* choose to eat on her own. FBT made sense to me. My husband wasn't so sure; it took him a while to get past the idea that we could reason our daughter out of the eating disorder. Once he understood that, he was all in, and we were able to work well together. The only problem was, the closest FBT therapists were 200 miles away. So we decided to give it a go ourselves.

ANNA: I remember not wanting to go away to residential treatment. But I also remember being terrified that my parents weren't medical professionals and how did I know that this was healthy and right. I recognize now a lot of that was the ED, but it was a very real and rational fear to me.

Growing up, especially in school, you're told over and over and over what you should be eating and doing, what is good and what is bad, this is. So I was being asked to not only go against everything society and my education and my eating disorder thought was healthy, but I was being asked to trust that my parents knew what they were doing. It was hard for me to accept.

HARRIET: And we had to act like we knew what we were doing. I mean, we did know, kind of, but like Anna we were so inculcated with the idea that doctors must always be right. And in this case the doctors, at least the ones we could find, were all telling us to go against our instincts. To sit at the table and let our daughter "choose" whether to eat. To watch her starve to death. I couldn't do it.

ANNA: I did trust my parents. I questioned, but they're my parents and we've always had a good relationship and I love them, and that helped me a lot. I always felt close to them. But there was definitely some conflict in my feelings. Looking back, it was very much conflict between me and the eating disorder.

There was always a part of me that wanted to get better. It just was so awful and overwhelming and consuming. I could want it but I didn't feel I had control or the ability to make it happen.

HARRIET: I could see that. And that's why FBT made sense to me. Of course on a literal level Anna did have to put the food into her mouth and eat it. Our job was to create an environment where she felt she had no choice but to eat, even though it went against the voice of the eating disorder. Even though we could see how much she paid for it afterward, in guilt and shame and fear. And even though that wasn't how we'd parented her up until then.

That was a truly terrible year for all of us. But it would have been infinitely worse if we'd been watching from a distance, or if we'd sent Anna away. She was our daughter, and she wanted to stay close. She needed to; she made that clear. We had to be the ones to help her.

Eventually we did find a wonderful therapist who was willing to support all of us through the re-feeding process. She and the pediatrician were our lifelines during that year and over the next four years, when Anna was better but not entirely well.

ANNA: The thoughts never really left. I kind of pretended. Things did get better, but I was never really recovered. I didn't realize it then, though, because I didn't think recovery was really possible. I thought the state I had hit was as good as it was going to get. And it was just going to suck.

HARRIET: I *knew* she wasn't really recovered, but no one believed me. Our pediatrician sat me down when Anna was 16 and told me that my anxiety was now the problem and maybe I was the one who needed treatment, that our daughter was fine. I felt terribly rebuked, and that made me quiet for a while. But I could tell, and so could my husband, that our daughter wasn't herself. So in a way it wasn't a huge surprise that she had a major relapse at 18, after graduating high school and living on her own for a few months.

ANNA: I'm not really sure exactly what happened. I don't remember purposefully starting to restrict or over-exercise. The eating disorder just kind of crept up on me. It was insidious.

HARRIET: That was the beginning of a very challenging couple of years. Anna came home, she went to college, she came back. She'd gain a few pounds and then lose them immediately; she was so scared, and so were we. We found an FBT therapist this time around, but it was three hours' round-trip every time we saw her. And while she's a wonderful professional, she wasn't a good fit for Anna. She helped support Jamie and me, but nothing really changed.

ANNA: I think it's my personality to not trust being open about very private things in my life. For my age I am very conservative. I don't post revealing things on social media. I don't want the whole world to know my life. I had a very hard time, and still do, trusting and relating to a therapist and letting them into my life. That was especially true when I was sick, because I felt even more judged and anxious than I normally do.

I was 18 and I didn't want to go through it all again. I didn't want to be sick again. I thought, *I did this already.* A big part of me was resigned. All along I'd been thinking, *Maybe this is just how it's going to be.* Everyone told me it wasn't true, that I could recover. My parents told me all the time. But no amount of anyone telling you it's possible to get better can ever make you believe it. You have to experience it for yourself.

HARRIET: In many ways the relapse was much worse than the first time. Anna wasn't a child anymore. She was 18 and 19 and 20 and she could walk out the door at any moment. She did walk out once, but she came back a few days later. I think on some level she always knew that, while there was a lot of conflict between us, we loved her and had her best interests at heart.

ANNA: I had lived away from my parents, so to give someone else control over my life was hard. It would be hard for anyone, let alone an 18-year-old sick with a disease that makes you feel like you have to control everything. And it was hard for me to differentiate between the illness and me at that point. I resented having to relinquish control. I didn't like it. But part of me knew there was no other way things could ever get better. I kind of felt like I didn't have a choice.

HARRIET: One of the most helpful things we did during this time was go out to an FBT-based ED program in San Diego and spend a week with the treatment team there. That was profoundly helpful for all of us for all sorts of reasons. I took Anna out, which gave Jamie and our younger daughter a break. I felt supported and validated by everything the team said and did. And best of all, Anna really connected with her therapist at the program.

ANNA: My therapist really got what it was like to have an eating disorder. You need a balance between someone who's going to understand and someone who's going to take you right back down that hole with them. I remember eating meals with my therapist, and her mediating between my mother and me, and helping both of us get through the things we found difficult about having a meal. To me, that was incredibly helpful.

HARRIET: To me too! Having a good FBT therapist was important in different ways the second time around. The first time we were focused on weight gain, and Anna was young enough and sick enough and shut down enough that therapy wasn't especially useful to her, though it helped Jamie and me. The second time around was much more emotionally complicated because we were dealing with a young adult now.

ANNA: My therapist made me feel safer, which let me express anxiety and work through it in a healthier way. After San Diego I came home and as much as the eating disorder still fought it, I had more of a sense of safety and trust in my parents, in what was going on. And that was important because while I don't remember a lot of specifics from that time, I do remember the feelings. I remember a lot of fear and anxiety and feeling hopeless. A lot of feeling like it was never going to get better and I was never going to live what I thought was a normal life. I was never gong to be able to make it through college, hold down a job, "succeed." Part of that came from the illness and part of that came from the need to be treated like a child in order to get better.

But I always trusted my parents on some level. I will be forever grateful to them for suffering through it with me. What we went through changed my life. It allowed me to *have* a life. Because at that point I could not wrap my head around the idea that I could wake up and not spend every second of every day feeling anxious about what I ate. I couldn't imagine not feeling physically uncomfortable all the time. I couldn't imagine my life not being run by this obsession. So there was a lot of getting close, then falling back a little bit, getting close, falling back a little bit, and that was because I would just give up. Not consciously give up, but I just felt hopeless about ever recovering and thought, *OK, this is what it is.*

HARRIET: At this point she was living with us and going to college in our town. So we were right there to watch her go through it again and again and feel helpless. It seemed like we could support her to gain a little weight but we couldn't keep her from dropping it again. We bounced around a lot during those years between trying to be very directive and controlling and giving her autonomy. I remember holding her hands and looking into her eyes and promising her that recovery was possible, that it would change her life. That it would give her back her life. But I don't think she could hear me. Not really. And I wondered if we would still be going around and around the same vicious cycle when she was 30.

ANNA: I think part of the reason it took me so long to recover was it took me years to accept that health didn't have to be this constant game of limiting, this holding yourself back. That our bodies are naturally programmed to be healthy. If you eat when you're hungry, if you eat carbs when you want them, if you listen to what your body wants to eat and how hungry you are, it kind of self-regulates. That concept was so foreign to me.

It took me a long time to believe that there is wiggle room, that it's OK to eat a cupcake once in a while. I don't usually see things in black and white. But the black and white thinking of the eating disorder was reinforced by everything and everyone around me. Every girl I've ever known, whether she has an eating disorder or not, feels to some extent that people are watching what they eat. People are judging you as a person and your lifestyle, how much you care about yourself and other people based on what's going into your mouth.

HARRIET: I've heard my university students say the same thing.

ANNA: I had to understand that the definition of healthy for me is different from what I'd been hearing.

HARRIET: That's where culture plays a huge role, especially as you get older. All the anti-obesity rhetoric plays right into the terror people feel when they're in the grip of an eating disorder. I felt like Jamie and I were trying to metaphorically out-shout not only the voice of the eating disorder but the voices that surround all of us that make us anxious about food and eating and weight. And I knew our voices couldn't possibly compete with all the others.

ANNA: My parents got me most of the way there and kept me there until I could figure out how to take the last few steps myself. There is a point where you realize that you can get helped 99 percent of the way, but those last few steps have to be on your own. You have to see through all the bullshit we get told about health and accept that everyone has a different definition of health and this is what yours is. That listening to how your body feels is the best gauge of what healthy is for you, not listening to everyone else.

Part of the turning point for me was having a boyfriend with a very destructive drug addiction. Watching someone I thought I knew, and thought I loved, destroy his life, despite being offered help over and over and over again. I had done my research. I knew what heroin addiction was and what the recovery rates were. I knew what odds he was facing and what kind of life he was facing if he didn't overcome it. And I saw very clearly for the first time that there was absolutely no way in hell no matter how much help he was offered that he was going to get better unless he wanted to and decided to. And that was a life-changing moment for me. It was the moment I said to myself, I can't let something like an eating disorder run my life. I can't let it ruin my life. I can't let it take any more years of my life away.

I also think being scared every day that I was going to find him dead gave me some perspective about how my parents felt watching me be ill. And that definitely helped me decide I was done. I was mostly weight-restored at that point. I had a couple pounds I was fluctuating, right on the border. But it was so much less about the weight at that point and more just a decision about how I was going to approach life. It's not like the eating disorder just stopped. It wasn't like, "Oh, I'm good now!" It took a lot of time. It wasn't that the thoughts went away; it was that when they came, I could take them and say, "I'm going to put these over there because I don't want them." I was able to take all the tools Roxie and my parents and other people had given me over the years and actually use them.

HARRIET: We could tell when things changed for Anna. We could almost see the switch flip. It was like getting her back after a very long absence.

ANNA: I'd say I'm closer to my parents now than a lot of people my age. I know I can talk to them about anything, and I do. I talk to them fairly frequently. I genuinely enjoy our conversations. I go to them when I have questions, concerns, conundrums, when I need to vent. I still feel safe being a kid with them. I definitely think that comes partly from going through FBT! I still feel like it's OK to call them at 4 in the morning if I'm sick or upset or just don't feel good.

As absolutely awful and hard as it was, I don't believe I would have recovered if we hadn't done FBT. And I do honestly think it made us closer. It sounds super cheesy, but being that sick for that long has given me a very different outlook on my life. I feel like I appreciate what I have a lot more, and that goes for our relationship as well. I want to be close to my parents because we had so many ups and downs, so many rough years. My mom sometimes says my senior year of college when I lived at home and was recovered felt like making up for lost time. And I loved it.

HARRIET: We did too. It was like getting a do-over for some of those earlier years when we were all so consumed by the eating disorder.

ANNA: The eating disorder very much shaped my personality. It was miserable but it gave me a strength a lot of people my age don't have yet, and gave me a lot of perspective. It gave me appreciation for the life I have, and made me realize there's no shame in struggling. Everybody struggles in some capacity or form, whether it's private or public. Now when I tell people what I've been through, they open up about the struggles in their own life that nobody knows about because this culture is so shaming about that. But I'm really not ashamed about it anymore. I don't have a fear about the world knowing.

18 Adolescent Impressions of Family Involvement in the Treatment of Eating Disorders

Erin Parks, Leslie Karwoski Anderson, and Anne Cusack

Introduction

Over the past 25 years, family-based therapy (FBT) has emerged as the first-line treatment for adolescent anorexia nervosa (AN) and has shown promise in the treatment of adolescents with bulimia (BN) (Le Grange, Lock, Agras, Bryson, & Booil, 2015) and young adults with eating disorders (Downs & Blow, 2013). One central premise in FBT posits that adolescents with eating disorders are often unable to make decisions that will foster recovery due to the ego-syntonicity, ambivalence, and treatment resistance that is so often inherent in eating disorders (Halmi, 2009), and thus parents must be empowered to lead their child's eating in order to restore weight and normalize eating patterns (Lock & Le Grange, 2012).

Regardless of the treatment modality, caring for a loved one with an eating disorder is an extremely stressful experience, with caregivers reporting high levels of burden, a desire for more information and skills to fulfill their role, and high levels of anxiety, depression, and stress (for a review, see Anastasiadou, Medina-Pradas, Sepulveda, & Treasure, 2014). In FBT, parents direct the children's recovery through managing the frequency, serving size, and content of meals and snacks with the child receiving increasing autonomy as their mental and physical health improves. While the process of parents feeding their children appears straightforward in principle, it can be very difficult to carry out and may result in family conflicts around meals and other activities. In FBT, the parents are encouraged to separate the eating disorder from the child, uniting with their child against the eating disorder as their common enemy (Lock & Le Grange, 2005). As patients face normative eating, they experience a high degree of anxiety and distress. Parents often report fearing that, by virtue of them requiring their adolescent child to undertake behaviors very difficult and distressing for them, the child may hold them responsible for their distress. Parents often fear that by challenging the eating disorder – either by confronting the irrational beliefs or by pushing them to eat more normally – the parent–child relationship will be compromised (ibid).

The emotional challenges that come up in caregiving for a child with an ED, specifically the fear of damaging the relationship with the child, may cause family members to act in ways that unintentionally exacerbate or enable the symptoms of the ED (Kyriacou, Treasure, & Schmidt, 2008). One of the ways in which this commonly happens is when parents are reluctant to challenge their child's eating disorder for fear of impacting their relationship. Parents might negotiate with the eating disorder, or refrain from firmly supporting the child to do what is needed in recovery because they are afraid of long-term consequences for the relationship.

As clinicians, we may be tempted to reassure parents that they need to relentlessly lead restoration of normal eating in their child, and the relationship will survive this conflict. However, little empirical data exist in detailing what actually occurs in the parent–child relationship after undergoing FBT for an eating disorder. To examine this idea, we interviewed adolescents who had been through family therapy for eating disorders to see how they felt about their parents' involvement after therapy terminated. Surveys were sent to adolescents who had graduated from a partial-hospitalization/intensive outpatient program as part of FBT to determine how they felt about their experience in therapy and their relationship with their family after the termination of therapy.

Methods

Participants

Adolescents who had completed a transdiagnostic partial-hospitalization (PHP) treatment program at the University of California, San Diego Eating Disorders Center for Treatment and Research were invited via email to participate in an online survey of their experiences with family involvement in their treatment. Invitations were mailed out to 104 email addresses, representing 64 families, belonging to either parents or adolescents who had consented to receive electronic notification of research studies. For families where we had only the parents' email addresses, it was requested that parents forward the survey to their child. Adolescents' responses were confidential and were unable to be reviewed by the parent or adolescent after the survey was electronically submitted. The study was conducted according to the Institutional Review Board regulations of the UC San Diego.

Treatment

All study participants and their families had participated in the PHP. Adolescents attended treatment for up to 10 hours per day, 5–6 days per week for an average length of stay of 4 months. Parents participated in the program for up to 13 hours a week. Family involvement in treatment included the interventions described below.

Family therapy sessions. Family therapy sessions occurred a minimum of one hour per week with the treatment modality of FBT for adolescent eating disorders. For adolescents with co-occurring impulsive behaviors, such as self-harm, suicidality or substance use, family sessions would incorporate more of a DBT structure and philosophy.

Family dialectical behavior therapy (DBT) skills groups. These multi-family skills groups followed an evidence-based (Linehan, 1999) traditional DBT 16-module format teaching skills in distress tolerance, mindfulness, emotion regulation, and interpersonal effectiveness.

Family experiential groups. Led by two masters- or doctoral-level therapists, experiential groups were attended by adolescents and at least one parent. The experiential groups are intended to provide psychoeducation on the neurobiology of eating disorders, separate the illness from the child, and/or strengthen DBT interpersonal and distress tolerance skills, and are based on emerging evidence-based models that integrate the neurobiology of AN into treatment delivery (Hill et al., 2012; Simic & Eisler, 2015; Treasure, 2007).

Parent process and psychoeducation groups. In these multi-family groups, topics included the neurobiology of eating disorders, nutrition, psychopharmacology, reintegrating children into school and sports, along with various other topics of interest and providing support to the families.

Parent management training. Offered weekly for 60 minutes, this group was led by a senior-level therapist and was attended exclusively by caregivers. This group was adapted from Kazdin's (2008) behaviorally-based parent management training.

Family sessions with treatment team. Parents could schedule sessions with their psychiatrist and dietician as needed, utilizing a consultation model. Most parents chose to meet with their treatment team members for a minimum of one hour per week.

Family group meals. Four meals per week were served as family group meals. Supervised by licensed dieticians, psychologists, and masters-level therapists, parents would take the lead in plating their adolescent's meal and the entire family would eat together. During the meal, the treatment team dined with the families and would offer in-vivo meal coaching.

Measures

While few studies have investigated adolescent impressions of family involvement, we utilized a mixed-method design with a *complementarity* intent consistent with the conceptual framework provided by Greene, Caracelli, and Graham (1989). As per Greene et al.'s guidelines, our quantitative and qualitative measures were interactively designed to measure the same phenomena using different methods with equal importance with the rationale of "increasing the interpretability, meaningfulness, and validity of constructs … by both capitalizing on inherent method strengths and counteracting inherent biases in methods" (p. 259). We found it particularly necessary to use two different methods of data collection given that the respondents were adolescents, were a heterogeneous group with respect to diagnosis and stage of recovery, and were being asked to both retrospectively reflect and comment on current feelings.

TODAY, when you look back at your time with UCSD, how do you NOW feel about...

	Very negative			Neutral			Very positive
Family Therapy	○	○	○	○	○	○	○
Family Groups	○	○	○	○	○	○	○
Family Meals	○	○	○	○	○	○	○
Your relationship with your family therapist	○	○	○	○	○	○	○
Your relationship with your parents	○	○	○	○	○	○	○
The helpfulness of family involment	○	○	○	○	○	○	○

Figure 18.1   Likert scale for rating impressions of multiple aspects of family involvement used at three time points

Participants were given seven open-ended writing prompts to share their impressions of family involvement in treatment. The following questions were asked:

- When you *first* started treatment, what did you think about having your family involved?
- How do you *now* feel about having had your family involved?
- What was *unhelpful* about having your family involved?
- What was *helpful* about having your family involved?
- Discuss your relationship with your parents over the course of treatment and recovery; how did your relationship change from before, and now after treatment?
- With regard to timing, do you think your family should have started treatment earlier? Later? When should your family have become involved?
- Do you have any other comments to make about your family's involvement in your treatment?

Participants also completed a 7-point Likert scale, rating their impressions of various aspects of family involvement from 1 (very negative) to 7 (very positive). We asked for their *current* impressions (see Figure 18.1), along with their retrospective assessment of their impressions during the first week of treatment (i.e. "In the *beginning*, when you *first* started treatment, how did you feel about...?"). Adolescents were asked for their impressions of family therapy, family groups, family meals, their relationship with their family therapist, their relationship with their parents, and the overall helpfulness of family involvement.

Eating Disorder Symptoms

To evaluate the effectiveness of treatment and adolescent impressions of treatment at the onset, we asked adolescents where they were currently at in their recovery, which eating disorder behaviors they were participating in at the beginning of treatment and in which eating disorder behaviors they were currently engaged. One of our hypotheses was that if a patient was engaging in minimal eating disorder behaviors, that was a proxy for effective treatment and thus they would have more favorable impressions of family involvement in treatment.

Results

Participant Characteristics

Twenty-nine adolescents completed the electronic survey. Ten (34%) had a diagnosis of anorexia nervosa–restrictive while in treatment, six (21%) had a diagnosis of anorexia nervosa–binge/purge, eight (27.8%) had a diagnosis of bulimia nervosa while in treatment, and five met criteria for other specified feeding or eating disorder (OSFED) while in treatment (17.2%). All participants were between the ages of 11 and 18 years when they entered partial-hospitalization treatment with us. At the time of the assessment, participants were between the ages of 12 and 21 years (mean = 16.6, SD = 2.21). When rating where they are at in their recovery on a 1 (not recovered) to 7 (recovered) Likert scale, participants responded between 2 and 7 (mean = 5.75, SD = 1.24) and seven participants reported "no" when asked if they "considered [themselves] in recovery." However, it is important to keep in mind the potential inaccuracies of adolescent self-reporting of recovery status (Murray, Loeb, & Le Grange, 2014), particularly when many adolescents typically do not want to be in treatment. As such, it is possible that participants were less recovered than they indicated on self-report measures. Participants were asked to report the ED behaviors they engaged in at the onset of treatment and the ED behaviors they are currently utilizing. Table 18.1 presents the number of participants that reported engaging in each eating disorder behavior.

Quantitative Impressions

Paired two sample *t*-tests were completed to compare the retrospective Likert scale ratings of treatment impression at the *onset* of treatment to *current* impressions since the termination of treatment. Results, shown in Table 18.2, demonstrated that adolescents have significantly more positive impressions of family involvement today, post-treatment, when compared to pre-treatment. Impressions were significantly more positive in all aspects of family involvement: family therapy, family groups, and family meals. Adolescents also reported a significant improvement in their relationships with their family therapists and their parents. Lastly, at the onset of treatment, adolescents did not believe family involvement would be helpful in their recovery; in fact, many of the qualitative responses indicated that the adolescents had initially resisted family treatment. Their impressions of the helpfulness of family involvement significantly increased, with the majority of adolescents now expressing appreciation of their families' involvement in treatment.

Table 18.1 Number of adolescents in the
sample reporting engagement in various
eating disorder behaviors (% of total sample)

Behavior	Before (%)	Now (%)
Restricting	28 (97)	8 (28)
Over-exercising	16 (55)	2 (7)
Binging	6 (21)	1 (3)
Purging	12 (41)	2 (7)
Laxative abuse	4 (41)	0
Self-harm	14 (48)	3 (10)
Substance use	1 (3)	2 (7)

Table 18.2 Adolescents ranked their impressions of various aspects of family involvement at the beginning of treatment and now (post-treatment)

t-test: Paid two sample for means (N = 29)

	Impressions of family involvement		
	Beginning	Now	P
Family therapy	2.66 (SD = 1.9)	5.00 (SD = 1.98)	< 0.0001
Family groups	2.34 (SD = 1.47)	4.62 (SD = 1.66)	< 0.0001
Family meals	2.55 (SD = 1.86)	5.28 (SD = 1.31)	< 0.0001
Relationship with family therapist	3.90 (SD = 2.24)	5.62 (SD = 1.80)	< 0.001
Relationship with parents	3.07 (SD = 1.81)	5.72 (SD = 1.28)	< 0.0001
Helpfulness of family involvement	3.00 (SD = 1.93)	5.62 (SD = 1.54)	< 0.0001

Note: Responses were recorded on a 7-point Likert scale ranging from 1 (very negative) to 7 (very positive).

Qualitative Impressions

Participants completed open-ended writing prompts about their impressions of family involvement. Their responses followed the same pattern demonstrated by those of the quantitative data, with more favorable impressions at the completion of therapy than when they first started. A sampling of the responses follows.

When you first started treatment, what did you think about your family's involvement?

With the exception of three adolescents, all participants expressed resistance to having their family involved in treatment. They expressed varying emotions, such as anger, fear and shame, related to the involvement of their family; for example:

- "It made me very uncomfortable, I did not want my family to see how bad I became [eating disorder-wise]."
- "I was very cautious about having my family involved. The main reason that I went to treatment was to avoid the eating disorder from ruining my relationship with my mom. I really wanted to just recover by myself and not have help."
- "I thought it was not going to be helpful and would just make things worse."

Looking back, how do you now *feel about having your family involved?*

With one exception ("I still don't like it"), all respondents expressed positive or dual emotions in relation to family involvement; for example:

- "I feel relieved. Even though it was an awkward transition at first, it helped in the long run because of how meaningful our relationship became and how much the support meant to me."
- "I thought it was valuable, even though I was annoyed."
- "They helped make sure I was eating my meals and they monitored everything, even when I didn't want them to. They definitely were a big part in recovery."
- "Looking back now, I'm glad my family was involved in my treatment because I was held accountable for my actions at home and was under constant supervision after and during meals. I'm also glad that they were present, because they were able to learn skills to help me and understood better how I was feeling and what I was working on in order to recover."

What was unhelpful *about having your family involved?*

Adolescents expressed a very diverse list of ways in which family involvement was unhelpful, but the overwhelming theme was difficulties around the loss of independence and perception of parents as "nagging" and intrusive when they were supervising ED behaviors. Some less frequent responses included critiques of how the parents could have done more and their guilt in reaction to their parents' worries; for example:

- "My parents often thought that they were to blame for my eating disorder. This is still very confusing and frustrating for me. I do not think that anyone at the program made them feel this way, but others have. Also, my family was extremely opinionated on things that I felt I needed to decide for myself. Their intentions were always good, but often the execution was poor."
- "I think that sometimes my parents, because they were involved so intricately in my treatment, felt that they could understand the "voice" of my eating disorder as perfectly as I could. As a part of the program parents are taught not to negotiate with the eating disorder voice coming from their

child, but sometimes I felt like my parents took this advice "too far" and would delegitimize my anxieties and concerns by saying, "Nope. This is your eating disorder talking and we don't want to hear it."

- "The potential of having them let you down for not taking their involvement seriously. It was disappointing and defeating when they wouldn't show up when asked to."

What was helpful *about having your family involved?*

Three respondents did not answer this question and the other adolescents (90%) all listed at least one thing that was helpful about family involvement. Of those who responded, the majority (50%) specifically discussed that, while they disliked the loss of independence, it was very helpful to have parents helping them eat at home. They described parents preparing meals, plating meals, and "making me eat" as helping them "stay on track at home." Additionally, respondents described the helpfulness of their parents being able to separate the ED from their child; for example:

- "It was really great to have my mother involved because she was very supportive and understanding when I was having trouble at home, due to all the information she received during my treatment there."
- "Even though it bugged me, as I look back I see how them being there would help me in later times when I was discharged, or I probably would have relapsed."
- "It was helpful to have someone to turn to when you needed it and have people to keep you accountable for your sleep hygiene plan, exercise plan, activity commitments, etc."
- "Having family groups on Saturday taught me many good coping skills and taught my parents to better understand what they needed to do to encourage me to be healthy."
- "Our entire relationship was saved."

Discuss your relationship with your parents over the course of treatment

With one exception, all respondents stated that their relationship with their parents is better now than at the onset of treatment. It should be noted that while the parent–child relationships started in different places, ranging from hostile to very positive, all but one participant described their relationship as better than before; for example:

- "During the beginning, I closed off from them, but through all of it and because of it we have grown closer."
- "Before [treatment] they did not know the extent of my struggles but we were close. During [treatment], they knew and things were hostile, but we were still close. Now we are closer than ever."

- "Before treatment, everyone walked on egg shells around one another. In family therapy we worked on "I" statements and validating others' feelings. Eventually, our relationships became easier to manage, with more open communication."
- "Before treatment it was very bad, during there was a lot of stress and obsessing over my recovery, and now there is still stress but I appreciate them so much and my respect for them is a lot higher."

Discuss timing – at what point should your family have become involved?

While many thought that the timing of treatment was correct, half of the responding participants stated that they wished their family had placed them in treatment earlier and/or they wished their parents had been involved in treatment earlier; three participants did not respond. Several wrote that they had been in other treatment facilities without family involvement and it would have been helpful if family involvement had occurred sooner; for example:

- "In hindsight, objectively, they should have begun a stricter treatment plan sooner."
- "My family should have started treatment earlier."
- "I think family therapy should start right away."
- "The family should maybe be involved a little later after the child has been involved for some time. I know my parents weren't too comfortable because they didn't know what to expect, and I couldn't give them any insight because we were going through it at the same time."

Discussion

Both the quantitative and qualitative data confirm what clinicians and parents have observed clinically – adolescents are initially resistant to including their parents in treatment. Our preliminary study suggests that this hesitance to involve the parents is motivated by a variety of reasons ranging from fear of hurting the relationship with their parents to ambivalence towards treatment. Regardless of their reasons for wanting to exclude their families from treatment, ultimately the adolescents typically reach the same conclusion upon discharge – family involvement was instrumental to recovery.

The adolescents demonstrated a significant change in opinion from the onset of treatment compared to now (post-treatment) on the helpfulness of all aspects of family involvement. This finding should encourage parents to participate in all aspects of treatment, regardless of initial reservations by their adolescent. Future studies may disentangle various forms of family involvement and the effects of each. One confounding variable in our study is the intensity of family involvement. Adolescents participating in treatment at UC San Diego spend up to 13 hours per week in treatment with their family, though practically it can vary based on family needs. Traditional FBT is an outpatient treatment, with families generally participating in treatment once a week for one hour. Thus, it is unclear if the adolescents in this study were reacting to the *idea* of having a parent in charge of their treatment, or to the number of hours of family involvement, or both.

Another possible confound to this preliminary study is the modality of family involvement. Although our treatment approach is primarily based on FBT, a few other approaches are incorporated, including DBT and parent management training. Thus it is not clear which aspects of family involvement our adolescents initially found aversive.

There are important methodological limitations to this study that must be acknowledged. The overall number of adolescents filling out the survey was small ($N = 29$), and represented 45 percent of the families contacted. There are numerous possibilities as to why there was a low response rate. One mother wrote an email in response to our survey request stating that she was choosing to not forward the survey to her adolescent:

> I have made the decision not to have my daughter participate. [She] has worked hard to beat anorexia. She has been able to maintain her weight since leaving the program ... I continue to monitor her weight, mood, what she is eating, and how she is feeling about eating. When she is having a hard time eating we work with her to get through it. Luckily those times are becoming fewer and are farther apart. I feel my participation in the program has been the reason she hasn't had to return to your program. I now know what to watch for and how to handle it. Bringing up the anorexia is very hard for my daughter so I have decided not to have her participate. I feel it will only bring up emotions that she has been able to work through.

In addition to parents not sharing the survey with their adolescents, it is unclear whether there were inherent biases in which adolescents chose to respond (e.g. those that had had a particularly good experience in treatment). The survey they filled out was entirely self-report, and although their answers were anonymous and confidential, they may have limited insight into their recovery status, a desire to "please" their former therapists by reporting positive impressions of treatment, or any number of other biases that could influence their responses. Further, the quantitative data in this study was based upon a set of questions that have not been psychometrically validated.

Our data also suggested that adolescents often have an initially negative impression of their family therapist. Even the most skilled clinicians can struggle with being disliked by their adolescent clients. This data suggests that even adolescents who dislike their family therapist and sometimes do not participate in the family sessions, may eventually have a more favorable impression and, more importantly, recover as a result of family therapy. This finding is consistent with research showing that therapeutic alliance is stronger for parents than for adolescents in FBT (Forsberg et al., 2014). It is also worth pointing out that research into other types of psychotherapy has shown that therapeutic alliance is not necessary to achieve clinical improvement, and may even improve over time as the patient experiences behavioral symptom reduction (Brown, Mountford, & Waller, 2013).

In addition to finding the family interventions to be helpful and even integral to treatment, the adolescents also reported that their relationship with their parents was strengthened as a result of family involvement. Both adolescents and parents worry about family involvement weakening their familial relationships. Adolescents expressed a fear of worrying their parents by sharing the extent of their eating disorder and parents expressed a fear of exacerbating a relationship already strained by the illness. These preliminary data suggest that, despite their understandable reservations about family treatment, parental inclusion ultimately strengthens their relationships. These findings will hopefully begin to assuage parents' fears as they courageously participate in treatment. It is helpful to remember that just as adolescents are not eager to include their parents, parents are also not necessarily eager to enter family therapy – they initially feel vulnerable and uncertain. Reducing this barrier to engaging in family treatment, such as data demonstrating improved outcomes *and* improved relationships, will hopefully help more families to take the courageous step toward family-inclusive interventions.

References

Anastasiadou, D., Medina-Pradas, C., Sepulveda, A. R., & Treasure, J. (2014). A systematic review of family caregiving in eating disorders. *Eating Behaviors*, 15(3), 464–477.

Brown, A., Mountford, V. A., & Waller, G. (2013). Is the therapeutic alliance overvalued in the treatment of eating disorders? *International Journal of Eating Disorders*, 46(8), 779–782.

Downs, K. J., & Blow, A. J. (2013). A substantive and methodological review of family-based treatment for eating disorders: The last 25 years of research. *Journal of Family Therapy*, 35, 3–28.

Forsberg, S., Lo Tempio, E., Bryson, S., Fitzpatrick, K. K., Le Grange, D., & Lock, J. (2014). Parent–therapist alliance in family-based treatment for adolescents with anorexia nervosa. *European Eating Disorders Review*, 22(1), 53–58.

Greene, J. C., Caracelli, V. J., & Graham, W. F. (1989). Toward a conceptual framework for mixed-method evaluation designs. *Educational Evaluation and Policy Analysis*, 11(3), 255–274.

Halmi, K. A. (2009). Perplexities and provocations of eating disorders. *Journal of Child Psychology and Psychiatry*, 50(1–2), 163–169.

Hill, L., Dagg, D., Hill, L., Dagg, D., Levine, M. et al. (2012). *Family eating disorders manual: Guiding families through the maze of eating disorders*. Columbus, OH: Center For Balanced Living.

Kazdin, A. E. (2008). *Parent management training: Treatment for oppositional, aggressive, and antisocial behavior in children and adolescents*. Don Mills, ON: Oxford University Press.

Kyriacou, O., Treasure, J., & Schmidt, U. (2008). Understanding how parents cope with living with someone with anorexia nervosa: Modelling the factors that are associated with carer distress. *International Journal of Eating Disorders*, 41(3), 233–242.

Le Grange, D., Lock, J., Agras, S., Bryson, S., & Booil, J. (2015). Randomized clinical trial of family-based treatment and cognitive-behavioral therapy for adolescent bulimia nervosa. *Journal of the American Academy of Child & Adolescent Psychiatry*, 54(11), 886–894.

Linehan, M. (1999). *Skills training manual for treating borderline personality disorder.* New York: Guilford Press.

Lock, J., & Grange, D. L. (2005). *Help your teenager beat an eating disorder.* New York: Guilford Press.

Lock, J., & Le Grange, D. (2012). *Treatment manual for anorexia nervosa: A family-based approach*, 2nd edition. New York: Guilford Press.

Murray, S., Loeb, K., & Le Grange, D. (2014). Indexing psychopathology throughout family-based treatment for adolescent anorexia nervosa: Are we on track? *Advances in Eating Disorders: Theory, Research and Practice*, 2(1), 93–96.

Simic, M., & Eisler, I. (2015). Multi-family therapy. *Family therapy for adolescent eating and weight disorders: New applications* (pp. 110–138). New York: Routledge.

Treasure, J. (2007). *Skills-based learning for caring for a loved one with an eating disorder.* Abingdon: Routledge.

19 A Qualitative Study on the Challenges Associated with Accepting Familial Support from the Perspective of Transition-Age Youth with Eating Disorders

Gina Dimitropoulos, Jessica Herschman, Alene Toulany, and Cathleen Steinegger

Body image concerns and disordered eating typically emerge in adolescence, increasing the risk for development of eating disorders (EDs) (Treasure, Stein, & Maguire, 2015). The peak age of onset for anorexia nervosa (AN) occurs during adolescence (14–18) (Pinhas, Morris, Crosby, & Katzman, 2011), and bulimia nervosa (BN) symptoms increase between the ages of 14–16 for adolescent girls (Abebe, Lien, & von Soest, 2012). EDs are associated with high rates of mortality across all ages (Arcelus, Mitchell, Wales, & Nielsen, 2011) due to life-threatening medical complications and suicide (Campbell & Peebles, 2014). The rise in eating disorders and the highest risk of mortality (Arcelus, Bouman, & Morgan, 2008) coincide with a developmental stage that is characterized by major life changes, including individuation from the family, relationship building, transferring from secondary to post-secondary education settings, and entering the workforce (Arnett, 2007).

Research has shown that only half of adolescents with EDs recover; the remaining half continues to experience either subclinical EDs or a chronic course of illness (Steinhausen & Weber, 2009). Since many young people experience EDs that persist into early adulthood, they will likely require a transfer from pediatric eating disorder programs (EDPs) to adult care settings for ongoing treatment and/or medical monitoring (Arcelus, Bouman, & Morgan, 2008; Winston, Paul, & Juanola-Borrat, 2012). Transfer has been conceptualized as the termination of the provision of child and adolescent mental health services and the establishment of a connection with adult mental health service providers (Paul, Ford, Kramer, Islam, Harley, & Singh, 2013). Transition-age youth (16–25 years) have high rates of dropout from adult mental health services (Paul et al., 2013), which may, in part, be explained by the lack of evidence-based practices on effective transfer of care (Singh et al., 2010).

Parental support during the evolution from adolescence to emerging adulthood has been recognized as vital to the successful development of autonomy and individuation (Cote & Bynner, 2008). Most adolescents incrementally move from a state of emotional dependence on their family to a state of increasing independence (ibid) and often experience significant ambivalence about adulthood (Nelson et al., 2007). Parental support provides young adults with assistance to work through a multitude of transitions, including the formation of their identity and developing friendships and romantic relationships (Helgeson, Mascatelli, Reynolds, Becker, Escobar, & Siminerio, 2014). There are no published studies examining how family support evolves during late adolescence and early adulthood for individuals with an ED.

Family-based treatment (FBT) is the dominant intervention model utilized in pediatric EDPs (Norris et al., 2013) and has been shown to be effective in achieving weight restoration in medically stable youth with short illness duration (Le Grange et al., 2012). FBT emphasizes parent involvement in addressing ED symptoms and fostering treatment adherence (Lock, 2011; Lock et al., 2010). This approach is characterized by the gradual re-allocation of responsibility for ED management from parents to the adolescent as symptoms abate (Lock & Le Grange, 2013). This typically includes parents making decisions for the adolescent about when and how much to eat and navigating treatment services. However, it may further extend to parents assisting with issues outside of the ED itself, such as social difficulties and academic challenges, to a greater degree than would be expected for adolescents without mental illnesses. As a result, adolescents with EDs may have had limited opportunities to practise eating with independence, accessing and using services for their illness on their own, and exploring becoming autonomous individuals (Dimitropoulos et al., 2015).

There is a dearth of research on the experiences of transition-age youth with EDs and no research regarding their expectations of parental support during the transfer between pediatric and adult services. Addressing this question is important in order to: (1) increase knowledge of the type of parental support young adults perceive as helpful, and (2) enhance understanding of parent–child interactions that young adults identify as undermining their efforts to achieve independence and skills to directly manage their own health. Improved knowledge and understanding of how adolescents experience the transfer process may help mitigate the uncoordinated and often abrupt movement from pediatric to adult providers. This study aims to provide an account of the experiences of young adults with EDs who had previously transferred from pediatric to adult care services, with a particular focus on understanding their perceptions of parental support during the transition period.

The central question guiding the qualitative interviews was: what were the experiences of young adults transferring from pediatric to adult EDPs, health, and/or mental health services? We further sought to develop an in-depth understanding of the perceptions of parental support and any challenges associated with accepting familial support during the crossover to adult services from the perspective of young adults with EDs. We also aimed to identify how young people conceptualize effective support from family members as they exit pediatric care and during the process of being transferred to adult services.

Methods

Setting and Participants

This study was approved by the Research Ethics Boards at the University Health Network and the Hospital for Sick Children (SickKids) in Toronto, Canada. Inclusion criteria for this study consisted of: (1) young adults (18–22 years) who had received treatment in a pediatric EDP and (2) had a history of DSM-IV-TR diagnosis of AN and/or BN. A convenience sample of 15 participants was recruited over a two-year period. All participants had received an ED diagnosis from a licensed psychologist or psychiatrist at the time of admission into a pediatric EDP and/or prior to being placed on a waiting list for an adult EDP. Eligible participants had transferred out of a pediatric EDP within two years.

All participants in the study were female, with an average age of 19.1 years (SD = 1.5). Among our sample, a range of ED subtypes was represented: seven individuals had AN restrictive subtype, five had AN binge-eating/purging type, and the remaining three had BN. The average reported age of onset for their EDs was 14.7 years (SD = 1.8) and the average length of illness was 4.2 years (SD = 2.3). See Table 19.1 for a more detailed account of the demographic details of the participants.

Procedures

The procedures for recruiting participants and the methods used to conduct the data analysis have been described elsewhere (Dimitropoulos et al., 2015). Briefly, young adult participants were recruited following their discharge from a pediatric EDP or while on a waiting list for intensive treatment in an adult EDP. Prior to conducting the interviews, formal consent was obtained and the importance of confidentiality reviewed. Interviews were approximately one hour in length and were carried out at a time that was convenient for participants.

Using grounded theory methodology (Glaser & Strauss, 1967), the research team conducted data collection and analysis simultaneously in an iterative process (Corbin & Strauss, 1990). This iterative process is characterized by the systematic generation of comparisons, which allows for the identification of similarities and differences among concepts formed. An open-coding system was developed inductively through a line-by-line analysis of each transcript. Constant comparative analysis allowed the research team to both review the themes generated from the interviews and determine new areas to be explored in additional interviews with participants. The research team also examined any discrepancies or diverging views in their interpretation of the data, which was processed extensively until consensus was achieved. Finally, an axial coding system was employed to connect thick descriptions with the major themes that emerged from the data. The sample size was determined by whether the data had reached saturation (Strauss & Corbin, 1990).

Table 19.1 Demographic and clinical characteristics

	Young adult		
	n	*Range (years)*	*M (SD)*
Total	15		
Gender			
Female	15		
Age		18–21	19.13 (1.51)
Duration of illness	15	1–8	4.2 (2.27)
Onset of illness	15	12–17	14.73 (1.79)
Diagnosis			
AN-restrictive	7		
AN-binge/purge*	5		
BN	3		
Marital status			
Single	15		
Living circumstance			
Alone	2		
With family	12		
With partner and family	1		
Disability	7		
Student			
Ethnicity			
Caucasian	7		

* One participant with AN-binge/purge subtype also had a diagnosis of diabetes.

Notes: BMI data is not reported due to the variance of treatment progression and diagnosis within a small *N*. It is also important to note that the cut-off age for receiving pediatric treatment varies slightly across tertiary care programs in Ontario, resulting in a few participants being older (19 or 20) when they transferred to adult health and mental health services.

Results

We aimed to understand and describe the experiences of young adults with EDs who transferred from pediatric to adult care, with a particular focus on the challenges and facilitators associated with accepting support from family members. First, a description of some of the family-related difficulties that arise during the transition phase from the perspective of the young adult is provided. Second, the ways in which participants conceptualize familial support as either helpful or unhelpful to recovery are outlined. See Table 19.2 for a summary of helpful and unhelpful aspects of family support.

Theme 1: Family-Related Challenges Associated with Transition

Our results reveal that transition produces uncertainty about who will assume responsibility for ongoing management of the ED following discharge from paediatric to adult care. Subsequent to leaving pediatric EDPs, 14 out of 15

Table 19.2 Summary of challenges and helpful and unhelpful aspects of familial support

Challenges associated with accepting familial support

Uncertainty about who assumes control over ongoing illness management during transfer of care produces conflict

Unclear expectations about adult care system on part of both young adults and family members

Young adults have mixed feelings about recovery; relapse represents both an opportunity and a threat during transfer of care

Young adults have mixed feelings about parental involvement in recovery; desire for both autonomy and ongoing support

Helpful aspects of familial support	*Unhelpful aspects of familial support*
Involvement in treatment	*Involvement in treatment*
• Assistance with physical and practical aspects of treatment and recovery	• Ongoing parental control over recovery, rather than supportive involvement
• Offers accountability and external motivation for recovery during initial stages of transition	
Emotional support	*Emotional support*
• Consists of talking, listening, validation	• Lack of understanding/knowledge about EDs
• Can be facilitated by group and family therapy, which fosters improved communication skills and increased understanding of EDs	• Emotionally volatile responses to relapses and/or setbacks
• Sibling support qualitatively different from parent support	

participants reported conflict with family members, as both adolescents and their parents disagreed about who would maintain control over illness management. At times, these young adults expressed a feeling of either obligation or desire to assume responsibility for their ED *because of* their chronological age and concomitant discharge from pediatric care. The following statements reflect this theme:

> When I left [pediatric hospital], I felt like I was ready to take it on myself.... I don't know if it was because it was like, I'm not a child anymore, I can't go to [pediatric hospital], so I have to take on those adult responsibilities.... I could have just been wrong and I wasn't able to take those things on, but it felt like I was.
>
> (B4)

> When I left the program, I was 17.... I felt like I had to do it on my own.
>
> (C1)

> As an adult, I feel I have a lot more autonomy and I don't have to do what she [my mother] says. I would always say, "as an adult, I don't have to listen to what you say. I can do it myself." I feel like she is not in charge anymore....
>
> (I16)

During transition, tensions between participants and their families emerge; while adolescents expect that adulthood (defined in terms of the chronological age limits of pediatric care) confers responsibility for ED management, participants perceived their parents as reluctant to relinquish control over their illness and recovery.

Some of the ambiguity surrounding the responsibility for ongoing ED management may be attributed, in part, to unclear expectations about the philosophy and type of treatments available in the adult care system. Participants consistently reported feeling either passive during or excluded from their treatment in pediatric EDPs, deferring instead to the authority of healthcare providers and family members. Adult care, in contrast, was characterized as independent and patient-directed. This abrupt shift in care cultures often left participants feeling bewildered and ill-equipped to assume responsibility for their recovery. As one participant explained: "There's no sort of, like, in between. You go from being guided blindly to like, this is the truth, it's naked in front of you, and you have to figure out how to deal with it, and like manage it, and stuff" (L14). Parents, in turn, were described as being similarly unprepared; another participant stated: "My mom expected it to continue like treatment at [pediatric hospital] where she was responsible and she was the one pushing me to do things" (B4). These comments suggest that both participants and their families lack a clear understanding of the adult care system.

Mixed feelings about recovery further complicate the question of who assumes control over ongoing ED management. Twelve participants expressed ambivalence about relinquishing their ED symptoms following discharge from pediatric EDPs. As one participant succinctly explained: "Part of me wanted to get better and part of me didn't" (A5). Because of their ambivalent feelings, these young adults tended to characterize the transfer of care as a stressful phase of their recovery; nine participants indicated that transition represented both an opportunity for relapse and its frightening prospect. Consider, for example, the following statements:

> I think it was a lot harder to remain motivated [after discharge from pediatric care] because there was that unknown where I could just completely – [trails off]. I didn't have to go to [pediatric hospital] anymore, I could stop the psychologist if I wanted to. I was an adult, I could make my own decisions.
>
> (A5)

> When I left, I was happy because … I wasn't going to be told what to do or how to eat or clean my plate, things like that. I think I was more scared at the same time because I knew I was going to be on my own and … how quickly I could kind of relapse again.
>
> (C4)

> As much as I wanted to get out, it was like, "Oh God, what's going to happen?"
>
> (E2-14)

Ambivalence about recovery, combined with ambiguity surrounding the locus of control over ongoing illness management, fosters anxiety about transition; relapse is conceptualized as both an opportunity and a threat during this phase.

Participants also conveyed mixed feelings about the nature of parental involvement in recovery throughout all of the interviews. Although these young adults wanted greater autonomy with respect to the management of their EDs, they simultaneously expressed either a desire or need for external monitoring. The following quotes capture this seemingly contradictory request for both independence and parental support:

> Just give me some space, like, let me do some things myself. But at the same time, offer some support. Kinda like, let me do it, but be there when I need help and like, keep watching me.
>
> (B17)

> If they want to take control of their own thing [i.e. recovery], they should have at least one person there with them, or have somebody kind of look over them in a way, but still let them have control.
>
> (IC14)

> Giving more independence, but not making it completely up to you. And still say[ing] that you have to do things. (F14)I feel like before she [my mother] was a bit overinvolved [because of] pressure from the program.... [Now] she's not really involved. She knows what's going on but she doesn't intervene or anything.... It's not really helpful, but it's not unhelpful.
>
> (G9)

It can be challenging for adolescents and their families to achieve an appropriate balance between seemingly opposed objectives; while these young people seek autonomy with respect to their recovery, the prospect of managing an ED independently may be overwhelming. Although external monitoring is desired, intensive scrutiny from family members can generate resentment.

Theme 2: Conceptualizations of Familial Support during Transition and Ongoing Recovery

Participants tended to describe two different types of familial assistance with recovery: *involvement in treatment* and *emotional support*. One participant eloquently distinguishes between these two modes of helping:

> Being involved in my treatment means she's [my mother] part of doing it to me: whether that means supervising meals, making meals, ... monitoring

me, all that stuff is being involved in the treatment. Being a support, I think, is just being there: I need to talk to you, I need to tell you, you need to offer me advice, and someone to listen and just remind me why I'm here, why I'm doing this. Stuff like that.

(K9)

While the former mode encompasses the physical and practical aspects of recovery, and may include an element of taking over the eating (i.e. "doing it to me"), the later entails emotional and moral reinforcement. Importantly, participants regarded both modes of helping as beneficial during the transition phase.

Nine out of fifteen participants viewed some parental involvement in the treatment and recovery process as helpful. This involvement consisted of activities such as meal planning, meal monitoring, portioning, facilitating communication among different healthcare providers, and transportation. Frequently, the words "push" (mentioned 24 times throughout the interviews) and "force" (mentioned 18 times) were used when describing this type of support. As one participant described:

We were on a nutrition plan, and so basically, when I was in the transition phase, we just kind of kept up with that and my parents just tried to follow that a little bit more until I was comfortable doing things on my own. That took a while too, but definitely that helped because I wouldn't have known what to do on my own.

(D5)

When undertaken collaboratively and sensitively, with the ultimate goal of developing independence in the young person, parental involvement in recovery can be an asset during the transition phase.

Participants indicated that their initial motivation for recovery tended to be external (rather than internal), underscoring the importance of a gentle, parental "push." Eight individuals indicated that feelings of obligation towards and/or a desire to appease family members promoted compliance with treatment. One participant, M7, explained: "I think initially it was good to really give me a push to eat and to try to normalize it, but at the same time, it wasn't for myself. It was for other reasons and it wasn't enough to really sustain the foundations of wanting to heal for myself." While an external "push" from parents may initially promote healing, long-term recovery must ultimately occur on the young adult's own terms.

Furthermore, it is imperative that family members distinguish between *involvement* and *control* during the transition phase. Parents' attempts to maintain rigid and unilateral control over recovery were perceived as unhelpful by a small number of participants ($n = 5$). When non-collaborative approaches limiting the autonomy of the young adults were utilized, these participants felt infantilized and deprived of responsibility for their wellness. Consider, for example, the following statements:

> My mom has always been a support. But I feel like sometimes she ... takes too much upon herself and she makes me feel like I'm a child. When it's like, I'm 21.
>
> (B14)

> I tell them this is my recovery, you can't do it for me. Like, I want your support, but that's not the same as you doing it for me.
>
> (I121)

> Especially at that age when you really want to start to gain independence, I felt like a child.... At some point, I felt like I really could be eating it on my own, and there was just no way that she would let me do that.
>
> (M9)

Four participants suggested that strict parental control actually promoted deceptive behavior, as young adults sought to perpetuate ED symptoms in secret. One participant, E10, described this mentality as follows: "[Your] parents are all over you, so how much can you get away with? Ultimately, parental involvement requires a delicate balance; while a "push" may provide companionship in and motivation for recovery during the transition phase, ongoing control can be disempowering and may perpetuate further conflict and concealment of symptoms rather than support.

Emotional support, therefore, was the more significant and enduring mode of helping, mentioned by 10 participants. This type of support consisted primarily of listening, talking, empathizing, validating efforts at recovery, and making one's emotional availability known to the young adult. The following quotes demonstrate the nature of emotional support that participants found helpful:

> I had my dad with me all the time, so I knew he understood my problem and he listened to my concerns if I had anything [sic] and he would give me advice.
>
> (C5)

> Now they're very supportive and my mom and dad always say to me, "If you ever want to talk about anything, we're here." And they'll check in once in a while and be like, "What's going on with you?" But it's never directly about the ED; it's just an open question. And I think they do that because they know now that it's not an issue, but they do let me know that they're there just in case.
>
> (D9)

> She [my mother] can sympathize and listen to me when I am having trouble, and try to distract me.
>
> (I16)

Being able to have someone listen, I guess, and checking in. Maybe even just asking how your day is going, or if they're noticing habits, like talking to you about it.

(M12)

Irrespective of the stage of treatment or recovery, participants consistently appreciated offers of emotional support from parents; this mode of helping conveyed care and understanding, which helped to reduce feelings of isolation during the transition process.

Six participants felt that a lack of knowledge about EDs on the part of parents was unhelpful, and further enhanced feelings of isolation and guilt in them. As one participant, C1, remarked: "During that time, it was really rough because I was basically on my own. I didn't really have any other support to look to except my parents, but I felt like my parents didn't really understand what was going on." Another participant, H3, shared a similar sentiment: "They [my parents] don't know what it [ED] is, they think it's really weird. They don't know this type of thing existed, they thought I was just kind of going through a rebellious phase." It is important that parents be equipped with a clear understanding of what EDs are, how they operate, and how they may impact young adults and family members.

Maintaining equanimity was another aspect of providing emotional support to young adults with EDs during the transition phase. Five participants indicated that emotionally volatile responses to setbacks in recovery were unhelpful; such "blow ups" or "freak outs" ultimately served to perpetuate conflict, as the following participants described:

The hardest part for my parents has been when I do experience a blip, they sort of go crazy.

(A16)

I'm glad she [my mother] was really on board and was worried at me, but at the same time, depending on the week – if I had lost or gained – then it definitely would affect how I was, you know, treated afterwards. And it was not, well, I didn't like that part of it.

(M4)

And my mom – our relationship is really, really good, and it's strengthened. But it's kind of also weakened because if something bad happens she totally flips out.

(P10)

While setbacks to recovery may be trying for family members, participants felt it unhelpful when these feelings were expressed impulsively and/or with anger.

Discussion

This study sought to examine the perceptions of young adults regarding parental support during the transfer from pediatric to adult services for EDs. Two themes were gleaned from the analysis. First, young people describe experiencing considerable *uncertainty* about whether they or their parent should assume responsibility for the management of their eating, meals, and recovery once they have transferred out of pediatric care. Second, young adults articulated the desire for ongoing parental support during the transfer of care, which they defined as emotional involvement, the provision of monitoring and supporting of eating and behavioral changes, and assistance with communicating their health and mental health needs with new professionals in the adult system. Young adults expressed that parental support should not be coercive and controlling, but rather collaborative in nature, as they are seeking to become more autonomous decision makers regarding their physical and mental health. In relation to theme 1 – family-related challenges during transition and who should assume responsibility – our study suggests that the transfer of care from pediatric to adult services for young adults with EDs produces uncertainty and often leads to conflict regarding who will assume responsibility for ongoing management. As recently reviewed by Murcott (2014), uncertainty and conflict may ensue in part as a result of the lack of education in and understanding of the distinct service designs, and cultural and philosophical differences between the pediatric and adult systems of care. The results of our qualitative study are congruent with those of other research demonstrating that young adults with mental health issues experience significant uncertainty about the adult system and the degree to which their families will remain involved in providing them with support (Lindgren, Soderberg & Skär, 2014; Murcott, 2014). The uncertainty experienced by young adults may partially be explained by limited knowledge of pediatric and adult providers about what occurs in each other's institutions and organizations, given that service providers from both systems of care express a lack of understanding about the policies, philosophies, and structures of each other's mental health services (Belling et al., 2014).

Among adolescents with mental health problems, individuals with a history of an ED are significantly less likely to make the transition from child to adult mental health services (Singh et al., 2010). This aligns with our finding that ambivalence about recovery in young adults with EDs is likely a unique and key contributor to poor transition in this vulnerable population. One of the reasons explaining why participants in our study had mixed feelings about the nature of parental involvement during transition from pediatric to adult care appeared to be their ambivalence regarding recovery. Unlike other illnesses, EDs are ego-syntonic in nature; individuals seek treatment when severe medical or mental health symptoms develop, but motivation is short-lived once weight gain is established and their ability to cope is challenged (Guarda, 2008). If left to be entirely independent in treatment decision making, young adults with EDs may refuse care entirely. Their ambivalence about gaining weight and increasing their food intake contributes towards and exacerbates the tensions that participants experience in desiring parental support while simultaneously resisting parents' provision of support with eating and assistance with linking them to specialized adult eating disorder providers.

One of the most difficult aspects of transition for young people with any chronic illness is the role shift with respect to self-management and responsibility (van Staa, Jedeloo, van Meeteren, & Latour, 2011). Many healthcare providers report that adolescents often lack responsibility for their care and parents have trouble relinquishing their caring role (Sonneveld, Strating, van Staa, & Nieboer, 2013), even though they agree it is necessary (van Staa et al., 2011). Supporting independence, responsibility, and self-management does not mean that parents should withdraw all support (Allen, Channon, Lowes, Atwell, & Lane, 2011). One of the key elements to successful transition is enabling adolescents to become equal and effective partners in their own care (Viner, 2008). In fact, readiness to transfer to adult care is highly dependent on the adolescent's attitude to transition and their level of self-efficacy in managing their chronic illness (van Staa et al., 2011).

In relation to theme 2 – conceptualizations of familial support during transition and ongoing recovery – the dual and sometimes contradictory desires for both autonomy and support from family members reflect the challenges associated with transitioning this complex population to adult services. Young adult participants with EDs identified two types of parental assistance during transition: (1) direct involvement in eating disorder treatment and (2) emotional support. Both types of support were viewed as important, yet also as sources of conflict. Although participants acknowledged the need for parental emotional and tangible support during the transfer to adult services, they expressed ambivalent feelings regarding parental assistance with meal monitoring and portioning of food. For example, participants identified the need for a "push", yet also negatively perceived parental "force" to eat. Since EDs are perceived to have benefits for the affected individual despite the enormous costs, it is not surprising that external pressure from parents is often required for recovery yet resented by the adolescent. It is also possible that the tension between parental involvement in assisting with the management of ED behaviors and treatment speaks to the general tensions that arise for adolescents and young adults as they strive for greater independence and autonomy and yet still depend on family for support.

Some of the participants recognized that keeping parents involved maintains an external motivation for recovery when their own desire to stay well dissipates during the transfer of care to adult services. While initially supportive, participants felt that direct involvement in ED care was less desirable if maintained as a long-term strategy. Ultimately, young adults perceived that they must identify internal motivations for sustained recovery, with the final parental role being the provision of emotional support.

Clinical and Research Implications

Young adults in this study articulated the profound challenges that arise as they launch into adulthood and begin the transfer from pediatric to adult care services. The responsibility for improving the transfer of care from pediatric to adult services should not be shouldered by young adults and their families alone. Policy makers, researchers, and clinicians should take up the challenge to create clinical pathways and dedicate clinical resources and services to better prepare young people and their families for the transfer to adult services. Based on the themes ascertained from the qualitative interviews with young adults, the following recommendations are provided for service providers. First, assessments should be conducted to identify the degree to which parents and young adults are managing illness behaviours together and their perceptions of how roles and responsibilities may change as a result of the transfer of care to adult services where an adult rather than a family-centered approach is promoted. Second, clinical interventions (either in the pediatric or adult system) should be provided that allow for the exploration of the perceptions of both the young adult and their parents regarding factors that may influence the division of responsibility for management of the illness and recovery. Transition programs for any type of illness must help young adults to become equal and effective partners in their own care and support them as they actualize their emerging capacity for self-management (Viner, 2008), particularly if the illness has stripped them of opportunities to practice becoming self-efficacious.

At least two areas of future research are needed to better understand the challenges associated with transitioning between pediatric and adult systems of care for EDs. First, research is needed to ascertain the perspective of parents regarding the division of responsibility for illness management, and regarding the process of having their child transition out of pediatric care to adult services. Second, longitudinal studies are needed to determine the outcomes of young adults transferring out of pediatric care, including standardized quantitative measures to quantify key outcomes (e.g. BMI, eating behaviors) and determine predictors of outcomes (e.g. nature and degree of parental support) in transition-age youth who transfer to adult services.

Strengths and Limitations

This study has a number of limitations that must be considered. First, the sample size is small. However, we only stopped recruiting when no new themes emerged in our interviews with participants. We reached saturation with the data on the two themes described above, which were clearly important areas of concern for young people with EDs. Second, it is worth noting that the sample consisted of individuals who had successfully transferred to specialized adult hospital-based services. The findings based on this sample are therefore not generalizable to participants who elected not to pursue needed mental health services for their ED as adults, or who were unable to access services due to long waiting lists or other systemic reasons. Furthermore, this sample was likely biased towards young adults with severe illness requiring more intensive treatment in a hospital setting. Young adults with less severe illness utilizing community-based mental health services may have different perceptions and needs regarding parental support during their launch into adulthood and transfer to adult services.

A third limitation of the study is that it captured a snapshot of the experience of participants during the period of the transfer of care. We cannot be sure if the themes predated the point of transition from pediatric to adult services. Research on adolescents at different time points in their illness trajectory, treatment, and stage of development are required to understand how perceptions of parental support, desire for autonomy, and independence may be influenced by factors other than the transfer to adult services.

Conclusion

The findings of our study revealed that the transfer of care from pediatric to adult services often produces conflict between individuals with EDs and their family members. This conflict stems from illness-related factors (such as ambivalence about recovery) and issues associated with emerging adulthood (i.e. a desire for both autonomy and ongoing support from family members). These young adults voice that families can play an important role in facilitating independence by providing emotional support, empathy, and understanding during the transition phase.

Acknowledgments

Research was conducted within the Eating Disorders Program, Toronto General Hospital, University Health Network, Canada.

References

Abebe, D. S., Lien, L., & von Soest, T. (2012). The development of bulimic symptoms from adolescence to young adulthood in females and males: A population-based longitudinal cohort study. *International Journal of Eating Disorders*, 45(6), 737–745. doi: 10.1002/eat.20950.

Allen, D., Channon, S., Lowes, L., Atwell, C., & Lane, C. (2011). Behind the scenes: The changing roles of parents in the transition from child to adult diabetes service. *Diabetic Medicine*, 28(8), 994–1000. doi: 10.1111/j.1464-5491.2011.03310.x.

American Psychiatric Association. (2000). *Diagnostic and statistical manual of mental disorders*, 4th edition, text revised. Washington, DC: American Psychiatric Association.

Arcelus, J., Bouman, W. P., & Morgan, J. F. (2008). Treating young people with eating disorders: Transition from child mental health to specialist adult eating disorder services. *European Eating Disorders Review*, 16(1), 30–36. doi: 10.1002/erv.830.

Arcelus, J., Mitchell, A. J., Wales, J., & Nielsen, S. (2011). Mortality rates in patients with anorexia nervosa and other eating disorders: A meta-analysis of 36 studies. *Archives of General Psychiatry*, 68(7), 724–731. doi: 10.1001/archgenpsychiatry.2011.74.

Arnett, J. J. (2007). Emerging adulthood: What is it, and what is it good for? *Child Development Perspectives*, 1(2), 68–73. doi: 10.1111/j.1750-8606.2007.00016.x.

Belling, R., McLaren, S., Paul, M., Ford, T., Kramer, T. et al. (2014). The effect of organisational resources and eligibility issues on transition from child and adolescent to adult mental health services. *Journal of Health Services Research & Policy, 19*, 169-176. doi: 10.1177/1355819614527439.

Campbell, K., & Peebles, R. (2014). Eating disorders in children and adolescents: State of the art review. *Pediatrics*, 134(3), 582–592. doi: 10.1542/peds.2014-0194.

Corbin, J. M., & Strauss, A. (1990). Grounded theory research: Procedures, canons, and evaluative criteria. *Qualitative Sociology*, 13(1), 3–21. doi: 10.1007/BF00988593.

Côté, J., & Bynner, J. M. (2008). Changes in the transition to adulthood in the UK and Canada: The role of structure and agency in emerging adulthood. *Journal of Youth Studies*, 11(3), 251–268. doi: 10.1080/13676260801946464.

Dimitropoulos, G., Toulany, A., Herschman, J., Kovacs, A., Steinegger, C. et al. (2015). A qualitative study on the experiences of young adults with eating disorders transferring from pediatric to adult care. *Eating Disorders, 23*(2), 144–162. doi: 10.1080/10640266.2015.1064276.

Glaser, B., & Strauss, A. (1967). *The discovery of grounded theory*. Chicago, IL: Aldine Transaction.

Guarda, A. S. (2008). Treatment of anorexia nervosa: Insights and obstacles. *Physiology & Behavior*, 94(1), 113–120. doi: 10.1016/j.physbeh.2007.11.020.

Helgeson, V. S., Mascatelli, K., Reynolds, K. A., Becker, D., Escobar, O., & Siminerio, L. (2014). Friendship and romantic relationships among emerging adults with and without type 1 diabetes. *Journal of Pediatric Psychology, 40*(3), 359–372. doi: 10.1093/jpepsy/jsu069.

Le Grange, D., Lock, J., Agras, W. S., Moye, A., Bryson, S. W. et al. (2012). Moderators and mediators of remission in family-based treatment and adolescent focused therapy for anorexia nervosa. *Behavioral Research and Therapy*, 50(2), 85–92. doi: 10.1016/j.brat.2011.11.003.

Lindgren, E., Söderberg, S., & Skär, L. (2013). The gap in transition between child and adolescent psychiatry and general adult psychiatry. *Journal of Child and Adolescent Psychiatric Nursing*, 26, 103–109.

Lock, J. (2011). Evaluation of family treatment models for eating disorders. *Current Opinion in Psychiatry*, 24, 274–279.

Lock, J., & Le Grange, D. (2013). *Treatment manual for anorexia nervosa: A family based approach*, 2nd edition. New York: Guilford Press.

Lock, J., Le Grange, D., Agras, W. S., Moye, A., Bryson, S. W., & Jo, B. (2010). Randomized clinical trial comparing family-based treatment with adolescent focused individual therapy for adolescents with anorexia nervosa. *Archives of General Psychiatry*, 67(10), 1025–1032. doi: 10.1001/archgenpsychiatry.2010.128.

Murcott, W. J. (2014). Transitions between child and adult mental health services: Service design, philosophy and meaning at uncertain times. *Journal of Psychiatric and Mental Health Nursing*, 21(7), 628–634. doi: 10.1111/jpm.12150.

Nelson, L. J., Padilla-Walker, L. M., Carroll, J. S., Madsen, S. D., Barry, C. M., & Badger, S. (2007). "If you want me to treat you like an adult, start acting like one!" Comparing the criteria that emerging adults and their parents have for adulthood. *Journal of Family Psychology*, 21(4), 665–674. doi: 0.1037/0893-3200.21.4.665.

Norris, M., Strike, M., Pinhas, L., Gomez, R., Elliott, A. et al. (2013). The Canadian eating disorder program survey–exploring intensive treatment programs for youth with eating disorders. *Journal of the Canadian Academy of Child and Adolescent Psychiatry*, 22(4), 310–316.

Paul, M., Ford, T., Kramer, T., Islam, Z., Harley, K., & Singh, S. P. (2013). Transfers and transitions between child and adult mental health services. *British Journal of Psychiatry*, 202(s54), s36–s40. doi: 10.1192/bjp.bp.112.119198.

Pinhas, L., Morris, A., Crosby, R. D., & Katzman, D. K. (2011). Incidence and age-specific presentation of restrictive eating disorders in children: A Canadian paediatric surveillance program study. *Archives of Paediatric Adolescent Medicine*, 165(10), 895–899. doi: 10.1001/archpaediatrics.2011.145.

Singh, S. P., Paul, M., Ford, T., Kramer, T., Weaver, T. et al. (2010). Process, outcome and experience of transition from child to adult mental healthcare: Multiperspective study. *British Journal of Psychiatry*, 197(4), 305–312. doi: 10.1192/bjp.bp.109.075135.

Sonneveld, H. M., Strating, M. M. H., van Staa, A. L., & Nieboer, A. P. (2013). Gaps in transitional care: What are the perceptions of adolescents, parents and providers? *Child: Care, Health and Development*, 39(1), 69–80. doi: 10.1111/j.1365-2214.2011.01354.x.

Staa, A. van, Jedeloo, S., Van Meeteren, J., & Latour, J. M. (2011). Crossing the transition chasm: Experiences and recommendations for improving transitional care of young adults, parents and providers. *Child: Care, Health and Development*, 37(6), 821–832. doi: 10.1111/j.1365.

Steinhausen, H.-C., & Weber, S. (2009). The outcome of bulimia nervosa: Findings from one-quarter century of research. *American Journal of Psychiatry*, 166(12), 1331–1341. doi: 10.1176/appi.ajp.2009.09040582.

Strauss, A., & Corbin, J. M. (1990). *Basics of qualitative research: Grounded theory procedures and techniques*. Thousand Oaks, CA: Sage.

Treasure, J., Stein, D., & Maguire, S. (2015). Has the time come for a staging model to map the course of eating disorders from high risk to severe enduring illness? An examination of the evidence. *Early Intervention in Psychiatry*, 9, 173–184. doi:10.1111/eip.12170

Viner, R. M. (2008). Transition of care from paediatric to adult services: One part of improved health services for adolescents. *Archives of Disease in Childhood*, 93(2), 160–163. doi: 10.1136/adc.2006.103721.

Winston, A. P., Paul, M., & Juanola-Borrat, Y. (2012). The same but different? Treatment of anorexia nervosa in adolescents and adults. *European Eating Disorders Review*, 20(2), 89–93. doi: 10.1002/erv.1137.

20 Multi-Family Therapy in Anorexia Nervosa

A Qualitative Study of Parental Experiences

Sofie Engman-Bredvik, Nivia Carballeira Suarez, Richard Levi, and Karin Nilsson

Anorexia nervosa (AN) is a serious eating disorder, often with psychiatric comorbidities. AN occurs in 1 percent of girls in the risk ages 13–18 years and in about 0.1 percent of boys in the same age group. It has a standardized mortality ratio of 5.86 (Arcelus, Mitchell, & Wales, 2014). In 10–20 percent of those affected, AN is refractory to treatment, thus leading to chronic suffering and psycho-social disturbances (Berkman, Lohr, & Bulik, 2007).

Parenting and caring for a teenager with AN can be extremely demanding. A previous study (Svensson, Nilsson, Levi, & Carballeira Suarez, 2013) explored such parental experiences, and found that parents reported unmet needs for support. High levels of caregiver distress and caregiver burden have been documented in several previous studies (Cohn, 2005; Graap & Bleich, 2008; Zabala, Macdonald, & Treasure, 2009). This becomes potentially critical, as family support is crucial for good outcomes (Nilsson & Hägglöf, 2006; Robinson, Strahan, Girz, Wilson, & Boachie, 2013). Families tend to reorganize in response to having an afflicted family member, whereby AN takes a central position for the family as a whole. Most relationships both within and outside the family will become disturbed, not only for the patient but also for the rest of the family (Dimitropoulos & Klopfer, 2009; Hillege, Beale, & McMaster, 2006).

Current therapeutic guidelines for recent-onset AN in patients aged 18 or younger prescribe family-oriented therapy (American Psychiatric Association, 2012; National Institute of Clinical Excellence, 2011; Watson, & Bulik, 2013), in particular the so-called Maudsley family-based therapy (Downs & Blow, 2013; Hurst, Read, & Wallis, 2012; Lock & Le Grange, 2013).

Multi-family therapy (MFT) has been proposed as an adjunct to traditional family-oriented therapy in the treatment of teenagers with AN (Carr, 2014; Eisler, 2005). It was pioneered in this function in Dresden (Scholz & Asen, 2001) and London (Dare & Eisler, 2000). It is now recognized as a valuable additional therapeutic tool in many countries. However, cross-cultural differences may influence the response to this type of intervention (Mehl, Tomanová, Kubĕna, & Papežová, 2013). Applicability in a specific socio-cultural context needs to be established, and cannot by default be generalized from positive experiences in another context.

MFT is a manual-based eclectic and comprehensive treatment approach that combines elements from several therapeutic schools. It is a group treatment for six to eight families with ten whole-day meetings spread out over a year. The main purpose is to improve and corroborate familial coping and intervention in the context of AN, and also to prevent social isolation and stigmatization (Asen & Scholz, 2010; Schmidt & Asen, 2005; Scholz, Rix, Scholz, Gantchev, & Thömke, 2005).

This study investigates MFT as part of AN treatment from a parental perspective. Specific research queries were:

- How was MFT perceived and accepted?
- Was MFT seen to be compatible with other treatments offered?
- How, specifically, did parents experience engaging with other parents?
- How, if at all, did MFT influence daily family life?
- Is MFT likely to be useful in the cultural context of northern Sweden?

Method

Design and Participants

Participants (i.e. parents of children/adolescents with AN) were recruited from a university department of child and adolescent psychiatry clinic in northern Sweden with a specialized team for eating disorders. Team members have different occupations, but all are specialized in treating eating disorders. The team uses structured interviews and questionnaires for assessment and treatment planning. Patients are under the age of 18. Family therapy is used as the first choice of treatment, mainly the Maudsley treatment model (Lock & Le Grange, 2013). There is also an inpatient unit, mainly for patients with prominent medical risks due to starvation. MFT was added to the treatment concept in 2013.

All parents who participated in MFT were invited to join the current study. Exclusion criteria were inability to communicate in the Swedish language, current alcohol or drug addiction, and/or major current psychiatric problems. A total of 14 parents participated in an MFT program, of whom 12 (6 mothers and 6 fathers) constituted the study group. Parents from one family declined to participate in the study as their child went into remission at an early stage. All parents lived together with their child (i.e. the patient). Disease duration varied between 1 and 4 years with a mean duration of 1 year and 11 months. The patients were six girls aged between 12 and 17 years (mean = 14 years, 11 months). Mean weight was 47.4 kg; mean body mass index (BMI) was 17.74; and mean resting pulse rate was 61.4. Global eating disorder psychopathology was measured by the Eating Disorder Examination Questionnaire (EDE-Q; Carter,

Table 20.1 Interviewer's guide

- How would you describe the experience of MFT and how easily was the treatment accepted?
- How did MFT work in conjuction with the usual treatment?
- Was working through the treatment process together with other families in a similar situation a significant experience?
- How do you perceive the influence of MFT on the family's everyday life?

Stewart, & Fairburn, 2001; Fairburn & Beglin, 2008), which yielded a mean global score of 2.68.

MFT commenced with four consecutive meeting days during one week and a fifth day after three weeks. The remaining five days of the program were spread out during the rest of the year, at gradually longer intervals. The participating staff had received special training on MFT, and had many years' experience working with eating disorders.

The MFT program comprised three phases: symptom oriented; relationship oriented; and future oriented. MFT used a combination of exercises, lectures, and discussions in whole-group and sub-group settings (Wallin, 2011). Some specific exercises, for example the "family sculpture," will be presented in the results section of this chapter, in order to facilitate the understanding of participant reports.

Follow-ups were conducted after MFT was completed. The final meeting was on December 2, 2013, when questionnaires and medical examinations for quantitative information were collected. Due to intervening winter holidays and the geographical dispersion of participants, the semi-structured interviews were carried out one to two months after the concluding MFT session. Interviews took place at the clinic or research department by the first author (SEB). All parents were interviewed individually. Open-ended questions were used to stimulate detailed accounts of parental experience (Table 20.1). The study was approved by the Regional Ethical Review Board at Umeå University, Sweden.

Analysis

1. Interviews were recorded and then transcribed verbatim for subsequent analysis according to an empirical, psychological, phenomenological method (EPP) (Lundberg, Styf, & Bullington, 2007). EPP focuses on the individual's experience of the phenomenon under study; that is, in this study, the parental experience of MFT as it was experienced after completion of one year of treatment. Data analysis was performed by three researchers following five consecutive steps:
1. Reading through all transcribed interviews to gain an overall impression and basic understanding of their contents.

2. Breaking the running narrative down into units of meaning.
3. Reformulating the units of meaning in the researchers' vocabulary in order to clarify the meaning of the text, attempting to use as much of the parents' own descriptions as possible. This step attempts to find the implicit and explicit meaning as the participant had experienced and described it in the protocol.
4. Transforming the text into so-called "situated structures," which comprise a synthesis of different meaning units, elucidating the experience of the participant interviewed.
5. Studying the situated structures alongside one another to identify general patterns and interesting differences. Analysis was considered complete when it was deemed that the material could not yield further themes supported by the data.

Results

Three major themes emerged and are explored below (see also Table 20.2).

Theme 1: Positive Experiences

Overall, MFT was perceived positively, as being instrumental for subsequent remission. The factors behind the positive experience were further qualified as follows.

De-Stigmatization

Participants found meeting other families in a similar situation most valuable. They felt less lonely, as they realized how common the disease is, and that other, otherwise completely "normal," families were sharing the struggle. This yielded a comforting experience of fellowship and belonging.

Participants could identify with the narratives of others, and thereby gain confirmation of their own thoughts and feelings. Several participants described the difficulty of explaining to outsiders how AN affects most aspects of life,

Table 20.2 Parental experiences during MFT – themes and sub-themes

Positive experiences	New perspectives	Improved family dynamics
De-stigmatization	Realism regarding disease duration and relapse risk	Improved competence in parental role
Relief from guilt and shame	Understanding the impact and manifestations of the disease	Improved parental collaboration
Empowerment	Understanding the child and the disease	Shared responsibility and new behaviors
Peer support	Insights concerning siblings	

and in many cases parents had stopped even trying. They also recognized the detrimental effects on relationships and social life for both patient and family. One participant said, "The best of all was to meet other parents. When you meet others, you hear that it is exactly the same. It is as if the youths have read the same instruction book."

Relief from Guilt and Shame

Some participants revealed feeling guilty and somehow responsible for their child's illness. One participant said that previously it had been a mystery why his child had "got this." During MFT they met "nice families" that nevertheless had also ended up in a similar situation, and this recognition was comforting and made them feel less worthless as parents. One participant commented on the benefit of receiving "affirmation that it was not my fault; we had not done anything evil. Nobody knows why it [AN] turns out this way. It just happens."

Participants also thought that their adolescents had been feeling guilty and full of shame, but during MFT the adolescents no longer had to maintain a brave face and matured as a result of talking openly in front of the group. After MFT some adolescents dared to speak to their friends about their disease for the first time.

Empowerment

The participants emphasized their need for support in the parental role. During MFT they derived strength from one another, even though the things they talked about were difficult. They got to follow each other's journeys and it was rewarding to subsequently see improvements. Recognising that people actually can get better gave them a sense of hope. Exercises and discussions concerning the future and dreams were appreciated. Participants reported that they never took the time to do that in their everyday lives. It gave hope. Together as a family, they got to talk about the future and show one another that it is possible to get well.

Peer Support

At all stages of MFT there was an open atmosphere, where parents felt that they dared to share experiences. The first days of therapy were considered tough and intense. This was the time when, typically, families for the first time openly discussed their situation in depth and became close to each other in a brief period of time. The participants perceived all to be in a similar situation and could thus acknowledge one another, in words or by a pat on the shoulder. Several moments were described as emotionally charged; for example, when patients were asked to verbalize their emotions and when they could see other parents hurting whilst opening up and sharing emotions. Parents could ask questions that were spot on and it was acceptable to shed a tear. They received endorsement from others regarding how they had acted, which was soothing and much-needed. It showed that one was on the right path and this promoted the resilience to persist. During MFT no one tried to diminish the gravity of the situation.

Theme 2: New Perspectives

Realism regarding Disease Duration and Relapse Risk

Among participating families, illness duration at the time of study varied between one and four years. Several participants initially believed that they would "fix this" rapidly within the family, but during MFT they realized that the process could be very long indeed. Insights into the complexity and risk of relapse were considered valuable since it made participants better prepared for subsequent drawbacks. Most parents expressed a wish that MFT should be commenced early in the course of the disease. Those who had lived with the disease for a longer period of time thought that they would have benefitted if they had had access to the treatment earlier on.

Understanding the Impact and Manifestations of the Disease

During MFT, participants got to hear about aspects of the disease that they had not been aware of previously. Revelations from other participants, such as children who had hidden food and who had been covertly working out, made parents more watchful. Some participants also began to realize how ill their child really was:

> The first day, I remember thinking, "Oh my God, she is really ill!" It was like … somehow, I think I had, so to say, turned a blind eye. I had denied it.

By observing each other, parents realized how AN affected the whole family. Their lives were hampered, for example, when it came to meals, social life, vacations, and trips with the family.

The parents started to reflect on co-dependency, for example distinguishing between behaviors that are truly supportive and those that merely reinforce the disease, which was a new perspective for many parents. On one occasion the adolescents had to describe how they wanted their parents to act when they had a hard time; this encouraged some of the parents to stand back more in these situations and to let go of some of the control.

Interaction with other families was reported to have contributed to a deeper understanding of "how the disease plants its seeds," and its effects on the patient and family.

The "family sculpture" exercise was particularly valued, as it aroused strong emotions and clarified family roles. In this exercise, parents and children (including siblings) depict their family dynamics before, during, and after the disease period, using members from the other families to play the role of the family under study. Persons are designated the role of mother, father, and sibling, and are physically placed in spatial relation to each other (e.g. close or far apart, facing towards or away from each other, at different levels). The sculpture visualized the family from the outside, that is, from a third-person perspective. This was often painful, but also served as a wake-up call.

Understanding the Child and the Disease

Participants described how it could be difficult to differentiate between manifestations of the disease and manifestations of the child's "true self." To aid in this, one family had named the disease (rather like naming an evil monster), something which several of the other families then also adopted. Thereby it became easier to communicate with the child about their frustration with the disease and, together with the child, work towards removing the "uninvited guest" from the house.

Overall, participants reported that they had learned to understand their children better as a result of MFT. In particular, exercises where the children acted as experts on their disease and parents asked their own child as well as the other children questions concerning the disease, provided useful new insights. Participants believed that their sick child benefitted from meeting children of the same age with the same kind of problems. They thereby felt less lonely and could empower each other. Although severity of illness as well as illness duration varied, all parents had experienced similar kinds of problems with food and anxiety, which were described as the most crucial problems. The anxiety of the child/patient was described as the most unbearable aspect of the disease for the parents, and also the most frightening and difficult thing to understand:

> It was very hard, with strict rules, during the common meals. The adolescents were to eat everything on the plate. There was a lot of anxiety concerning the food, but after the meal you got to talk about it right away. At home you never do that. Here, I had the support.

Insights concerning Siblings

Parents of children with the longest disease duration all brought siblings to MFT and found that a positive experience. The siblings then had an opportunity to talk to each other during the MFT, which in some cases led to improved relationships between the siblings. These parents stressed the importance of acknowledging the siblings, regardless of age, since they were also affected and sometimes neglected. During some exercises parents could see very clearly how siblings had had to step aside.

MFT provided an opportunity for siblings to talk and share their thoughts, opinions, and feelings, which had not been possible before. They could improve their insight into how the disease affects its sufferers:

> I believe that it is difficult for a 15-year-old boy to have understanding [of AN]. He says, "Isn't she going to get well soon so that we can get away from this?" and "How long is it going to last?" But maybe he now has a greater understanding that it is not she [his sister] who reacts in a certain way; rather, it is the disease that takes her over.

In families where their child had been sick for a shorter period of time, views on involving the siblings varied. Some families started to think more about the importance of involving the siblings in the therapeutic process and not excluding them, while others chose not to bring the siblings. Regardless of whether the parents chose to involve the siblings or not, they were all satisfied with their decision.

Theme 3: Improved Family Dynamics

Improved Competence in Parental Role

MFT gave participants a new perspective on their children's behaviors. Seeing and hearing examples from other families made them more able to distance themselves from pathologic behaviors and feel safer in their parental role. As a result, they were able to handle critical situations in a better way. Some of the parents became calmer and more patient because they knew that there were other families that had been through the same or worse.

Improved Parental Collaboration

Several participants described strained parental relationships. Many recognized the phenomenon as a venting of frustration on each other rather than on the root cause, that is, the sick child and their disease:

> It starts with our daughter doing something, but it ends with me and my wife fighting … that is somehow what this disease does.

In several cases MFT had a positive effect on the collaboration between the parents. They became more "on the same page," and also improved their understanding of their partner.

Shared Responsibility and New Behaviors

Participants reported that MFT led to greater shared responsibility for the disease. In several families it was primarily the mother who had taken responsibility for the disease, but after MFT fathers became more active. Some mothers believed that the fathers gained a more profound understanding of the seriousness of the condition and the importance of their active involvement in their child's recovery. At the same time, the mothers had to learn how to let go of some of the control in order to facilitate cooperation between the parents. Both mothers and fathers liked being divided into groups of mothers and fathers, because they found it easier to understand other participants of the same gender. Some mothers believed that MFT was especially rewarding for the fathers since they had not been able to speak about their situation before. Often the mothers had been more open to friends and co-workers even before MFT:

> I think that it has been good for both fathers and mothers, but especially for fathers … it is like men do not talk to each other in the same way as women do, so for the fathers it has been very important.

The meetings and comparison of issues with other families resulted in a larger toolkit of strategies to try at home. MFT provided insights that affected ways of both thinking and behaving, which resulted in practical changes in everyday life, such as avoiding discussions of sensitive issues during meals. A shared responsibility between parents put less burden on the mothers. Two mothers described the realization that shared responsibility between the parents allowed them to strengthen themselves individually. They learned to think more about themselves.

Discussion

There are few studies on parental experiences of MFT in AN, which is why this was chosen as the main focus of the present study. Furthermore, the utility of MFT in the treatment of AN may well be culturally dependent, thus making it critical to assess its usefulness in various cultural spheres. In summary, this study demonstrates that MFT was very well accepted by the parents as a useful adjunct to the other treatment modalities. MFT contributed to a deeper understanding of the disease manifestations and ways of coping with them. Peer support provided a sense of empowerment, and relief from guilt and shame. These findings were also reported by Coomber and King (2012) and Linville, Brown, Sturm, and McDougal (2012). The emotional and reflective quality of MFT, also discussed by Voriadaki, Simic, Espie, and Eisler (2015), empowered the parents to reflect on how they might consolidate or modify constructive family interactions.

We propose interpreting the findings of this study in such a way that parents can be seen as undergoing a five-step process as they participate in MFT (see Figure 20.1). This process comprised providing peer support as participants experienced feelings leading to the normalization, recognition, and acknowledgment of AN, reduced guilt and self-doubt, decreased social isolation, and improved communication. It also yielded an understanding of how vicious

Figure 20.1   Hypothesized parental process during one year of multi-family therapy

circles could develop and be avoided. All of these elements led to a fresh outlook on the parental role in combatting AN. The process culminated in a redistribution of control and responsibility in the family and, beyond that, new and more functional behaviors.

This study is part of a broader study in which patient outcomes will be presented. So far we have not collected enough data to offer conclusive findings; however, preliminary analysis indicates encouraging results. In particular, parents of children with a short illness duration at the time of MFT stressed the importance of the intervention to their child's recovery. Parents of children with the longest disease duration were less able to identify whether or not MFT had helped their child. This is also in accordance with our preliminary outcome analysis. If this impression holds, it will add further support to the notion of the importance of early intensive intervention in AN (see also Treasure & Russel, 2011).

Strengths and Limitations

Qualitative research methods involve the systematic collection, organization, and interpretation of textual material derived from conversation or observation, and the observer is a participating subject. To minimize the effect of subjective bias in this study, the following measures were taken: reflection on the researchers' own pre-understanding, explicitly describing the methodological steps and co-judging of the data (triangulation).

The interviews and analyses were carried out by researchers who were not involved in the treatment of the families, thus allowing for participants to be open and honest. In addition, this study will be followed by a quantitative study of the outcome.

There are also noteworthy limitations to this study. As it includes only one therapy group, generalization of results must be made with caution. However, phenomenological, hermeneutical study methods are not primarily designed for that purpose, but rather, in this case, for investigating subjectivity as a way of enhancing understanding of parental experiences of this method of treatment. We interviewed 12 parents individually with the purpose of investigating the experiences of MFT from a parental perspective. The empirical phenomenological psychological (EPP; Lundberg et al., 2007) method is well suited to this purpose and this sample size.

Conclusion

According to the participating parents, MFT provided significant value in terms of their ability to cope with having a child with AN in their family. Analyzing results according to the EPP method demonstrates that these positive subjective experiences could be specified and thematized. Thus, the usefulness of MFT was corroborated and further specified by this study, which also supports the applicability of MFT in a cultural setting that has not previously been investigated.

References

Arcelus, J., Mitchell, A. J., & Wales, J. (2014). Mortality rates in patients with anorexia nervosa and other eating disorders. *Archives of General Psychiatry*, 68, 724–731.

Asen, E., & Scholz, M. (2010). *Multi-family therapy: Concepts and techniques*. London: Routledge.

Berkman, N., Lohr, K., & Bulik, C. (2007). Outcomes of eating disorders: A systematic review of the literature. *Journal of Eating Disorders*, 40, 293–309.

Carr, A. (2014). The evidence base for family therapy and systemic interventions for child focused problems. *Journal of Family Therapy*, 36, 107–157. doi: 10.1111/1467–6427.12032.

Carter, J. C., Stewart, D. A., & Fairburn, C. G. (2001). Eating disorder examination questionnaire: Norms for young adolescent girl. *Behaviour Research and Therapy*, 39, 625–632.

Cohn, L. (2005). Parents' voices. What they say is important in the treatment and recovery process. *Eating Disorders*, 13, 419–28. doi: 10.1080/10640260591005317.

Coomber, K., & King, R. M. (2012). Coping strategies and social support as predictors and mediators of eating disorder carer burden and psychological distress. *Social Psychiatry and Psychiatric Epidemiology*, 47, 789–796. doi: 10.1007/s00127-011-0384-6.

Dare, C., & Eisler, I. (2000). A multi-family group day treatment programme for adolescent eating disorder. *European Eating Disorders Review*, 8, 4–18.

Dimitropoulos, G., & Klopfer, K. (2009). Caring for a sibling with anorexia nervosa: A qualitative study. *European Eating Disorders Review*, 17, 350–365. doi: 10.1002/erv.937.

Downs, K. J., & Blow, A. J. (2013). A substantive and methodological review of family-based treatment for eating disorders: The last 25 years of research. *Journal of Family Therapy*, 35, 3–28. doi: 10.1111/j.1467-6427.2011.00566.x.

Eisler, I. (2005). The empirical and theoretical base of family therapy and multiple family day therapy for adolescent anorexia nervosa. *Journal of Family Therapy*, 27, 104–131. doi: j.1467-6427.2005.003/j.1467-6427.2005.00303.x/full.

Fairburn, C. G., & Beglin, S. J. (2008). Eating disorder examination questionnaire (EDE-Q 6.0). In C. G. Fairburn (Ed.), *Cognitive behavior therapy and eating disorders* (pp. 309–313). New York: Guilford Press.

Graap, H., & Bleich, S. (2008). The needs of carers of patients with anorexia and bulimia nervosa. *European Eating Disorders Review*, 16, 21–29.

Hillege, S., Beale, B., & McMaster, R. (2006). Impact of eating disorders on family life: Individual parents' stories. *Journal of Clinical Nursing*, 15, 1016–1022. doi: 10.1111/j.1365-2702.2006.01367.x.

Hurst, K., Read, S., & Wallis, A. (2012). Anorexia nervosa in adolescence and Maudsley family-based treatment. *Journal of Counseling & Development*, 90, 339–345. doi: 10.1002/ j.1556-6676.2012.00042.x.

Linville, D., Brown, T., Sturm, K., & McDougal, T. (2012). Eating disorders and social support: Perspectives of recovered individuals. *Eating Disorders*, 20, 216–231. doi: 10.1080/10640266.2012.668480.

Lock, J., & Le Grange, D. (2013). *Treatment Manual for Anorexia Nervosa: A family based approach*, 2nd edition. New York: Guilford Press.

Lundberg, M., Styf, J., & Bullington, J. (2007). Experiences of moving with persistent pain: A qualitative study from a patient perspective. *Physiotherapy Theory and Practice*, 23, 199–209. doi: 10.1080/09593980701209311.

Mehl, A., Tomanová, J., Kuběna, A., & Papežová, H. (2013). Adopting multi-family therapy to families who care for a loved one with an eating disorder in the Czech Republic combined with a follow-up pilot study of efficacy. *Journal of Family Therapy*, 35, 82–101. doi: 10.1111/j.1467-6427.2011.00579.x.

National Institute for Health and Clinical Excellence. (2011). *Eating disorders: Core interventions in the treatment and management of anorexia nervosa, bulimia nervosa and related disorders*. London: NICE.

Nilsson, K., & Hägglöf, B. (2006). Patient perspectives of recovery in adolescent onset anorexia nervosa. *Eating Disorders*, 14, 305–311. doi: 10.1080/10640260600796234.

Robinson, A. L., Strahan, E., Girz, L., Wilson, A., & Boachie, A. (2013). "I know I can help you": Parental self-efficacy predicts adolescent outcomes in family-based therapy for eating disorders. *European Eating Disorders Review*, 21, 108–114. doi: 10.1002/erv.2180.

Schmidt, U., & Asen, E. (2005). Does multifamily day treatment hit the spot that other treatments cannot reach? *Journal of Family Therapy*, 27, 101–103.

Scholz, M., & Asen, E. (2001). Multiple family therapy with eating disordered adolescents: Concepts and preliminary results. *European Eating Disorders Review*, 9, 33–42.

Scholz, M., Rix, M., Scholz, K., Gantchev, K., & Thömke, V. (2005). Multiple family therapy for anorexia nervosa: Concepts, experiences and results. *Journal of Family Therapy*. 27, 132–141. doi: 10.1111/j.1467-6427.2005.00304.x.

Svensson, E., Nilsson, K., Levi, R., & Carballeira Suarez, N. (2013). Parents' experiences of having and caring for a child with an eating disorder. *Eating Disorders*, 21, 395–407. doi: 10.1080/10640266.2013.827537.

Treasure, J., & Russell, G. (2011). The case for early intervention in anorexia nervosa: Theoretical exploration of maintaining factors. *British Journal of Psychiatry*, 199, 5–7. doi: 10.1192/bjp.bp.110.087585.

Voriadaki, T., Simic, M., Espie, J., & Eisler, I. (2013). Intensive multi-family therapy for adolescent anorexia nervosa: Adolescents "and parents" day-to-day experiences. *Journal of Family Therapy*, 37, 5–23, doi: 10.1111/1467-6427.12067.

Wallin, U. (2011). *Multifamiljeterapi vid anorexia nervosa* [*Multifamily therapy of anorexia nervosa*]. Lund, Sweden: Behandlingsmanual.

Watson, H. J., & Bulik, C. M. (2013). Update on the treatment of anorexia nervosa: Review of clinical trials, practice guidelines and emerging interventions. *Psychological Medicine*, 43, 477–500.

Zabala, M. J., Macdonald, P., & Treasure, J. (2009). Appraisal of caregiving burden, expressed emotion and psychological distress in families of people with eating disorders: A systematic review. *European Eating Disorders Review*, 17, 338–349. doi: 10.1002/erv.925.

21 Parents' Experiences of Having and Caring for a Child with an Eating Disorder

Elin Svensson, Karin Nilsson, Richard Levi, and Nivia Carballeira Suarez

Eating disorders (EDs), including anorexia nervosa (AN), bulimia nervosa (BN), and "eating disorder not otherwise specified" (EDNOS), are all potentially serious conditions and also commonly comorbid with other psychiatric disorders such as depression. AN is additionally associated with an increased mortality risk, and in up to 10–20 percent of sufferers the condition is refractory to treatment and becomes chronic (Berkman, Lohr, & Bulik, 2007; Fairburn & Harrison, 2003; Steinhausen, 2002).

Having and caring for a child with an ED can be extremely demanding (Cottee-Lane, Pistrang, & Bryant-Waugh, 2004; Nilsson, Engström, & Hägglöf, 2012), as it is associated with high levels of distress and caregiver burden (Cohn, 2005; Graap et al., 2007; Zabala, Macdonald, & Treasure, 2009). At the same time, the family is typically very important to the person with an ED (Linville, Brown, Sturm, & McDougal, 2012; Nilsson & Hägglöf, 2006). Families with a child suffering from an ED tend to reorganize, giving the illness a central position in the family (Whitney & Eisler, 2005). The relationships within the family, between parents and patient, between siblings and patient, and between siblings and parents, are all commonly affected (Dimitropoulos, Klopfer, Lazar, & Schacter, 2009; Hillege, Beale, & McMaster, 2005). Adverse emotional reactions to the challenges that arise due to an ED may cause family members to act in ways that unintentionally aggravate its symptoms (Kyriacou, Treasure, & Schmidt, 2008). Different perceptions of the burden among family members can increase the difficulties (Coomber & King, 2013). Recently, Linville, Brown, Sturm, and McDougal (2012) examined how social support could be helpful and/or hurtful during the ED recovery process. However, research findings are still limited regarding the precise ways in which families can usefully cope with the disease and help the child to recover. Indeed, the family should be viewed as a resource and an important part of the recovery process (Le Grange, Lock, Loeb, & Nicholls, 2010) and family-based treatment (FBT) is the first-line treatment recommended for children with AN (Lock & Le Grange, 2011).

To our knowledge, the lived experience of having a child with an ED has not been documented to any extent in Sweden. In the present study, a qualitative phenomenological-hermeneutical method was used (Karlsson, 1993) in order to promote insight into EDs from the perspective of parents.

Table 21.1 The interviewer guide

Can you give examples of concrete situations that occurred due to your child's eating disorder?
Have you experienced changes in life due to your child's eating disorder? Can you give examples?
What have you done to cope with the situation? What has helped you?
What do you, as a parent of a child with an eating disorder, need to best help your child? What support is needed from health professionals?
Can you describe how you, as a parent, have experienced your child's illness?

Method

The study was approved by the Research Ethical Committee of Medicine at Umeå University, Sweden. Participants were recruited from a department of child and adolescent psychiatry of a university hospital in Sweden. Twenty parents of ten adolescents with severe EDs (i.e. requiring intensive specialist treatment) for at least one year were invited. Ten parents (six mothers and four fathers) of seven female patients 16–18 years old agreed to participate. For three of the patients, both mother and father participated. Parents in this study had participated in FBT. Four patients were diagnosed as having AN and three with an EDNOS. Illness duration varied between one and four years at the time of the interview. This study was part of a broader research effort; both used self-assessment questionnaires.

Participants were initially contacted by a letter describing the project. Follow-up phone calls were made to schedule the interviews.

Semi-structured interviews were carried out, recorded, and transcribed verbatim for analysis. The interview guide is shown in Table 21.1.

Analysis

Data were analyzed using a phenomenological, hermeneutical method, putting aside ("bracketing") former knowledge in search of the phenomenon under study (Karlsson, 1993). In this case, the phenomenon under study was the "experience" of having a child with an ED. The analysis was performed by three researchers following five consecutive steps:

1. Reading through all transcribed interviews to gain an overall impression and basic understanding of their contents.
2. Breaking the running narrative down into units of meaning.
3. Reformulating the units of meaning in the researchers' vocabulary in order to clarify the meaning of the text.
4. Transforming the text into "situated structures" showing the experience of the parent interviewed.
5. Studying the situated structures alongside one another to identify general patterns and interesting differences. The analysis was completed when it

was deemed that the material could not yield further themes supported by the data.

Results

The lived experiences of having a child with an ED were found to be diverse. However, a few major themes emerged. These are presented under three headings: social disruption, emotional impact, and coping (see also Table 21.2).

Theme 1: Social Disruption

Overall, parents' lives were reported to be profoundly affected by the child's ED. The socially disruptive changes could be further categorized under the following sub-themes:

Isolation. The child's disease was reported to become the parents' chief priority. The ED dictated how the parent's days had to be spent, and severely limited time available for other activities. Parents felt that they acted as if they were again caring for a toddler. There was a constant focus on the sick child at each meal. As a consequence, families decreased socializing with others and consequently experienced isolation.

The child's refusal to eat diminished the social value of sharing meals with others. Parents felt uncomfortable as they expected critical comments from others concerning their child's eating behavior. Furthermore, controversial topics became actualized by the child's aberrant behavior, e.g. others posing questions regarding the psychiatric implications of EDs. Described one parent:

> We have been quite active in [our] church, me and my husband, but we [have] quit this altogether, really ... she [the daughter with an ED] needed our constant attention around mealtimes. And also, you lose energy; you don't have what it takes to engage in other things at all.

Food and physical exercise-related situations and conflicts. Incidents related to food and physical exercise occurred frequently, according to the parents. Typical

Table 21.2 Lived experiences of having a child with an eating disorder

Social disruption	Emotional impact	Coping methods
Isolation	Worry and anger	Talking about the situation
Food- and exercise-related situations and conflicts	Guilt and shame	Being aware of the inherent resilience of the family
Effect on spousal relationship	Frustration	Accepting the situation
Effect on siblings		Taking periods of rest
Negative effect on work and financial situation		Acquiring facts

situations comprised an increased focus on the child's meals, possible changes in menu, and other efforts towards facilitating food intake, but also overt conflicts being triggered by meals. One parent found it difficult to eat herself, whilst her husband instead over-consumed food in order to compensate for the child's restricted intake. Others still felt awkward about having to fully monitor each of the child's meals, including school lunches.

Strained spousal relationships. Due to the intense focus on the child's ED, the time parents could spend with each other as spouses became very restricted. One parent described the large toll being separated for lengthy periods took on her marriage, as one of them constantly had to accompany their child in hospital:

> Me and my husband were apart for many weeks. One of us was at the [hospital] ward, and one was at home [in another city]. On one occasion, we "changed guards" [on the highway] in separate cars, and gave each other a hug and that, well it was horrible.

Effect on Siblings. Some parents voiced concerns regarding how the sick child's siblings were affected by the ED, how the sick child controlled whether the siblings were allowed to bring friends over, and how they had to witness repeated food-related fights and arguments. One father described how the older siblings and the one suffering from the ED almost fell out because of lack of understanding of the sick child's behavior. He thought the older siblings considered the sick child to be "acting crazy" on purpose rather than genuinely suffering from an illness:

> [T]he siblings were hesitant to bring friends over because at our place it was like a world war [going on] and shouting and doors being slammed, and one of the siblings had told a friend to come to our place ... the friend just stopped outside and heard the yelling from inside [our house] and I think turned around...

Effect on work and financial situation. The parents reported adverse consequences concerning their work. They either had to reduce their workload or take periodic sick-leave. One parent could work from home and one reported repeated short-term absences. An unemployed mother reported economic difficulties and trouble getting reimbursements from the Swedish Social Insurance Agency:

> When she [the daughter with an ED] was admitted, we started living every other week with her in the hospital ward and every other week I was at home, working. But that wasn't maintainable for long, so I went on sick-leave ... it was so hard to be with her at the ward, then go and be nice and perform at the workplace the next day; it was too much.

Theme 2: Emotional Impact

A wide range of negative emotional consequences was reported by parents in response to their experience of caring for the sick child.

Worry and anger. Many parents reported being worried for their child, and also for other family members indirectly affected by the situation. First was worry about the sick child's behavior, for example over-exercising and refusal to talk to health professionals. Second was worry for the future of the child, for example that the child would have to struggle with the consequences of the condition for a long time and the possibility of relapse. Third was fear of the child dying. Fourth was anger triggered by the sick child's behavior:

> Early on in her illness, she ran off, out. And that was very hard in some ways and you knew she was ... feeling bad ... I never knew where she went. It was incredibly worrisome.

Guilt and shame. When it comes to guilt, some parents said outright that they carried a sense of guilt or a feeling that they had done something wrong or perhaps had been bad parents, that is, that they somehow were responsible for causing the child's ED. Others conveyed this feeling in more subtle ways:

> What she [the daughter with an ED] can say is just "It's never someone else's fault; it's my own," ... and that ... that may be, but as a parent you'll never think like that ... you'll always think why didn't I do something, or why didn't I notice? Why didn't I care at first?

Some said that there was shame associated with having a child with an ED. One parent said he did not like to talk much about it and felt it to be taboo to talk about "psychiatric conditions such as this," especially since others adhered to the theory that the parents were to blame:

> All psychiatric disorders are a bit ... it's a bit shameful.... If you're in pain or have diabetes or cancer, you can talk about having that kind of disease. It [a psychiatric disorder] is more taboo.

Frustration. Frustration was a word frequently used by the parents to describe their perceived powerlessness in relation to the illness. How, no matter what they tried, the child failed to improve and sometimes became sicker. Discussions and reasoning with the child were felt to be impossible and hopeless.

Several parents described a feeling of inadequacy. One mother described how it was of utmost importance to her child's recovery to increase the child's self-esteem and self-confidence. She, as a mother, found it hard to help in this matter as her child, after all, was now a teenager. Another parent found maintaining constant vigilance of her child very challenging, and stated that as soon as her focus shifted for just a minute, something happened. Yet another parent could not act as advisor and therapist for her child due to her own emotional reactions. She felt too close to her child to be of help, and wished her child would accept the help from professionals that she had been offered:

> Well, very frustrating, very frustrating not to reach [her], not being up to it, to always finish second in every race, to not be enough, yes, frustrating.

In addition to that, descriptions such as "a hell," "a nightmare," and "a time of darkness" were used. One parent described it as one of the most difficult times in her life and compared it to having lost another child. Another used the picture of "falling off a cliff and not knowing when you would land." Some described the situation as chaotic, or that everything had been turned upside down. One parent said she did not recognize her child; another that it was like having a stranger in the house: "It's like living in a bubble ... it's a bit unreal, the world outside, at least in the beginning."

Theme 3: Coping

The parents reported many different ways of attempting to cope with the situation.

Talking about the situation. Most of the parents reported having found talking to others very helpful and felt that it was very important to have a working support system in place. Some mainly talked to the health professionals at the hospital; others talked to people in their social networks. Being open with the situation was described as being very helpful and as reducing the sense of shame. Another positive aspect of talking was the relief of letting it out instead of keeping it to yourself: "It got a lot easier once we could talk a bit more openly about this. It was like a crossroad."

Another way in which parents attempted to cope was by expressing feelings and thoughts concerning the ED in a diary or blog.

To talk to and hear from other parents in a similar situation was felt to be very valuable to some. It felt reassuring to know that things were just as crazy for others, and it made it easier to handle the situation. Many mentioned talking to their spouse or the child's other parent both in and out of treatment sessions as being important. Some felt very fortunate to be able to talk with their child, and that everything was discussable. Talking to the child helped the parent understand their child's thinking.

Most of the parents interviewed found it helpful to talk to the health professionals at the treating clinic. Most reported being positive and thankful for the help they had received, whereas some found the support to be insufficient. Positive things mentioned were the confidence the team brought to the treatment process and a sense of trust. Support and encouragement was found to be very valuable. Some thought they received clear directives on how to act, whereas others wished for firmer guidance and coaching.

Inherent resilience of the family. Faith in the inherent ability of the family and in one's competence as a parent was mentioned as a further important aspect of managing the ED. Spousal support was also vital to some of the parents:

> [It is crucial t]hat the family works well otherwise. It's very important. If you have frictions when entering something like this [having a child with an ED], it can break any marriage.
>
> When I've been down, [the child's mother] has supported me in this, and the other way around. We have had good support from each other.

Acceptance of the situation. Accepting the current state of affairs was reported to be helpful by some of the parents. It was mentioned especially in the context of temporary drawbacks and during critical stages of the ED. About half of the parents interviewed said they tried to be patient, take one day at a time, make the best of the situation, and "keep hanging on in there." One father said he tried to take the "drama" away from the situation and to accept it as a part of everyday life.

Furthermore, parents stated that they were able to maintain hope that their child would get well and ultimately grow stronger as a result of the illness:

> Somewhere deep inside I think like this, that she ... I think she will make it, I really think she will. She will probably get kind of strong from this. She will be the strongest of us all I think. She is ... that's what I hope she will be. I hope she will become the strongest of [us] all.

Periods of rest. Spending time alone was reported as valuable by some. They felt the need to take a break in the midst of everything and think about something else. One mother pointed out that it was important to take a walk and have some time alone when spending most of the time with the child on the ward. Others found being actively sent home from the ward a positive experience when staff saw that they could not help the child just there and then, that it was too much for them emotionally:

> When you can't stand it yourself, when you feel that no, to leave ... and say that no, now it's your turn, I don't have the energy. I have to get out and just do something else ... not even see anyone else.

Acquiring facts. Searching and finding more information about EDs via the internet or books was reported to have been helpful to some parents. Yet others had tried in vain to find information on the parental perspective. Most parents did not have any idea how long the recovery process would take and many stated that they never could have imagined it taking so long:

> It's like you start walking, and you think you're near the goal, but still you have a good distance to go. It takes such a long time. I read ... that ... you

must expect it to take around two years. You think that this will take two months, one month; you just have to fix it. To [make her] start eating.... If someone had said from the start that it will take two years, you wouldn't have been able to understand. It's a long process, it really is.

Discussion

This is the first study focusing on parental experiences of having and caring for a child with an ED in Sweden. As the parents indisputably are a potentially important resource in the treatment of EDs, it is clearly relevant to gain insight into their experiences. Generally, we found that parents shared several common concerns and many parents described this period as a "difficult journey," "a hell," "a nightmare," and "a time of darkness."

Consequences of Social Disruption and Emotional Impact

We found some interesting similarities with previous studies. For example, demanding and challenging situations, social isolation, financial difficulties, worry for siblings, and strained spousal relationships were all noted by Cottee-Lane, Pistrang, and Bryant-Waugh (2004).

As in Whitney et al. (2005) and Whitney and Eisler (2005), we found reports of powerlessness, hardship, and other negative emotional reactions and situations. Our study and others (Goddard et al., 2011) have identified themes of self-blame and shame. Parents in our study blamed themselves for being the cause of the illness, although they did not connect this with inconsiderate words from others, as Hillege, Beale, and McMaster (2005) reported. The Academy for Eating Disorders (Le Grange, Lock, Loeb, & Nicholls, 2010) and other guidelines (National Institute for Clinical Excellence, 2004) recommend that parents should be included in treatment as an important resource and it should be clearly stated that they are not the cause of the illness. This recognition facilitates acceptance of the diagnosis, treatment, referral, and interventions, and also minimizes undue stigma associated with having the illness.

Our findings also fit well with the model of interpersonal maintaining factors described by Treasure et al. (2008). This model describes how unhelpful attributions can fuel a variety of emotional reactions that cause family members to become less helpful to the sick person. The most difficult situations described in our study were those focused on conflict related to food and exercise. The constant attention needed could drain the parents' energy.

The manualized family-based treatment of adolescent AN (Lock & Le Grange, 2011) is evidence-based and recommends that parents take control of food and exercise in the first phase of the treatment. However, this can be a difficult task for the parents, and there is little research into the experiences of the parents in this demanding situation. Ellison et al. (2012) found that the core parental objectives in family-based therapy that predicted weight gain for the patient were taking control, being united, not criticizing the child, and externalizing the illness. Parental control was the strongest predictor of outcome. In our study the parents tried to take control in food- and exercise-related situations as instructed and supported by professionals. Nevertheless, they reported often feeling powerless and drained of energy in these situations. This makes us assume that not only do parents need to be included in treatment but also that they need support and guidance during the different phases of the illness.

Coping

In spite of the hardships and difficulties reported, we also found that parents used many different ways in which to cope well with the situation. The parents found talking about the situation meaningful, as well as utilizing the support they could gain within the family. Belief in the resilience of the family was important in terms of being able to endure difficult days. Sometimes it was a relief just to be able to accept the difficult situation as it was. Particularly important were having periods of rest to regain energy; parents working together; and acquiring factual information about different aspects of the illness. These results can be compared with those of Raenker et al. (2013), whereby caregivers reported that helping them cope with their concrete responsibilities was more helpful than the provision of emotional support. In our study, we found that parents were much occupied with meals during the starvation phase and during that phase they really needed to be periodically relieved of this duty.

Clinical Implications

Parents in our study all received FBT. We found that the parents appreciated this help and support. From the results we could see that there was still a need to lessen the isolation and emotional impact that they experienced. Since parents are an important part of the treatment process, it is important to support them, for instance by using interventions such as multi-family therapy that reduce their isolation (Eisler, 2005). It is important to focus on parent solidarity as a means of helping them support each other (Treasure, Whitaker, Todd, & Whitney, 2012) and to include both primary and secondary caregivers in treatment (Sepulveda et al., 2012).

The parents wanted to gain more information about the illness. Some information can be given by the clinicians, but initially it can be difficult to provide an accurate prognosis. It may also be difficult for parents to internalize information during the chaotic period of the illness.

The parents in our study worried about siblings. Research concerning siblings (Dimitropoulos, Klopfer, Lazar, & Schacter, 2009) does not seem to offer any clear guidelines to parents. However, a recent study (Ellison et al., 2012) found that sibling support did not predict weight gain but higher levels of sibling support were found to significantly predict increased parental control. We think there is a need to take the situation of the siblings into consideration and to include them in treatment as well.

We also found that there can be financial problems when parents have to stay at home and take care of their child. There is free healthcare in Sweden and when a parent must take care of a seriously ill child, the parents can gain reimbursement from the social insurance system. Still, we found that finances nevertheless may be strained, especially if a parent is unemployed. Thus, the financial consequences should be included in the total assessment of the clinical situation, especially if there is a long duration of the illness.

Strengths and Limitations

In this study we met both fathers and mothers and the parents were not in the most acute phase of the illness and could thus look back and reflect on the situation. Because we met the parents and conducted open interviews, we were able to obtain rich narratives regarding the problems they faced and the methods they used to cope with them. In this way, we were able to account for the complexity of the lived experience.

The interviews were carried out by people who were not treating the families, and we think the parents were thus able to be open and honest. A rigorous and open approach to analysis was followed.

There were also noteworthy limitations to this study. A sample of 10 parents is obviously too small to allow generalizations to all parents and all clinical situations. This, however, was not the aim of this phenomenological, hermeneutical study. Different study methodologies complement each other by analyzing different aspects of the state of affairs under study. The method used in this study focused on subjectivity, with the primary goal of enhancing understanding of what it is like to experience having a child with an ED. Obviously, more quantitative and operationalized methods will provide valuable data of a different kind.

Conclusion

The present study focused on EDs from the perspectives of the parents with the intention of describing the lived experiences of having and caring for a child with an ED in Sweden. Our results concur with those of other studies by clarifying the various difficulties experienced and the need for more effective interventions to reduce the strain and hardship parents experience. They need to become more empowered in terms of taking control of the ED and to reduce the concomitant isolation and negative emotional impact. There was an expressed need for more information about the illness and its impact on the family as a whole. As parents and siblings are typically very involved in treatment and may act constructively or destructively, and as their ability to act constructively depends on their own psychological well-being, we feel that the results of this study further underscore the need for ED programs to include the whole family in treatment protocols.

References

Berkman, N. D., Lohr, K. N., & Bulik, C. M. (2007). Outcomes of eating disorders: A systematic review of the literature. *International Journal of Eating Disorders*, 40, 293–309.

Cohn, L. (2005) Parents' voices: What they say is important in the treatment and recovery process. *Eating Disorders*, 13, 419–428.

Coomber, K., & King, R. M. (2013). Perceptions of carer burden: Differences between individuals with an eating disorder and their carer. *Eating Disorders*, 2, 26–36. doi: 10.1080/10640266.2013.741966.

Cottee-Lane, D., Pistrang, N., & Bryant-Waugh, R. (2004). Childhood onset anorexia nervosa: The experience of parents. *European Eating Disorders Review*, 12, 169–177.

Dimitropoulos, G., Klopfer, K., Lazar, L., & Schacter, R. (2009). Caring for a sibling with anorexia nervosa: A qualitative study. *European Eating Disorders Review*, 17, 350–365. doi: 10.1002/erv.937.

Eisler, I. (2005). The empirical and theoretical base of family therapy and multiple family day therapy for adolescent anorexia nervosa. *Journal of Family Therapy*, 27, 104–131.

Ellison, R., Rhodes, P., Madden, S., Miskovic, J., Wallis, A. et al. (2012). Do the components of manualized family-based treatment for anorexia nervosa predict weight gain? *International Journal of Eating Disorders*, 45, 609–614. doi: 10.1002/eat22000.

Fairburn, C. G., & Harrison, P. J. (2003). Eating disorders. *The Lancet*, 361, 407–416.

Goddard, E., Macdonald, P., Sepulveda, A. R., Naumann, U., Landau, S. et al. (2011). Cognitive interpersonal maintenance model of eating disorders: Intervention for carers. *British Journal of Psychiatry*, 199, 225–231. doi: 10.1192/bjp.bp.110.088401.

Graap, H., Bleich, S., Herbst, F., Trostmann, T., Wancata, J., & de Zwann, M. (2007). The needs of carers of patients with anorexia and bulimia nervosa. *European Eating Disorders Review*, 16, 21–29.

Hillege, S., Beale, B., & McMaster, R. (2005). Impact of eating disorders on family life: Individual parents' stories. *Journal of Clinical Nursing*, 15, 1016–1022.

Karlsson, G. (1993). *Psychological qualitative research from a phenomenological perspective*. Stockholm: Almqvist & Wiksell.

Kyriacou, O., Treasure, J., & Schmidt, U. (2008). Understanding how parents cope with living with someone with anorexia nervosa: Modelling the factors that are associated with carer distress. *International Journal of Eating Disorders*, 41, 233–242.

Le Grange, D., Lock, J., Loeb, K., & Nicholls, D. (2010). Academy for Eating Disorders position paper: The role of the family in eating disorders. *International Journal of Eating Disorders*, 43, 1–5.

Linville, D., Brown, T., Sturm, K., & McDougal, T. (2012). Eating disorders and social support: Perspectives of recovered individuals. *Eating Disorders*, 20, 216–231.

Lock, J. (2011). Evaluation of family treatment models for eating disorders. *Current Opinions in Psychiatry*, 24, 274–279.

Lock, J., & Le Grange, D. (2015). *Treatment manual for anorexia nervosa: A family-based approach*, 2nd edition. New York: Guilford Press.

National Institute for Clinical Excellence. (2004). *CG9 eating disorders: NICE guideline.* Available online www.nice.org.uk/CG009NICEguideline (accessed July 19, 2012).

Nilsson, K., & Hägglöf, B. (2006). Patient perspectives of recovery in adolescent onset anorexia nervosa. *Eating Disorders,* 14, 305–311.

Nilsson K., Engström I., & Hägglöf, B. (2012). Family climate and recovery in adolescent onset eating disorders: A prospective study. *European Eating Disorders Review,* 20, e96–e102.

Raenker, S., Hibbs, R., Goddard, E., Naumann, U., Arcelus, J. et al. (2013). Caregiving and coping in carers of people with anorexia nervosa admitted for intensive hospital care. *International Journal of Eating Disorders,* 46, 346–354. doi: 10.1002/eat22068.

Sepulveda, A. R., Graell, M., Berbel, E., Anastasiadou, D., Botella, J. et al. (2012). Factors associated with emotional well-being in primary and secondary caregivers of patients with eating disorders. *European Eating Disorders Review,* 20, e78–e84. doi: 10.1002/erv.1118.

Steinhausen, H.-C. (2002). The outcome of anorexia nervosa in the 20th century. *American Journal of Psychiatry,* 159, 1284–1293.

Treasure, J., Sepulveda, A. R., Macdonald, P., Whitaker, W., Lopez, C. et al. (2008). The assessment of the family of people with eating disorders. *European Eating Disorders Review,* 16, 247–255.

Treasure, J., Whitaker, W., Todd, G., & Whitney, J. (2012). A description of multiple family workshops for carers of people with anorexia nervosa. *European Eating Disorders Review,* 20, e17–e22. doi: 10.1002/erv.1075.

Whitney, J., & Eisler, I. (2005). Theoretical and empirical models around caring for someone with an eating disorder: The reorganization of family life and inter-personal maintenance factors. *Journal of Mental Health,* 14, 575–585. doi: 10.1080/09638230500347889.

Whitney, J., Murray, J., Gavan, K., Todd, G., Whitaker, W., & Treasure, J. (2005). Experiences of caring for someone with anorexia nervosa: Qualitative study. *British Journal of Psychiatry,* 187, 444–449.

Zabala, M. J., Macdonald, P., & Treasure, J. (2009). Appraisal of caregiving burden, expressed emotion and psychological distress in families of people with eating disorders: A systematic review. *European Eating Disorders Review,* 17, 338–349.

22 Mothers' Experiences of Home Treatment for Adolescents with Anorexia Nervosa

An Interpretative Phenomenological Analysis

Jessica Bezance and Joanna Holliday

Introduction

Background

Adolescence is the most common period for the onset of anorexia nervosa (AN), which is most frequent in females (Kjelsas, Bjornstrom, & Gunnar Gotestam, 2004; Le Grange & Loeb, 2007). In recent years the disadvantages of inpatient treatment for anorexia have received attention. Research in adolescents with AN indicates adverse effects on self-esteem and self-efficacy (Gowers, Weetman, Shore, Hossain, & Elvins, 2000), a negative impact on family life and social support (Green, 2002), and the acquisition of new unhelpful illness behaviors (Boughtwood & Halse, 2010) following inpatient admission. Hospitalization also has a poor outcome (Gowers et al., 2007), and is more costly, compared to outpatient care (Meads, Gold, & Burls, 2001). The National Institute of Clinical Excellence (2004) now recommends specialized outpatient intervention for AN rather than inpatient treatment wherever possible.

Research also favors the involvement of the family in the treatment of adolescent AN. A family-based approach, known as the Maudsley Model or family-based treatment (FBT), is recommended for adolescents with AN and has accrued a substantial evidence base (Lock, Le Grange, Agra, & Dare, 2001). FBT is a problem-solving approach that views the family system as fundamental to recovery. FBT involves significant commitment from families; it is time-intensive and carers need to become skilled in supporting their adolescent to eat and regain weight. Treasure and colleagues (2007) have also pioneered a family-based treatment that aims to empower parents to help their child eat by teaching and sharing the therapeutic skills used by professionals.

Intensive Community Treatment

Along with the development of specialized outpatient interventions for AN, there has been a move towards providing intensive community support. This aims to reduce the need for inpatient admission. Intensive community support is based on the bio-psycho-social model and is derived from both the wrap-around model (VanDenBerg & Grealish, 1996) and intensive home-based models of psychiatric care (Woolston, Berkowitz, Schaefer, & Adnopoz, 1998). Its philosophy is that a small change for a young person in their own environment is more significant and worthwhile than a larger change in an environment that is alien to them, such as an inpatient unit. A number of different intensive community support programs have been developed for adolescents with mental health difficulties, including assertive community treatment, crisis resolution teams, and home treatment (Lamb, 2009; York & Lamb, 2005).

Home treatment (HT) refers to a child-focused, family-centered approach (Schmidt, Lay, Gopel, Naab, & Blanz, 2006), which aims to address the adolescent's psychological and developmental needs in the home and family environment (Woolston et al., 1998). It is designed to empower and support family members, reduce the caregiving burden, and enable the family to live as normal a life as possible.

Home treatment for AN is a recent development, and is not widely available. Services tend to have developed idiosyncratically, depending on local need and service structure, and there is little research on the most effective way to deliver it. Two studies have described the positive effects of HT on hospital admission rates for adolescents with AN (Darwish, Salmon, Ahuja, & Sleed, 2006; Jaffa & Percival, 2004).

Family-based treatment for AN suggests that empowering parents to support their child to eat is key to success of interventions for AN. In inpatient programs, therapeutic meal support has been highlighted as one of the most important components of the treatment program (Desantis, 2002; Holliday & Woolrich, 2007). In relation to eating and weight gain, HT has the advantage of enabling parents to support mealtimes in the home on a frequent basis, which unsurprisingly presents the greatest strain for carers and siblings of adolescents with AN (Cottee-Lane & Pistrang, 2004).

Carer Burden

In line with government directives highlighting the needs of carers (Department of Health, 1995, 2004), there has been growing research interest in the experience of caregiving in mental health. In HT of AN, carers (usually parents) retain the main caring responsibility. It is important to understand this experience given that the burden of care is very high in AN (Eisler, 2005). Anxiety and depressive symptoms, for example, are widespread amongst carers of those with AN (Zabala, Macdonald, & Treasure, 2009).

Nevertheless, despite the caring responsibility involved for parents in HT for adolescents with AN, little is known about the impact of HT on those parents. The literature suggests that parents of children and adolescents with AN should be involved throughout the treatment process (McMaster, Beale, Hillege, & Nagy, 2004). However, parents report feeling neglected

(Highet, Thompson, & King, 2005) and shut out by professionals (McMaster at al., 2004).

The aim of the current study was to explore the experiences of mothers receiving HT as part of treatment for their daughters' AN. In order to create a homogenous sample, it was felt that mothers' experience of HT would differ from fathers' given that mothers are usually the primary caregivers.

Method

Design

A qualitative research design was used and semi-structured interviews were conducted to collect data.

Context

Two HT teams from the same trust evolved from recognition that some young people with AN needed intensive support in the community and at home as an adjunct to the typical tier 3 Child and Adolescent Mental Health Services (CAMHS) treatment package. The home treatment team is a multidisciplinary team consisting of psychiatric nurses, occupational therapists, and a clinical psychologist with psychiatry input. The aim of HT is to reduce risk to physical health, reduce carer burden, and empower carers to support their child at home. The HT treatment program includes intensive monitoring, supervision of meals at home, and/or additional individual/family support that usually lasts approximately eight weeks.

Participants

Nine biological mothers living with their adolescents meeting the study criteria were included. The inclusion criteria were as follows:

1. The adolescent must have been referred from CAMHS to HT and be engaged with HT for at least 2 weeks within the last 18 months.
2. According to ICD-10 (World Health Organization, 1993) conducted by the clinician in the service, the adolescent had a primary diagnosis of anorexia nervosa or eating disorder not otherwise specified of an AN-type (EDNOS-AN).

Interview Measure

A semi-structured interview schedule was developed specifically for this study. The interview included a series of open-ended questions (for example: what was your experience of the home treatment team?) to gather retrospective and current accounts of participants' experience of HT.

Ethical Considerations

Approval was obtained from the Oxford Doctoral Course in Clinical Psychology and the Oxford Research Ethics Committee prior to commencement of the study.

Data Analysis

Interview transcripts were analyzed using Interpretative Phenomenological Analysis (IPA). The primary goal of IPA is to try to understand the lived experience of the participants and how the participants themselves make sense of their experiences (Larkin, Watts, & Clifton, 2006). It is phenomenological and explores an individual's personal perception or account of an event or state as opposed to attempting to produce an objective record of the event or state itself. The analysis followed a series of considered steps (Smith & Osborn, 2003). First, transcripts were read and re-read and tentative comments generated. Second, ideas were clustered together in order to form themes within transcripts. Third, themes from all transcripts were clustered and integrated to form a list of master themes that conveyed the shared experience of the participants.

Quality Measures

Several steps were taken to ensure rigor in the data analysis, in line with guidelines promoting high quality qualitative research (Elliott, Fischer, & Rennie, 1999; Willig, 2001). The researcher was interviewed twice by another IPA researcher to gather information on the researchers' personal, academic, clinical, and research background and to explore pre- and post-interview their expectations and predictions regarding the outcome and findings of the study. In addition, a reflective diary was kept throughout the research process to collate thoughts, observations, and ideas about the research and data (Huberman & Miles, 1994).

Credibility checks were undertaken with the research supervisor to review emerging themes during the analytic and reflective processes to provide an audit trail.

Results

Situating the Sample

Participants ranged from 40 to 63 years old. At the time of HT, their adolescents with AN were between 13 and 16 years of age. Five of the nine adolescents received inpatient treatment after HT. The length of HT varied from 2 to 12 weeks. Participant ethnicity is not included due to concerns regarding preserving participant anonymity but the majority were white British.

Becoming Enmeshed

This superordinate theme conveys participants' accounts of becoming increasingly enmeshed with their daughters and AN. The three subordinate themes capture different aspects of this experience.

Accommodation of anorexia nervosa. Mothers' narratives were dominated by the extent to which living with and caring for their child with AN had taken over their lives. For many, monitoring food and exercise was the first thing they thought of in the morning and the last before they went to bed. As Amanda stated, it "completely took over my life, absolutely completely," and this sentiment is echoed by Felicity, who felt that she had "slaved to this anorexia." Samantha described how it impacted on her family's life and how they organized their lives around AN; for example, "we didn't go out together because we wouldn't leave her on her own." A number of participants described a complex relationship in which they often felt manipulated: "She is fooling me in a way. She needs to make sure I am doing what she wants" (Sarah). Similarly, Emily found it difficult to remain boundaried and strong:

> When you have that emotional tie and your daughter's sobbing, it is so easy; to … you can bend the rules. "You have to have a banana…" and she would say "oh mum look, have half with me" and I did it, and that was just a mistake.

Loss of identity. As the condition progressed, participants' sense of who they were appeared to diminish. Amanda reflected:

> I was very clear that there was some kind of enmeshment going on between the two of us. But she was becoming like a mollusc to me. It was becoming difficult to define who was her and who was me.

Participants became consumed in their daughters' AN and neglected their own needs. Sarah described how "the important thing was [name of adolescent] putting on weight. So I was putting myself, you know, aside and therefore completely forgot about who I was or what I was doing." Similarly, Sam understood her own health to be secondary: "You see, I don't think as a mother you think about yourself. You think about your daughter…. [Name of adolescent] is ill so I can't be ill."

Interestingly, participants described how their enforced change of role as a mother also appeared to alter their sense of self. Prior to the AN, participants were often working and parenting a relatively independent teenager. The arrival of AN meant that participants had to make sacrifices in their own lives to accommodate the needs of their daughter, as Felicity illustrates:

> It's like having a baby that you've got to feed, change nappies, burp them, and get them to sleep. And then you're starting again, it's the same thing. So yeah work became pretty secondary and my business suffered, definitely.

Feeling alone. As a result of enmeshment and caring responsibilities, most participants described a pervasive sense of loneliness and isolation from support. They felt distanced from other family members, and this contributed to the intensity of the mother–daughter dynamic:

> I just felt that … it was just me and her. And my family were just going away from it because they didn't know how to deal with it…. And it was just like me and [name of adolescent] to one side and the rest were just doing their own thing.
>
> (Helen)

Sam described feeling distanced from friends and the stigma of mental illness:

> It is lonely … because friends were frightened to come. When someone has a broken leg, you get "Get well" cards. When somebody has anorexia, you don't. People are, because it is a mental illness, they are frightened of it.

Reaching Rock Bottom

All participants described an acute phase of the journey of caring when they reached rock bottom. This phase was commonly experienced immediately prior to the start of HT. The arrival of professional help then seemed to allow participants to express and acknowledge how desperate they had become.

Despair and exhaustion. All participants described a breaking point when they felt overwhelmed by the emotional and physical impact of caring. Felicity reported:

> I just stopped sleeping [cries]. I was a complete wreck. My husband thought … if she wasn't admitted, then I would be pretty soon. You know, which one of us was going to be first was how he … was what he wanted really.

Participants described days spent "constantly crying" (Helen), "feeling really worried and anxious" (Sarah), and being "desperate" (Emily). Emily said "it is strangling me and you can't relax or whatever you do…. And you lose the motivation, it totally exhausts you… .You're not buzzing, you don't feel like buzzing." Many participants had given up work, had lost weight, or were going to their GP for medication.

Helplessness/powerlessness/sense of failure. A profound sense of helplessness and powerlessness pervaded participants' accounts. Most had tried a plethora of strategies to increase food intake, but most were unsuccessful:

> Just trying to get her to eat actually doesn't work at all. So you just leave her to eat whatever she wants and let her get on with it [but] that doesn't work. So, I kind of think that nothing I do helps really.
>
> (Rachel)

Feeling powerless and helpless led to a sense of failure, despite a powerful maternal responsibility to ensure that their child was eating. For some mothers, needing HT support signified failure:

> One of the hardest things is you feel like you have failed your daughter ... I think that's ... to have to get somebody else involved in your child is quite hard. But at the end of the day you get so desperate.
>
> (Emily)

Changed person. Most participants described how difficult it was to witness the change in personality and behavior of their daughter:

> After every meal, breakfast included, she would chuck herself on the floor, scream, thump the floor, you know. "You don't understand me. You bitch mother." All hell coming out of my daughter's mouth [laughs] ... like she was possessed.
>
> (Felicity)

As a result of extreme mood swings, aggression, and verbal abuse, participants found they could no longer recognize their daughters: "It's like the devil that's got into my daughter" (Emily); she "looked like a wild woman" (Isobel); "She was alien" (Helen). This was overwhelming and unbearable and led to feelings of shame when these behaviors were witnessed by others, notably HT staff.

Fear of death. Many participants gave traumatic accounts of the moment they realized that their daughter could or "was going to die" (Amanda). The impact of this was profound. Isobel reported:

> I thought the stress was going to kill me. I really, I wanted to die.... Because I couldn't bear looking at how ill she was ... I didn't wish she could die but I wished I could die so I could just be away from the misery that it must have been for her and for us.

Experience of Help

Participants' experience of HT was informed by their previous journey through services and by their individual philosophy and values. Mothers described a need for containment, learning skills, and rediscovering strength and confidence when reflecting on their experience of HT.

When help is needed. Participants' accounts of HT were embedded in the wider experience of seeking and receiving professional help. In most cases, the journey started with a struggle to access the right help. Sarah described how her initial attempts to seek help from her GP were unsuccessful and her concerns were invalidated: "He said that I was, you know, I was making too much fuss and you know she was a teenager and that she was fine."

When HT was first offered, most participants experienced an overwhelming sense of relief:

> It felt like a huge relief that actually somebody has realized that this is a real sort of crisis for us and they were coming to do something about it. It was also most like the cavalry … coming to try and help us.
>
> (Christine)

Conversely, the end of HT often provoked feelings of disappointment, fear, and anxiety for the future, even when an inpatient admission had been averted:

> And now we're getting her back a little bit. But there is that fear that we might have a slide. I said to my husband, I don't want outreach to leave us until she is, until she has recovered completely. I don't want them to hand us back to CAMHS.
>
> (Sam)

Rachel felt strongly that an eight-week program was not sufficient:

> I think it's really difficult as HT is only there for a certain amount of time … umm where she is in a really worse place at the moment. It's going to withdraw her support at a time when she is in crisis.

Several participants whose daughters ended up receiving inpatient care felt that HT was offered too late; for example:

> Crisis [home treatment] tried to get involved before [name of adolescent] went to the inpatient unit. I had been seeing the CAMHS and they tried to get a diet plan together but she was too ill…. It was too late to be able to turn it around or make it work.
>
> (Emily)

Need for containment. All participants described a need for containment. They felt helped and reassured by the provision of information, experienced a sense of expertise from professional involvement, and said that consistency in the treatment was important.

Christine described how a meeting with the HT team provided her with a clear understanding of what the treatment entailed and what the aims were:

> They were very good at setting us at ease and explaining what they were and … what they were there to do, and laying out exactly what was going to happen going forward … you certainly felt at the end of it that, oh these are people who know what they're doing. They're gonna come and help us.

In contrast, Amanda felt "in no man's land" as she was not given a clear idea of what to expect:

> And so we sat down with him and said, "Well, what does this mean?" And he said, "Oh I've no idea." "[I've] not really come across it in this way," is how he put it.... So I didn't really have that much explanation as to what they would do when they came in.

Once HT had commenced, containment was facilitated by a consistent approach from experienced staff. For most participants, inconsistency between staff members and a change in the person visiting had a negative impact. For example:

> There was a lot of this sort of, erm, quite a few people came just once and you know it just didn't enable any relationship. It was a lot of hard work then to develop any sort of, erm, trust before the meal took place.
>
> (Christine)

Finding strength and skills. Despite difficulties, most participants described how they were able to develop and recover strength through HT. Most described benefitting practically and emotionally: "I felt that in the darkness somebody was holding my hand" (Sarah).

On a practical level, mothers learned "how to be around [their daughters]" (Felicity) and "different things to try" (Emily) to help manage their daughters' eating. However, some did not find this sufficient and several wanted more advice and information. Rachel described little direct contact with the HT staff and remained desperate for feedback and "advice on how to support [my daughter] in-between appointments … cos' obviously at the end of the day they are with you." Helen described how she "went on the internet just to find out the information, how to deal with certain situations with her. Because they [HT] didn't really offer that kind of advice for a parent on how to deal with certain situations." Isobel requested:

> a little more education about certain aspects of behavior of the anorexic and how to deal with them. I mean one book, which was very good. But I think maybe just talking to me, you know, without even [name of adolescent] being here…

When successful, intensive support at home enabled mothers to reinstate boundaries and move away from the enmeshed and accommodating position described earlier (see superordinate theme 1), as these mothers illustrate:

> I learnt … to be a lot tougher, a lot stronger with [name of adolescent], not to give in to her, because I did use to just allow it.
>
> (Helen)

> I think it is having the support to know that you're not being cruel to your daughter; that you are doing it for her sake because you can so easily give in.
>
> (Emily)

As well as providing hope, HT reduced carer burden, increased confidence, and built up carers' strength. There was also a sense from some participants that support from HT had helped them regain a sense of themselves, as Sarah illustrates:

> Somehow they took away from me that anxiety I had ... [They] did teach me to feel a bit more strong. To go out and do my hair or look after me instead of waking up in the morning and not even washing my face because [name of adolescent] needed me ... they made me feel like ... it's not just [her], there is actually me here somewhere if you look around.

Sam reflected, "they were our carers as well as [name of adolescent]'s carers." Felicity described the benefits of having respite from the trauma of mealtimes:

> [I felt] reenergized ... and a lot more confident about dealing with her and um, yeah I, um, I sort of felt far more my old self. I felt like I could cope again, I wasn't about to lose it. Yeah, just happier I suppose.

Philosophy and values. For all participants the experience of HT was mediated by the extent to which the intervention fitted with the philosophy and values of their family.

Motivation. It was evident from the interviews that the young person's motivation to change and engage in HT was crucial. Sarah and Felicity both felt there were "moments, chinks of light here and there" (*Felicity*) which signaled a willingness to recover and engage with HT. These moments provided hope and were crucial in whether or not inpatient treatment was avoided.

In contrast, Amanda described her daughter's "unspoken entrenched attitude" as signifying reluctance to engage in HT. This manifested itself in a number of ways, including adolescents staying in their room when the HT team member visited, refusing to see HT staff, or refusing to eat with parents alone. When adolescents failed to engage, it was felt that their needs were greater than the support HT could offer:

> They became increasingly ineffective as time went by and that was down to her ... putting up the shutters really. It was getting harder and harder to get her to eat ... just one visit for the sort of couple of hours that they had, just wasn't enough.
>
> (Christine)

The bottom line felt by many whose daughters ended up receiving inpatient treatment was that "it's got to come from her … you try and mend and until she's ready or she wants to, there's no hope" (Emily).

Collaboration versus intrusion. Nearly all participants described some element of "feeling threatened" by HT. It was important for participants to feel that they could relate to the HT staff. Felicity shared her initial concerns:

> When I met them, I was surprised that they were really nice young people. Not scary old biddies, you know. Men in white coats … I suppose subconsciously it was a scary thing; it was almost, these mental health workers were going to come in and what were they going to look like and how were they going to be?

Some families were able to see visiting staff almost as "part of the family" (Sarah), whereas others felt their presence was intrusive and made maintaining a sense of normality difficult:

> I think they [two older daughters] found it an intrusion. It's quite difficult to have people you really don't know sitting round a table … it's the five of us and suddenly you've got another couple.
>
> (Emily)

Feeling observed by HT staff generated anxiety amongst mothers. Isobel described an experience where she felt anxious about planning meals, "making sure everything was ready for when HT arrived," anxious about how she would respond to her daughter while they were there, and pressure to "conform." Helen experienced some HT staff as having an authoritarian approach that made her feel judged: "I just felt like I was being looked on as if I wasn't doing my role properly as a parent."

What is my role? For many participants, there was confusion and uncertainty regarding the part they needed to play in HT. For Helen, this led to feeling redundant:

> It got to the stage when I was cooking the food, they were in the kitchen with me, they were watching my portion size I was giving her. And umm, you know it just felt like I wasn't being able to do my job properly as her mum.

Similarly, Rachel expressed frustration that she was not provided with feedback or guidance on her role. As a consequence, she "kept completely in the background" and, in times of crisis, was not sure what to do or whom to contact.

It was vital for participants to be part of the treatment, specifically the feeding process; as Amanda stated,

> You can't ignore the parent and the parent's feelings…. They have to realize how powerless you are. That actually you don't necessarily want that power to be taken, to be further eroded.

Discussion

This is the first study to explore mothers' experience of HT for adolescent AN. Three broad themes emerged from the data: becoming enmeshed, reaching rock bottom, and the experience of help.

Becoming Enmeshed

A vicious cycle was evident whereby, in supporting their daughters, mothers unwittingly became more entangled in the AN and more distanced and isolated from others. This led to mothers losing a sense of themselves and becoming further drawn into a problematic relationship with their daughter. The mothers' accounts resonate with models of caring in AN and the maintenance cycles that can develop (Eisler, 2005; Schmidt & Treasure, 2006).

The experience of feeling enmeshed in particular echoes Minuchin, Rosman, and Baker's (1978) systemic theory of AN, which describes families of teenagers with AN as enmeshed and rigid, accompanied by a strong sense of over-protection towards the adolescent. While Minuchin and colleagues imply a causal relationship between enmeshment and AN, more recent theorists see enmeshed families as a consequence of AN and the immense burden this places on carers (Schmidt & Treasure, 2006). Family-based approaches to the treatment of AN (FBT, structural family therapy) aim to support parents to return to a normal family structure.

In relation to HT, enmeshment is likely to affect how HT is perceived by mothers and how well they are able to engage in treatment. Providing an opportunity for parents to reflect on the impact of AN on family functioning and relationships is likely to be beneficial both in engaging and supporting mothers at home and safeguarding their mental health and that of siblings. Similarly, staff should be aware of the context within which they will be working and the possible likelihood of a mother's enmeshed relationship with her daughter.

Reaching Rock Bottom

The theme of reaching rock bottom conveyed the extreme levels of desperation and despair experienced by mothers that often preceded HT. This high level of stress is consistent with previous research demonstrating high levels of anxiety and depression in mothers (Zabala et al., 2009). It adds to existing research by communicating the qualitative experience of this group of carers. The finding illustrates the potential risk of overlooking the mental health needs of mothers who are asked to take on a significant role in their daughters' recovery and highlights the need for separate carer assessments (Department of Health, 2004). Family-based treatments require parents to take control of feeding their child. In order to be effective, it is crucial that parents are helped to rediscover their own strength and resources as individuals. This may necessitate separate support for parents alongside that offered to their child, for example carer support groups, workshops (Treasure et al., 2007), or individual therapy.

Contributing to mothers' feelings of despair was the sense that their daughters had been taken over or changed significantly. This echoes parents' narratives describing the eating disordered personality as having "exorcist-type demon" qualities (Brown, 2011). Similarly traumatic were the feelings mothers experienced when they realized their daughter might die. These experiences were associated with raw emotions of fear, horror, and desperation.

Despite evidence for psychological distress in families with AN (Zabala et al., 2009), little research has been conducted exploring the potentially traumatic nature of caring for a family member with AN. The nature and intensity of the experiences described in this study echo those in models of vicarious trauma/compassion fatigue (Figley, 1995) and would benefit from further exploration in future studies.

Experience of Help

The superordinate theme of "experience of home treatment" described mothers' experience of HT and their journey through services. Seeking help was generally an arduous process, which is consistent with findings in the wider literature (Haigh & Treasure, 2003; McMaster et al., 2004). In addition, many mothers felt that HT was offered too late and that the duration was insufficient.

This finding suggests that reviewing the timing and length of HT for adolescents with AN is important. In particular, the transition from HT to CAMHS requires consideration and an understanding of how to help mothers feel equipped and empowered to continue when treatment intensity reduces needs.

Mothers described a need to feel held and reassured by HT. Provision of consistent information from professionals was key; however, several mothers described a lack of information about care and what to expect. This supports previous findings that parents often feel excluded and ill-informed throughout the treatment process (McMaster et al., 2004). This is important given that providing information has been found helpful for parents of adolescents with AN (Honey & Halse, 2006) and can reduce the distress they experience (Treasure et al., 2007).

Where HT was experienced as consistent and available, this had a positive impact on relationships among staff, mothers, and adolescents. However, frequent change in staff led to confusion and was considered a hindrance in the development of a good therapeutic alliance. Variability in staff approach and style, described by most participants, may reflect the lack of accepted guidelines for HT and for supported mealtimes (Long, Wallis, Leung, & Meyer, 2012), which need to be developed. Training for staff should include clear aims of HT, how to prepare families for HT, and how families can best be supported at mealtimes. Consulting the literature on nurses' experiences of supported mealtimes in inpatient units may also be useful in training HT teams (Holliday & Woolrich, 2012).

Two key benefits of HT were (1) acquisition of skills to support their daughter and (2) practical and emotional support to restore their own resources and take back control. These findings add credence to treatment approaches that aim to support parents, practically and emotionally, as they feed their offspring with AN. Both Treasure et al.'s (2007) skills-based training and FBT (Lock et al., 2001) have the ultimate aim of empowering parents to support re-feeding at home, albeit using slightly different methods.

The fit between HT and the values and beliefs held by the family influenced the experience of help. Such factors are rarely considered in treatment research but in the current study they had an important impact on engagement and treatment success. For mothers, beliefs about how HT fits into their family mediated their experience of help; staff either became "part of the family," collaborative and safe, or were seen as threatening and intrusive. Mothers also expressed concerns regarding the impact of HT on other family members, specifically other children. Research indicates that siblings are affected by living with AN (Garley & Johnson, 1994) and may play an important role in treatment and recovery from AN (Lock et al., 2001). The current findings suggest a need to involve the whole family in HT.

Mothers' experience of HT was also mediated by how HT teams positioned themselves in the family system and mothers' understanding of their own role. Ambiguity, confusion, and perception of their role as the mother being undermined by HT were experienced negatively and exacerbated feelings of powerlessness. These findings are consistent with research reporting that parents' evaluation of clinicians, services, and practices are related to whether the system supported or ignored the parents' role as the primary carer (Honey, Clarke, Halse, Kohn, & Madden, 2006). It seems crucial that HT teams discuss the position they hope to take in relation to the family and are explicit in how this will be achieved.

Interestingly, skills-based training for carers (Treasure et al., 2007) and FBT (Lock et al., 2001) adopt subtly different stances; the former adopts an expert position, offering information and caregiving skills and the latter adopts a non-authoritarian stance of empowering parents. Mothers' confusion regarding their role in HT may reflect this dilemma. It may be that one of these approaches offers a better fit with a particular family's culture, beliefs, and expectations than the other and this should be considered at the start of HT involvement.

Research Limitations and Areas for Future Study

The current research has a number of limitations. The study investigated the experience of HT in a single health trust. There are a number of variations of HT in the UK (Lamb, 2009; York & Lamb, 2005) and there is no current universal model for its implementation. Therefore, it is necessary to be cautious in drawing conclusions about other services from this study.

Given IPA requires a homogenous sample, mothers were interviewed about their experiences of HT following CAMHS treatment. Some adolescents experience HT following inpatient care and it would be useful to compare and contrast mothers' experiences in the two different situations, as well as to also consider the experiences of fathers, siblings, and adolescents.

The retrospective nature of this study could be seen as a limitation due to the possibility of inaccurate recollection. However, IPA assumes that the important reality is what people perceive it to be (Willig, 2001); therefore, the nature of such bias should be minimal. What may be more relevant, however, is whether participants' experiences of HT were influenced by the outcome; for example, was mothers' experience of HT informed by whether or not their daughter subsequently experienced inpatient treatment.

Finally, given that HT is presented as an alternative to inpatient admission, further research is required to assess whether it is a viable alternative, building on the promising cases reported in the literature (Jaffa & Percival, 2004). For five of the adolescents in this study, HT was insufficient to avoid an inpatient admission. This could be as a result of a number of variables: severity of AN, motivation of adolescent, mother's capacity and so on, and these factors need to be explored in order to understand how and why HT may or may not be successful.

References

Boughtwood, D., & Halse, C. (2010). Other than obedient: Girls' constructions of doctors and treatment regimes for anorexia nervosa. *Journal of Community and Applied Social Psychology*, 20, 83–94. doi: 10.1002/casp.1016.

Brown, H. (2011). A parent's perspective on family treatment. In D. Le Grange & J. Lock (Eds.), *Eating disorders in children and adolescents: A clinical handbook* (pp. 457–463). New York: Guilford Press.

Cottee-Lane, D., & Pistrang, N. (2004). Childhood onset anorexia nervosa: The experience of parents. *European Eating Disorders Review*, 12, 169–177. doi: 10.1002/erv.560.

Darwish, A., Salmon, G., Ahuja, A., & Sleed, L. (2006). The community intensive therapy team: Development and philosophy of a new service. *Clinical Child Psychology and Psychiatry*, 11, 591–605. doi: 10.1177/1359104506067880.

Department of Health. (1995). *The Carers (Recognition and Services) Act*. London: Stationery Office.

Department of Health. (2004). *The national service framework*. London: Stationery Office.

Desantis, A. (2002). Therapeutic mealtime support: A treatment strategy for disordered eating. *Pulse*, 21, 4–5.

Eisler, I. (2005). The empirical and theoretical base of family therapy and multiple family day therapy for adolescent anorexia nervosa. *Journal of Family Therapy*, 27, 104–131. doi: 10.1111/j.1467-6427.2005.00303.x.

Elliott, R., Fischer, C. T., & Rennie, D. L. (1999). Evolving guidelines for publication of qualitative research studies in psychology and related fields. *British Journal of Clinical Psychology*, 38, 215–229. doi: 10.1348/014466599162782.

Figley, C. R. (1995). *Compassion fatigue: Coping with secondary traumatic stress disorder in those who treat the traumatized*. New York: Brunner/Mazel.

Garley, D., & Johnson, B. (1994). Siblings and eating disorders: A phenomenological perspective. *Journal of Psychiatric Mental Health Nursing*, 1, 157–164.

Gowers, S. G., Clark, A., Roberts, C., Griffiths, A., Edwards, V. et al. (2007). Clinical effectiveness of treatments for anorexia nervosa in adolescents: Randomised controlled trial. *British Journal of Psychiatry*, 191, 427–435. doi: 10.1192/bjp.bp.107.036764.

Gowers, S. G., Weetman, J., Shore, A., Hossain, F., & Elvins, R. (2000). Impact of hospitalisation on the outcome of adolescent anorexia nervosa. *British Journal of Psychiatry*, 176, 138–141.

Green, J. (2002). Provision of intensive treatment: Inpatient units, day units and intensive outreach. In M. Rutter & E. Taylor (Eds.), *Child and adolescent psychiatry, modern approaches*, 4th edition. (pp. 1038–1050). London: Blackwell.

Haigh, R., & Treasure, J. (2003). Investigating the needs of carers in the area of eating disorders: Development of the Carer's Needs Assessment Measure (CaNAM). *European Eating Disorders Review*, 11, 125–141.

Highet, N., Thompson, M., & King, R. M. (2005). The experience of living with a person with an eating disorder: The impact on the carers. *Eating Disorders*, 13, 327–344.

Holliday, J., & Woolrich, R. (2007). A qualitative exploration of supervised meal time experiences amongst adults receiving inpatient treatment for anorexia nervosa. Unpublished doctoral thesis, University of Oxford, Oxford, UK.

Honey, A., & Halse, C. (2006). The specifics of coping: Parents of daughters with anorexia nervosa. *Qualitative Health Research*, 16, 611–629. doi: 10.1177/ 1049732305285511.

Honey, A., Clarke, S., Halse, C., Kohn, M., & Madden, S. (2006). The influence of siblings on the experience of anorexia nervosa for adolescent girls. *European Eating Disorders Review*, 14, 315–322. doi: 10.1002/erv.713.

Huberman, A. M., & Miles, M. B. (1994). Data management and analysis methods. In N. K. Denzin & Y. S. Lincoln (Eds.), *Handbook of qualitative research* (pp. 428–444). Thousand Oaks, CA: Sage.

Jaffa, T, & Percival, J. (2004). The impact of outreach on admissions to an adolescent anorexia nervosa inpatient unit. *European Eating Disorders Review*, 12, 317–320.

Kjelsas, E., Bjornstrom, C., & Gunnar Gotestam, K. (2004). Prevalence of eating disorders in female and male adolescents (14–15 years). *Eating Behaviours*, 5, 13–25. doi: 10.1016/S1471-0153(03)00057-6.

Lamb, C. E. (2009). Alternatives to admission for children and adolescents. Providing intensive mental healthcare services at home and in communities: What works? *Current Opinion in Psychiatry*, 22, 345–350.

Larkin, M., Watts, S., & Clifton, E. (2006). Giving voice and making sense in interpretative phenomenological analysis. *Qualitative Research in Psychology*, 3, 102–120.

Le Grange, D., & Loeb, K. L. (2007). Early identification and treatment of eating disorders: Prodrome to syndrome. *Early Intervention in Psychiatry*, 1, 27–39. doi: 10.1111/j.1751-7893.2007.00007.x.

Lock, J., Le Grange, D., Agra, W. S., & Dare, C. (2001). *Treatment manual for anorexia nervosa: A family-based approach.* New York: Guilford Press.

Long, S., Wallis, D., Leung, N., & Meyer, C. (2012). "All eyes are on you": Anorexia nervosa patient perspectives of inpatient mealtimes. *Journal of Health Psychology,* 17, 419–428. doi: 10.1177/1359105311419270.

McMaster, R., Beale, B., Hillege, S., & Nagy, S. (2004). The parent experience of eating disorders: Interaction with health professionals. *International Journal of Mental Health Nursing,* 13, 67–73. doi: 10.1111/j.1447-0349.2004.00310.x.

Meads, C., Gold, L., & Burls, A. (2001). How effective is outpatient care compared to inpatient care for the treatment of anorexia nervosa? A systematic review. *European Eating Disorders Review,* 9, 229–241. doi: 10.1002/erv.406.

Minuchin, S., Rosman, B., & Baker, L. (1978). *Psychosomatic families: Anorexia nervosa in context.* Boston, MA: Harvard University Press.

National Institute for Clinical Excellence. (2004). *Eating disorders: Core interventions in the treatment and management of anorexia nervosa, bulimia nervosa, and related eating disorders.* Leicester: British Psychological Society.

Schmidt, M. H., Lay, B., Gopel, C., Naab, S., & Blanz, B. (2006). Home treatment for children and adolescents with psychiatric disorders. *European Child and Adolescent Psychiatry,* 1, 265–276. doi: 10.1007/s00787-006-0531-x.

Schmidt, U., & Treasure, J. (2006). Anorexia nervosa: Valued and visible. A cognitive interpersonal maintenance model and its implications for research and practice. *British Journal of Clinical Psychology,* 45, 343–366. doi: 10.1348/ 014466505X53902.

Smith, J., & Osborn, M. (2003). Interpretative phenomenological analysis. In J. Smith (Ed.), *Qualitative psychology: A practical guide to research methods.* London: Sage.

Treasure, J., Sepulveda, A. R., Whitaker, W., Todd, G., Lopez, C., & Whitney, J. (2007). Collaborative care between professionals and non-professionals in the management of eating disorders: A description of workshops focussed on interpersonal maintaining factors. *European Eating Disorders Review,* 15, 24–34. doi: 10.1002/erv.758.

VanDenBerg, J. E., & Grealish, E. M. (1996). Integration of individualized mental health services into the system of care for children and adolescents. *Administration and Policy in Mental Health,* 20, 247–257.

Willig, C. (2001). *Introducing qualitative research in psychology: Adventures in theory and method.* Buckingham: Open University Press.

Woolston, J. L., Berkowitz, S. J., Schaefer, M. C., & Adnopoz, J. A. (1998). Intensive, integrated, in-home psychiatric services: The catalyst to enhancing outpatient intervention. *Child and Adolescent Psychiatric Clinics of North America,* 7, 615–633.

World Health Organization. (1993). *The ICD-10 classification of mental and behavioural disorders: Diagnostic criteria for research.* Geneva, Switzerland: WHO.

York, A., & Lamb, C. (2005). *Building and sustaining specialist CAMHS: A consultation paper on workforce capacity and function of tier 2, 3 and 4 child and adolescent mental health services.* London: Royal College of Psychiatrists.

Zabala, M. J., Macdonald, P., & Treasure, J. (2009). Appraisal of caregiving burden, expressed emotion and psychological distress in families of people with eating disorders: A systematic review. *European Eating Disorders Review,* 17, 338–349.

Part V
"How I Practice"

23 The Venus Flytrap and the Land Mine

Novel Tools for Eating Disorder Treatment

Laura L. Hill and Marjorie M. Scott

Introduction

In the last decade, genetic and neurobiological research has increased our understanding of eating disorders (EDs), allowing us to view these illnesses from the inside out, and pointing toward a new paradigm for treatment (Frank, 2015). We now know that there are altered brain responses that fire differently in persons with EDs compared to those who do not have EDs (Kaye, Fudge, & Paulus, 2009).

Genetic research helps explain why some people have a higher vulnerability to developing EDs over others, while neurobiological studies indicate how the gene expression plays out in brain response (Steiger, Labonté, Groleau, Turecki, & Israel, 2013). As we increase our understanding of EDs through the lenses of functional magnetic resonance imagery (fMRI) and positron emission tomography (PET) studies, a new model emerges that describes nature/nurture influences on EDs, and lays a foundation and framework for new ED treatment tools.

Neurobiological research describes where and how ED symptoms occur in the brain. At our ED center, nearly every patient and family member report that upon learning these neurobiological findings, they feel less guilt and increased relief that there is a biological explanation to this illness. It is as important for families to learn this as it is for ED patients, because whenever possible the family plays a central role in supporting their loved one and can be a vital part of the solution, instead of the problem.

Metaphors are a wonderful tool to simplify complex topics, while simultaneously having the capacity to introduce novelty and hope to a painful experience. Consider the Venus flytrap. It is a carnivorous flower that has teeth-like projections on the top and bottom petals. When a fly is drawn to the flower and walks into the depths of its petals, the flower closes and devours the fly.

Nature/Nurture Model

The Venus flytrap is a metaphor for the nature/nurture influences on EDs. The "teeth" on the bottom petal represent genetic traits that trigger neurobiological alterations, increasing one's vulnerability to developing an ED. Each tooth is a different trait such as: perfectionism, avoidance or inhibition anxiety, obsessionality, impulsivity, and competitiveness (Kaye, Wierenga, Bailer, Simmons, & Bischoff-Grethe, 2013).

Each tooth on the top petal is an environmental/social influence such as: "be thin," "eat only 'healthy' foods," "be the thinnest," "eat less than everyone else," or "exercise more than others." The diet is the fly. As the fly lands on a petal of the Venus flytrap and walks into the flower, the flytrap closes, thus capturing the fly and consuming it. So too, as a diet becomes more restrictive, the body becomes increasingly strained from too little energy intake, causing self-destructive behavioral responses.

If there are several ED genetic traits or "teeth" in place, dietary restriction triggers identified genes to "turn on," creating a new level of brain and hormonal responses, "entrapping" thoughts and behaviors, and devouring the body (Klump et al., 2010). As the Venus flytrap closes, a diagnosable eating disorder has developed. The person is "locked" into destructive perceptions of body image, feelings, and actions that confine daily life.

On the other hand, if the Venus flytrap had missing genetic or environmental "teeth," the fly could maneuver its way out. In like manner, for those who have fewer genetic precursors or are not exposed to as many environmental triggers that encourage the diet to increase, the person is freer to step away from the diet. The question becomes: how can those who have been caught in the flytrap and held by a wall of genetic and environmental teeth, get out? How does this metaphoric nature/nurture model inform new treatment?

Psychotropic medications could "soften" the inside tissue of flytrap petals, just as they impact neurochemical receptors allowing the person with an ED to have more cognitive and emotional strength to push harder from the inside to lift the petal and fly away (Peterson & Mitchell, 1999). While some medications may hold promise, they are not currently effective as stand-alone treatments for most patients. The patient pushing alone with medication is usually not enough to force the flytrap to release the fly. The environmental and genetic teeth hold too much power without equal or increased force countering the teeth-like hold. Since there is no proven device or mechanism to open the flytrap currently, it must be opened manually. "We" need to push and pull from the outside of the flytrap to "pry open the petals," while the patient pushes from the "inside."

The "we" is key in ED treatment. The ED treatment team needs to actively broaden its forces. It is usually not enough for a clinician to treat ED patients solo and assume the Venus flytrap will open with ease. Even a multidisciplinary treatment team is sometimes not enough. Whenever possible, the "we" needs to include the family, so as to have the team pushing from the outside while the medication and patient with a detailed meal plan push from the inside in a combined effort to pry open the flower together.

In order to keep the patient from becoming exhausted or wanting to give up, we need to be more specific, directed, and detailed. The patient cannot see the larger picture when entrapped, nor identify where to push, how much, and when. The family and treatment team can do for their loved one what the patient cannot do for themself. We need to push, pull, and maneuver in coordination with the patient to help them squeeze through or bend the "teeth" or pry open the petal to crawl out. Otherwise, the patient becomes discouraged or upset and the family steps back. In most cases, the family members appreciate detailed ED information and desire neurobiological tools to help inform their actions.

The Land Mine Activity: A Neurobiologically-Informed Treatment Tool

New neurobiological treatment tools are needed for clinicians, families, and patients to use in the process of recovery. The tools should help the family and patient more fully understand how the brain responds when one develops an ED and when one is trying to escape its entrapment. Brain circuitry responses have been identified and inform us of pathways that are under- and over-firing compared to those without an ED (Wagner et al., 2010), providing the team (clinical, dietary, medical, family, patient) with opportunities to develop creative methods to pry open the Venus flytrap and maneuver out together.

Hunger and fullness signals in the insula appear to be under-firing or not firing at all as the illness progresses (Kaye et al., 2013). The person with an ED comes to the table with low to no insular signals that provide interoceptive awareness of hunger and fullness, and at times taste. There appear to be reduced signals of pleasure from eating for those with anorexia nervosa (AN), and the same after the first few bites for those who binge eat (Stice, Yokum, Blum, & Bohon, 2010; Wagner et al., 2010). It could be said that a person with an ED is "blind" to eating due to reduced activity in these specified brain areas.

How can a person approach a meal if these basic sensations are not firing well enough to know what, how much, and when to eat? In addition, it appears that thoughts become a loud, noisy, chaotic cacophony of indecision: "Should I eat this?", "What do I do?", "Eat it all?", "Vomit later!" The metaphor rises again to serve as a heuristic tool for action to help patients and their families explore ways to compensate for areas of brain "blindness" in EDs. Our group has developed a new tool with input from ED patients, families, and other support people called the "Land Mine Activity."

This tool can be administered with a group of ED patients and is best experienced with both patients and their families or other support people. The families experience what it is like to move through and complete a meal, while blindly walking through a field of eating disorder "land mines." To begin, the patient is asked to stand on one side of the room. The opposite side is identified as the completion of an unplanned meal. The patient is then asked to share with the group the thoughts, feelings, and ED urges that typically get in the way of completing the meal. Peers and family members in the group are assigned to be the voices of the identified thoughts and feelings.

The patient is told to close their eyes, to mimic areas of brain blindness while walking through the field. The patient is informed that all the "noise" or thoughts/feelings about the meal and body size are going to be yelled continuously as they walk forward. After the patient's eyes are closed, but before they begin to walk, objects are placed on the floor randomly (books, balls, any object in the room that could be stepped on). If the patient steps on, or touches, one of these land mines, all noise ceases and the patient steps back five steps. The reversal in steps represents acting on an ED behavior, and the quiet represents relief from the mental noise. As the patient resumes walking forward through the field of land mines, the mental noise begins again. The goal is to get through the field of land mines while ED noise is being shouted. Patients win the game if and when they navigate through the field of land mines, meaning they complete the meal.

Experimentation is necessary in this game, as in life. At first the "blind" ED patient usually tries to walk through the field of land mines alone, only to realize it is nearly impossible to get through the field or unplanned meal unaided. After several tries, when the patient realizes they cannot do it alone, they are asked, "What do you need to get through the land mine field?" They almost unanimously choose to seek support. This validates the central role of the family in maneuvering around the land mines. The therapist instructs the patient to specifically identify who they want to support them to get through the field.

Once support is identified, the patient is asked to instruct the family members, "What I need from you is…." ED patients report a range of needs, from asking for words of encouragement as they walk to asking family members to guide them around the land mines by giving clear instructions. Families have responded by offering the requested methods of support, relieved to know what their loved one wants and needs. Some family members have tested additional creative responses such as holding their loved one's arm or stepping in front of the land mines themselves. One mother and father actually picked their adult loved one up and carried her over the first few mines.

After getting through the land mine field, reaching the goal of completing the meal, the patients and family members are asked to describe their feelings and experiences. The therapists draw upon their answers to identify individualized actions that can be applied during meals at home that were playfully experimented with and acted out. The patients often realize that the key is to keep going, to move forward, as awkward and difficult as it may be, in order for them to push through the "teeth" of the illness.

It is recognized early in the game that stepping on land mines is inevitable, just as an ED behavior is expressed when challenged with many unknowns. In many ED cases, there appears to be no easy way to escape the genetic and environmental teeth alone. If possible, creating a united force with the family and clinical team results in greater power to maneuver *with* the patient through the ED urges.

Summary

In summary, a new paradigm is emerging that explores the nature/nurture model of eating disorders. It acknowledges and actively applies new neurobiological findings to transform treatment into individualized actions that involve the patient, family, and multidimensional treatment team. Traits are constant throughout life, as are the teeth of the Venus flytrap. Traits that have contributed to EDs are not eliminated; rather, they are transformed by pushing and pulling them to bend and shift from self-destructive traits to "teeth that bite into life activities," in order to eventually engage in work and a life with purpose beyond the ED.

Currently, it appears nothing less than active involvement of the family along with the patient and the treatment team, together pushing and pulling through the teeth, will lead to ED recovery. The land mine activity is an example of an experiential treatment tool founded on concepts from neurobiological ED research. It provides an opportunity for the patient to identify what is needed while the family can walk beside their loved one in a playful game and explore how to maneuver around cognitive and emotionally painful reactions to food, eating, and body shape. On a larger scale, it is not just the patient and family that are transforming their responses in this new treatment approach; the entire ED field is transforming its overall paradigm as it integrates new neurobiological and genetic findings into a more comprehensive and balanced approach to this illness.

References

Frank, G. K. (2015). Recent advances in neuroimaging to model eating disorder neurobiology. *Current Psychiatry Reports*, 17, 559. doi: 10.1007/s11920-015-0559z.

Kaye, W. H., Fudge, J., & Paulus, M. (2009). New insights into symptoms and neurocircuit function of AN. *Nature Reviews Neuroscience*, 10, 573–584.

Kaye, W. H., Wierenga, C. E., Bailer, U. F., Simmons, A. N., & Bischoff-Grethe, A. (2013). Nothing tastes as good as skinny feels: The neurobiology of anorexia nervosa. *Trends in Neurosciences*, 36, 110–120.

Klump, K., Burt, S. A., Spanos, A., Mcgue, M., Iacono, W., & Wade, T. (2010). Age differences in genetic and environmental influences on weight and shape. *International Journal of Eating Disorders*, 43, 679–688.

Peterson, C. B., & Mitchell, J. E. (1999). Psychosocial and pharmacological treatment of eating disorders: A review of research findings. *Journal of Clinical Psychology*, 55, 685–697.

Steiger, H., Labonté, B., Groleau, P., Turecki, G., & Israel, M. (2013). Methylation of the glucocorticoid receptor gene promoter in bulimic women: Associations with borderline personality disorder, suicidality, and exposure to childhood abuse. *International Journal of Eating Disorders*, 46, 246–255.

Stice, E., Yokum, S., Blum, K., & Bohon, C. (2010). Weight gain is associated with reduced striatal response to palatable food. *Journal of Neuroscience*, 30, 13105–13109.

Wagner, A., Aizenstein, H., Venkatraman, V. K., Bischoff-Grethe, A., Fudge, J. et al. (2010). Altered striatal response to reward in bulimia nervosa after recovery. *International Journal of Eating Disorders*, 43, 289–294.

24 Behavioral Contracts for Eating Disorders

A Tool to Enhance Motivation and Elicit Change

Stephanie Knatz Peck

As the field of eating disorders (EDs) advances, we continue to gain an improved understanding of the status of our current treatments and their relative efficacy in improving the medical and psychological welfare of the clients that we treat (Watson & Bulik, 2013). Overall, significant advancements have been made in terms of delivering improved treatments to our clients, and simultaneously, new and improved treatments are desperately needed. Even in our most highly regarded treatments, there continues to be a substantial proportion of clients who do not respond favorably and certain subpopulations for which there are no effective treatments (Hay, Touyz, & Sud, 2012; Watson et al., 2013), leaving much to be desired of our existing treatment base.

Behavioral contracting is a treatment strategy adopted from other fields of behavioral treatment and further developed for eating disorders. Although not a novel tool in the field of psychology, the application of behavioral contracts to our field stems from the consideration that specific neural mechanisms known to be at play in these illnesses can be targeted by applying behavioral contracts. With an updated understanding of how individuals with eating disorders make decisions to approach or avoid a behavior (Harrison, Treasure, & Smillie, 2011), and how these decisions are affected by altered reward processing and set-shifting abilities (Holliday, Tchanturia, Landau, Collier, & Treasure, 2014; Wierenga et al., 2014), we have modified and updated the application of behavioral contracts so that they can be applied to eating disorders in a way that addresses neural dysfunctions specific to these illnesses. Behavioral contracts have been used and tested at the UCSD Eating Disorder Treatment and Research Center as part of a broader treatment program and preliminary data suggests promising outcomes for both adults and adolescents (Hill, Wierenga, Knatz, & Liang, 2015; Marzola et al., 2015). In qualitative acceptability surveys, parents of adolescent participants of our program recognized behavioral contracts as the most helpful component of a larger treatment program (Marzola et al., 2015).

This chapter provides a brief background on the use of behavioral contracts for psychological issues and an empirically supported rationale for their suitability with EDs. Clinical tools, including a clinician worksheet and a contract template, are then presented to demonstrate methods for implementing behavioral contracts with eating disorder clients across the age spectrum.

Applying Behavioral Contracting to Eating Disorders

The advent of behavioral contracts emerged directly from the behaviorism movement and has been studied for decades in relation to a variety of psychological issues as a tool to promote behavior change, including substance use, depression, and a variety of adolescent behavioral problems such as oppositional defiant disorder, conduct disorder, and delinquency (Kazdin, 2012; McLean, Ogston, & Grauer, 1973; O'Farrell, 1993; Stanger & Budney, 2010). Contracts are used to systematically enact operant principles of conditioning in order to effect change in behavior. The most substantive elements of a behavioral contract include both the specification of a target or desired behavior in concrete terms, and its related contingencies. For example, a parent might implement a contract that specifies that an adolescent must clean their room by the end of every week (target behavior) and that they will receive money for doing so (contingency). Within the context of ED recovery, a parent or caregiver might specify, as an example, a target behavior of needing to complete three meals and two snacks per day, and a related contingency of a walk privilege should this be achieved. Certainly operant reinforcement and punishment are not novel ideas and often are already being used in recovery, particularly because there are a variety of natural contingencies that occur as a result of being ill with an ED (e.g. being removed from sports by the medical team due to low weight; being hospitalized and removed from school/work due to a low heart rate). Furthermore, recovery plans are enacted regularly amongst treatment providers and clients. The primary difference, however, between a behavioral contract based on operant behavioral principles and a recovery plan or verbal contingency plans is the potent, additive benefit that comes from constructing a written document that operationalizes specific target behaviors that are necessary to achieve recovery and providing a tool that allows for contingencies to be delivered consistently to motivate change. Additionally, a written agreement enhances the likelihood of involved parties following through and can make goals more tangible by deconstructing them into smaller and more immediate steps. Doing so allows for clients to rely on a predictable and consistent plan for achieving what is valuable to them. These contributions are significant for clients given that change and unpredictability, something that a behavioral contract prevents by specifying detailed rules and expectations, are often difficult to tolerate and can lead to increased anxiety (Frank et al., 2012). A contract outlines a specific rule set and/or goal set to which a client can habituate if followed and delivered consistently.

Additionally, as providers, we often encounter a lack of motivation to recover in our clients, a symptom unique to EDs that can make clients difficult to engage with and treatments difficult to enact (Waller, 2012). To combat this, a contract is designed to be constructed around the goals and objectives of value to the client as a way to enhance motivation by summarizing a clear set of rules that will place them on a trajectory to meeting these goals. For example, if a client has the goal of attending college, an expectation that may be set by a treatment provider in conjunction with the client's parents may be to achieve and maintain a minimum weight by a certain date. As opposed to simply stating this, as often would be done in treatment, a behavioral contract can be constructed that stipulates more short-term and specific rules that the client can follow to achieve this long-term goal. For example, the expectation that a client follows their meal plan on a daily basis and gains a certain amount of weight on a weekly basis are ways to ensure a successful path to the long-term goal. Outlining specific rules and expectations also provides a way for us as treatment providers to hold ourselves accountable to ensuring that we are specifying treatment expectations that are in line with the current recommended standards, as well as using a therapeutic tool to enhance motivation, a key ingredient for recovery that many treatment formats overlook.

Behavioral contracts can also function as a means to ensure that carers and support persons are involved with their loved ones in recovery in ways that enhance recovery. Having a method for involving carers in productive ways can be of critical value in an era where many carer-supported interventions are emerging as effective, and more are being explored (Watson et al., 2013). A behavioral contract allows for support persons and caregivers involved in recovery to be aware of recovery-promoting behaviors, and provides specific instruction for responding in ways that reinforce and promote recovery. Eating disorders are complex illnesses that are often difficult for carers to understand and respond to. Due to their secretive nature, carers are often kept unaware and remain uninvolved, precluding them from opportunities to learn how to respond to behaviors in functional ways. As a result and without even being aware, carers may cope using avoidance or with responses that inadvertently reinforce or enable the illness. Constructing a behavioral contract can facilitate functional involvement from carers by specifying ways in which those offering support can be involved (e.g. partner will be present at dinner and ensure that client is meeting meal plan), and providing a method for supportive others to respond in ways that are consistent, predictable, and, most importantly, effective (e.g. if weight goal is not met, then partner will eat lunch with client).

Why do Behavioral Contracts Work for Eating Disorders?

The use of brain imaging techniques, such as fMRI, in EDs has allowed us to understand neural circuitry that underlies ED behaviors. Findings about neurobiological alterations have informed the way in which we apply behavioral contracts to EDs, and help explain why they may be so effective with this population. Neurobiological findings have uncovered hard-wired personality traits and specific brain circuitry that, when considered, guide the way in which behavioral contracts can be enacted to maximize their efficacy. Specific findings that have been taken into account when applying contracts to EDs include information about altered reward processing and differences in set-shifting abilities in individuals with EDs. Reward circuitry in the brain, which is involved in decision-making processes related to eating behavior, has been shown to be altered in both AN and BN (Wierenga et al., 2014). This circuitry, which evaluates the rewarding and punishing properties of engaging in a behavior, guides whether we engage in or inhibit a response, and thus has important implications for our behavior. Due to alterations in the balance between reward appraisal and inhibition, those with AN exhibit an enhanced ability to delay reward and an exaggerated sensitivity to punishment. Individuals with BN exhibit the same disturbance in valuating rewards, but demonstrate difficulty in inhibiting their behavior (Wierenga et al., 2014). These processes are thought to contribute to ED psychopathology. Behavioral contracts are an optimal tool to address this neural anomaly because they are specifically designed to enhance motivation to engage in a behavior by appealing to the way in which we factor rewards and consequence into our decision making. Furthermore, information about reward and punishment sensitivity in ED populations can be used to formulate a contract that is tailored to the relative reward and punishment sensitivity of a specific client. For example, if we know that individuals with AN are difficult to engage in treatment due to reward insensitivity, which explains the lack of motivation that is commonly seen in clinical settings, then it is necessary for practitioners to be thorough and diligent in helping the client identify that which is of utmost value to them in their life, and to pursue the construction of a contract that stipulates specific behaviors which will lead to achieving this goal (or not). Since we understand that individuals with AN may be more attuned to consequences or losses, it may also be important to frame the contract in terms of opportunities lost versus gained. As an example, if a client is working towards leaving their family home to study at an out-of-state college, you may work with them and their family to operationalize specific and measurable goals that must be achieved in order to leave the house, and directly specify that the inability to achieve these goals would result in them staying home for an extra semester. Conversely, for a client with BN who has difficulty in controlling their responses but may be more sensitive to rewards, you may assist in setting up a contract that rewards the client on a more immediate basis (such as a daily reward) for engaging in a positive behavior stipulated in the contract, such as following their meal plan.

In addition to considering contingencies, when applied to eating disorders, it is equally important for behavioral contracts to delineate a concrete and predictable rule set for each target behavior specified (for an example, see Figure 24.1). Individuals with EDs have also been shown to experience difficulty in set-shifting abilities, that is, the ability to shift back and forth between tasks, sets, or operations (Roberts, Tchanturia, & Treasure, 2010). These differences in information processing are thought to underlie behaviors that are routinely observed clinically such as inflexible, rigid,

Contract

Objective: To ensure your safety, prevent inpatient hospitalization and prevent weight loss. Help client to be free from an eating disorder and enjoy a healthy, active life.

Meals and Snacks

1. Client must eat 100% of meals and snacks as recommended by her medical team's dietician at each stage of her treatment. Patient's parents or another trusted adult will be present for all meals.
2. All meals and snacks will be chosen, prepared and plated by Client's parents or a person picked by parent.
3. Client will finish all meals within 30 minutes and snacks within 15 minutes.
4. Client will not negotiate or change the meals after they have been plated by the parent.
5. Meals include caloric drinks such as milk, Gatorade, juice.
6. Client must have 4 cups of fluid every day.
7. Client will be supervised for 1 hour following the meal.
8. When Client returns to school, lunch at school will be supervised by parent or another trusted adult.
9. SUPPLEMENTING:
   (a) If Client eats more than 50% but less than 100%, she will drink 1 Boost plus.
   (b) If Client eats less than 50%, she will drink 2 Boosts plus.

Weight

1. Client will aim to reach a healthy weight range gaining at least 1–2 pounds each week, based on the treatment team's recommendation.
2. If Client does not gain weight as predicted by dietary plan and historic pattern or loses any weight, parents will increase the amount of nutrition/food given.
3. If Client loses more than 2 lbs for 2 consecutive weeks, she will be moved to a higher level of care.

Daily Rewards

For each day that Client meets all of his/her goals (and follows rules above, he/she will receive:

Weekly Rewards

When Client meets weekly weight goal, he/she will earn:

Long-term Rewards

When Client reaches: _____, he/she will receive:

Daily Consequences

If Client violates any of the rules above, or fails to meet daily goals, he/she will lose the following privileges:

Figure 24.1   Contract template: meals and snacks

Weekly Consequences

If Client fails to meet weight goal, then he/she will lose the following privileges:

Long-term Consequences

If Client is in violation of the contract for 3 consecutive weeks, and/or fails to meet weekly goals for 2 consecutive weeks, then:

Contract will be revisited after 4 weeks and modified as needed

Parent Signature_____   Date_____
Client Signature _____   Date_____

Figure 24.1   (cont.)

and repetitive behavior and difficulty with tolerating change, particularly around eating and weight (Tchanturia et al., 2012). Behavioral contracting may hold particular utility for EDs because it allows for the construction of a set of predictable, pre-established rules and response patterns from support persons, thus appealing to this particular neurobiological trait. Contracts are designed to be delivered with consistency, and for target behaviors and contingencies to be predictable and devoid of uncertainty. Although initially a contract may present a significant change and be difficult for clients to accept, their temperament may be particularly suited to following an established set of rules that are delivered consistently; habituation to such a contract may thus be helpful. A contract also helps to ensure that rules are followed and that support persons are responding and remaining involved with recovery in consistent ways.

Enlistment of Support Persons

Behavioral contracts require that another party be responsible for delivering contingencies and assist with overseeing established guidelines, and thus are most often applied in carer-supported interventions. They are highly compatible with other carer interventions and can be delivered in conjunction with other treatments. Behavioral contracts are extremely well suited to adolescents and should be considered a supplement to family-based treatment (FBT), as they can be framed as an additional tool to enhance both parent and adolescent engagement, and thus support the directives of FBT. The contract can also be used as a behavioral supplement to assist support persons of adults with both understanding appropriate expectations for recovery and choosing response sets, whether natural or arbitrary contingencies, that are reinforcing to recovery. If a client is receiving only individual treatment, behavioral agreements can be a way to enhance the individual therapy by enlisting other support persons in the client's life, which can include partners, other family members, and close friends. Finally, if support persons are not available, a contract can also be established between a client and the therapist as an agreement to be followed to achieve positive results in treatment (see Figure 24.2 for examples of ways in which to construct a contract).

Behavioral Contract Worksheet

(COLLABORATORS)

This agreement, beginning on _____ is between _____ and _____.
                          (date)   *(client name)*   *(parent(s), therapist,*
                                                                        partner, other)

(TIME FRAME)

and will be in effect for / until _____.
                                   ((#) weeks / months, or major goal marker (Ex..fall semester of college))

(LONG-TERM GOAL)

The purpose of this agreement is to ensure that _____
                                                 (client)

- *achieves / is able to (*reward sensitive):* <u>*Ex.: attend college in the fall, participate in sport, attend school*</u>
                                                (Identify and specify salient client goal)
- *avoids (*consequence sensitive):* <u>*Ex.: avoid a higher level of care*</u>
                                      (Identify and specify salient client consequences & natural consequences)

*Therapist to work in collaboration with supports and client to identify target behaviors.

1. **Identify and list all problem behaviors.**
2. **Choose 3 most important behaviors.**
   Ex's: Not following meal plan, purging after meals, losing weight
3. **Convert problems into rule sets.**
   Ex: <u>*Problem:*</u> *Not following meal plan*
   <u>*Rule set:*</u> *1) Client will eat 100% of meal plan. 2) Support person will receive copy of plan and be present during (specify meals) to ensure this. 3) Client replace any food not eaten with a supplement drink.*
4. **Identify contingencies for each rule set**. *(*Common categories of rule sets include meals / snacks, physical activity, weight).*
   - *If client achieves above goal, then he / she will receive / be able to (*Rewards):* <u>*Ex. 15 minute walk*</u>
   - *If goals aren't achieved, then (*Consequences):* <u>*Ex. Supervision during meals will be increased*</u>
5. **Identify long-term contingency plan based on long-term goal**.
   - *If client is able to achieve _____, then he / she will be able to _____.*
                                (Insert primary marker of recovery)   *(Insert long-term goal)*
                        (Ex: weight restoration, minimum weight criteria, meals with no purging)
   - *If client is unable to achieve _____, then he / she will _____.*
                                    (Insert primary marker of recovery)   *(Insert long-term consequence)*

Figure 24.2   Behavioral contract worksheet

Summary

Eating disorders can be difficult to treat and novel treatment strategies are needed to improve outcomes. Behavioral contracts have the potential to be a potent treatment tool because they address specific neural mechanisms that underlie ED behavior. Contracts can be applied either as a stand-alone treatment, or as a supplement to other therapies to enhance client motivation and engagement, something that is currently a significant barrier to treatment and not well addressed by existing therapies. Behavioral contracts achieve this by operationalizing the expectations for recovery and reducing them into a specific and concrete plan for achieving recovery that frames progress in terms of what is most valued by clients. Furthermore, as our field continues to explore the benefits of involving carers in ED treatment, treatment strategies that facilitate productive collaboration amongst carers and clients are needed, something that a behavioral contract achieves, as it is based on eliciting the engagement of another interested party.

References

Frank, G. K., Roblek, T., Shott, M. E., Jappe, L. M., Rollin, M. D. et al. (2012). Heightened fear of uncertainty in anorexia and bulimia nervosa. *International Journal of Eating Disorders*, 45(2), 227–232.

Harrison, A., Treasure, J., & Smillie, L. D. (2011). Approach and avoidance motivation in eating disorders. *Psychiatry Research*, 188(3), 396–401.

Hay, P. J., Touyz, S., & Sud, R. (2012). Treatment for severe and enduring anorexia nervosa: A review. *Australian and New Zealand Journal of Psychiatry*, 46(12), 1136–1144.

Hill, L., Wierenga, C., Knatz, S., Liang, J., & Kaye, W. (2015). *Neurobiologically enhanced with family eating disorder trait response treatment for adults with anorexia nervosa.* Poster presentation from the Eating Disorder Research Society, Taormina, Sicily.

Holliday, J., Tchanturia, K., Landau, S., Collier, D., & Treasure, J. (2014). Is impaired set-shifting an endophenotype of anorexia nervosa? *American Journal of Psychiatry*, *162*(12), 2269–2275.

Kazdin, A. E. (2012). *Behavior modification in applied settings.* Long Grove, IL: Waveland Press.

Marzola, E., Knatz, S., Murray, S. B., Rockwell, R., Boutelle, K. et al. (2015). Short-term intensive family therapy for adolescent eating disorders: 30-month outcome. *European Eating Disorders Review*, 23(3), 210–218.

McLean, P. D., Ogston, K., & Grauer, L. (1973). A behavioral approach to the treatment of depression. *Journal of Behavior Therapy and Experimental Psychiatry*, 4(4), 323–330.

O'Farrell, T. J. (1993). *A behavioral marital therapy couples group program for alcoholics and their spouses.* New York: Guilford Press.

Roberts, M. E., Tchanturia, K., & Treasure, J. L. (2010). Exploring the neurocognitive signature of poor set-shifting in anorexia and bulimia nervosa. *Journal of Psychiatric Research*, 44(14), 964–970.

Stanger, C., & Budney, A. J. (2010). Contingency management approaches for adolescent substance use disorders. *Child and Adolescent Psychiatric Clinics of North America*, 19(3), 547–562.

Tchanturia, K., Davies, H., Roberts, M., Harrison, A., Nakazato, M. et al. (2012). Poor cognitive flexibility in eating disorders: Examining the evidence using the Wisconsin Card Sorting Task. *PlOS One*, 7(1), e28331.

Waller, G. (2012). The myths of motivation: Time for a fresh look at some received wisdom in the eating disorders? *International Journal of Eating Disorders*, 45(1), 1–16.

Watson, H. J., & Bulik, C. M. (2013). Update on the treatment of anorexia nervosa: Review of clinical trials, practice guidelines and emerging interventions. *Psychological Medicine*, 43(12), 2477–2500.

Wierenga, C. E., Ely, A., Bischoff-Grethe, A., Bailer, U. F., Simmons, A. N., & Kaye, W. H. (2014). Are extremes of consumption in eating disorders related to an altered balance between reward and inhibition? *Frontiers in Behavioral Neuroscience*, 8, 410.

25 Going around in Circles

Circular Questioning and Family Therapy for Eating Disorders

Stuart B. Murray

The difference between a straight line and a circle, depending on how one interprets the question, may be both strikingly straightforward and remarkably complex. On paper, the difference is immediately discernible. However, when applied to the relationship between human-to-human interactions and symptomatic behavior, the distinction between a straight line and a circle heralded one of the most significant paradigmatic shifts in the history of family therapy. A linear school of thought prevailed in psychotherapy for many years, postulating that A causes B, which in turn causes C, and that problematic behaviors may therefore be treated once the root cause is identified. This linear notion of causality had clear implications for the delivery of mental health treatment, and underpinned a diverse array of therapeutic modalities, including behavioral, cognitive-behavioral, and psychodynamic psychotherapy, which have been woven into the tapestry of eating disorder (ED) treatment over the last several decades.

However, the advent of general systems theory introduced an alternative framework to conceptualize family organization, and processes related to problematic behaviors. Systems theory emphasizes the importance of systemic stability over time but, crucially, acknowledges the circular and mutual influence that individual parts of a system (i.e. family members) have on one another, and on the overall system of which they are a part (i.e. the family). In essence, systems theory postulates that influencing and being influenced within the family system happen recurrently and bi-directionally. Crucially, this located all symptomatic behaviors in the context of a broader system of interactions. An important effect of this paradigmatic shift for family therapists related to the adjustment from linear to circular causality, which embedded problematic or challenging behaviors in a social and systemic context, with each behavior or interaction being inherently connected to its broader context. Reflecting this shift, the therapeutic toolbox of family therapists evolved, with an increasing array of techniques being oriented towards uncovering circular as opposed to linear processes. These circular questions are oriented towards illustrating the patterns that connect people, actions, perceptions, feelings, and ideas, in recurrent feedback loops, as opposed to investigating direct cause and effect.

Circular questioning is particularly salient in the context of EDs, where (1) a multitude of family therapy-based approaches have demonstrated promising efficacy, and (2) empirical evidence illustrates that the presence of ED symptomatology within families results in broader systemic changes within family structure. Perhaps more importantly for clinicians working with EDs, (1) ED symptoms can quickly become the focal point of family interactions, serving to narrow family interactions and amplify challenging dynamics, resulting in systemic "stuckness" (Whitney & Eisler, 2005), yet (2) family therapy is predicated on the well-defined roles allocated to each family member throughout treatment. Thus, circular questions may likely assist in identifying and overcoming potential systemic barriers that may undermine the effective delivery of evidence-based family therapy for EDs.

While many psychotherapy graduate schools and training programs offer comprehensive training in individual therapy, much less regard is typically afforded to family therapy training, and the transition from individual to family therapy settings is a challenging one for many therapists. Again, this may be particularly relevant in the context of EDs, where, upon completing graduate school or clinical training, therapists wishing to practice evidence-based treatment are likely to quickly encounter family therapy. In moving from individual to family work, perhaps the biggest transition may be connected to the shift from linear to circular hypothesizing and questioning.

Circular Questioning

Circular questions are oriented towards the underlying systemic framework that connects people and behaviors/symptoms within a family. For instance, circular questions may aim to gather information relating to the unwritten rules within families, determine who is closest to whom, who can turn to whom for support, and how challenging behaviors impact people differently in the family. This information is critical in the context of ED-focused family therapy, when all family members are mobilized and allocated an active role throughout treatment (Lock & Le Grange, 2013).

Perhaps most fundamentally, circular questions, instead of asking *what*, more typically focus on *how*, *why*, or *who*. When woven into the delivery of evidence-based family therapy in the context of EDs, these circular questions may add several layers of important additional data to the therapeutic encounter. For instance, when working with a family that is stuck in the re-feeding phase of family-based treatment (FBT; Lock & Le Grange, 2013), linear discussions of parental interventions may result in the development of excellent concrete behavioral strategies, but may offer little insights as to why these strategies are unable to be implemented, as the child continues to lose weight. Alternately, circular conversation with parents around potential barriers to implementing their ideas may reveal broader systemic barriers. I recall one such circular conversation with parents who had not implemented the behavioral strategies they had devised, which revealed the mother's own experience of severe child abuse at the hands of both parents, which stymied her ability to "hold firm" with their daughter as it violated her belief system around the type of parent she vowed to be herself. In concert with this, the father perceived the mother as "being the good cop," leaving him to overcompensate and "become the bad cop" in being firm with their daughter. This in turn replicated the mother's own father, and she withdrew from her husband to instinctively protect their daughter, causing further overcompensation on the part of the father. This case serves as one example of a broad array of complex systemic processes that may undermine the effective delivery of evidence-based practice, which may not be immediately discernible through linear questioning. Table 25.1 outlines the distinct approaches adopted during linear versus circular questioning.

In addition to uncovering important systemic processes, circular questions may also be inherently more connecting and interventive than linear questions (Tomm, 1988). That is, as each person constructs their own reality within the family system, open circular conversations within families are often highly effective in revealing each person's different perceptions and understanding of events in the family system, which in itself can be a powerful determinant in the change process. This articulation of other people's understanding and viewpoints around particular patterns helps promote "news of difference" within an otherwise stuck family system, which can assist in breaking through homeostatic patterns of interactions. For instance, as opposed to linearly asking person A what they were thinking or feeling at a particular time when tracking a sequence of events, opting to ask person A who they think might be the best-placed and least well-placed person to share insights on their thoughts and feelings may open up a series of powerful circular conversations. For instance, asking a brother and a sister how they think their anorexic sister might describe their thoughts and feelings may yield important information that may (1) provide the anorexic sibling with feedback relating to the broader perception of their thoughts and behaviors within the family system; (2) illustrate any important discrepancies in how well their thoughts and feelings are understood within the broader context of those around them; (3) help the brother and sister gauge how well-connected they are to their anorexic sibling's thoughts and feelings; and (4) help the therapist identify patterns that connect people within the family.

I can recall one particularly stuck family pattern involving two siblings, an older sister with entrenched AN and a younger sister who had become withdrawn and depressed. Each felt rejected by the other, and each mourned the loss of their previously close relationship. When circularly asking each person their thoughts on how the other person may describe their withdrawal from the friendship, each sister blamed themselves for the fracture of their relationship, yet held hostile attitudes about the other's role in rejecting them. Upon hearing her younger sister's perception of their relational fracture being due to her not being good enough to be close to her any more, the adolescent with AN tearfully described how she had made the incredibly difficult decision to "step back" from her close relationship with her younger sister, who she knew looked

Table 25.1 Clinical examples of linear versus circular questions in the context of eating disorder-focused family therapy

Linear question	Circular question alternatives
To parents: What was it that made your daughter's/son's weight go up this week? What did you do differently?	To father: If I were to ask Mum what percentage she feels as though she's been in control over the eating disorder this week, what might she say? What things do you think she might refer to as important milestones in your family's journey this week? Who do you think Mum might say has most noticed these milestones? How might she say these changes became possible?
To adolescent patient: What scares you most about your weight going up?	To adolescent patient's sibling: How might your parents notice if your sister/brother becomes more frightened about their weight going up? If the eating disorder had a voice, what do you think it might be telling your sister/brother as their weight changes? How might your sister/brother say this eating disorder voice affects them? Who would be most likely to notice if she/ he became more frightened?
	To adolescent patient: What was your sibling most on track with?
To adolescent patient: What do you think might have prevented weight gain this week?	To parents: Can you recall any instances this week in which the eating disorder strengthened itself? Who was affected by these instances? Why might the eating disorder have targeted this person? How were they affected? Who do you think may be the first person to notice if this person was targeted again? What do you think the internal dilemma for this person might have been when they were targeted?

up to her, in a bid to shield her from the influence of her ED. Whilst having vowed never to disclose this information, it was this circular conversation and hearing her younger sister's thoughts on how she thought her elder sister blamed her for the fracture that prompted her to convey the meaning behind her actions. This conversation was hugely impactful in the construction of a new meaning surrounding the fracture in their relationship, which was healed throughout treatment as both sisters learned to support each other in a way that was helpful to one another.

These examples may serve to illustrate the relevance of circular questions in the treatment of eating disorders. Certainly, as family therapy assumes an increasingly central role in the treatment of eating disorders, it is important to not overlook the broader systemic processes impacting the family, and the treatment. As such, it appears that going around in circles may not be such a bad thing after all.

References

Lock, J., & Le Grange, D. (2013). *Treatment manual for anorexia nervosa: A family-based approach*, 2nd edition. New York: Guilford Press.

Tomm, K. (1988). Interventive interviewing: Part III. Intending to ask linear, circular, strategic, or reflexive questions? *Family Process*, 27, 1–15.

Whitney, J., & Eisler, I. (2005). Theoretical and empirical models around caring for someone with an eating disorder: The reorganization of family life and inter-personal maintenance factors. *Journal of Mental Health*, 14, 575–585.

Index